NEW ORLEANS ARCHITECTURE

VOLUME VIII:

The University Section

2 Audubon Place.

NEW ORLEANS ARCHITECTURE

VOLUME VIII:

The University Section

Joseph Street to Lowerline Street
Mississippi River to Walmsley Avenue

By The Friends of the Cabildo

Compiled and edited by:
ROBERT J. CANGELOSI, JR., A.I.A.
DOROTHY G. SCHLESINGER

Contributing Authors:
ROBERT J. CANGELOSI, JR., A.I.A.
HILARY SOMERVILLE IRVIN
BERNARD LEMANN
SAMUEL WILSON, JR., F.A.I.A.

PELICAN PUBLISHING COMPANY
GRETNA 2000

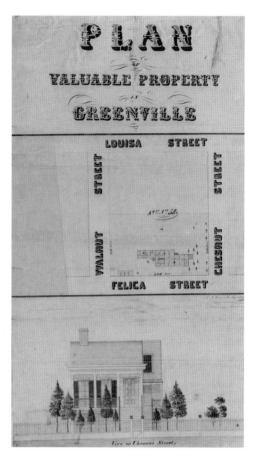

"Plan of Valuable Property in Greenville,"
Square 58 facing Chestnut, by C.A. Hedin and
L. Reizenstein, November 14, 1857. (Courtesy
Notarial Archives for the Parish of Orleans,
hereafter NA)

International Standard Book Number: 1-56554-235-5

First printing, May 1997
First paperback printing, September 2000

Library of Congress Cataloging-in-Publication Data
(Revised for volume 8)

Friends of the Cabildo.
    New Orleans architecture.

    Vol. 4 compiled by R. Toledano, S. K. Evans, and
M. L. Christovich.
    Includes bibliography and index.
    Contents: v. 1. The Lower Garden District.—
v. 2. The American sector (Faubourg St. Mary)—[etc.]—
v. 8. The University Section.
    1. Architecture—Louisiana—New Orleans.
2. New Orleans (La.)—Buildings, structures, etc.
I. Wilson, Samuel, 1911-   . II. Christovich, Mary
Louise, ed. III. Toledano, Roulhac, ed. IV. Title.
NA735.N4F74 1971   720'.9763'35   72-172272

Library of Congress Cataloging-in-Publication Data

ISBN 0-911116-51-6 (v. 1)

Printed in Korea

Published by Pelican Publishing Company, Inc.
1000 Burmaster Street, Gretna, Louisiana 70053

CONTENTS

Fig. 1. 5800 St. Charles, lake side, circa 1905. Rotograph Co. post card.

PREFACE AND ACKNOWLEDGMENTS

Rebuilding the Cabildo after the disastrous 1988 fire took precedence over a great deal of the pre-publication work for Volume VIII. From the initial organizational planning to the selection of buildings in the inventory, subsequent title research, choice of illustrations, editing, and a myriad of related details, the progress has been slow but relentless.

Countless hours have been spent in the major research centers of New Orleans. It has been gratifying to have had the assistance of many professionals in these primary source repositories. Without their help, this work could not have been accomplished. We are grateful, and recognize:

The Historic New Orleans Collection, Museum/Research Center:
Pamela Arceneaux, Jan White Brantley, Alfred Lemmon, John Magill, Jude Solomon, Jessica Travis.

Louisiana State Museum Historical Center:
Burt Harter, Kathrine Page.

New Orleans Conveyance Office:
Gasper Schiro.

New Orleans Notarial Archives:
Stephen P. Bruno, Sally K. Reeves.

New Orleans Office of Property Management, Division of Real Estate and Records:
Thomas McGoey, George Kaltenbach.

New Orleans Public Library, Louisiana Division:
Collin B. Hamer, Jr., Ernest "Tito" Brin, Wayne Everard, Mac Sintes.

Tulane University, Howard-Tilton Memorial Library:
Louisiana Collection:
Joan Caldwell, Richard Campbell, James Powell, Martha Tanner, Shannon Freeman.
Rare Books and Manuscripts Division:
Wilbur Meneray.
Southeastern Architectural Archive:
William Cullison, Gary Van Zante, Kevin Williams.

University of New Orleans, Earl K. Long Library, Archives and Manscripts:
D. Clive Hardy.

Meticulous title research was done by Judy Bethea, Robert Cangelosi, Dorothy Schlesinger, and Helen Wetzel.

The generosity of Caroline Dreyfous Weiss has helped defray pre-publication expenses.

John Geiser III carefully copyread the text, and Linda Dawson undertook the task of entering the manuscript and inventory on computer.

Others who have been supportive are: Herman J. Abry, Dennis Alonzo, James Blanchard, Arthur Carpenter, Edward D'Antoni, Sister Dorothy Dawesop, Margene Dawson, Bryce and Elroy Eckhardt, Susann Gandolfo, Robert Merrick, A.L. Schlesinger, Jr., Eric Smith, Charles Stich, John Walker, Constance and Casey Willems, and Koch and Wilson Architects.

Fig. 2. "A Buggy Ride in Audubon Park under an Alley of Live Oaks Covered with Spanish Moss," circa 1895. (Courtesy Library of Congress)

FROM THE PRESIDENT

In its forty years of existence, the Friends of the Cabildo, Associates of the Louisiana State Museum, has had as part of its mission the laudable goals of preservation and education. With the aid of a large, active membership, the Friends of the Cabildo has developed into an excellent educational resource, stimulating interest and concern in preserving our state's heritage and culture. Nowhere in the many activities of the Friends is this more apparent than in the publication of this acclaimed New Orleans Architecture series, which celebrated its twenty-fifth anniversary in 1996. From *Volume I: The Lower Garden District*, published in 1971, to

Fig. 1. J. Raymond Samuel. (Courtesy Martha Ann Samuel)

the present, the documentation of New Orleans' many diverse neighborhoods, whether in jeopardy or not, continues to serve as an invaluable asset in the ongoing battle to preserve and educate.

During the seven years of work on Volume VIII, the Friends of the Cabildo has mourned the loss of two former presidents who left their mark on this organization and the City of New Orleans. The Friends of the Cabildo dedicate this book to the memory of those men—J. Raymond Samuel and Samuel Wilson, Jr.

J. Raymond Samuel, known to one and all as Ray, was a founding member of the Friends of the Cabildo, and as its president from 1970 to 1972 was instrumental in getting the first volume of this architectural series·published. Deeply committed to a better state museum, Ray recognized the need for a full-time, professional director of the Louisiana State Museum and worked toward upgrading the museum and its personnel. As one of the founders of the Louisiana Landmarks Society, he helped save the Pitot House. Ray also served as president of the Louisiana Historical Society for many terms. In the foreword of *Volume I: The Lower Garden District*, he wrote of the dedication of the Friends of the Cabildo volunteers who had a hand in the production of the book and urged readers not to let it sit on the "coffee table," but to use it to get involved in a cause he loved—historic preservation.

Sam Wilson, noted preservation architect and author, was also a founding member of the Friends of the Cabildo. Between 1979 and 1981, he served as president of the Friends, and he was on the board of directors for almost twenty years. A tireless contributor to the New Orleans Architecture series, Sam wrote articles for almost every volume, and *Volume VI: Faubourg Tremé and the Bayou Road*, was released during his presidency. In addition to publishing over 175 books and articles on regional architecture, Sam was instrumental, along with his partners, in restoring and preserving many local landmarks and several museum properties, including the Cabildo. Active in other community organizations, Sam was a founding member of the Louisiana Landmarks Society, Save Our Cemeteries, Orleans Parish Landmarks Commission, and Preservation Resource Center. In 1991 the Friends of the Cabildo awarded

Fig. 2. "The New Orleans Exposition—The Approach to Horticultural Hall," from *Harper's Weekly,* January 3, 1885. (Courtesy Frank Mapes)

Fig. 3. Samuel Wilson, Jr. (Courtesy Times-Picayune Publishing Corporation)

Sam, one of its greatest supporters, the History Maker Award for his years of commitment to the organization.

The Board of Directors of the Friends of the Cabildo expresses its sincere appreciation to the editors and their associates and assistants who have volunteered hundreds of hours of their time to make this volume possible. Already at work on Volumes IX and X, *Carrollton* and *The Vieux Carré*, these dedicated Friends of the Cabildo volunteers will be documenting our architectural heritage well into the next century.

Fran Phillips Tessier, President
Friends of the Cabildo

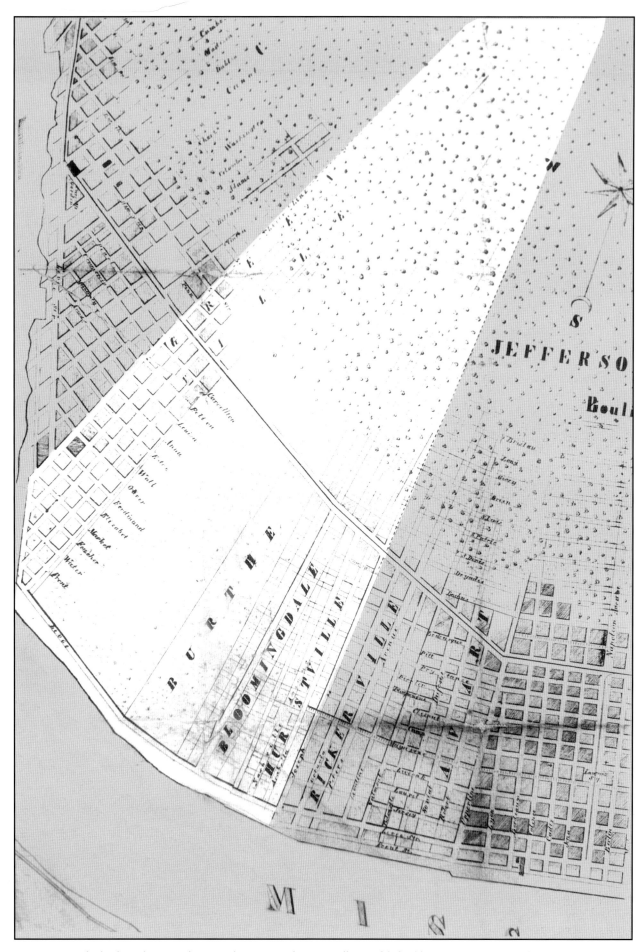

Fig. 1. Detail of "Plan of New Orleans and Environs," by W. Walker, published by A. Bronsema, 1885. (Courtesy TULC)

INTRODUCTION

DOROTHY G. SCHLESINGER

Anchored by Audubon Park and further secured by many educational and religious institutions, the Uptown sector of New Orleans designated as the University Section has long been considered one of the most stable and prestigious residential areas of the city. Many years ago, the Fourteenth Ward (Jefferson Avenue to Lowerline Street) was dubbed with the now-obsolete name "Silk-Stocking Ward," denoting its elegance and wealth. Numerous Times-Picayune Loving Cup recipients and Carnival kings reflect the prominence and civic involvement of many residents.

Uptown, from Louisiana Avenue to Lowerline, is now on the National Register of Historic Places as part of the Uptown National Historic District. Vigilant neighborhood organizations have been vociferous guardians of their surroundings, and commercial encroachment has been kept to a minimum, with the exception of Magazine Street. The housing stock runs the gamut from mansions to modest "box" houses.

Upriver from the area that became Jefferson City in 1850 were six faubourgs (suburbs) (Figure 1) dating from the early 1800s. **Hurstville**, the 1832 enterprise of Cornelius Hurst, extended from Joseph Street to a line between Eleonore and State streets (still referred to in legal documents as the Bloomingdale line). Two years later, John Greene (Green) acquired property from Julie Avart which comprised both sides of State Street and was known as **Bloomingdale**—from the Bloomingdale line to a line between State and Webster streets. That line was the lower boundary of **Burtheville**, the plantation of Dominque François Burthe, who acquired the property from Bernard Marigny in 1831. It extended to the lower line of the Foucher property now known as Audubon Park. Sandwiched in between the Foucher property and Lowerline Street (the lower line of the Macarty property, now Carrollton) was **Greeneville**, the 1836 undertaking of James Ogilvie, Oliver Aiken, and John Greene.

In 1837 the land at the rear of Greeneville from Long (Freret) Street to Claiborne Avenue (then a canal) was divided into squares and lots in accordance with an agreement between James Ogilvie, Noel Barthelemy LeBreton, and Charles Derbigny and his wife, Josephine Eulalie LeBreton, and was named **Friburg**.

Not precisely Uptown, but interesting to mention here, is one parcel of land—Marly, or **Marlyville**. Pierre Marly was a free man of color, but little else is known about him. According to records, Marly purchased Lot I of Macarty's plantation from the New Orleans Canal and Banking Company, Samuel Kohn, Laurent Millaudon, and John Slidell on June 4, 1833, and it appears at the rear of Friburg on an 1869 map compiled for Gardner's *New Orleans Directory*. But the 1855 "Plan of the City of New Orleans" by L. Pessou and B. Simon (Figure 2) describes the area of Marly and much more as "Vacant Land." The original plan has been lost or destroyed, but an 1894 survey by George Grandjean and H.W. Reynolds indicates the property to be "unimproved palmetto lands" from the end of Friburg to the Illinois Central Railroad line.

In 1846 the Borough of **Freeport** was established, extending from Toledano to the Bloomingdale line (between Nashville Avenue and State Street). The following year, Hurstville and Bloomingdale seceded from the borough, reducing Freeport's boundary to Joseph Street. The 1850 session of the state legislature incorporated the remaining area—Toledano Street to Joseph Street—as Jefferson City.

The six uptown faubourgs and the Foucher tract became a part of New Orleans in 1870 and were designated as a major portion of the Fourteenth Ward in the Sixth Municipal District.

Some of the same factors that spurred the development of Jefferson City (see Volume VII) are applicable to our subject area: the uptown side of Joseph Street to the downtown side of Lowerline Street. That great transportation artery, the Mississippi River, along with the New Orleans and Carrollton Rail Road (Figure 3) and the relatively "high and dry land" from the river back to "the woods," as well as such factors as the financially disastrous World's Industrial and Cotton Centennial Exposition of 1884 and the advent of the automobile all played a part in the evolution of this prime real estate. The late 1800s and early 1900s saw development of an effective mechanical drainage system of sewerage and a filtered water supply, which greatly enhanced the livability of the entire city.

Nineteenth century maps depict significant development of the area. The 1835 "Topographical Map of New Orleans and Environs" by Charles Zimpel accurately delineates the

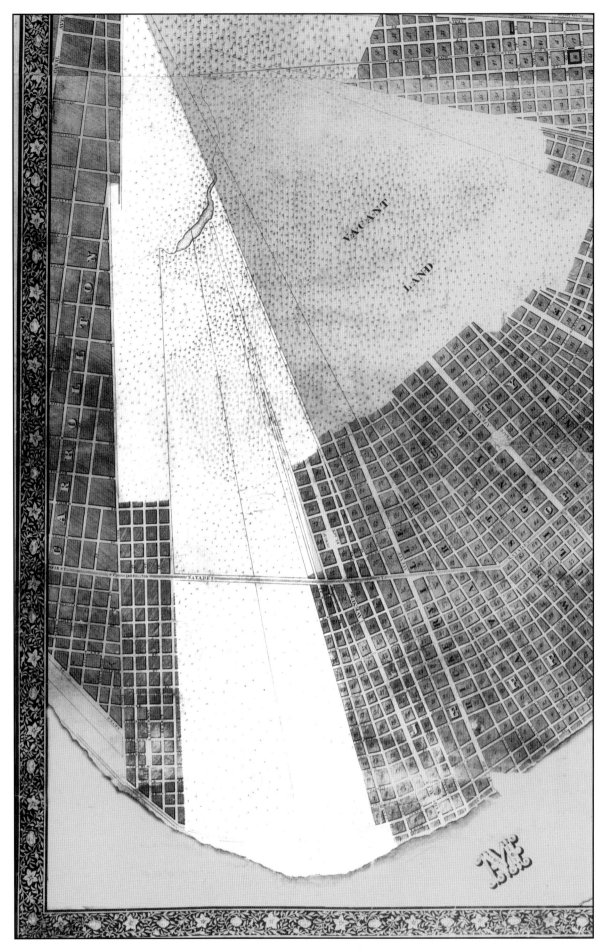

Fig. 2. Detail of "Plan of the City of New Orleans," by L. Pessou and B. Simon, 1855. (Courtesy Historic New Orleans Collection, Museum/Research Center, hereafter HNOC, Acc. No. 1959.201.24)

Fig. 3. 5900 block of St. Charles Avenue, 1889, showing steam engine and car operated by the New Orleans & Carrollton Rail Road. (Courtesy TULC)

Foucher plantation and that of Dominque François Burthe but omits the home of Cornelius Hurst that he had built in 1832, shortly after he acquired the property. Belle Point Race Course is a prominent feature on the Zimpel map, but outside of Nayades Street (later St. Charles Avenue) and the surveyed streets of Hurstville, no other streets of our subject area are designated.

A map of the "South Eastern District of Louisiana East of the Mississippi River" (Figure 4) dated June 29, 1843, from the Surveyor General's Office shows surveyed areas of Hurstville and Greeneville, with the land in between tagged "Farm," "Pasture," "Undergrowth," and "Batture."

With the publication of Elisha Robinson's *Atlas of the City of New Orleans* in 1883 (based on circa 1877 information supplied by C.A. Braun), there are depicted uptown squares divided into lots with the owners' names clearly shown in many cases. Most of the large residences facing St. Charles Avenue are gone. Two in the square bounded by St. Charles, Nashville, Hurst, and Eleonore remain, and two others have been moved—one to face Arabella Street, and

the other to face Lowerline Street. Only one building (now an attractive private residence) remains of the German Protestant Orphan Asylum in the square bounded by State, Webster, Camp, and Chestnut streets. The Louisiana Retreat for the Feeble Minded, now DePaul Hospital, occupied one square fronting on Calhoun Street and backed by City (now Audubon) Park, Plaquemine (Coliseum), and Chestnut streets. The Hebrew Cemetery, bounded by Joseph, Arabella, Pitt, and Garfield streets, is extant, but the two plant nurseries in the neighborhood, Bloomingdale Nursery and Mt. Ararat Nursery, are no longer in existence. St. Mary's Dominican Convent (Figure 5) at St. Charles and Broadway is now owned by Loyola University, and Leland University is presently the site of Newcomb Boulevard.

Insurance Maps of New Orleans, Louisiana of 1896 and 1909 by the Sanborn-Perris Map Company of New York have been invaluable sources of information. These maps are accurate and show not only the footprint of each structure, but also the number of levels, building materials used, and, in most cases, the house number.

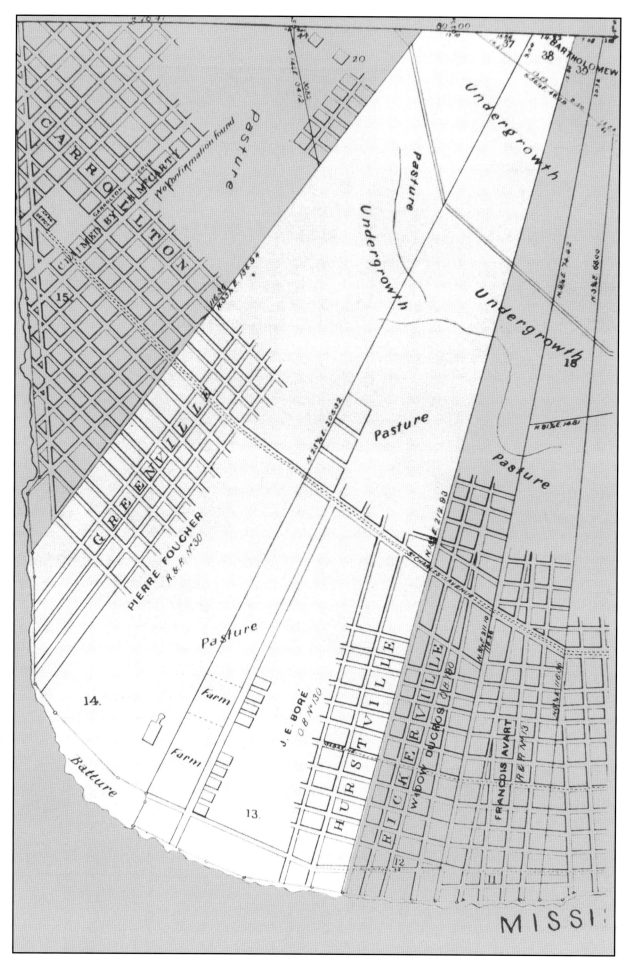

Fig. 4. Detail of "South Eastern District of Louisiana East of the Mississippi River," Surveyor General's Office, January 26, 1872. (Courtesy TULC)

Fig. 5. 7214 St. Charles Avenue, St. Mary's Dominican Convent, William Fitzner, architect; G. Murray, builder, 1882, from *The City of New Orleans*. (Courtesy Koch and Wilson Architects, hereafter K&W)

The 1896 Sanborn map indicates that there were few paved streets in the area. Many, like Tchoupitoulas Street, were "part planked," or covered with "Rosetta gravel." St. Charles Avenue was gravel-paved on the lake side and asphalt-paved on the river side. Henry Clay Avenue was covered with "vitrified brick" while Magazine Street had "cobblestone" paving. State Street was "macadamized" and Pine Street was "shelled," as indicated on the 1909 Sanborn map—which also reveals that Nashville Avenue was not paved and had an 8-foot-5-inch-wide drainage canal in the center of the street from near St. Charles Avenue to Claiborne Avenue.

Many private homes had outbuildings identified as greenhouses, giving credence to the probability that not only flowers, but also fruits and vegetables were home-grown. At least four sizeable nurseries are depicted—one with the additional information, "Florist" (Figure 6). Until the 1960s, the Kraak family maintained a nursery and flower shop on Eleonore Street, between Garfield and Pitt streets, now the site of two private residences.

Three dairies are shown on the 1909 Sanborn map—one in the square bounded by Broadway, Pine, Maple, and Hampson streets; another on Calhoun Street backed by Tulane University, between Freret and Howard (LaSalle) streets; and the third on South Robertson, backed by Magnolia, between Calhoun Street and Tulane University.

The Crescent City Rail Road Company's Magazine Street electric car barn (Figure 7) (still located on Magazine, be-

tween Arabella and Joseph streets, backed by Constance Street) is described on the 1896 Sanborn map as an iron building with structural steel beams and girders, corrugated iron sides with pine boards under an iron roof, with bricks to the eaves on the front and back and to a height of eight feet on the sides. For insurance purposes, it was important to note that there were electric lights, eight hydrants with a 50-foot-21-inch linen hose attached to each, fire pails, barrels of water, and a night watchman. By 1909 city water was pumped by electricity into two tanks thirty feet high. The adjacent riverside square had a blacksmith shop.

By 1909 the Louisiana Retreat for the Feeble Minded consisted of three small, one-story buildings. A two-story barn and a two-story storage building were "to be moved 80' back from street" to a large area designated as a "truck farm."

Fig. 6. 6037 Hurst Street, E. Valdejo Nurseries and Greenhouse, from *New Orleans, Louisiana: The Crescent City*. (Courtesy K&W)

Fig. 7. New Orleans Railways Co. Arabella Barn (Magazine Street Electric Car Barn) from *New Orleans, Louisiana: The Crescent City*. (Courtesy K&W)

Fig. 8. Touro-Shakspeare Alms House, from *Artwork of New Orleans*. (Courtesy TULC)

The Shakspeare Alms House (Figure 8) on South Rampart (Danneel) Street, between Joseph Street and Nashville Avenue, had a detached kitchen and dining room, separate male and female wards, a separate Negro ward, a hospital building, and a small building identified with the letters "wc" (water closet).

It was not unusual in 1896 for schools to be heated by stoves and illuminated by oil lamps, as noted for Leland University and St. Mary's Dominican Academy. Henry W. Allen School, built in 1904 (bounded by Nashville Avenue, Joseph, South Franklin [Loyola], and South Liberty streets), Lasalle School (bounded by Webster, Perrier, State, and Coliseum streets), and Rudolph T.P. Danneel School (in the square of Nashville Avenue, Arabella, Annunciation, and Laurel streets) all were steam heated, but only Danneel School had electric lights. Audubon School (facing Broadway, backed by Audubon, between Elizabeth [Chestnut] and Meadow [Camp] streets) was heated by stoves and had no lights.

On the corner of Pine and General Hood (Perrier) streets, backed by Broadway and Wall (Prytania) streets, J.P. Hecker owned a building with the intriguing identification "Inventors-Experimental Shop."

A building similar to the Audubon Golf Club House is depicted on the 1909 Sanborn map, but the Audubon Golf Club, founded in 1901, is not labeled as such. It is to be noted that the site of Langenstein's, the popular Uptown grocery store on the corner of Pitt and Arabella streets, backed by Prytania Street and Nashville Avenue, was once the location of a boarding stable before the advent of automobiles.

The extant "Fire Engine House" facing Arabella Street (bounded by Prytania, Perrier, and Joseph streets) housed ten men, five horses, one steamer, one hose wagon, one chemical engine, and a 650-foot hose.

There was, and in most cases still is, a proliferation of shotgun doubles in the 5900 block of Laurel; the 6000 blocks of Tchoupitoulas, Annunciation, and Patton streets; the 400-600 blocks of State, Webster, and Calhoun streets; and the 1000 block of Joseph Street.

The *Daily Picayune*, in its 1893 "Columns of Brick and Mortar," reported that new construction in the Sixth District led the city. There were 310 new buildings costing $604,720 and repairs to 142 buildings totaling $49,327. Two years later, it was noted that the Sixth District was second only to the First (Central Business) District in the amount of repairs and building construction for the preceding two years, from May 1893 to May 1984 and from May 1894 to May 1895.

In recent years, there has been a renewal of the quality of life in the University Section. Many fine, old homes have been restored and enhanced. Young couples are finding the large, high-ceilinged homes attractive, commodious places to raise families in convenient neighborhoods. In the past few years, innovative landscape designers have created beautiful gardens, adding another lovely dimension to the Uptown scene.

As in Volume VII, we have limited our inventory of the University Section to structures built before World War II, narrowing our choices to buildings of historical interest and architectural significance, both typical and atypical.

The *raison d'etre* for this architecture series was to call attention to the increasing loss of our architectural heritage and to preserve our many historic neighborhoods. Having been on the cutting edge of the preservation movement and nearly accomplishing our initial objective, our mission has added a new dimension: to foster and stimulate interest, knowledge, and pride in our heritage and culture. Virtually all severely threatened neighborhoods have been examined. Surely the University Section is not endangered, as were most of the subject areas of the previous seven volumes, but it is a part of the grand plan to inventory all of New Orleans. The series continues with a proactive goal of preserving and protecting our precious inheritance for future generations.

NEW ORLEANS ARCHITECTURE

VOLUME VIII:

The University Section

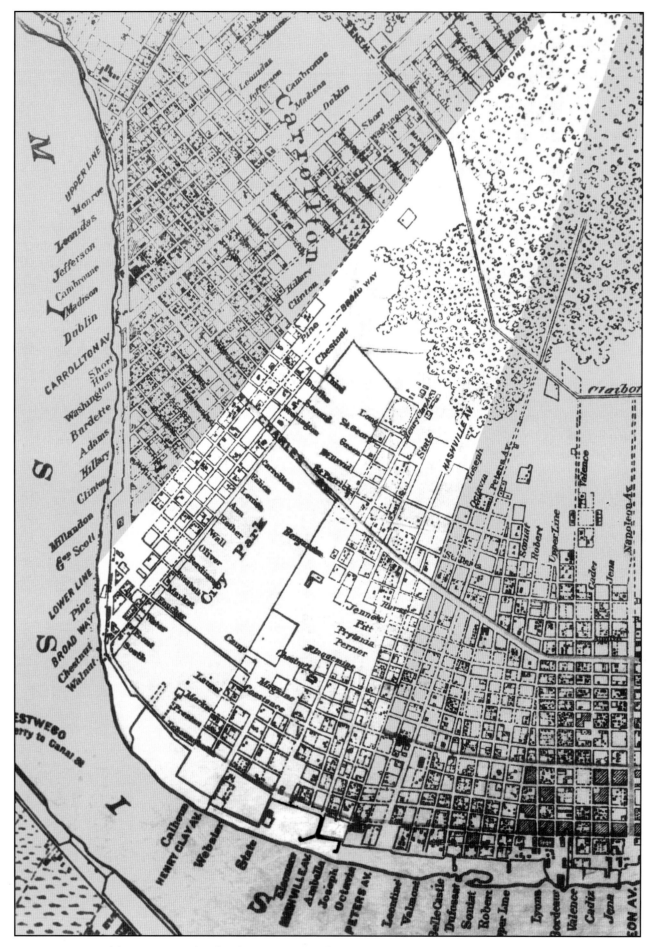

Fig. 1. Detail from "Topographical and Drainage Map of New Orleans," by T.S. Hardee, 1880. (Courtesy TULC)

AMBIENT REVIEW

BERNARD LEMANN

The part of New Orleans sometimes familiarly known as the University area is the uppermost district of the Uptown sequence. It begins at Joseph Street, where we left Jefferson City (Volume VII). It ends at Lowerline Street, the margin of Carrollton, a noteworthy historic community and one-time seat of the neighboring parish, still recognized in the consciousness of its inhabitants. In contrast, our present topic, the group of small, suburban settlements (Hurstville, Bloomingdale, Burtheville, and Greenville) surrounding Audubon Park and the universities, have been long-since forgotten as individually distinct entities by the general public—much like Jefferson City itself. Excluding the "City of Carrollton" as a separate subject, the topic of this Volume VIII stands as a counterpart of the American Sector (Volume II), the first and lowermost of the Uptown sequence as viewed by inhabitants below the wide division of Canal Street. In depth, all sectors seem to merge and disappear as the arpents of early survey lines, normal to the river, converge in the backwoods of the last century (Figure 1). The resulting pattern of plantation properties or streets creates a few interesting shifted alignments, small, residual parks, or irregular plots amid the dull grid of city squares.

The city's historic housing stock is so vast that a full treatment of Uptown has crowded out a single volume of references. This has necessitated excluding the University Section from previous volumes of the New Orleans Architecture Series. In general character, the University Section is related to all of Uptown, especially all above the Garden District. Any attempt to summarize a broad definition of the area as distinctive and apart from the adjacent Jefferson City must be expressed in subtly relative, even tentative or ambivalent terms. Careful investigation may disclose a valid contrast, responding to the sightly younger feeling of this upper phase of the Uptown development. The differences are noticeable if we scan upward along the central spine, St. Charles Avenue, as well as outward from the avenue on either side.

What observations might be relatively valid to justify this separate treatment of the later Uptown? First of all, the area is an almost untouched, consistent whole package of three or four graduated levels of cityscape, but nevertheless a tightly tied-in package. There have been fewer demolitions of these newer houses, fewer moving of structures to adjust to a new site. The individual buildings exist comfortably together in the street fabric.

In general these newer types of compatible street scenes belong to a slightly later era (as compared to prevalent styles in Jefferson City). There are virtually no double-galleried "Old South" types dating earlier than the delimiting parenthetical dates of our area, say 1895-1925. Only a small count are exceptions outside the other end of the parenthesis—the newer modernists. The old central-hall types of plans, both for cottages or multi-level houses, are much less numerous (Figures 2 and 3). Open plans, particularly the irregular, asymmetrical ones, are more common. One enters the house into a so-called "living hall" (actually more for dancing than ordinary living), or a "stair hall." This scheme of large houses is often imitated pretentiously on a smaller scale.

The late Victorian houses (largely outnumbered by newer neighbors) still cling to fantasies of irregular galleries, staggered freely with balconies, bays, bulges, or turrets in a fandango of heavy woodworkings (Figure 4). The early-twentieth century house front tends to assume a more subdued character—a simple, vaguely traditional paraphrasing of early New England, Georgian, Mediterranean, or Petit Château elegance. History-oriented commentators, sometimes at a loss to answer the demand for stylistic vocabulary, resort to a broadly approximate term, such as "eclectic," or possibly "traditional" (Figure 5). This consciously intellectual "architect's styling" is a determining factor in the predominantly early-twentieth century streets of the University Section. The objective, as expressed, for example, in *The Honest House* by Ruby Ross Goodnow and Rayne Adams (1914) was "to create a house . . . consistent in all of its parts, true to a chosen style or character, and containing throughout the elements of good design."

It is remarkable how, even before air conditioning, front galleries were sacrificed in the interest of refined taste in favor of plain, carefully moderated fronts, in the manner of such fashionable journals as *House Beautiful*. The comforts of a new style of living called for inconspicuous rear or side solariums or screened porches with overhead fans. Electric power began in the 1880s, but at first for street

Fig. 2. 7306 St. Charles (demolished), from *The City of New Orleans.* (Courtesy K&W)

Fig. 3. 1468 Nashville (demolished). (Courtesy Helen Schneidau)

Fig. 4. 7030 St. Charles Avenue, from *New Orleans Illustrated in Photo Etchings.* (Courtesy K&W)

Fig. 5. 5801 St. Charles Avenue, from *Hansell's Photographic Glimpses of New Orleans.* (Courtesy K&W)

lighting, and only gradually for residences. Through the late 1890s, houses often had wall-light fixtures and chandeliers piped for gas concurrently with the electric system, as a backup in case of power failure. So, in a very broad view, we could place the period style of the University Section buildings as predominantly between early electricity and the advent of air conditioning.

The vague terminology of eclectic or traditional design and the loose adaptations of various historic flavors leaves us with no appropriate language or architectural analysis. As we turn from Victorian living and approach twentieth

century conditions, the mode of indwelling might be a more convenient descriptive keynote. We can characterize the graduated levels of the whole package of University-Uptown in terms of socioeconomic evaluations. In that case, it would be necessary to devise a self-determined terminology, roughly as follows:

Type A: Elitist Syndrome (as in St. Charles Avenue, private streets, parts of State Street, Henry Clay and Palmer avenues). Large lots, living halls, third-floor servants' quarters, central heat, often with ground-level furnaces, and laundry space (Figures 6A, B, C, D, E, and F).

A

B

C

D

Fig. 6. Elitist Syndrome: Edmond Burthe House, St. Charles and Calhoun, destroyed by fire, circa 1897. A-Exterior, B-Entrance Hall, C-Music Room, D-Library, *(on opposite page)* E-Parlor, F-Dining Room. (Courtesy Bernard Lemann)

Fig. 6E. Edmond Burthe House, Parlor.

Fig. 6F. Edmond Burthe House, Dining Room.

Type B: Upper Comfortable (Nashville Avenue, Audubon Street). Like the above, but slightly less; butler's pantries, powder rooms, multiple baths, smaller stair halls (Figure 7).

Type C: Moderate Comfortable (Joseph Street, Arabella Street). Much as above, but on a smaller scale, on narrower lots; double-parlor effects with bookshelf division, catalog fireplaces (Figure 8).

Type D: Modest (toward the river and Broadway). Row housing, bungaloid shotguns; late-Eastlake and late-Colonial Revival detailing (Figure 9).

Fig. 7. Upper Comfortable: 1112 State Street (demolished), John Woodville residence, from *New Orleans, Louisiana: The Crescent City*. (Courtesy K&W)

Fig. 8. Moderate Comfortable: 1600 block Pine Street.

AT RIGHT: Fig. 9. Modest: 1100 block Joseph Street.

These categories are intended to apply to houses, not necessarily to neighborhoods or streets throughout their entire lengths. Streets do tend to be consistent, or at least graduated in house types.

Only one area does not presently seem to know where it is going—the hospital, dockside, and industrial developments in nearby groupings, where clients of the Lighthouse for the Blind with their walking sticks must cope with eighteen-wheelers making awkward turns in heavy traffic. With completed construction, thoughtful planning, and a few shifts, this can become a well-ordered district of the city, even with a few surviving landmarks.

One other result of the farther Uptown and later development may be the greater number of large swaths of land that were available. Besides Audubon Park and the universities (which have their own special histories, reported elsewhere), there emerged a number of institutional plots of ground acquired early in the history of the area. The list is as follows:

1. Marine Hospital, now Adolescent and Children's Mental Health and Substance Abuse Hospital (between State Street and Henry Clay Avenue, backed by Tchoupitoulas Street).

2. Home for the Incurables, now New Orleans Home and Rehabilitation Center (Henry Clay Avenue, Calhoun, Patton, and Constance streets)(Figure 10).

3. German Protestant Orphan Asylum, now subdivided, but

Fig. 10. Home for the Incurables. (Courtesy TULC)

with new houses trying to join the neighborhood (State, Webster, Camp, and Chestnut streets).

4. Louisiana Retreat for the Feeble Minded, now DePaul Hospital (Exposition Boulevard, Henry Clay Avenue, Coliseum and Chestnut streets) (Figure 11).

5. Poor Clare Nuns (Henry Clay Avenue, Calhoun, Magazine, and Constance streets).

6. Touro-Shakspeare Alms House—originally funded in 1882 by donations of professional gamblers in lieu of licensing; subdivided into lots in 1939 (Danneel and Joseph streets, Loyola and Nashville avenues).

Fig. 11. Louisiana Retreat for the Feeble Minded. (Courtesy TULC)

Fig. 12. 1415 Exposition Boulevard, A.M. Halliday residence (demolished), C. Milo Williams, architect, from *Architectural Art and Its Allies*, June 1909. (Courtesy TULC)

7. Sophie Gumbel School, now the Association for Retarded Citizens (Nashville Avenue to Joseph Street on Loyola Avenue).

8. Ursuline Convent (State Street and Nashville Avenue, between Willow Street and Claiborne Avenue).

Narrow Gilmore Park straddles State Street between Eleonore and Webster streets at a widening of Laurel Street and its extension that was once named Market Street. The park was established by and named for Samuel Louis Gilmore (1859-1910), a prominent attorney, civic leader, and congressman. Gilmore Park was reworked and rededicated in 1991. Corresponding to this Laurel Street park, Annunciation Street widens at Eleonore Street and continues thus to a few steps beyond Alonzo Street. There is no apparent explanation for these small, park-like layouts. Once called Eleonore Playground, the widened Annunciation

Street space has been renamed in honor of Alma Peters (1896-1973), whose house is at the playground site and who is remembered for her activities with the children of the neighborhood for more than forty years. An employee of New Orleans Recreation Department, she was designated a supervisor of the playground.

Extensive inquiries have not revealed the name source for Alonzo, the small street at the terminus of the Alma Peters Playspot. The name appears on early maps, and records show that the already existing street was extended across Tchoupitoulas Street to the river by a city ordinance in 1895. Some Alonzo family members believe a family legend that their antecedent was associated with the pirate Jean Lafitte, but not one can supply a clue about the street name.

One final eccentricity is that Exposition Boulevard (Figure 12) has no street way, only a pedestrian walk at the

Audubon Park margin. According to a hearsay report, a street way was omitted in response to the wish of a property owner, although a published map associated with the 1884 Exposition indicated a horse-car line along this boundary. A nameless alley is inserted behind Boulevard houses for access and trash pickup. This arrangement is rare in New Orleans, though not uncommon in other cities—for example, Philadelphia, Galveston, Milwaukee, and Seattle.

The private street arrangement, like Audubon Place or Rosa Park, is a familiar concept in St. Louis, where local people believe it is unique to St. Louis.

What is the appearance of our presently studied upper segment of Uptown, considered in relation to the entire inner city? New Orleans, viewed as it were from outer space, is essentially a nineteenth century city (surrounded indeed by the recent sprawl of speedways, parking lots, and relative facelessness). The Vieux Carré, the old center of the original settlement, is presently datable as dead-center nineteenth century, averaging early to late, with a sprinkling of barely a dozen late-eighteenth century structures and a comparable negligible spillover of twentieth century. The inner city, ranging from early to late from its historic core, has a spread of nineteenth century neighborhoods (excepting the business district, which since World War II has progressively lost much of its nineteenth century feeling). Extended at the far end of the radiating urban pattern is our upper stretch of Uptown, where nineteenth century developments are extra late, and a minority. Yet, this extended part of the pattern belongs recognizably to the essential New Orleans, a nineteenth century American city.

Allowing for a buffer of fifty years, which has become technically the measure for historicity, the area is already on the National Register of Historic Places. It is not difficult to foresee that in another half century or less the area will have accumulated a number of cherished associates as well as a special appreciation for its environmental beauties and interesting historic features. The corridor of St. Charles Avenue, where it widens to the spaciousness of the park and colleges, has acquired the quality of a coordinated urban center that is outstanding among American cities. Like the symbolically central image of Jackson Square, it developed out of a favorable series of considered design decisions and possibly also a few happy accidents.

Other streets in the vicinity have an overall sense of comfort and distinction. Already some neighborhoods can be seen as consistent artifacts, as completely representative of an historic phase in comparison with any corresponding parts of the Garden District. A drive or walk in these shaded surroundings can induce feelings of well-being and visual satisfaction.

Here and there a few objects that might be called "street furniture" contribute to the scene. Bollards at corner curbs or gutters to ward off wheels of turning traffic have almost entirely disappeared. Their thin walls of cast iron were friable, and so readily destroyed over the years. A few on Palmer Avenue were recently demolished. Others appear in Gilmore Park. The ambivalent, solid bollards at the welcoming gateway to Audubon Park are paradoxical and should go. There are better ways of handling traffic circulation.

The thin metal of streetlight standards is also succumbing to the onslaught of modern traffic. The old, sputtering carbon-arc lamps that prevailed at the turn of this century were gradually replaced by incandescent lighting during the 1920s. Along St. Charles Avenue, the handsome, bronze columns topped by milk-glass spheres were maintained until the early 1950s, even though their glass shades made targets for mischievous sports. The base and capitals of these classic standards remain, the column modified by elongation and the fixture stretched like a gooseneck to accommodate mercury-vapor light bulbs, and now sodium lamps that give more lumens per dollar, but also give off a deathly glow. A few of the classic, unstretched columns may be found about the city, some near City Park and on the Tulane University campus. These observations on street lighting and fixtures have been confirmed in consultation with John Bendler of Tulane University, assistant director emeritus of physical plant.

The appealing qualities of these University Section neighborhoods are their gracious spaces and the prevalent plant life—spreading greenery, color, and perfume of flowering shrubs, columnar palms, and above all, the area's crowning delight, a filigree roof of outspread, aging oaks. Coming generations in retrospect will cherish this comfortable ensemble as a historic Upper Garden District.

THE UPTOWN FAUBOURGS

SAMUEL WILSON, JR., F.A.I.A.

HURSTVILLE

Hurstville, the first of the faubourgs or suburbs of uptown New Orleans, above the old City of Jefferson, extended from Joseph Street to the Bloomingdale Line, a line between State and Eleonore streets. It was named for Cornelius Hurst and in its original plan, as shown on the Zimpel map of 1834 (Figure 1), ran from an unnamed street (now Joseph) marked "proposed railroad" and extended upriver four blocks and back 7½ blocks beyond Nayades (now St. Charles). The streets perpendicular to the river were, on Zimpel's map, named Arabella for Hurst's daughter, Eleonore for his wife, and Alonzo. The first street parallel to the river was to be the riverfront route of the proposed railroad that was to tie in with the New Orleans and Carrollton Rail Road at Nayades. Next was Front Street, followed by Tchoupitoulas, Jersey, Laurel, Live Oak, and Magazine.

The long, narrow strip of land that became Hurstville had been part of the plantation of Jean Baptiste François LeBreton that was bought by Cornelius Hurst, Pierre Joseph Tricou, and Julie Robert Avart. The ten-arpent plantation, once part of that of Etienne Boré, was sold before notary Felix de Armas on May 25, 1831. On February 8, 1832, before notary Carlisle Pollock, the three purchasers divided it into three equal parts, Hurst receiving the downriver third, and then on the following September 11, he acquired Tricou's center tract. Thus it was that the lower two-thirds of the former LeBreton Plantation became Hurstville.

Hurst House

Soon after acquiring his first part of the LeBreton plantation, and probably before he began to consider the possibility of developing a new faubourg, Cornelius Hurst began the construction of the splendid residence (Figure 2) which has since been known by his name. The site was near the lower boundary of the tract, facing the river, which eventually became the square bounded by Tchoupitoulas, Arabella, Annunciation, and Joseph. The LeBreton tract was still a plantation, but it is not known if Hurst thought of his new home as a plantation house or as a suburban residence.

The name of the architect of the house is unknown, but the work was carried out under the superintendence of William Cochran, who contracted with William Maples and James Bozeman for the brickwork and Rausburgh and McCurrie for the framing, the carpentry, and possibly the elaborate millwork found throughout the exterior and interior of the house. The Doric colonnade that surrounds the house was evidently done by someone who was familiar with such books as Asher Benjamin's *The American Builder's Companion* with its plates on "Grecian Architecture." The entablature with its triglyph frieze and cornices and the Palladian windows (Figure 3) in the gable ends are all exceptionally well detailed, and the interior door and window casings (Figure 4) with carved flower corner blocks and reeded frames with carved acanthus leaves are of unusual elegance. The marble mantels with Ionic columns were probably brought down from New York. Contained in a lawsuit between Maples and Hurst is much information concerning the construction of the house. One of the carpenters, William L. Slaughter, testified that the framing was "unusually difficult and expensive" and "a great deal more than is done on a common house."

Cornelius Hurst did not long reside in the new mansion, for on March 6, 1835, before notary William Boswell, he leased it to Clement Biddle Penrose, with its outbuildings and structures on the batture "consisting of a Steam Saw Mill and engine, driving one upright and nine cross cut saws, an iron corn and cob mill and a large pair of stones, complete; a large eating house, kitchen, store house and blacksmith's shop. . . . Also eight negro cabins and a lot of ground on said plantation, three hundred feet square, together with a large brick dwelling house, brick kitchen, servants rooms, stable, smoke house and a chicken house of wood." This lease to Penrose, a relative of the Wilkinson family, was for the term of five years, from February 21,

Editors' Note

This article is being published posthumously. Wilson, who died in 1993, had not completed his final editing of the article. The editors have chosen to publish it in the form he left it, with only minor corrections and editing.

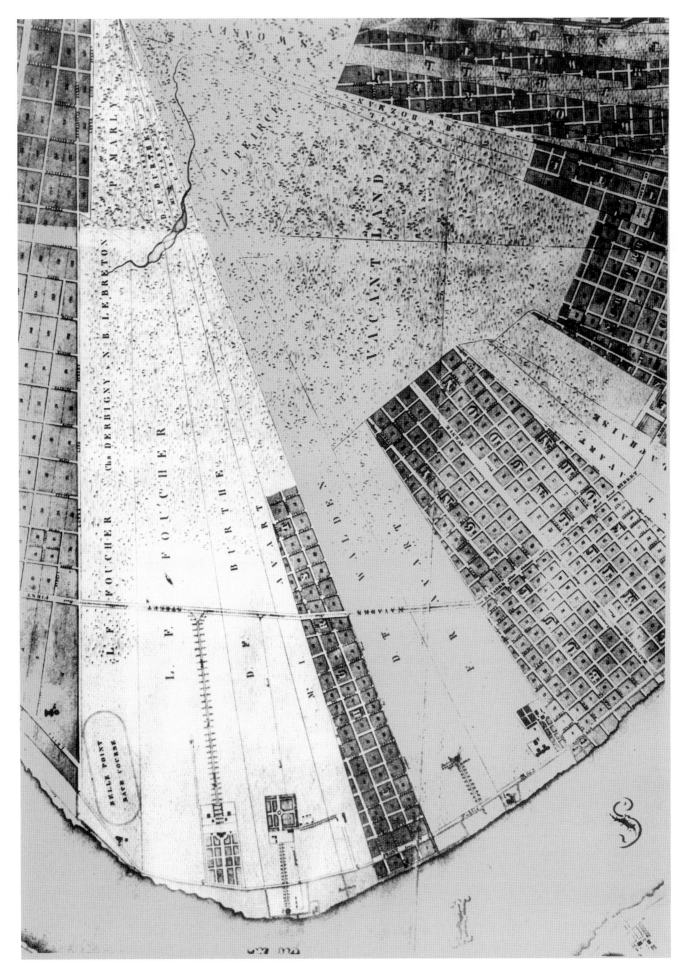

Fig. 1. Detail from "Topographical Map of New Orleans and Its Vicinity, 1834," Charles F. Zimpel. (Courtesy K&W)

Fig. 2. 5619 Tchoupitoulas, now 3 Garden Lane, Hurst House, Charles Franck, photographer. (Courtesy K&W)

Fig. 3. Palladian Window in Gable End, Hurst House. (Courtesy K&W)

AT RIGHT: Fig. 4. Gib Window and Frame, Hurst House. (Courtesy K&W)

Fig. 5. Dormer, Hurst House. (Courtesy K&W)

which reduced the width of the 300-square-foot lot mentioned in the lease to 280 square feet so that a new street, Nashville Avenue, could be added to the center of the plan to accommodate the proposed New Orleans and Nashville Rail Road. On March 20, 1837, a lengthy, two-column advertisement appeared in the *Louisiana Courier,* announcing that there "will be sold on Tuesday, the 28th instant . . . that valuable and eligibly situated property called Hurstville." The New Orleans and Carrollton Rail Road was already in operation across the rear of the property, making lots away from the river desirable, especially along Nayades (now St. Charles Avenue).

Cornelius Hurst finally lost his Hurstville house and property to his creditors, and it was sold by the sheriff on April 15, 1840. It was purchased by Louis B. Salomon and Louis Auguste Neal, two of the principal creditors, for $28,000. Then on November 15, 1841, they sold the house to Alexander Parker Gray. He owned it only until June 5, 1844, when he sold it to a business associate, Edwin Campbell, who on March 3, 1849, sold it to Jean Ursin Lavillebeuvre. The architect-diarist Thomas K. Wharton visited the house on May 3, 1855, and wrote:

> I give a sketch from the bank of the river about 4 miles above New Orleans when we all went out together to get a mouthful of fresh air. It shows one of those old plantation houses which are fast disappearing, but some of which still remain to link us with the time when the now populous region lying between the city and Carrollton was laid out wholly in quiet farms and rich plantations. Many a splendid group of foliage and fine grazing tracts still exist but the corn and sugar-fields are all gone.

He marked the sketch (Figure 6) "M. Lavillebeuvre's old plantation house on the river 4 miles above N. Orleans." The house was then less than twenty-five years old. Lavillebeuvre may have had trouble meeting his payments on the notes on the house and it was advertised for sale, the following advertisement appearing on the front page of the *Daily Picayune* on January 3, 1852:

Delightful Residence and Garden near the River
at Hurstville, Parish of Jefferson.

BY J.A. BEARD & MAY, Auctioneers—On SATURDAY, Jan. 3, 1852, at 11 o'clock, will be sold at Banks' Arcade, without any reserve—

All that well known and delightfully situated property at Hurstville, formerly the residence of J.U. Lavillebeuvre, Esq., between the railroad and the river, comprising two fine squares of ground, highly improved, with a large and roomy dwelling, kitchens, barns, chicken house, stables, &c., with a garden well stocked with fruit trees, evergreens, choice shrubs, and about 600 sweet orange trees; and particularly desirable for a gentleman's residence or market garden, as any extent of cultivated land can be obtained immediately adjoining. The facilities of reaching the property is easy both by railroad or omnibus. The property to be sold

1835, at the rate of $5,000 per year. It was specified "that the said Hurst is to have the use of one half of the lot of three hundred feet square with the buildings thereon and shall also have the right of removing the eight negro cabins either to the batture or to the lot immediately back of the dwelling house."

Penrose did not long enjoy the Hurst house, for on August 5, 1837, he again appeared before notary Boswell and abrogated the lease of March 6, 1835. He and Hurst agreed "that the said Clement B. Penrose shall forthwith deliver up to the said Cornelius Hurst, the batture saw mill, negro cabins and all other buildings on said leased premises, with the exception, however, of the dwelling house and all outhouses situated on the square of three hundred feet which are to be delivered on the fifteenth day of September next."

Perhaps this abrogation of the lease was due to Penrose's health, for he died in 1839, or it may have been for Hurst's benefit, for that year he had had a new plan for Hurstville drawn up by Benjamin Buisson, dated March 17, 1837,

Fig. 6. "Old Plantation House on the River 4 miles above N. Orleans," May 3, 1855, by Thomas K. Wharton. (Courtesy New York Public Library)

without reserve, to close a joint interest. The improvements are insured for $2500.

Terms—The purchaser will assume the payment of two notes of $1125 each, payable April 1, 1852 and 1853, with interest of 6 percent from April, 1850; balance in cash.

Act of sale before A. Mazureau, notary public, at the expense of the purchaser.

It is not known if this sale ever took place, but on March 28, 1853, Lavillebeuvre retroceded the property, including the house and sawmill, to Alexander Parker Gray. Lavillebeuvre may have continued to live in the house, for his address in the 1859 city directory is still listed as Hurstville. Gray sold the house during the Civil War on December 26, 1864, and it passed through a succession of owners until it was acquired on April 19, 1921, by Herman Brunies. Then on July 14, 1921, the house was sold to Isaac H. Stauffer to be removed from the land. The house was dismantled under the direction of the architects Armstrong and Koch and re-erected where it still stands at No. 3 Garden Lane, overlooking the golf course of the New Orleans Country Club.

Paul Cook House

Among other important early houses in Hurstville was that of Paul Cook, which occupied the entire block on St. Charles Avenue between Joseph and Arabella back to Danneel. Cook had bought this block and four additional adjacent squares from George W. Huntington and Thomas A. Clarke on April 7, 1860, for $15,000, before notary W.L. Poole. He then engaged the services of his friend, architect-diarist Thomas K. Wharton, to design a splendid mansion which unfortunately is no longer standing, nor are any photographs of it known to exist. Wharton visited the site of the new house and wrote in his diary on March 29, 1861: "It is a noble square, very high and dry, about 250 x 500

feet and beautiful, planted with choice fruit trees, vegetables, etc." Apparently no buildings existed on the square. The building contract for the house was awarded on April 18, 1861, to James Keating, builder, for $18,685. Another contract was given to Keating the following October 14 for $3,500 for a stable building behind the house. The work was carried out under Wharton's close supervision and was completed in November 1861. It was Wharton's last major work, for he died on May 24, 1862.

Paul Cook sold his mansion (Figure 7) on February 8, 1869, to Miss Mary Amanda May, who sold it at auction on March 21, 1874, to the widow of John Gauche, who had built the Gauche mansion at Royal and Esplanade in 1856. The Cook house was the residence of Mrs. Gauche until her death, when it was sold by her heirs in 1893. It was later bought by William T. Coats, who in 1913 built the house that still stands on the site at St. Charles and Arabella.

When the Cook house was auctioned in 1874, it was described as

that superb Brick Mansion of Miss Mary A. May . . . The Most Complete Family Residence in the South . . . The improvements thereon are of an unusually superior character, combining elegance of finish with the most substantial durability. The mansion and outbuildings are all in brick, in perfect and complete condition, with gas and water works and containing the most modern improvements and conveniences.

The grounds and gardens have been improved at great expense. The walks and banquettes in front are of the finest German stone. Clusters of natural oak, orange, magnolia and other evergreen trees shade the property. Shrubbery of great variety, and exotics of the rarest description, are planted in plats and ornament the grounds, and a rich iron palisade encloses the property from St. Charles Avenue. For style, beauty and comfort it is unsurpassed by any property in the city.

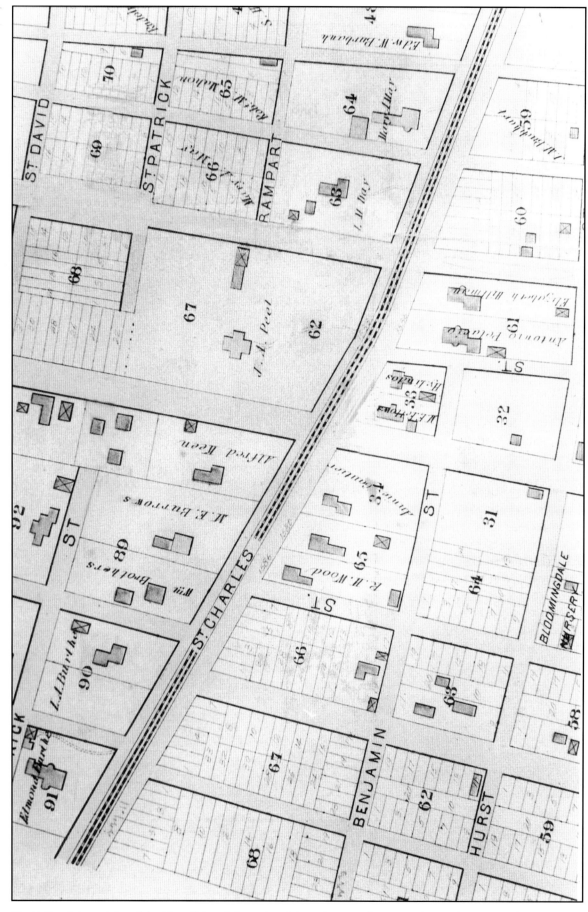

Fig. 7. Detail from *Atlas of the City of New Orleans,* by Elisha Robinson, illustrating the Cook-May Residence, Square 64; Benjamin-Day residence, Square 63; Palacios and Hillman residence, Square 61; Peel residence, Squares 62-67; Fellows and Lindop residences, Square 33; Wood residence, Square 65; Gautier residence, Square 34; Keen residence, Square 89; Burrows and Williams residences, Square 89; L. Burthe residence, Square 90; and E. Burthe residence, Square 91. (Courtesy K&W)

In 1903 an imposing Colonial Revival mansion was built in the side yard of the Cook house for Timothy H. Mc-Carthy, now the residence of the Robert Schoen family.

Judah P. Benjamin House

In the block above the Paul Cook house on St. Charles Avenue between Arabella and Nashville in the 1850s stood a house that Judah P. Benjamin (Figure 8) and his brother Joseph bought as a home for their widowed sister, Rebecca Benjamin Levy, and unmarried sister, Harriet. On April 30, 1835, the Benjamin brothers and their friends, George W. Huntington and Thomas A. Clarke, bought ten squares of ground near Nayades (St. Charles Avenue) for $32,500 from George May. In this transaction, the Benjamin brothers received this square No. 63 between Arabella and Nashville valued at $9,650. The adjacent square, No. 64, on which the Cook house was later erected, was also valued at $9,650 and went to Huntington and Clarke, from whom Paul Cook bought Square 64 and four other squares in 1860.

Judah P. Benjamin had often visited with his sisters at Belle Chasse plantation, below the city on the west bank, which he owned jointly with Samuel Packwood and to whom he sold his interest in April 12, 1853, a few weeks before he bought the Hurstville property. Benjamin, however, maintained his residence with his friend George W. Huntington on Polymnia Street near Coliseum, although it is said that he dined almost every day with his sisters who prepared his favorite dishes. He was elected to the United States Senate in 1852 and in 1859, and during the Civil War served in the cabinet of Jefferson Davis, Confederate president. His sister, Rebecca, and her daughter and sister, Harriet, continued to live in the St. Charles Avenue house until after the fall of New Orleans and its occupation by Federal forces. Mrs. Levy's daughter, Mrs. Popham, gave the following account of the Federal seizure of the house, published in Pierce Butler's *Judah P. Benjamin* (Philadelphia, 1907):

"One night in the summer of 1862," said she, "about nine o'clock, there came a knock on the door that startled the family. Riley, the colored dining room man, went to answer it, and returned with fear in face and accent, to announce that 'there's a Yankee right at the door.' Mrs. Levy and Miss Harriet fled, leaving me to face the young Federal lieutenant whom I found there, and who told me that he had merely been sent to warn us that the house was needed by the military authorities, and would be taken possession of in the morning and used as a hospital for General Weitzel's men. 'This will do,' he said, after inspecting the rooms with a candle while I followed, protesting vainly. 'If you wish to leave at once, you may take away such things as you absolutely need; a squad of men will be sent to protect you to-night.' We began packing up at once, and fortunately,

Fig. 8. Judah P. Benjamin. (Courtesy A.L. Schlesinger, Jr.)

when the dreaded soldiers came, the men proved to be Germans who had known Mr. Popham. By humoring them and plying them with what was left of some rare old Bourbon and Cognac, once highly prized by Mr. Benjamin and his guests, we prevailed upon them to move nearly all of the furniture to the house of a neighbor, kindly put at our service, which was practically empty. Owing a small amount to the German groceryman whose yard adjoined ours, I pulled some palings off the fence and drove the cow into his yard. By this payment in kind, our only debt was cleared.

"All through the night we worked, packing and moving. In the morning, as Mrs. Levy was sitting on a bundle of our belongings, almost the last, on the front porch, another squad of soldiers, with an insolent young fellow in command, came to relieve the complaisant guard of the past night. 'Madame,' said the officer, 'are you the sister of the arch rebel, Benjamin?' Mrs. Levy timidly admitted that she was. 'Then you are not to remove anything from this house. It is a military necessity.' Fortunately this individual was relieved later in the day by a more reasonable officer, who permitted us to remove the few remaining things that we needed."

On August 20, 1863, the Supervising Special Agent of the Treasury Department reported receiving from Capt. J.W.

McClure "subject to confiscation . . . in Square No. 63, Hurstville, Nashville Station on Carrollton R.R., one house & Lot, valued at $6,600, occupied by George P. Bowes. The above property is claimed to be the property of J.P. Benjamin and brothers of New Orleans."

In 1864 the property was sold by the sheriff for taxes to James Madison Wells, Louisiana lieutenant governor and later governor, who sold it less than a year later to L. Madison Day. It later became involved in legal controversy in Fifth District Court in the suit of *T. Micou vs. Judah P. and Joseph Benjamin and L. Madison Day*. As a result, it was again sold by the sheriff on July 21, 1874, for $8,500 to James E. Zuntz. It then passed through a succession of owners until it was purchased for $15,000 by John M. Bonner on March 21, 1887. Bonner decided to remove the Benjamin house and subdivide the property into several lots. On April 17, 1891, he sold a lot 75 feet on Arabella Street by 120 feet in depth, plus the house and its contents in the center of the square to Carrie Newsom, wife of Alphonse O. Pessou. She moved the house to the Arabella Street site where it still stands in a somewhat different form (see "Selective Architectural Inventory," 1630 Arabella).

Fabacher Residence

The front part of the square, on St. Charles between Arabella and Nashville, was acquired by Lawrence Fabacher (Figure 9), president of the Jackson Brewing Company. An article in the *Daily Picayune* reports that Fabacher

> on this St. Charles Avenue square, built a house, or rather, bungalow, with casino, stables and a conservatory. From an artesian well 1,200 feet deep he drew up a stream of pure salt water. For this he built a marble swimming-tank, with Roman baths surrounding it. The remainder of the square he covered with a lawn, flower gardens, vegetable gardens, patches of corn, okra and table vegetables of many kinds.
>
> The result is an elysium. Paradise on the St. Charles Belt is hardly too vigorous a term. It is a pioneer of its kind. There is nothing else in New Orleans like it, though it is safe to predict that there will be soon.
>
> Mr. Fabacher has ideas of his own on the subject of domestic architecture. He employed skilled help to work his designs into workable shape, of course, but the originals were emanations from his own fertile brain. The Casino, most comfortable of his creations, was his own idea, as was the Roman bath. The peculiar style of the house was also originally conceived by him.

The *Picayune* article is illustrated with photographs of the house, the casino, the pool, and other buildings. The house was later demolished, and on half of the site was built a house based on the design of "Tara," from the movie *Gone With the Wind* (Figure 10). This house, which still stands, was built in 1941 for George Palmer, the architect

Fig. 9. Laurence Fabacher, from *The City of New Orleans.* (Courtesy K&W)

being Andrew W. Lockett (see "Selective Architectural Inventory," 5705 St. Charles Avenue).

Following the Civil War, several other important houses were built along the river side of St. Charles Avenue in Hurstville and are still standing. Among these are the house designed by noted architect Henry Howard for Antonio Palacios and erected by builder Daniel Fraser in 1867 at the corner of Eleonore and St. Charles (Figure 7), now the residence of the F. Evans Farwell family (see "Selective Architectural Inventory," 5800 St. Charles Avenue). Next to it is the somewhat similar house at the corner of St. Charles and Nashville, built for John Hillman, who bought the site in 1869. In the block below, between Nashville and Arabella, are two Queen Anne houses built by architect Louis Lambert (see "Selective Architectural Inventory," 5718 and 5726 St. Charles Avenue), and in the block between Arabella and Joseph are two mansard-roofed houses in the French Second Empire style (see "Selective Architectural Inventory," 5604 and 5624 St. Charles Avenue), all of the late-nineteenth century.

According to a survey dated December 6, 1858, by William W. Williams, surveyor for Jefferson Parish, Magazine Street was then extended from Rickerville, where it

Fig. 10. 5705 St. Charles Avenue, Fabacher residence. (Courtesy Edward D'Antoni)

ended in a plank road, across Hurstville and Bloomingdale, where it had been laid out by Benjamin Buisson in the 1830s, and across the Burthe and Foucher plantations to Greenville, which had been laid out in streets and squares. Magazine was then called Foucher Street. The Magazine Street extension was shown as turning into Broadway in Greenville for two blocks, then returning on Elizabeth Street and diagonally across the Foucher tract to meet Magazine Street at the Burthe property line. The diagonal extension was never constructed, nor was it or the Broadway-Elizabeth street part included in the surveyor's list of distances across the other properties.

BLOOMINGDALE

The smallest of the uptown faubourgs was the one called Bloomingdale, which embraced the upper third of the ten-arpent plantation of Jean Baptiste François LeBreton which had been purchased on May 25, 1831, by Cornelius Hurst, Pierre Joseph Tricou, and Julie Robert Avart. Madame Avart retained this third of the plantation while Cornelius Hurst developed the other two-thirds as Hurstville. She then sold her third on May 4, 1834, before notary Felix de Armas to John Green.

Benjamin Buisson made a plan dated November 12, 1836, for subdividing the property which extended up-river from the line of Hurstville to the line of the D.F. Burthe

plantation which became known as the Bloomingdale line, running through the squares between State and Webster streets. State Street ran through the middle of the subdivision, from the river to beyond St. Charles (Nayades). The beginning of this street at the river follows approximately the line of the road from the river road that led to the Le-Breton-Boré, sugar mill, as shown on the Zimpel map of 1834 (Figure 11). The streets parallel to the river were the same as those of Hurstville. The fourth street from the river was widened across the width of the property to provide a site for a market and was named Market Street (now Laurel). The market site is now a small park.

Although the plan for Bloomingdale was made by Buisson in 1836, little building activity took place in the area until after the Cotton Centennial Exposition of 1884 in what later became Audubon Park. The Robinson *Atlas* of 1883 shows only twenty-eight houses on the entire tract, other than the buildings for the German Protestant Orphan Asylum.

This institution purchased the square facing State Street between Camp and Chestnut, running back across the Bloomingdale line to Webster Street, in 1867. On it then was a two-story frame house which served as the only asylum building until June 15, 1869, when the asylum signed a contract before notary Joseph Cohn with a builder, Henry Friedrich, to erect a three-story brick dormitory with a

Fig. 11. Detail from "Topographical Map of New Orleans and Its Vicinity, 1834," by Charles F. Zimpel, showing LeBreton-Boré Sugar Mill and Boré Plantation. (Courtesy K&W)

Fig. 12A and 12B. German Protestant Orphan Asylum, 1869, Henry Friedrich, builder; Charles Hillger, architect. (Courtesy New Orleans Historic District Landmarks Commission)

gallery in front on each floor (Figures 12A and 12B). This building was designed by New Orleans German architect Charles Lewis Hillger and cost $11,650. A second, matching building was soon built, forming a court behind the original building. In the rear, along Webster Street, a two-story brick stable was built. In 1904 the original frame building was replaced by a two-story brick administration building. The two dormitory buildings and the stable were given landmark status in 1978 by the city's Historic District Landmarks Commission.

The asylum ceased operations in 1976 and the entire property was sold and subdivided into twenty-one building lots. The two brick dormitory buildings had their landmark status revoked and they were demolished. The stable building was retained and converted into a handsome residence in 1980 (see "Selective Architectural Inventory," 919 Webster).

Most of the early Bloomingdale residential development occurred along St. Charles Avenue where the property was easily accessible by the New Orleans and Carrollton Railroad. The Robinson *Atlas* of 1883 shows only one brick house in all of Bloomingdale (Figure 13) . This was the residence of J.A. Peel that occupied the entire square between Nashville and State on the river side of St. Charles. The cross-shaped brick house stood on the Bloomingdale half of the square, while the stable was on the Hurstville half, near Nashville Avenue. John A. Peel is listed in Edwards' 1873 city directory as being a partner in the firm of Peel and Reid, wholesale grocers and liquor merchants, 13-15 North Peters. His residence was then the brick

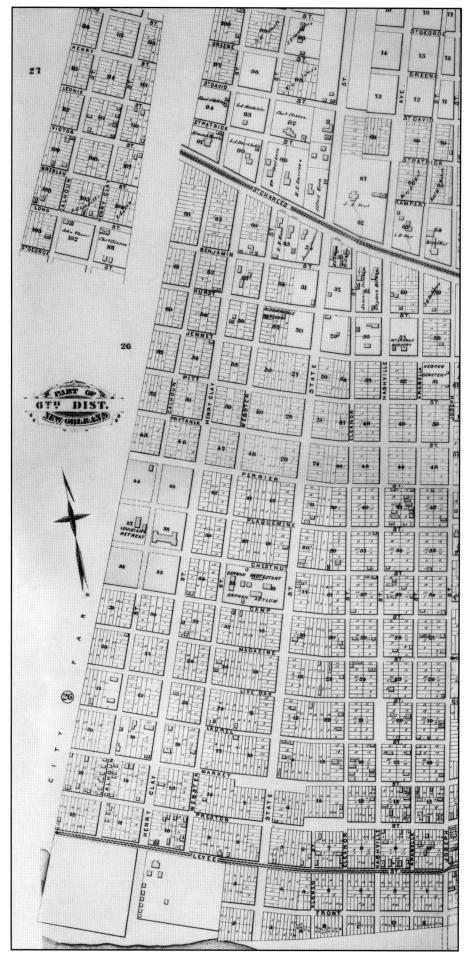

Fig. 13. *Atlas of the City of New Orleans,* by Elisha Robinson, 1883. (Courtesy K&W)

house on St. Charles between State and Nashville. According to the 1869 directory, Peel was then living in Jefferson City and probably built the brick house between 1868 and 1873. He had bought the entire property on St. Charles between State and Nashville from the heirs of R.W. Godwin and wife on May 27, 1868, before notary T.O. Starke. When Peel bought this property, he assumed the mortgage that Godwin had given to J.V. Lavillebeuvre, from whom he had bought it on May 20, 1867. On August 16, 1873, John Peel's wife, Fanny Burgess, died while in Europe, and an inventory of the property, appraised at $21,000, was made by Andrew Hero, Jr. on September 11, 1875. It was about this time that Peel apparently defaulted on the note he still owed to Lavillebeuvre, and the property was seized and sold by the sheriff. Simon Hernsheim, a prominent tobacco merchant, was the successful bidder at $12,000.

Hernsheim, who then lived farther up St. Charles at Pine Street, never lived in the Peel house, but on April 8, 1882, made an exchange of property with Mrs. Minerva Ann Scott, widow of Richard Flower and mother of Walter C. Flower, later mayor of New Orleans. Mrs. Flower then owned and lived in a house at St. Charles and Seventh which she gave to Hernsheim with $6,000 in exchange for the Peel property on St. Charles between Nashville and State. The house at Seventh Street had been built by Richard Flower in 1872 in the Second Empire style and burned in 1984. Hernsheim kept it only a few weeks before selling it. Mrs. Flower and her son, Walter, then moved into the Peel house, where he is listed as residing in the 1883 city directory.

The next owners of the Peel property were Durant da Ponte and John M. Bonner, who bought it on March 30, 1887, from Mrs. Flower for $32,000. They then, in 1891, developed the Hurstville half of the property as Rosa Park, named for da Ponte's wife, Rosa Salomon da Ponte. On June 15, 1893, da Ponte and Bonner sold the site of the Peel house, lots M and H at St. Charles and State, and lots 21 and 20 behind them on State Street to Joseph Tanner, who a few months later on June 6, 1894, sold lots M and H to Henry Plauché Dart before notary J.C. Wenck for $12,000. It was probably about this time that the Peel house was demolished, and Henry Dart had an elaborate French château style, two-story brick mansion erected in its place (Figure 14). In 1913 Dart sold his splendid house to Marie Louise Schmidt, wife of Hugues de la Vergne, for $54,000. It was the de la Vergne residence for many years. After the death of Hugues de la Vergne, his widow married

Fig. 14. 5931 St. Charles Avenue, Henry Dart residence (demolished), 1897, Toledano and Reusch, architects, from *New Orleans, Louisiana: The Crescent City.* (Courtesy K&W)

Henry Landry de Freneuse, and after her death the house was sold and demolished.

Across St. Charles Avenue, opposite the Peel house, according to the 1883 Robinson *Atlas,* were the residence of M.E. Fellows at the corner of St. Charles and State and that of Henry Lindop at the corner of Eleonore, both properties extending back to Benjamin Street (Figure 7). The 1873 city directory lists E.T. and E.J. Fellows, attorneys-at-law, with offices at No. 12 Exchange Place, upstairs, and both residing at State Street at the corner of St. Charles. In the 1890s, the house was the residence of John McEnery (1833-1891), who had served as governor from 1872 until his administration was overthrown in 1874 by the Federal authorities. His brother, Samuel, was elected governor in 1884, the year the World's Industrial and Cotton Centennial Exposition opened in nearby Audubon Park.

Early in 1906, the First Presbyterian Church on Lafayette Square purchased the old Fellows property from Mrs. John McEnery with the idea of erecting a church to be known as Palmer Memorial in memory of its noted pastor, the Reverend Benjamin Morgan Palmer (Figure 15). Palmer had lived nearby on Henry Clay (Palmer Avenue), beyond St. Charles, and in 1902 died as a result of being struck by a streetcar at the corner of St. Charles and Henry Clay. The name of Henry Clay beyond St. Charles has been changed to Palmer Avenue in his honor. The idea of a church in his memory was abandoned, and the old house was used for the Sunday school that the church had established in the area in 1905.

In 1911 the First Presbyterian Church then erected on the site a concrete block building, designed by W.W. Van Meter, architect, which in 1920 became the St. Charles Avenue Presbyterian Church. In 1924 a Sunday school building was erected in the rear of the "Little Church," at the corner of Benjamin Street. In 1928 construction was begun on the present church at the corner of St. Charles and State Street, also designed by architect W.W. Van Meter (see "Selective Architectural Inventory," 5914 St. Charles Avenue). The "Little Church" was demolished some years later when the Sunday school building was enlarged in 1949, Favrot and Reed being the architects, with Earl L. Mathes associate.

The 1873 city directory lists Henry Lindop, importer of slating, with an office at 112 Carondelet and a residence on St. Charles, between Eleonore and State. The same directory also lists Aime Gautier, cotton weigher, as living on St. Charles at the corner of State (Figure 7). The 1883 Robinson *Atlas* also shows a single frame house on the large lot bounded by St. Charles, State, Benjamin, and the Bloomingdale line belonging to "Annie Gautier." Opposite this, across St. Charles Avenue at State Street, on a large lot is shown a frame house of Alfred Keen (Figure 7), but his

Fig. 15. The Reverend Benjamin Palmer, from *Jewell's Crescent City Illustrated.* (Courtesy K&W)

name does not appear in the 1881 directory. In 1883, however, Fred F. Keen, a clerk with Forstall, Ross and Clayton, ship and steamship agents, is listed as living on State between St. Charles and St. Patrick. None of these St. Charles Avenue houses, the principal houses in Bloomingdale, has survived.

Much of the Bloomingdale land beyond St. Charles Avenue first developed as nurseries and dairies. On December 23, 1875, E.F. Lavillebeuvre, who had several squares in Bloomingdale on State Street behind the Peel property, inserted the following advertisement in the *Daily Picayune:*

> TO GARDENERS AND MILKMEN — To rent, on a long lease, ten squares of ground, measuring together about twenty arpents of high and superior land, under fence, with gardener's house, situated in the Sixth District, between State and Nashville Avenue, commencing at the second square from St. Charles street in the rear and adjoining the residence of John A. Peel, Esq., thirty minutes distance from Canal street by the Carrollton cars, and in proximity to the city markets. There is on the place a number of bearing fruit trees, such as orange, plum, fig and scuppernong vines. Soil light and easy to work. Ten squares more next adjoining could be added to the above if desired. Terms suitable to the times.

The 1883 Robinson *Atlas* shows the Bloomingdale Nursery on Webster between Hurst and Jeannette (now

Garfield), probably extending back to State Street. In 1904 the Steckler Seed Company moved its nursery and garden from the Bayou St. John area to Nashville Avenue and Pitt Street. Bloomingdale is now one of the best residential sections of New Orleans.

BURTHEVILLE

The last of the uptown faubourgs to be subdivided and laid out in streets and squares was Burtheville, the plan of which (by the surveyor Numegger) is dated January 24, 1854. This plantation of Dominique François Burthe extended from the Bloomingdale line to the lower boundary of the L.F. Foucher plantation, now Audubon Park. The wide central avenue was named in honor of Henry Clay and the parallel streets on each side for John C. Calhoun and Daniel Webster, the three noted statesmen who had died in 1850 and 1852. Calhoun and Webster streets did not extend to the river, but began at Tchoupitoulas Street, then known as Levee; Calhoun Street beyond St. Charles was known as Edmond, for Edmond Burthe, whose residence was at the corner of St. Charles and Edmond (Calhoun). Henry Clay beyond St. Charles was renamed Palmer Avenue about 1898 in honor of the Reverend Benjamin Morgan Palmer, minister of the First Presbyterian Church from 1856 until his death in 1902.

The entire area of Burtheville, as well as Bloomingdale and Hurstville, had once been the plantation of Jean Etienne Boré, (Figure 16), who first granulated sugar successfully here in 1795. His extensive buildings and gardens were located in the area now bounded by Annunciation, Henry Clay, Constance, and Calhoun. Boré, had received this plantation on October 1, 1781, from the widow of Juan Piseros in exchange for a plantation that he owned on the German Coast. Piseros had acquired it on March 18, 1774, from Don Juan Lafite and Don Francisco Langlois. At the time of the sale before notary J.B. Garic, this twenty-one-arpent plantation had a house, buildings, gardens, and other features. Boré first grew indigo on his plantation about four miles above New Orleans and in 1784 gave 1,400 pounds of indigo to Bertrand Dingirart of the German Coast in exchange for thirty-four slaves. When Boré's title to the plantation was confirmed by the United States in 1812, it was stated that the "said land had been successively transferred by several proprietors thereof, since the year 1729, down to the present claimant." In 1729 it was part of the extensive plantation of Jean Baptiste le Moyne de Bienville, the city's founder.

In 1796, Boré's plantation was visited by the French General Victor Collot, who wrote:

His establishment consists of a mill, drying room and shed (the whole built of bricks and covered with tiles), including cylinders and kettles. It cost him but $4,000. It is

Fig. 16. Jean Etienne de Boré. (Courtesy Rare Books and Manuscripts Division, Howard-Tilton Memorial Library, Tulane University)

true that the labor was done by his own negroes, forty in all, men and women. It is also true that the bricks, tiles, lime and carpenters' wood were all prepared by his laborers, on his plantation, and the entire construction was finished by them in eighteen months.

In 1798, Boré received a visit from the Duke of Orleans, the future French king, Louis Philippe, and his two brothers. In 1803 Pierre Clement de Laussat, the French Commissioner whom Napoleon sent to take Louisiana back from Spain and to transfer it to the United States, appointed Boré as mayor of New Orleans. Laussat wrote that in looking for a qualified person to fill the post of the city mayor, he had his eye on "Boré, a Creole from a distinguished family, a former musketeer in France, one of the strongest and ablest planters of Louisiana, and a man well known for his patriotism and the unshakable independence of his character."

Laussat also wrote of his visit to Boré's plantation in May 1803:

The residence of M. Boreé [sic] . . . was quite attractive, surrounded by lovely gardens with magnificent lanes of orange trees loaded with abundant blossoms as well as with fruit in every stage of ripening. It was in this place that the first attempt to raise sugarcane in Louisiana was made and sustained. This cultivation is still carried out successfully there and has had, since, many prosperous imitators in the neighboring area.

In the following months, Laussat again visited Boré:

I invited myself to dinner at M. Boré's. I had refused invitations to his formal dinners, and I surprised him at home with his family. He gave me a tour of his properties, his gardens, his walks lined with trees, his sugarcane fields, and his establishments. His last sugar crop [1802] had been about eighty thousand pounds of sugar, which was considered of premium quality in lower Louisiana.

In July 1806 William C.C. Claiborne, first American governor of Louisiana, wrote to President Thomas Jefferson of a visit he had made to this important plantation: "Between Col. Macarty's farm [Carrollton] and the city resides Mr. Boré; he is a neat planter and has evinced much taste in the arrangement of his garden and yards."

In *Harper's* magazine for March 1887, Boré's grandson, Louisiana historian Charles Gayarré, in his article entitled "A Louisiana Sugar Plantation of the Old Regime," gives a picture of life on the Boré plantation, where he spent much of his childhood. He describes the approach to the house from the river road and its gardens:

A magnificent avenue of pecan-trees led from the public road alongside the bank of the river to the vast enclosure within which stood the house of M. de Boré, with its numerous dependencies. That part of the enclosure which faced the river presented a singular appearance. . . . It was that of a fortified place, for there was to be seen, with a revetment of brick five feet high, a rampart of earth about fifteen feet in width and sloping down to large moats filled with water and well stocked with frogs, fish, and eels. This rampart was clothed in clover, and at its foot, on the edge of the moats, there grew a palisade of the plant known in Louisiana under the name of "Spanish-daggers" . . .

This picturesque and uncommon line of fortified enclosure extended a good deal more than three hundred feet on both sides of the entrance gate that opened into the courtyard at the end of the pecan avenue. . . . On the opposite side, in front of this line of enclosure, there was another consisting of a well-trimmed and thick orange hedge four feet in height. Beyond were the gardens and several alleys of superb grown-up orange-trees, gorgeous in turn, according to the season, with their snowy blossoms and their golden apples. . . .

This plantation was sagaciously and tastefully laid out for beauty and productiveness. The gardens occupied a large area, and at once astonished the eye by the magnificence of their shady avenues of orange-trees. Unbroken retreats of myrtle and laurel defied the rays of the sun. Flowers of every description perfumed the air. Extensive orchards produced every fruit of which the climate was susceptible. By judicious culture there had been obtained remarkable success in producing an abundance of juicy grapes.

Jean Etienne Boré (whom his grandson always referred to as de Boré although Boré never used the "de" in his writings

or on his tombstone) served as the first mayor of New Orleans, from 1803 to 1804. He died on his plantation on February 2, 1820, and the inventory, begun March 22, 1820, gives the following description of

The Principal House of the said Plantation.

This house is constructed with as much elegance as solidity; it is truly a beautiful and good building. It is built on sills set on brick piers, bricked between posts, and besides it is covered with planks on three sides. A gallery runs along the front toward the yard. The perron and stair of the principal entrance of the house are brick, having a peristyle above them. All the rooms are planked top and bottom; the drawing room (salle de compagnie) has a plaster ceiling. This fine house is divided as follows:

It really forms two main buildings which have each their own roof, but these two units are linked by a spacious covered passage, so that the whole forms in fact but a single house. The principal unit whose facade is on the yard is composed of a drawing room with fireplace; three cabinets, two of which have beds set up, consequently serving as bed chambers. The passage which has been spoken of above opens on the drawing room which was just mentioned and takes up there and leads to a dining room which is part of the second unit. This passage is fitted at right and left with a fixed jalousie; it is ceiled in planks and surmounted by an upper story forming a pretty bed chamber. The second unit includes a large and fine dining room having a fireplace, a fine bed chamber with fireplace, also a pantry; a cellar whose walls are of brick, an office and finally a small passage for communicating within the garden and other places on the rear of the said house.

Then follows a description of the numerous outbuildings of the plantation, including the billiard room; the milk house; a small apartment serving as a distillery; the kitchen; a seed storehouse; the coach house; the stables; the negroes' kitchen; a milling room for corn and rice; the sugar works; the mill and the refinery; the cattle shed; the workshop kitchen; a building formerly serving as a rum distillery; the negro huts or cabins, thirteen huts, each 12 feet by 18 feet, and five double cabins 12 feet by 36 feet, of posts in the ground; the forge; a storehouse serving also as a coach house and stable, 25 feet by 100 feet with a long gallery ten feet wide; two pigeon cotes, 12 feet square on brick piers; the hospital; the master kitchen, serving also as lodging for the servants; two cabins for the use of the domestics of the principal house; and five huts serving as chicken houses. This was indeed a plantation of major importance.

Boré's wife, Jeanne Marguerite Marie Destrehan, whom he had married in Paris in November 1771, had died in New Orleans in 1814. When Boré died in 1820, the plantation was inherited by his two surviving daughters and by the two sons of his diseased daughter. His daughter, Francisca Isabel, wife of Pierre Foucher, owner of the neighboring plantation, now Audubon Park, inherited one-third of the estate, as did his other daughter, Marie Elizabeth, widow of Charles Gayarré. A third daughter, Jeanne Marguerite, had died, leaving her two sons, Jean Baptiste François LeBreton and Jean Barthelemy Edmond Dechapelles LeBreton, heirs each to one-sixth of Boré's estate.

On May 22, 1820, the Fouchers sold their one-third interest in the estate to their LeBreton nephews, leaving them and their aunt, the widow of Charles Gayarré, owners of the entire Boré plantation. Madame Gayarré and her two nephews then on May 5, 1820, made an agreement to operate the plantation for the next four years. One of the brothers, Jean Barthelemy Edmond LeBreton, and Madame Gayarré died soon after, and her son, Charles E.A. Gayarré, and his cousin, Jean Baptiste François LeBreton, the sole heirs, divided the property between them. Gayarré took the half adjacent to the Foucher tract and on April 23, 1825, sold two arpents of it to his uncle, Pierre Foucher. Then on August 6, 1829, he sold the remaining eight arpents, one toise, to Gustave Marigny. Marigny died soon after, and Bernard Marigny, buying the property from Gustave's succession on June 3, 1831, sold it the same day to Dominique François Burthe for $38,000. This was the land that became Burtheville when subdivided in 1854.

The property was later inherited by Edmond Burthe, but little had been accomplished in the way of development.

After the Civil War, a case was brought in the Second District Court, No. 2921, involving the succession of D.F. Burthe, *Edmond Burthe vs. Union Insurance Co. of New Orleans,* for a partition. As a result, most of the property was put up for auction on May 29, 1867, with the following advertisement appearing in the *Daily Picayune:*

AUCTION SALES
BY J.B. WALTON & DESLONDE
GREAT SALE
OF VALUABLE AND IMPROVING PROPERTY,
ON LONG CREDIT AND ON EASY TERMS.
SIXTY-NINE SQUARES OF GROUND, SUB-DIVIDED
INTO FOURTEEN HUNDRED AND NINETY-TWO LOTS
IN BURTHEVILLE.
Embracing all the Property between Levee street and six squares back of St. Charles street and the Carrollton Railroad, and between Bloomingdale and Foucher. To close an estate and for partition.

By this time, the extensive buildings of Jean Etienne Boré, located mostly in Squares 14, 19, and 22, had apparently disappeared, and these squares were being offered for sale, each containing twenty-four or twenty-six lots (Figures 17 and 18). When the Robinson *Atlas* was published in 1883, only about a dozen insignificant buildings existed on the main street, Henry Clay Avenue, between Tchoupitoulas and St. Charles. The only brick building besides the

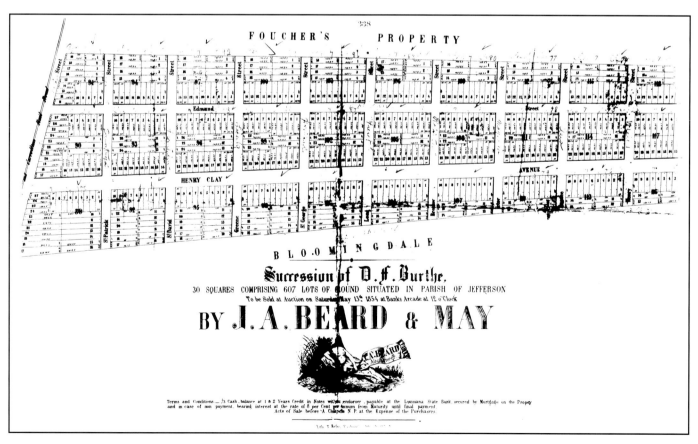

Fig. 17. "Succession of D.F. Burthe, 30 Squares to be Sold at Auction May 13, 1854." (Courtesy Lawyer's Title Insurance Company)

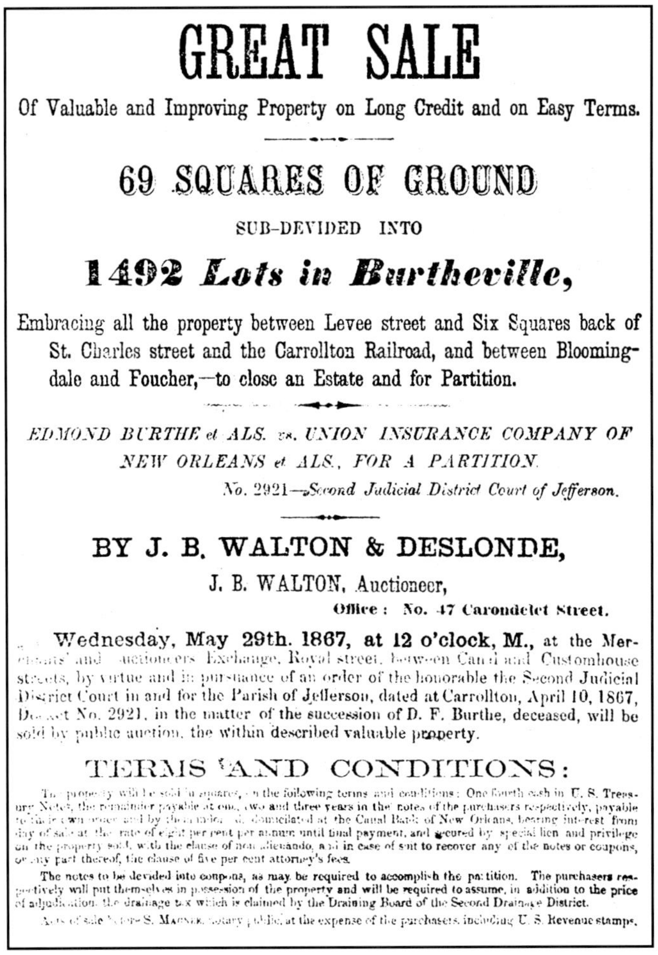

GREAT SALE

Of Valuable and Improving Property on Long Credit and on Easy Terms.

69 SQUARES OF GROUND

SUB-DEVIDED INTO

1492 *Lots in Burtheville*,

Embracing all the property between Levee street and Six Squares back of St. Charles street and the Carrollton Railroad, and between Bloomingdale and Foucher,—to close an Estate and for Partition.

EDMOND BURTHE et ALS. vs. UNION INSURANCE COMPANY OF NEW ORLEANS et ALS., FOR A PARTITION.

No. 2921—*Second Judicial District Court of Jefferson.*

BY J. B. WALTON & DESLONDE,

J. B. WALTON, Auctioneer,

Office : No. 47 Carondelet Street.

Wednesday, May 29th. 1867, at 12 o'clock, M., at the Merchants' and Auctioneers' Exchange, Royal street, between Canal and Customhouse streets, by virtue and in pursuance of an order of the honorable the Second Judicial District Court in and for the Parish of Jefferson, dated at Carrollton, April 10, 1867, Docket No. 2921, in the matter of the succession of D. F. Burthe, deceased, will be sold by public auction, the within described valuable property.

TERMS AND CONDITIONS:

The property will be sold in squares, on the following terms and conditions: One fourth cash in U. S. Treasury Notes, the remainder payable at one, two and three years in the notes of the purchasers respectively, payable to their own order and by them made, domiciled at the Canal Bank of New Orleans, bearing interest from day of sale at the rate of eight per cent per annum until final payment, and secured by special lien and privilege on the property sold, with the clause of non alienando, and in case of suit to recover any of the notes or coupons, or any part thereof, the clause of five per cent attorney's fees.

The notes to be devided into coupons, as may be required to accomplish the partition. The purchasers respectively will put themselves in possession of the property and will be required to assume, in addition to the price of adjudication, the drainage tax which is claimed by the Draining Board of the Second Drainage District.

Acts of sale before S. Magner, notary public at the expense of the purchasers including U. S. Revenue stamps.

Fig. 18. "Great Sale of Valuable and Improving Property on Long Credit and on Easy Terms," May 29, 1867. (Courtesy Lawyer's Title Insurance Company)

Fig. 19. 6145 St. Charles Avenue, M.E. Burrows residence (demolished). (Courtesy HNOC, 1982.57.4)

stable of the German Protestant Orphan Asylum on Webster Street was the large mental hospital, the Louisiana Retreat, on Henry Clay, between Coliseum and Chestnut. This institution, which still occupies the same site, became De Paul Hospital, owned by the Sisters of Charity of St. Vincent de Paul of Emmitsburg, Maryland. In 1888 on January 30, before notary J.J. Wolfe, the sisters contracted with Ferdinand Reusch for an additional brick building here, for which Albert Diettel and Son were the architects, the cost $50,057, for the "Louisiana Retreat Asylum."

As in Bloomingdale, the most important residential construction, as shown in the Robinson *Atlas,* was along St. Charles Avenue. Only two houses were indicated on the river side of the avenue in Burtheville—that of R.H. Wood, at the corner of Webster (Figure 7), its grounds extending back to Benjamin Street, and, between it and the Bloomingdale line, another large frame house. Across St. Charles, opposite these two houses, was the residence of M.E. Burrows, a large brick house with a rear frame wing (Figure 19), and next to it, at the corner of Henry Clay (later Palmer), was the residence of William Brothers (Figure 7). Across the street, taking up half the square between Henry Clay and Calhoun, was the large frame residence of L.A. Burthe, and across Calhoun was the large house of Edmond Burthe. None of these names appears in the city directory of 1883 except L. André Burthe, with the firm of Chalard and Hoffman, commission merchants, but his residence was then at 207 North Rampart Street.

In the *Daily Picayune* of April 12, 1884, the other half of the block, which was the side yard of the L.A. Burthe house, was advertised for sale:

FOR FOREIGN OWNER'S ACCOUNT
ADMIRABLE BUILDING SITES
Opposite the Upper City Park,
THE
HALF SQUARE OF GROUND,
Planted with Shade and Orange
Trees,
BELOW THE RESIDENCE OF COL. THOS.
HUNTON AND ADJOINING THAT OF
A. GOMILA, ESQ.
The Entire Square of Ground
BEING THE SECOND EAST OF ST.
CHARLES AVENUE,
FRONTING THE LOWER LINE OF THE
UPPER CITY PARK,
BETWEEN HURST AND BENJAMIN
STREETS.

The residence of Anthony Gomila, of Gomila and Company, produce and commission merchants, was the one shown in the Robinson *Atlas* as the home of L.A. Burthe, and the home of Thomas Hunton, lawyer, was that shown as Edmond Burthe's (Figure 7). Both Gomila and Hunton are listed at these Burtheville addresses in the 1883 city directory. Temple Sinai now is on the site of the Gomila residence.

At the river end of Burtheville, the Robinson *Atlas* shows a large house with symmetrical, detached rear wings at the corner of Tchoupitoulas (Levee) and Henry Clay, with a row of cabins back of it, extending along Henry Clay to the river. This large tract extended from the Bloomingdale line to Henry Clay and from Tchoupitoulas to the river. This became the site of the United States Marine Hospital, which was first opened here in April 1885. The site was purchased by the federal government on April 5, 1883, from Celestine Louise La Branche, widow of Polycarpe Fortier, for $55,000. It had been the Fortier family home since the purchase of the site. Polycarpe Fortier had bought it from Dominique François Victor Burthe, administrator of the succession of Dominique François Burthe and his wife, Louise Delord Sarpy, on June 1, 1857, before notary Selim Magner. The elder Burthes for some years had lived in the notable Delord-Sarpy house on Howard Avenue, between Camp and Magazine, that was destroyed for the Camp Street ramp of the Mississippi River bridge.

Meloncy C. Soniat, who married Fortier's daughter, Exilée, wrote an important article, "The Faubourgs Forming the Upper Section of the City of New Orleans," published in the *Louisiana Historical Quarterly* of January 1937. In discussing Burtheville, he states that in purchasing the property from Burthe, Fortier obtained "the exclusive use of a space of twenty-five feet wide in the middle of Henry Clay Avenue. A branch railroad was constructed on this tract of land to connect the brick-yard with the Carrollton Railroad. The old home of the Fortiers is still in existence and is now occupied by one of the surgeons of the Marine Hospital."

When the Marine Hospital (Figure 20) opened in 1885, the *Daily Picayune* carried a lengthy article describing the buildings, only one of which still stands (see "Selective Architectural Inventory," 210 State Street). The others were demolished, and the present main building was erected in the 1930s. The *Picayune's* reporter wrote on April 23, 1885:

> The hospital is built from plans furnished by the Surgeon General, Marine Hospital Service, approved by the supervising architect, and carried out under the general supervision of Col. J.W. Glenn, the Government Architect at this port. It is built in the pavilion style, affording plenty of light and air, and making all the departments within easy access of each other. The pavilions are one-story in height, the other buildings two stories. The kitchen is of brick and all other structures of double weather-boarding, with

Fig. 20. United State Marine Hospital, from *New Orleans, Louisiana: The Crescent City*. (Courtesy K&W)

water-proof paper between the boards. Facing the river is the executive building, or office of the hospital. . . .

The hospital is one of the best arranged in the South, and will be among the future points of interest in the city.

THE FOUCHER PLANTATION

The plantation between the upper line of Burtheville and the lower line of Greenville has become Audubon Park and the site of Tulane and Loyola universities and Audubon Place. This was the ten-and-one-half-arpent plantation bought by Pierre Foucher from Jacques Fontenot on November 18, 1793, before notary Pedro Pedesclaux. Foucher was married that year to Francisca Isabel Boré, daughter of the owner of the neighboring plantation, Jean Etienne Boré. After Boré's death in 1820, Foucher bought two arpents of the Boré plantation from his wife's nephew, Charles Etienne Gayarré, who inherited part of the Boré plantation from his mother. The act of sale of this two-arpent tract was passed before notary Hugues Lavergne on April 23, 1825. The Foucher plantation remained in the Foucher ownership at twelve and one-half arpents until it was finally sold in 1871.

As shown on Charles F. Zimpel's 1834 "Topographical Map of New Orleans and its Vicinity" (Figure 11), the buildings and gardens of the Foucher plantation were even more extensive and elaborate than those of Boré. The large, symmetrically planned house was approached from the river road through an enormous parterre garden about four blocks in depth and two in width, terminating in a semicircular area in front of the main house, which was flanked by symmetrical outbuildings, probably dovecotes. Behind the house were the service yards, stables, and probably large kitchen gardens. The buildings and service areas occupied an additional space of about two blocks by two blocks. From the center of this area, a long, straight road through an alley of trees led all the way to St. Charles Avenue to a railroad that connected to the New Orleans and Carrollton Rail Road.

This was apparently the second house that Pierre Foucher had built on his plantation, which then included the additional seven arpents that later became Greenville. In an article that William H. Williams wrote on the history of Carrollton in 1876, he indicates that the original Foucher house was in the upper part of the plantation, and it will be included in the section on Greenville. Of the later house, shown on the Zimpel map of 1834, Williams says that Foucher had left the earlier house "for the much more imposing residence he had afterwards built on the lower side of his plantation, and which was destroyed during the late war to make room for a military hospital. The ancient building survived the new one" (Figure 21).

Boré's daughter, Francisca Isabel Boré, wife of Pierre

Fig. 21. Camp Sedgwick. (Courtesy Library of Congress)

Foucher, died on October 28, 1830, and was buried from St. Margaret's Chapel on Delord Street. This small frame chapel had been built by Pierre Foucher. When he died two years later, on September 13, 1832, in his will he "recommended that a lot of thirty-eight feet of front, a bit near to Delord street and extending in depth as far as the limit of Mme Poeyfarre, as well as the little wooden chapel constructed by him on this lot should continue after his death to serve the usage of the Catholic cult, but that the property should remain to his family."

Pierre Foucher's heirs were his son, Louis Frederic Foucher, and daughter, Marie Antonine Foucher, wife of Philippe Auguste Delachaise. On July 15, 1833, before notary Theodore Seghers, they donated usage to the wardens of the St. Louis Cathedral "in lieu of the land and of the Delord street Chapel, in full ownership, in the same square as the other lot, under the condition that the said Wardens would construct thereon a chapel and a house to serve it." On this lot the first St. Patrick's parochial school with its chapel was constructed. St. Theresa's Church, built in 1847, later succeeded the Foucher's Delord Street chapel.

In the partition between Louis Frederic Foucher and his sister, he received the uptown plantation, and it remained in the Foucher ownership until 1871. It is said that the plantation had served as the campgrounds of Andrew Jackson's Army of Kentucky and Tennessee before the Battle of New Orleans in 1815, and from 1862 to 1867 it was occupied by troops of Union Gen. Benjamin Butler after the fall of New Orleans in the Civil War. Louis Frederic Foucher died in Paris in 1869.

In one of a series of articles entitled "The Environs of New Orleans" in the New Orleans *Daily Crescent* of June 13, 1866, the anonymous writer gives a vivid description of the Foucher plantation and its neighbor that became Greenville:

We recollect . . . some of the really beautiful country seats in the upper districts . . . these actually enchanting abodes of the then very wealthy residents of those mansion houses. Among some of these fine rural estates, we remember particularly that belonging to the Foucher family, a little above, if not immediately adjoining the plantation of Mr. Noel LeBreton. . . . These two country farms, established upon the most extensive scale, were at the distance of some six or seven miles from the old city of New Orleans, upon the site formerly called the Canadian Point, below Maccarty's plantation. . . .

Here in summer as well as in the midst of winter, the eye would be delighted with a profusion of evergreen vegetation. Upon these plantations, besides the common orange hedges, which served as an inclosure around the very extensive gardens, field and camp districts, we noticed that the owners had, besides the ordinary cypress board fences, used a species of evergreen cactus plant, armed with a covering of multiplex prickles, so as to exclude most substantially all ingress of roving porkers or other intruding

cattle. This was, no doubt, a very great consideration, for the protection of these fine kitchen gardens, the beautiful flower parterres, and the numerous fruit orchards, containing a variety of plums, apricots, peaches, figs, oranges, granates, citrons, lemons—in fact such an assortment of Southern fruits that it took a considerable time for a visitor to come back from his astonishment in seeing such a paradise.

We shall not speak of the long rows of rose bushes, the alleys of myrtle and acacia, shrubberies, etc. Let the reader, who has seen our miniature flower parterre in Jackson's square, imagine this area increased ten fold in size and variety and he will then approximate the beautiful, extensive views beheld in these charming country farms. . . . The United States government, properly estimating the beautiful and healthy location of that vicinity, has thereabout established a military health recruiting station, or an asylum for military invalids.

Five years after this article was published, the Foucher plantation was sold by Mrs. Marguerite F. Burthe, widow of Louis Frederic Foucher, Marquis de Circé, and Mrs. Aline Delachaise, wife of F. Dugué, sister of L.F. Foucher, on May 6, 1871, before notary E.G. Gottschalk to Malek A. Southworth and Robert Bloomer for $150,000. Southworth sold part of his interest to C.E. Gerardy and Company on August 12, 1871, and two days later these investors sold it to the city for $800,000 to become Upper City Park, now Audubon Park. On October 22, 1871, an advertisement appeared in the *New Orleans Republican* in which the Board of Commissioners of the New Orleans Park asked for proposals "for the furnishing of all materials and the construction of a wire railing around the City Park Grounds." Nothing more appears to have been done until the park became the site of "The World's Industrial and Cotton Centennial Exposition" in 1884.

The part of the Foucher plantation beyond St. Charles Avenue was purchased in 1889 by the Reverend John O'Shananahan, S.J., Superior of the Southern Jesuits, to become the site of the Jesuits' Loyola University and the Church of the Most Holy Name of Jesus. An earlier wooden church was built by the Jesuits and served as the parish church from 1892 until it was dismantled in 1922 and re-erected in Westwego, across the river.

GREENVILLE

The town of Greenville, the last of the uptown faubourgs below the town of Carrollton, was once part of the plantation of Pierre Foucher, who had bought the seven-arpent tract on January 15, 1800, at the public sale by the creditors of the succession of Bartholomé Lebreton, before notary Carlos Ximines. The sale was actually made in the name of Pierre Foucher's brother, Louis Foucher, who acknowledged before notary Pedro Pedesclaux on July 23, 1805, that he had made the purchase for his brother, who added

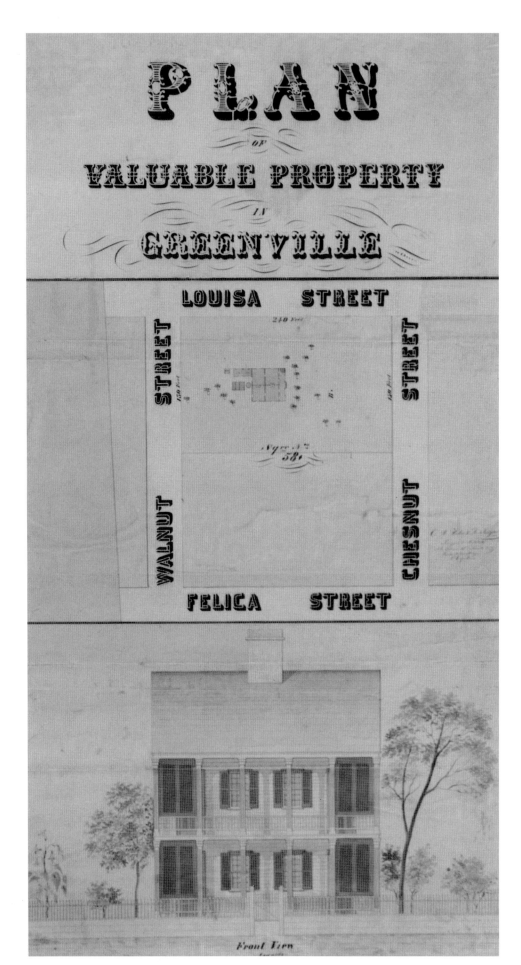

Fig. 22. "Plan of Valuable Property in Greenville , Square 58 Facing Chestnut," by C.A. Hedin and L. Reizenstein, November 12, 1857. (Courtesy NA)

these seven arpents to the ten and one-half arpents he bought in 1793.

In his 1876 article, "History of Carrollton," William H. Williams states that when Pierre Foucher owned this seven-arpent tract, his residence was located on it. He wrote:

> On the upper part of this plantation and near the river, stood till within a few years, perhaps the first and oldest building ever put up in this whole neighborhood of plantations. This was the dwelling known as the William Young house, which was burned down a few years ago. It was a structure of ancient style and time-worn complexion, and seventy years before Greenville was planned, had been the plantation residence of Pierre Foucher, the father of the late owner of the property; built by the ancestor and occupied by him for many years. . . . After being abandoned as a residence, it was occupied for many years as a school or college; and there are old residents now in Jefferson and neighboring parishes who there went to school.

Charles Gayarré, a nephew of Pierre Foucher, attended this school and thus mentions it:

> On the Foucher plantation, and near its upper limit, there was a very large house, occupied by one Lefort, who kept a school that was very well attended by the children of the planters on both sides of the river. It was there that I learned my A B C. . . . This Lefort was a man of culture, but rather rough, and unmercifully addicted to striking his pupils. I was six years old when I attended his school, and I have not yet forgotten, after so many years, the blows which he used to give me because my young and imperfect organs of speech could not properly pronounce the English [word] the. He was very fat and pot-bellied.

On October 14, 1816, L.F.J. Le Fort inserted the following advertisement in the *Louisiana Courier:*

> Full of gratitude for past favors, and resolved to use his best endeavours to deserve new ones, the subscriber makes it known to the public at large and his friends in particular that his academy will be opened for the reception of young gentlemen, on the 4th of November, at his former residence on Mr. P. Foucher's estate.
>
> Cards announcing his terms may be had at Messrs. Bouchon's, Maspero's & Laignel's stores.

Just behind this house was a racetrack, probably laid out by Pierre Foucher and shown on the Zimpel map of 1834 as the Belle Point Race Course (Figure 1). Horse racing was a popular sport then, as it still is in New Orleans.

After the death of Pierre Foucher in 1832, this seven-arpent tract, the Lebreton plantation, was sold on February 27, 1836, by Foucher's son, Louis Frederic Foucher, to James Ogilvie before notary Theodore Seghers. The same day, Ogilvie made an agreement with Oliver Aiken and John Green to develop this land, and as Meloncy Soniat records:

> James Ogilvie caused a plan of the front part of the plantation to be made by Benjamin Buisson, Surveyor, dated April 16, 1836, whereby the estate was subdivided. The subdivision was called "Greenville," no doubt after John Green, one of the partners. It was bounded below by the property of Mr. Foucher, now Audubon Park, and above by Carrollton, Lowerline Street, in front by the River and in the rear by Third, now Elm [Freret] Street.
>
> The rear of the plantation beyond Third Street was at a later date laid out into lots and squares and was called "Friburg."

The plan as laid out by Buisson divided the land into streets and squares, as shown in the 1883 Robinson *Atlas.* The streets perpendicular to the river were parallel to the lower line of Carrollton, this first street still called Lowerline. The broad center street was called Broadway, the others named for trees. The street on the upper side was called Pine, the one next on the lower side of Broadway being Chestnut, and the one nearest the Foucher tract being Walnut. Chestnut was later changed to Audubon. The first two blocks of Broadway off Magazine were widened, apparently to provide a site for a public market; these two blocks were bisected by Market Street. The lower line of Greenville runs at a slight angle so that near the river there is, between Walnut Street and the Greenville-Foucher line, space for about six lots; this is gradually reduced so that at St. Charles there is only a sliver of land.

One of the earlier houses in Greenville is the one at 515 Broadway, the site of which was acquired in 1839 by Christian Roselius, one of New Orleans' most prominent nineteenth century lawyers. The house originally occupied all of Square No. 62, bounded by Broadway, Dominican (formerly Carrollton), Audubon (formerly Chestnut), and Benjamin (formerly Felicia). This square, 300 feet by 240 feet, consisting of twenty lots with improvements, had been bought by Roselius from Josette Dorian, widow of Jacob Bundy, on May 29, 1839, for $12,000. She had bought it from James Ogilvie, the developer, on December 15, 1837. Sometime after 1839, Roselius erected a country residence here, but maintained his principal house on Dumaine, between Royal and Bourbon. Then in 1852 he made the Greenville house his permanent residence until his death in 1873. He served as dean of the Law Department of the University of Louisiana (now Tulane) from 1865 until 1872. His only surviving daughter, Mary Roselius, wife of Godfroy Bouny, inherited the house, which was sold by her succession on May 24, 1888.

The house was originally a raised house of one story, but was later raised to a full two stories. The stables, kitchen, and garden were located in the adjacent square. The house was described in 1877 as "a large two story dwelling and elegant well cultivated grounds and is known as The Roselius Homestead." It has since passed through several ownerships, being sold in 1919 with only half its original square of ground. When owned by Dr. George B. Crozat between 1925 and 1967, it was remodeled inside, the architect being Douglass V. Freret. After it was bought in 1967 by Barbara Ann Schreier Edisen, it was again extensively remodeled by Richard Koch and Samuel Wilson, Jr., Architects (see "Selective Architectural Inventory," 515 Broadway).

Another of the early Greenville residences is the one said to have been built in 1867 for Frederick Fischer, who with his son, Frederick Fischer, Jr., owned the Picayune Saw Mills at the foot of Canal Street (now Carrollton Avenue) in Carrollton. This one-story raised cottage originally faced St. Charles Avenue at the corner of Lowerline, its grounds taking up half the square and extending along Lowerline from St. Charles to Carrollton (now Dominican). The other half of the block along Pine Street was occupied by the large residence of Simon Hernsheim, a prominent tobacco importer and wholesale dealer. The Fischer house was moved around to a smaller plot facing Lowerline Street, No.

535 (see "Selective Architectural Inventory," 535 Lowerline). When this house was offered for sale in 1909, it was described as "the splendidly built raised cottage . . . the desirable and commodious residence, 535 Lowerline Street, containing wide front gallery, large hall, double parlors, library, dining-room, kitchen, 8 bedrooms, bathrooms, etc. Two story stable on rear of lot. House nicely papered and in tip top condition. One of the best built residences in the Sixth District."

Across Broadway from the Roselius house was another early house at 514 Broadway (Figure 23), as shown in the 1883 Robinson *Atlas*. It also occupied an entire square, marked in the name of Justin Frankey. This handsome one-story attic frame house, surrounded by many large trees, was later the Waldo family residence and was demolished around the 1940s.

Robinson's *Atlas* also shows at least eight other large houses occupying a whole or half square in Greenville, and many other squares in single ownerships but not yet built upon. The square on St. Charles between Broadway and Audubon was advertised in 1882 as a

> valuable square of ground . . . with a neat cottage home and orange orchard . . . enclosed in front by an open iron fence, and having an extensive orchard of orange trees and pecan and other trees. The Cottage is one story, with front and rear galleries, hall in centre and some 8 or 10 rooms, rear buildings, stables, 3 cisterns, etc. . . . . This property fronts the Dominican Convent and is near the fine residences of Bouny, Gogreve, Werlein, Fischer and Hernsheim.

This was probably typical of the mid- and late-nineteenth century residences of Greenville. The Gogreve residence still stands on Broadway, between Garfield and Pitt, and was extensively remodeled in the 1930s with a new classical, four-columned portico front designed by the office of Moise H. Goldstein, architect (see "Selective Architectural Inventory," 460 Broadway).

One of the best descriptions of a mid-nineteenth century Greenville residence was in the advertisement for the sale of the "Splendid and Delightful Property Situated and Fronting on the Railroad, Greenville," which appeared in the *Daily Delta* for November 17, 1849:

> That very valuable COUNTRY-SEAT, lately the Residence of Jas. A. Beard, Esq., in the delightful village of GREENVILLE, only 15 minutes' run by the Railroad Cars from the City.
> The Property comprises two good Frame Dwellings, Two Story each, with all the comforts requisite for a respectable family. The Out Buildings are very extensive, having Kitchens, "Negro Quarters," Coach-house, Stables for four Horses, the Cow-house for ten Cows, six Cisterns, and two Wells—all in good order.
> The Grounds are laid out in the best style, and stocked with the choicest assortment of Plants, Shrubs, Flowers selected in the United States, Europe and Asia. The Vegetable

Fig. 23. 514 Broadway, Waldo residence. (Courtesy NOPL)

Fig. 24. H.R. Gogreve, from *The City of New Orleans.* (Courtesy K&W)

Garden is in the finest order, and a fine Crop now growing. The Hot-House Plants comprise a large assortment of the choicest specimens of Flowers, Plants, Evergreen Shrubs, &c. &c., and can be had at valuation by the purchaser of the Property.

Persons desirous of viewing the Property are notified, that the Gardener is on the premises to receive them.

The large block facing St. Charles, between Broadway and Pine Street and backed by Dominican Street, on which the principal buildings that housed the former St. Mary's Dominican College stand, was designated as Square 66 on the original Buisson plan of Greenville (see "Selective Architectural Inventory," 7214 St. Charles Avenue). The front part, 300 feet on Broadway and Pine streets, belonged, with other Greenville properties, to the widow of Jacob Klein, who, represented by James Ogilvie, the original developer of Greenville, sold it to John Green on August 5, 1853, before notary E.L. Lewis for $4,000. The same day, before the same notary for a similar price, John Green bought the rear part of the block from William Frederick Vigers. Green may then have built a house upon it, for on January 22, 1855, before notary Theodore Guyol, he sold the entire Square 66, "with all the buildings and improvements thereon," to Jean Charles Felix Mace for $13,000.

Here the Maces opened a school for girls, first known as Madame Mace's School. In 1857 the St. Charles Institute,

established in 1854, had sixty pupils who, it is said, were met each morning at the New Orleans and Carrollton Railroad stop and conducted safely to the school and similarly returned at four o'clock in the afternoon. *Mygatt & Co.'s Directory* for 1857 carried a full-page advertisement for the school, then known as the "St. Charles Institute, Greenville near Carrollton, Jefferson Parish, La." It was a "boarding, half boarding and day school for young ladies, conducted by Madame C. Mace." The advertisement continues:

This Institution, already favorably known to the public, having attained so great a degree of prosperity, Madame Macé found it necessary to purchase the beautiful property, which she has occupied now two years, in order to extend the accommodations, and to carry out improvements essential for an establishment of learning on an extensive scale.

In pursuance of this object spacious school-rooms, vast and airy dormitories with other additions to the former buildings, have just been completed, all of which have been constructed with the most scrupulous regard to the health of the pupils.

The SAINT CHARLES INSTITUTE, situated undoubtedly in one of the most salubrious localities of Louisiana, sufficiently remote from the City to be free from its noise and attractions, so prejudicial to study, and receiving the advantages of instruction afforded by the most distinguished professors, offers great opportunities for the attainment of a liberal and enlightened education.

Religious instruction is imparted with all the care its importance demands, and every pupil is allowed the most perfect freedom in the profession of her particular faith.

During the Civil War, as the result of a suit of *George H. Brown vs. Mrs. Clara Mace,* the property was seized and sold by U.S. Marshall Cuthbert Bullitt. It was then, on January 6, 1865, purchased by the New Orleans Dominican Female Academy, which continued to operate in the old Mace buildings. Mrs. Mace reopened the St. Charles Institute on Bourbon Street and married one of her French teachers. The 1873 city directory lists the "St. Charles Institute, Mrs. Clara Mace-DeFranc, principal, 104 and 106 Bourbon." It is last listed in the 1881 directory at 143 St. Ann, with Miss O. Labranche as principal.

The Dominican Sisters, Congregation of St. Mary, from Cabra, Dublin, Ireland, arrived in New Orleans in 1860 and began a school at the church of St. John the Baptist on Dryades Street, of which this new Greenville academy, a boarding school, was a branch. It was listed in the 1873 directory as "St. Mary's Dominican Convent and Academy for Young Ladies, Sister Geneviève, superioress." In 1882 a new, three-story frame structure with a cupola, designed by New Orleans German architect William Fitzner and built by the Murray Construction Company, replaced the old Maces' buildings, and is still standing. In 1911 a large,

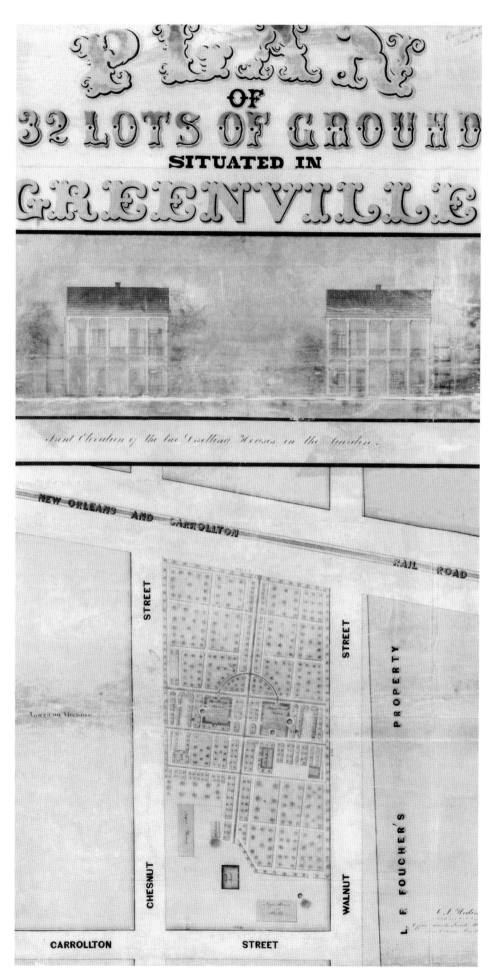

Fig. 25. "Plan of 32 Lots of Ground Situated in Greenville, Square 68 facing St. Charles," by C.A. Hedin, May 12, 1847. (Courtesy NA)

circular-head dormer, flanked by two similar but smaller ones, was added to the third-story facade. Part of the Fitzner building was at first used as a convent for the nuns and the rest for the school and chapel. The building was then known as St. Mary's Hall, but in 1960 the Dominican sisters moved to their new convent on Broadway, and the old building was renamed Greenville Hall.

On November 30, 1898, architects Toledano and Reusch completed plans for an annex to St. Mary's Hall, which was built along its upper side along Pine Street and connected to it by a two-story corridor (Figure 26). The new building was a three-story frame structure with a large stair hall in the center projecting as a semi-octagon bay on the Pine Street facade. The annex contained a chapel, classrooms, dormitory rooms, and an art department. This handsome structure in the Gothic style was demolished in the 1970s and replaced by tennis courts when a new dormitory building was built in front along Broadway.

In 1910 the academy became St. Mary's Dominican College, a liberal arts school for women. The college operated successfully and expanded into the adjacent square across Pine Street. By 1983, however, it faced severe financial difficulties, and the board of trustees decided to close the school in June 1984. Most of the property, including historic Greenville Hall, was sold to Loyola University.

LELAND UNIVERSITY— NEWCOMB BOULEVARD

The area of Greenville on St. Charles between Audubon Place and Audubon Street now occupied by Newcomb Boulevard was for many years the site of Leland University. This Negro school was established during the Reconstruction period by the American Baptist Home Mission Society for the promotion of Christian education, its specific purpose being to prepare "ministers and teachers, and to qualify men for business," especially among the recently freed slaves. It is said that the federal government, through the Freedmen's Bureau, gave $17,500 toward the erection of the first building.

The prime mover in establishing Leland University was Deacon Holbrook Chamberlain, a retired New York slave merchant who made generous contributions to the school.

On April 6, 1870, Chamberlain, a member of the board of trustees of Leland University, under authorization by the

Fig. 26. Dominican College, circa 1903, with demolished 1898 "Annex" and original attic window on main building. (Courtesy St. Mary's Dominican Archives)

board, purchased four squares of ground facing the New Orleans and Carrollton Rail Road (St. Charles Avenue), between the Foucher line and Chestnut (Audubon) Street, four blocks back to Freret Street. The first block off St. Charles, Square 69, was bought from Mrs. Elizabeth Ogden, wife of William F. Ogden, who had acquired it from the succession of Julia Ogden, wife of Abner N. Ogden, on February 16, 1866, before notary A. Commandeur. The price for this large, apparently vacant square was $7,000. The next three squares, 76, 77, and 84, were purchased for $18,000 from Abner Nash Ogden. Square 76, between what are now Hampson and Maple streets, was sold "together with the improvements thereon, consisting of a large dwelling house, outhouses, and improved grounds." Squares 77 and 84 were vacant. The large house on Square 76 probably became the first home of Leland University. Squares 76 and 77 had been bought by Ogden from William T. Hepp on December 15, 1865, before Selim Magner, notary. He had bought Square 84 from Robert and William E. Murphy on February 18, 1860, before Hugues Pedesclaux.

A large, two-story brick building with a raised basement and a dormered, mansard roof crowned by a square, mansard-roof cupola, was built on Square 69 facing St. Charles Avenue (Figure 27). This main building, called Leland Hall, had a columned gallery across the front reached

by an elaborate double flight of steps in the center. This was a conspicuous object on the avenue for some forty or more years. It was lighted by oil lamps and heated by stoves, probably pot-bellied, cast iron, coal-burning stoves in each room. The 1873 Edwards city directory lists "Leland University and Chapel. Free Mission Baptist, Rev. Charles Satchell, pastor and trustee, Chestnut, cor St. Charles." The Reverend Satchell had been one of the trustees when the Ogden property was purchased for the university in 1870.

On September 1, 1884, the *Daily Picayune* in its report on building activities in the city stated that "a three story building with a finished attic for Leland University is under construction on St. Charles Avenue, opposite the Park. It was planned by Sully and cost $15,000." This building, near Maple Street, had a raised basement with two stories above and a dormered, finished attic. A projecting central bay was flanked by gabled, projecting end bays with a gallery between them, across the front, reached by a broad, straight flight of steps in the center. It also was lighted by lamps, but heated by steam. This building, named Chamberlain Hall in honor of the university's benefactor, Holbrook Chamberlain, was a dormitory and contained dining and kitchen facilities in the basement. The *Times-Democrat,* also on September 1, 1884, reported that "Mr. Thomas Sully, during the year, has constructed the following buildings on St. Charles street, opposite the Exposition buildings, for the Leland University. This building will have 100 rooms, and be steam heated." The Robinson *Atlas* of 1883 shows the location of this dormitory with smaller frame buildings in front and behind it, probably the buildings that existed at the time of its sale to the university in 1870. They no doubt were demolished when the new dormitory was completed; they do not appear on the Sanborn map of 1896.

Leland University continued its operation in this rapidly developing, fashionable residential section adjoining Audubon Place until its buildings were severely damaged by the disastrous hurricane of September 29, 1915. The *Times-Picayune* of October 10, 1915, reported that "Leland University, the negro school in St. Charles avenue . . . has been abandoned. No more classes will be heard there and the fine piece of property has been put [up] . . . for sale by the trustees who reside in New York." The property was finally sold for $175,000 on June 22, 1916, before notary G.A. Llambias. The purchaser was Robert F. Werk, who developed the property as a private street which he called Newcomb Boulevard. Leland College reopened in 1923 in Baker, Louisiana, where it was located until 1959.

Fig. 27. Leland University, from *Hansell's Photographic Glimpses of New Orleans, 1908.* (Courtesy K&W)

FOUCHER TRACT

HILARY SOMERVILLE IRVIN

Edging from the city's central downtown core, today's streetcar moves westward along the route first established by the New Orleans and Carrollton Rail Road in 1833. Mimicking the movement of the nineteenth century push toward the outlying, undeveloped plantation lands, it passes through the historic residential neighborhoods of the Lower Garden District, the Garden District, Jefferson City, and on to the University Section. Spatial arrangements change on the trek—from the densely settled areas of the Central Business and Lower Garden Districts, to the verdant lots of the Garden District, to the liberal grounds of the oftentimes large estates constructed for the barons of the city's "Gilded Age." Predominating architectural styles also change in reflection of the various stages of development—from Federal and Greek Revival style townhouses, to Italianate villas, to eclectic style mansions from the turn of the century.

A pleasant urban sprawl, without a defined locus, remains throughout most of the six-mile upriver stretch from the downtown area. The streetcar moves past Jefferson Avenue, then State Street, and arrives at an opening which gently directs the viewer toward the natural features of park and river on one side and, on the other, toward the man-made solidity of church and academia. This urban space—comprised of Audubon Park and the Mississippi River across St. Charles Avenue from the masonry structures of Holy Name of Jesus Church, Loyola University, and Tulane University—has come to symbolize the center of uptown New Orleans, just as surely as Jackson Square and its aggregate of parochial and secular structures mark the focal point of the Creoles' Vieux Carré.

The abandoned plantation of Louis Foucher came to its fruition in the late 1800s and early 1900s when it became the site of a public park based on the designs of the landscaping firm established by Frederick Law Olmsted, a Catholic church and Jesuit college, and a university established to be non-sectarian and non-political by an eccentric old man from Princeton, New Jersey (as well as of the site of the elite residential streets known as Audubon Place, Audubon Boulevard and Versailles Boulevard). These institutions have given their name to the desirable neighborhood, referred to interchangeably by real estate agents and others as the University, Audubon Park, and Holy Name Parish sections.

From "Dead Sea" to World's Fair Site

The Foucher Plantation was small and fan-shaped, measuring $12\frac{1}{2}$ arpents on the river and extending back 70 arpents or more toward Marly and the swampy hinterlands. Pierre Foucher acquired the first $10\frac{1}{2}$ arpents in 1793 from Jacques Fontenot and 2 arpents in 1825 from his wife's (Francisca Isabel Boré) nephew, historian Charles Etienne Gayarré. After Pierre Foucher died in 1832, his son Louis Frederic became the owner of the uptown tract. At best, lassitude surrounds the early history of the Foucher tract for many years after the death of the elder Foucher; at worst, greed and corruption apply. As a plantation, the Foucher land was unprofitable and poorly managed. In 1837 Louis Foucher tried to profit from the germinal uptown expansion by building a racetrack on his land and attempting to have a railway spur constructed there. Neither scheme succeeded. Thus, before the Civil War, Foucher abandoned his plantation, assumed a new persona in France as the Marquis de Circé, and never returned to Louisiana.

During the Civil War, both sides used the deserted plantation. In April 1861 the Confederates gained control of the Foucher tract, which they named Camp Lewis; after the fall of New Orleans in 1862, the Union troops under the command of Gen. Benjamin Butler moved in and erected a temporary hospital called Camp Sedgwick on the site, where they remained until 1867. After the war ended, Foucher filed a claim, as a French citizen, with the federal government for $88,449 in war damages. Foucher's succession records note that "during the military occupation, buildings and improvements thereon, the ferries, outhouses, bricks and brick sheds, and other material either [were] removed or destroyed by said troops or used by them in the erection of said property of Sedgwick Hospital and Barracks, which buildings were afterward removed or sold by the troops" (Civil District Court # 2036). After Foucher's death in 1869, Foucher's widow, née Marie Marguerite Félicie Burthe, and Arthur Denis, the executor of her estate, continued to press for reparation. Finally, in

Fig. 1. Stern gates, Audubon Park, Moise Goldstein, architect, 1921.

1883, the government awarded the estate $9,200 plus 5 percent interest from April 1, 1865.

By 1870 most owners of the uptown plantations had divided their property into city lots, though actual construction was scant. The Foucher Plantation alone remained to be acquired and developed. Indeed, the Foucher land was an eyesore, called a "dead sea" by a Carrollton newspaper, which further complained of the absentee owners' neglect. Madame Foucher offered the property for sale, and in 1871 two post-war speculators, Robert Bloomer and Malek A. Southworth, bought the site, forlorn and far upriver from the center of town.

No idealists who dreamed of creating green spaces for weary city dwellers, Bloomer and Southworth concocted a profitable but shady scheme which ultimately contributed to the impeachment of Reconstruction Gov. H.C. Warmouth. Providing only a fraction of the funds needed for the purchase of the Foucher tract, Bloomer and Southworth lobbied the state legislature to acquire the site for a public park on the river side of St. Charles Avenue and for a new state capitol on the lake side. The duo further sweetened the deal by suggesting that the legislators could acquire and build new homes on St. Charles Avenue's prime building lots. The legislature responded by naming a commission to choose a capitol site and another for selecting a park site on the Foucher tract. Southworth served on the latter board. By stealth, the pair of developers acquired the Foucher tract and resold the portion on the river side of St. Charles Avenue for a substantial profit to the park commission for

$800,000. A few months later Southworth, the majority shareholder, sold part of the tract on the lake side of the avenue for $150,000 to the firm of Camille E. Giraudey. In 1886 Southworth, at the time living in the state of New York, sold the remaining portion of his share of the tract to William Henry and Samuel Blanc; and Robert Bloomer sold his smaller share to Joseph Hernandez, who also bought an additional share from the Giraudey firm in 1889. Henry, Hernandez and Blanc then directly sold their land to the Jesuits and Tulane University.

The commission mortgaged the downtown City Park (the present City Park) to raise funds for a down payment on the new park, and a special park tax was levied to cover this mortgage. Revelation of the corrupt deal, payment for which was borne by the city's taxpayers, soured the public on the concept of municipal parks for many years to come. In 1877 the first park commission was abolished. In 1879 the city council established the Upper City Park Commission, charged with operating a park on the site. Neither city nor state, however, offered any financial assistance to the new board. The chief source of revenue came from the leasing of the park grounds for grazing.

The World's Industrial and Cotton Exposition of 1884-85

Upper City Park would have likely remained a swampy wasteland for many years, as did Lower City Park, if the site had not been chosen for the World's Industrial and Cotton Centennial Exposition of 1884-85 (Figure 2). This event,

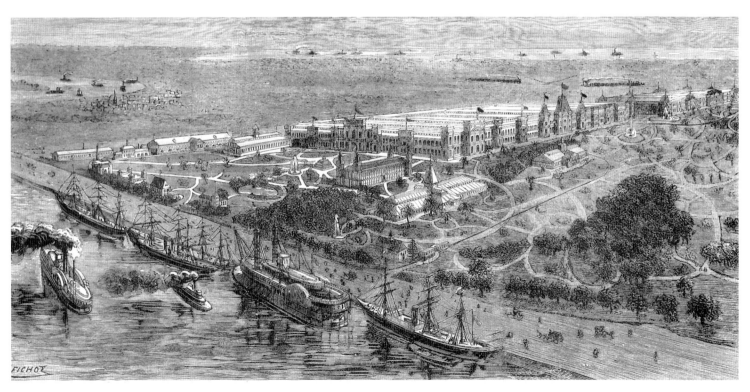

Fig. 2. "The New Orleans Exposition," by C.H. Fichot. (Courtesy A.L. Schlesinger)

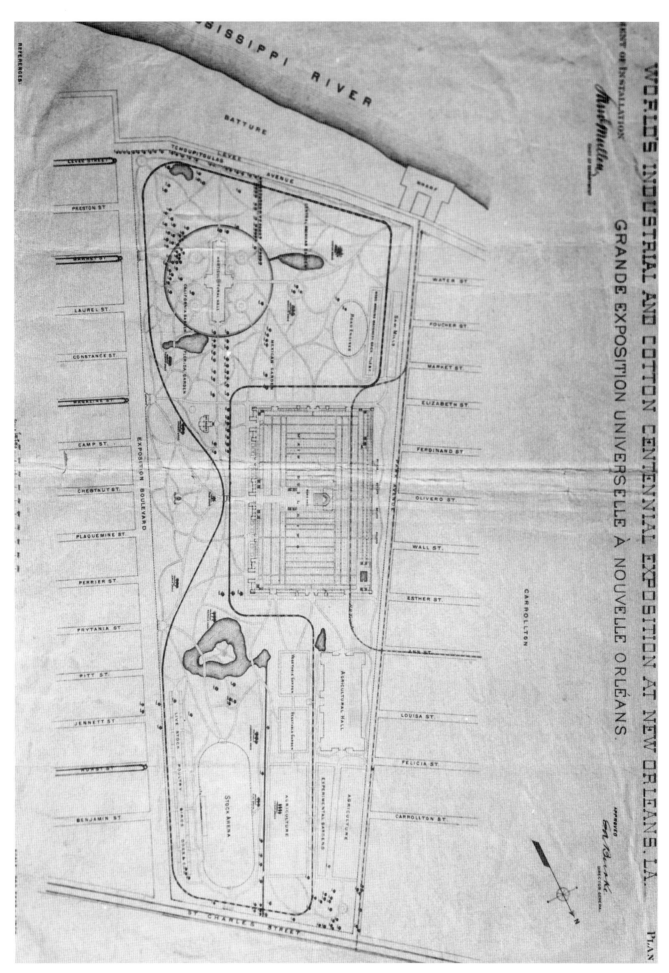

Fig. 3. "World's Industrial and Cotton Centennial Exposition at New Orleans, La." Site Plan. (Courtesy TULC)

planned to show off the "New South," as well as to commemorate the first shipment of cotton from the United States in 1774, ranks as a distinct financial failure. Yet the positive impact of the fair on New Orleans, especially on the Foucher tract and the immediately adjacent neighborhood, continued for many years after the fair had ended. Historian John Smith Kendall wrote in 1922 of these ramifications:

> It advertised to the world the fact that the city was now over the troubles which for over a quarter of a century had given it a sinister reputation. It had, moreover, the effect of drawing the attention of the people of New Orleans to the upper portion of the city as a desirable place of residing. Immediately after the exposition a movement began to build up this vast area, with the result that New Orleans gained very largely in population and in attractiveness.

Without the decision to have the exposition in this city, on the old Foucher estate, the Olmsted-inspired park, two important universities, and a large church might have been located elsewhere. Transportation improvements made to facilitate fair visitors, as well as the attention drawn to the yet undeveloped area, immediately brought an onrush of prosperous new residents. This growth of an influential population contributed immeasurably to the subsequent development of the park and its neighboring aggregate of educational and religious institutions. The notion of holding a cotton centennial came from outside New Orleans—from political economist Edward Atkinson in a letter published in the *New York Herald.* Small exhibitions had been held in Atlanta and Louisville before, in the parlance of the day, "progressive agriculturists and industrialists of the south" and some prominent New Orleanians united in an effort to hold a major exhibition in the Crescent City, where historical and geographic ties with Latin America could serve to attract participation from these southern neighbors.

An 1883 Act of Congress created a partnership between the federal government, the National Cotton Planter's Association, and the city chosen for the exhibition for the purpose of holding a national and international exposition in which "cotton, in all its conditions of culture and manufacture, will be the chief exhibit, but which is designed, also, to include all arts, manufacture, and products of the soil and mine." A national board was then named to choose the host city, among other things. Support in New Orleans lagged for the celebration, which would require the city to contribute $500,000, until the cause was taken up by Maj. Edmund A. Burke, editor of the *Times-Democrat* and treasurer of the State of Louisiana. Burke later became the exhibition's director general.

Invigorated by the support of Burke and other prominent local businessmen, plans for an exhibition in New Orleans moved ahead. At first the specific site for the event

had not been determined. Then when the city's contribution had not been sufficiently raised, Burke proposed that the city donate the Upper City Park for the site to offset the required expenditure. Although the park still left a bitter taste in the mouths of those who remembered the circumstances of its 1871 purchase and although the bonds for this purchase had not yet been paid, the city council voted to not only offer the park rent-free, but also to allocate $100,000 for the construction of a permanent building as the city's pavilion. The city council then quietly retired the park debt by issuing new twenty-year bonds. Influential in the decision to use the uptown park site was the insistence and proffered financial assistance of the St. Charles, Magazine, and Tchoupitoulas streetcar lines, which correctly read the opportunity to stimulate uptown expansion.

The fair's developers faced a herculean task in readying the swampy wilderness for the international celebration. Historian Kendall described the site: "Magnificent avenues of live oak trees, relics of one or more large plantations of an earlier period, trees standing like hoary sentinels draped in gray Spanish moss, were its only adornment." The land was cleared, infill soil brought in, and crude drainage ditches dug. The refinements of architecture, landscaping, and lighting ensued. Because the enabling congressional act stipulated that the celebration was to be held in 1884, the opening gala took place on December 16, 1884. Visitors found there a spectacle of mud and a raw, uncompleted fair site, devoid of promised lush, tropical flora. By spring, winter rains subsided, and mud gave way briefly to paved walks and dazzling lights.

With the exception of the city's pavilion, Horticultural Hall, the exhibition's wooden buildings were impressively scaled but ephemerally constructed. The largest of these was Main Building (Figure 4), which faced eastward toward downtown New Orleans, near the center of the site near Walnut Street. This structure, touted as having the largest exhibition space constructed at that time, covered nearly thirty-two acres. Designed by the Swedish-born, Mississippi-resident architect Gustav M. Torgerson, Main Building housed "foreign machinery and agricultural exhibits." Nearby was the smaller Factories and Mills Building in which was shown "cotton in all stages of manipulation from the boll to the bale." A field of cotton was planted near the latter building. An 11,000-seat-capacity music hall, with a gigantic organ, was located in the Main Building.

The departments of the federal government showed their exhibits in the United States and States Building, extending over twelve acres of ground near the corner of St. Charles Avenue and Exposition Boulevard. Special exhibits displayed the work of women and black Americans. The official program of the exposition noted: "One of the most important features will be the exposition of the colored race

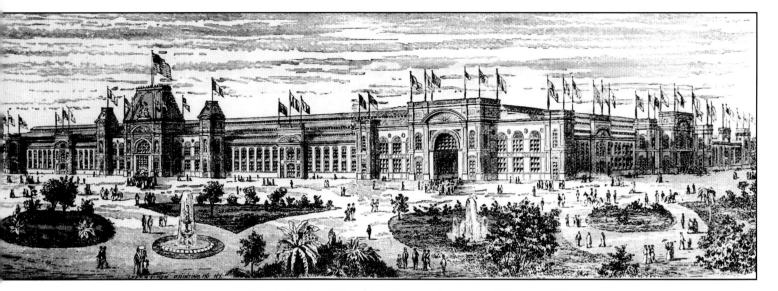

Fig. 4. "Main Building, New Orleans Exposition." (Courtesy TULC)

in the south. This is the first public opportunity that has been given to them, to show the world the progress they have made for themselves since their liberation from slavery." Sadly, after the close of the fair, Jim Crow laws tightened, leading to the exclusion of black American visitors from the park until recent decades. Horticultural Hall, "the largest conservatory in the world" (Figure 5), the Art Gallery, the Grand Rapids Furniture Pavilion, and two Mexican buildings were other significant fair buildings (Figure 6).

Whereas contributions made by European countries disappointed the fair's officials and visitors, Mexico had a major input. Her pavilions included the cast iron Mexican National Building (Barracks), which housed the country's cavalry and infantry members, fair workers, official representatives, a splendid array of birds and foliage, as well as the immensely popular Mexican Eighth Cavalry Band. This large troupe, along with a group of Mayas, captivated the city and performed at a number of social events in the

Fig. 5. "Interior of Horticultural Hall," by C.B. Mason. (Courtesy Robert Cangelosi, Jr.)

Fig. 6A and 6B. "The Mexican National Buildings and Mexican National Headquarters," from World's Industrial and Cotton Centennial Exposition. (Courtesy K&W)

community, even at Mardi Gras' Rex ball. The continuing influence of this musical group inspired an outpouring of popular sheet music with Latin American themes and well may have played a role in the development of New Orleans' evolving ragtime and jazz music forms. A separate Mexican building, an octagonal Moorish-style structure known as Alhambra Palace, displayed Mexican minerals and ores.

The Cotton Exposition closed in June 1885, setting a dismal record of attendance and lack of financial profit. Promoter Edmund Burke fled the country before the discovery of funds missing from the state's coffers (perhaps diverted to the strapped exhibition account). In November 1885 a new exhibition organization—the North, Central and South American Exhibition—leased the site, reopened the fair, and quickly failed. In early 1886 the old exposition company sued the American Exposition Company for uncollected funds. A public auction was held in May 1886 and almost everything was sold and hauled away from the site. Secondhand dealers in building supplies took away all sorts of materials, including the entire government building. Horticultural Hall, located near the river on high ground amidst live oak trees, did not survive for long as the city's permanent exhibit: the 1915 hurricane completed the destruction begun by a tornado in 1909 to the shoddily constructed building.

The only known remnant in the park today of the short-lived exhibition is the "meteorite," a massive piece of iron ore left from the Alabama exhibit. Additionally, a ghostly indentation on the golf course perhaps outlines Main Building's foundations. Mexico's exuberant Alhambra Palace was transported to one of Mexico City's parks only to be subsequently removed to make room for a roadway. The music hall's grand organ was taken to the downtown Jesuit church on Baronne Street but was later removed to be stored in an uptown location, only to deteriorate. Salvaged timber is scattered here and there in the neighborhood where it was used to supply the building boom that followed the exposition.

A few structures in various Louisiana and Mississippi locations are proudly rumored to have once been part of the exposition. A statue, Goddess of History—Genius of Peace, was bought from the centennial commission and taken to

ABOVE: Fig. 7. "The New Orleans Exposition: Mexican Pavilion and Main Building," from *Scribner's Magazine*, Vol. 18, July-December 1895. (Courtesy Louisiana State Museum)

AT LEFT: Fig. 8. "The New Orleans Cotton Exposition," from *Scribner's Magazine*, Vol. 18, July-December 1895. (Courtesy Louisiana State Museum)

a small park in the 2200 block of Esplanade Avenue (see Volume V), appropriately dedicated to historian Charles Gayarré, once an owner of the park site. The statue existing today is a replacement for the original, which was vandalized in the 1930s. The effects of the exhibition, however, did not subside in 1886, but went on to stimulate the immediate development of the area as a fashionable neighborhood for the city's burgeoning bourgeoisie, one that was eventually endowed with its own lush urban oasis—Audubon Park.

A Neighborhood Park: 1886-1915

The City of New Orleans: The Book of the Chamber of Commerce and Industry boasted in 1894 of the great spurt of construction taking place in uptown New Orleans after the close of the exposition:

> That district of the city surrounding the "Exposition Grounds," now known as "Audubon Park" presents unmistakable evidence of the advantage the city has derived from its building and loan societies. This was acreage a few years ago, used chiefly for pasture lands; today it is a district of homes—the homes of the thrifty, and even the aristocracy.

Although the exposition established Upper City Park as a place for recreational activities and attracted newcomers to its neighborhood, a landscaped park, as Audubon Park appears today, took years of effort. The ultimate push for such a park came eventually not from public or governmental agencies but from a private group—the Audubon Park Improvement Association—made up of affluent residents who moved "uptown" during the late-nineteenth century.

Significantly, private citizens, lobbying surely on their own behalf as well as from a spirit of altruism, made the real push for the development of the park. Therefore Audubon Park can be said to have developed as a neighborhood park rather than as a "park for the people." At the vanguard of the proponents for a well-designed urban space were two successive presidents of the appointed Audubon Park Commission, John Ward Gurley (1886-1903) and Lewis Johnson (1903-9). Gurley, a lawyer who served as district attorney until an assassin's bullet felled him in 1903, lived nearby at 6211 St. Charles Avenue. Johnson, president of Johnson Iron Works and head of the Sewerage and Water Board, however, had his home in the Lower Garden District.

Immediately after the close of the fair, the park site mostly lay fallow. In May 1886 the New Orleans City Council created a new park commission and charged the twenty-five-member board with operating the park and maintaining the St. Charles Avenue median ground. This board soon changed the name from Upper City Park to Audubon Park, after the naturalist-painter, John James Audubon, mistakenly believed to have been of Louisiana rather than West Indian origin. This Commission managed some accomplishments despite a lack of public funding: John Bogart, a New York park planner, was hired to design carriage drives in the park; and money was raised by renting the river-fronting wharf, selling hay from the park meadows, and leasing the arena left from the exposition as a racetrack. In 1888 the Louisiana Science and Agricultural Association secured a ten-year lease (later extended) of a fifty-acre tract near the river for use as an important sugar

experimentation station, which New Orleans architect James Freret designed in 1889 (Figure 9). In the 1920s, after the closing of the station, this tract became the site of the swimming pool, tennis courts, and a portion of the zoo.

After the organization in 1890 of the Audubon Park Improvement Association, private funding and enthusiasm quickened the move toward a properly landscaped park. In 1892, $5,000 was allocated by the city to be divided between the two city parks; and in 1894, $20,000 was granted to Audubon Park. This latter sum went toward badly needed improvements and repairs to Horticultural Hall (Figure 10) and the drainage system, the paving of St. Charles Avenue in front of the park, and the purchase of a narrow strip of land at the Walnut Street and St. Charles Avenue end of the park. Despite this increased funding, the Audubon Park Commission's 1895 annual report included an "Address to the People," urging widespread public support:

> The commissioners realize that without a popular influence on behalf of the park they can not hope to make any great improvement. It is a true saying that one generally gets what he deserves. This is the people's park. If they have not a lively interest in its development into the beautiful expanse for which nature has furnished so grand a foundation, the progress toward this desirable result will be very slow and uncertain, and they can blame none but themselves.

Finally, in 1896, the efforts of the two park commissions led to the state legislature's directive to the city of New Orleans to give $15,000 annually to each of the parks.

Armed with a portion of the 1896 appropriation, Gurley and Johnson began the search for a professional designer to effect a master plan for the park's development. Fortuitously, in 1897 Johnson attended a park convention in Louisville and there met John Charles Olmsted, scion of the great landscaping firm of Olmsted and Brothers. This meeting came at an opportune time for the New Orleans group. This famed firm—largely responsible for redefining the concept of urban parks from formal, didactic places to naturalistic spaces for contemplative recreation—faced a crisis point in 1897: the 75-year-old Frederick Law Olmsted suffered from mental and physical deterioration; the third partner, Charles Eliot, had just died; and John Charles Olmsted, both Frederick's nephew and stepson, was left largely in charge. (Frederick Law Olmsted, Jr. was then only twenty-seven.) John Charles welcomed the opportunity to work on a project of his own, especially one located in the South. Because of his personal eagerness, John Olmsted endured long delays and numerous skirmishes over design concepts before actualization of his plans. Standing with him during these struggles were commission presidents Gurley, Johnson, and later Jacob K. Newman, who all shared a commitment to the Olmstedian park philosophy.

Fig. 9. "State Agricultural Experiment Station," from *New Orleans, Louisiana: The Crescent City*. (Courtesy K&W)

Fig. 10. Horticultural Hall. (Courtesy Robert Cangelosi, Jr.)

Fig. 11. Audubon Park gates. (Courtesy TULC)

Upon the invitation of the commission board, John Charles Olmsted arrived in New Orleans to survey what must have been, on a November's day, a dreary site. Yet he did not see a flat, barren expanse, devoid of landscaping except near Horticultural Hall, but a place ripe with promise and graced with oak trees. He wrote that it is "difficult to exaggerate the value of such noble trees for park purposes." In addition to the ancient trees, Olmsted recognized the benefits offered by the fecund, alluvial soil, coupled with a semitropical climate. Above all Olmsted was struck by the positioning of the site, which opened to a vista of the wide Mississippi River. Returning home to Brookline, Massachusetts, the planner made preliminary "before and after" sketches which convinced the commission to hire Olmsted and Brothers as the park's designers. These early sketches evince the following features, definitive of the evolved Olmstedian concept of parks: a system of waterways, a central meadow for passive recreation, and a naturalistic setting provided by graceful undulations of ground and new plantings, arranged to hide requisite roadways and neighboring buildings.

Although Olmsted's master plan was substantially complete by 1898, implementation took another twenty years. Lack of money was the major factor in the delay: only $25,000 was in hand for the million-dollar project. Olmsted, however, did not back away from the project, but only requested that the plan be followed while work progressed. Even before any work began, arguments and debates erupted on all sides. For example, some residents wanted a roadway along the lower side of the park; Olmsted, Gurley, and Johnson did not. The proposed lagoons and lakes fueled the shrillest arguments between park leaders and neighbors who feared an infestation of disease-carrying mosquitoes. Most disagreements, however, resulted from the means taken to increase revenues. The Corps of Engineers leased the park's riverfront, and the Illinois Central Railroad won the right to construct tracks along a new levee near the river. These decisions nixed Olmsted's grand riverfront promenade for many years to come. The board also allowed concessions, such as one for a miniature train, extended the lease of the sugar experiment station, and turned over a large portion of the park (Olmsted's "meadow") to the Audubon Golf Club. Since 1898 the playing of golf has remained a very visible activity in the park. Although altered and enlarged over the years, the existing golf club dates from 1912 and was designed by DeBuys, Churchill and Labouisse.

Finally, in 1900, the initial phase of the park began. The improvements took place on a thirteen-acre site near the front of the park and included extensive plantings along the park's borders, an entry road and gate, and a children's wading pool and sand shelter, the latter clearly catering to the local residents. After this small beginning, work halted, not to resume for over ten years. Gurley, the great defender of the Olmstedian plan, was murdered in 1903, and Lewis Johnson took over as the board's president. Disagreements over design philosophy intensified with the change of leadership. The Audubon Tea Room, a carousel (Figure 12), and a polo club were soon added. Significantly to the subsequent development of the park, the bitter fight over locating an art museum (clearly in contravention of the Olmstedian precept of a "landscaped park foremost") in the park ended in 1909 when Isaac Delgado decided to place his largesse in City Park.

Returning to New Orleans in 1909, John Olmsted faced the factious board. Although gravely ill, board president Johnson garnered support for the master plan, so arduously protected over the years by him and his predecessor Gurley. The board then asked the planner to prepare a step-by-step plan for implementation. Within a few months Johnson was dead, and Jacob K. Newman became president. While supporting the Olmstedian principles in general, Newman was willing to make whatever compromises he deemed necessary to push forward the landscaping.

A Park for the People

The Olmstedian duality of parks as scenic, contemplative places "offering the most agreeable contrast to that of the rest of the town" and as democratic places where people of all classes can come together "for the single purpose of enjoyment" contains an inherent contradiction. This contradiction is clearly shown in the development of Audubon Park. In the process of evolving from a neighborhood park for its middle-class residents to becoming a park where people of varied backgrounds wanted to come for recreational pursuits, compromises were made to the original Olmstedian design. Various structures, usually donated by patrons as memorials, and facilities for active recreation such as swimming, tennis, and soft ball were added. In his push for the implementation of the park plan in 1916, Newman advocated the first of the major compromises made to the original plan—the confining of the lagoon to the upper portion of the park.

Once the reluctant designers accepted the modified plan, Newman worked successfully toward passing a $100,000 state bond issue for the park improvements. Announcing

Fig. 12. Audubon Park carousel. (Courtesy TULC)

Fig. 13. "Lovers Lane," J. Earl Rogers Co., 1907. (Courtesy Robert Cangelosi, Jr.)

Fig. 14. "Entrance to Audubon Park and Avenue of Live Oaks," circa 1916. (Courtesy Robert Cangelosi, Jr.)

that work had finally started on the modified plan, the *Times-Picayune* on August 16, 1916, ran an article describing the original plan "with its beautifully encircling lake, with its trees grouped along the borders, and with its green little islands scattered here and there like emeralds," and the modified plan with the lake sweeping down the lower side of the park and "so around to the river side." Opposition from the Audubon Golf Club's influential membership stymied the completion of even the modified plan, so the lake today does not extend to the upper side of the park.

Once the lake was filled and the lush landscaping in place, private donations came, enabling the addition of some of the familiar features that still distinguish the park today: Moise Goldstein's neoclassical St. Charles Avenue entrance (1921), given by Mrs. Maurice Stern in honor of her husband and with marble work provided by Weiblen Marble and Granite Company; the arts-and-crafts-style gazebos on the lake's shores; Emile Weil's Newman bandstand (1921), "Dedicated to music in memory of Isidore Newman, Rebecca Kiefer Newman"; the Gumbel fountain (1918); the Hyams wading pool (1921) (Figure 15); and the Popp floral gardens (1921), the latter two just

across Magazine Street in the lower park. Both the Gumbel and Hyams fountains have bronze sculptures by Austrian-born sculptor Isidore Konti (1862-1938). The Gumbel fountain, located directly behind the Stern entrance, is dedicated to Sophie and Simon Gumbel. The Hyams fountain bears the inscription, "Given to the Little Children of New Orleans by Sara Lavinia Hyams MCMXIV," and further notes that Hyams left her jewels to Audubon and City parks, the proceeds of which were to build a "Testimonial of her love for her Home City." Thus, the design for the upper portion of the park was essentially complete when its tenacious designer died in 1920. The younger members of the firm, headed by Frederick Law Olmsted, Jr. (1870-1957), continued to advise the park board until the outbreak of World War II.

The popularity of the park as a fun destination for people from the city's neighborhoods grew during the 1920s and 1930s. In the early 1920s the commissioners refashioned the portion of the lake near the bandstand in the upper portion of the park, near Magazine Street, into the Bobet Natatorium (Figure 16), made deep enough for safe swimming. The board then reclaimed the fifty-acre site formerly leased

Fig. 15. Hyams Wading Pool, 1921.

to the sugar experimental station in 1924, thereby opening this expanse for new uses. Baseball fields were placed there, as well as the Audubon Park swimming pool, which opened in 1928. The zoo would also be added to the abandoned site. Native New Orleanian Mary Lou Widmer recalled her childhood outings during the depression years to the uptown park:

> A day was set aside, the family was collected, and the long ride began. Our old car wove in and out of those unfamiliar uptown streets, loaded with kids, a picnic lunch and our cooler of root beer. . . . What a pool Audubon Park had! . . . The bathhouse was a wonder in itself. I remember the endless rows of lockers, the changing booths, and the huge, mirrored room with hair dryers in the wall. I loved the sky-lit cement path inside the bathhouse, lined with those various facilities. I enjoyed changing my clothes in a private booth, wearing my jingling locker key pinned to the belt of my bathing suit, and running through the hallway of shower jets that sprayed me just before I entered the revolving doorway to the pool. These were all spiffy new things we did not have at the City Park pool.

John Olmsted's plan for a grand riverfront promenade was stymied until only recently. The batture had been increased over the years by its use as a city dump. Therefore, during the 1930s Olmsted Brothers made plans for extended landscaping of the area, but funding provided only for the filling-in of the batture with river sand and the construction of Monkey Hill before the outbreak of the war. A protracted legal battle over control of the batture halted further development until the late 1960s when work began on a riverfront park, now redesigned to be more in keeping with John Olmsted's vision of a promenade as "the most delightful place for enjoying the ever varying, enlivening river views."

Audubon Zoo

To many of the city's visitors and residents, Audubon Park denotes the zoo, with its spacious, airy landscape and an intriguing variety of animal specimens healthfully exhibited in ecological settings, often equipped with natural barriers. A trip to the zoo today results in a pleasant educational experience. Memories of the zoo of the past, before its massive remodeling began in the 1970s, may well evoke less agreeable images—scratching, caged animals, steamy, unshaded paved walks, foul smells ripening in the heat, and a moth-eaten stuffed bear, offered as a prop by a grumpy photographer, there to capture the summer's day fun on film. The Olmsted Brothers firm would surely have approved of this modern-day transformation from animals on display to zoological gardens.

Fig. 16. Bobet Natatorium.

Animals as providers of entertainment figured early in the history of Audubon Park. A racetrack stood on Louis Foucher's plantation; exotic birds and animal species drew spectators during the Cotton Exposition, and Buffalo Bill Cody's circus took place on the grounds in the late 1800s. In 1916 the *Times-Picayune* described the about-to-be-improved park site as the "old-time pasture ground, where the cattle grazed undisturbed, and where the gentle showman unfurled his tents and spread his sawdust, and the quiet of uptown was broken by the hoarse roar of the wildest African lion in captivity." Some animals continued to be housed and shown in the park, usually in and around Horticultural Hall, until 1913 when the commissioners announced that animals would no longer be kept in the park, a pronouncement in keeping with the principles of the Olmsted firm. The concept of a park without animals, however, did not appeal to the public. In 1916 the commission accepted the suggestion of architect Samuel Stone, also a board member, to use the $10,000 insurance money received for the storm-damaged Horticultural Hall for a flight cage. This new construction was in place by the end of 1916 and may be considered as the beginning of Audubon Zoo. The origin of the zoo, then, was simultaneous with the implementation of the Olmsted park plans.

After the lagoon was filled and brimming with water, a public campaign took place to fund a zoo in the park. Daniel D. Moore, manager-editor of the *Times-Picayune* and the newly elected president of the Audubon Park Commission, headed this drive, toward which he contributed the first $500; soon after, the New Orleans Zoological Society was organized. Accepting the inevitability of a zoo in the park, the planners wisely suggested that its location be on the grounds recently abandoned by the sugar station. The commission, however, chose the highly visible area just off Magazine Street, near the oak alley remaining from the Foucher Plantation and the formal garden, newly endowed by John H. Popp (1921). The development of the zoo gained momentum, with private donations steadily coming in during the prosperous 1920s. Sigmund Odenheimer, president of Lane Cotton Mill and a most generous benefactor, enabled (in addition to a monkey cage) construction of the neoclassical aquarium (Figure 17) (Favrot and Livaudais, architects) and sea lion pool (Figure 18) (Samuel Stone, architect), connected by a walkway embellished with a fountain of Hygeia. On an axis with the Newman bandstand just across Magazine Street, the Odenheimer complex today serves as the focal point of the lower end of the park and, with the alley of ancient oak trees, reminds the viewer of the site's antecedents as the grounds of a plantation house.

Despite private donations, the zoo lacked permanent funding, several attempts to secure public appropriations having failed. After the stock market crash of 1929, even the private sources dried up. Earlier in 1929, however, Valentine Merz, president of New Orleans Brewing Company, offered a $50,000 contribution to be made available after the death of his wife. This legacy served as the starting point for the zoo of the 1930s. Even more contributory to the creation of the Merz Memorial Zoo, which opened on May 15, 1938, was the enormous financial aid made available through the New Deal's Works Progress Administration. The proposal submitted to this federal agency was prepared under the leadership of Moise Goldstein, local architect and park commissioner.

Using the funding from the Merz donation, the board charged the Olmsted firm with making plans for the relocation of the zoo to the southwestern section of the park, previously recommended by the firm as a proper zoo site. A general landscape plan was then devised for the zoo, and the restoration of the park grounds near the Odenheimer complex was accomplished. Over $250,000 in federal money made possible the construction of the features remembered by anyone over thirty-five years old as the "Audubon Zoo," in reality a memorial to the New Deal. Moise Goldstein designed five buildings in the zoo's first stage of development—a monkey house, a tropical bird-house, a large animal house, a small animal house, and a barn (1935). The next year, cages for bears, raccoons, birds, and turtles were funded. Despite this great outlay, the park board continued to have problems with sustained funding for the zoo, which eventually deteriorated into a run-down place with poorly kept animals, dubbed in a 1958 *New Orleans Magazine* article by David Kleck as a "zoological ghetto." Only after the emergence in the late 1960s of a private, activist group—the Audubon Zoological Society—were steps taken toward zoo reform. In 1972 New Orleans voters approved a millage tax and bond issues for expanded and improved zoo facilities, resulting in today's acclaimed Audubon Zoological Gardens.

Holy Name Parish

Eight years before John Charles Olmsted came to New Orleans to survey the desolate park site, the Catholic church arrived in the neighborhood to establish a new parish. Just as the Jesuits had done when they arrived early in the history of French colonial New Orleans, so too did they bring their missionary zeal to the uptown suburb. The Reverend John O'Shanahan, S.J., Superior of the Southern Jesuits, saw the almost instantaneous swelling of the area's population after the opening of the Cotton Exposition as an opportunity to foster a new parish and to found educational institutions. In the words of the Superior:

> In the very early part of 1886, after consultation I proposed to the Very Rev. Father General of the Society of

Fig. 17. Odenheimer Aquarium.

Fig. 18. Sea Lion Pool. "One of the most recent additions to the New Orleans Zoo and Aquarium attractions in Audubon Park is the beautiful Odenheimer Sea Lion Pool. The Graeco-Roman architecture of this open air pool makes it a center of interest, and a beautiful addition to the park. Several California specimens disport themselves in its waters." (Courtesy Robert Cangelosi, Jr.)

Jesus, the prospect of soliciting a parish at the side of Carrollton which might also be a location of a future college and serve as a house of retreat for men.

During the Christmas holidays of 1889, the Jesuits bought from Joseph Hernandez a lower section of the Foucher tract, measuring 447 feet frontage on St. Charles Avenue and extending back beyond the Claiborne Canal, a distance greater than two miles. Hernandez had acquired his portion of the Foucher tract in a partition between himself, the heirs of Samuel P. Blanc, and the heirs of William Henry (James Fahey, N.P., April 10, 1889). At the time of the Jesuit purchase, the land was used for little other than grazing and some truck and dairy farms. One year later, in November 1890, the *Daily Picayune* noted that the purchase price of $22,500 seemed quite low, considering "the future possibilities of St. Charles Avenue."

In a speech at the ground breaking ceremonies for Loyola University's Marquette Hall twenty-one years after the 1889 purchase, O'Shanahan said that at the time of the Jesuit acquisition no one would touch the Foucher tract because they thought it had a questionable title. Future Supreme Court Justice Edward Douglass White, however, researched the title for the Jesuits and found that not only was the title clear but the whole tract could be gotten for only $75,000. O'Shanahan noted that he regrettably did not follow White's advice because, at the time, it looked like "commercial buying, which is forbidden to the Jesuits."

In 1890 the Catholic church named a parish for the new mission territory—Holy Name, the boundaries of which went from Leontine to Pine streets and from Prytania Street to the swamps (South Claiborne Avenue). Work then began on the first Church of the Holy Name and an adjacent priests' residence (Figure 19), placed near the downtown Foucher line, facing the park. The "Little Jesuits," as the church came to be called to distinguish it from the downtown Jesuit church on Baronne Street, stood as a frame, vernacular Gothic structure, described by the *Daily Picayune* of July 19, 1910, as "totally a Louisiana product," with the carpentry work done by the priests according to the plans of Clayton Company of Galveston, Texas. On May 28, 1892, the priests celebrated Mass in this picturesque church, the first of an impressive grouping of institutional buildings which would occupy the expansive portion of the Foucher tract on the lake side of St. Charles Avenue.

Soon after the parish was created, a school for younger children was established, with classes held in the rectory. Between 1901 and 1909, the Notre Dame Sisters operated the parish school on adjacent property between the Foucher line and Calhoun Street, on streets now known as Cromwell and LaSalle places. The Sisters of Mercy then

Fig. 19. Holy Name rectory and church. Photo by E. Claud. (Courtesy Loyola University, hereafter LU)

assumed the operation of the schools, using their money to buy nearby property that would become the site of the Most Holy Name of Jesus School and Mercy Academy. Holy Name of Jesus School still operates today at 6325 Cromwell Place in a 1932 Gothic Revival structure designed by Rathbone DeBuys and built by Lionel Favret.

Loyola University

By 1890 the downtown Jesuit College of Immaculate Conception (now the site of the Pere Marquette Building) (see Volume I) was cramped, with classes spilling over into Gallier Hall. In 1904 a preparatory school was opened by the Jesuits in a frame building (Figure 22) on Saratoga Street (Marquette Place) near Holy Name Church. Father Albert Biever, S.J., issued a letter (dated August 21, 1904) to the public that began:

> Your attention is respectfully invited to the new school by the Jesuits in the garden district of the city, on St. Charles Avenue near Audubon Park. It is the earnest purpose of the Jesuit Fathers to so conduct this new institution as to deservedly entitle it to the name of a high grade school. . . . Pending the erection of College buildings, the classes will be conducted for the present in one of the elegant and spacious residences lately acquired by the Jesuit Fathers.

Eventually this uptown academy and the downtown college merged to form Loyola College (Figure 23). The Marquette Association for Higher Education, a laymen's association, was founded to build and maintain a Catholic university in New Orleans. The *Times-Democrat* of September 1, 1905 reported:

> Probably the most ambitious undertaking underway just now is the building of a college plant, opposite Audubon Park, upon ground which adjoins Tulane University. Just two years ago Loyola College, under the direction of the Jesuits was opened in the rectory of the Church of the Holy Name of Jesus.. The building was not considered suitable at the time, but a start was made and the money is rapidly accumulating for the erection of a great structure, which will fill the growing needs of the college and be an ornament to the avenue and a monument to Catholic zeal and liberality.

In 1909 the Jesuits held a design competition for a new main campus building. *Architectural Art and Its Allies* (December 1909) published the resulting designs. Favrot and Livaudais produced a Mediterranean design; Francis Mac-Donnell a "Chateauesque" one; Diboll, Owen and Goldstein a Renaissance Revival one; and Toledano and Wogan a Gothic one. Rathbone DeBuys of the firm of DeBuys, Churchill and Labouisse produced the winning design, in the "Tudor Gothic" style, which was used for both the brick and limestone Marquette (Figure 24) and Thomas (Figure 25) halls. On November 13, 1910, the cornerstone of Marquette Hall was laid, following the construction of the Burke Seismographic Observatory, constructed in 1909 and

Fig. 20. Interior of "Little Jesuits" (Holy Name Church). (Courtesy LU)

Fig. 21. Faculty residence, former rectory of Holy Name. (Courtesy TULC)

AT LEFT: Fig. 22. Loyola Hall. (Courtesy LU)

BELOW: Fig. 23. Sketch for "New Buildings for Church of the Holy Name of Jesus and Loyola College," by Diboll and Owen. (Courtesy TULC)

Fig. 24. Marquette Hall, from *Architectural Art and Its Allies.* (Courtesy TULC)

Fig. 25. Thomas Hall.

given by Mr. and Mrs. W.P. Burke in memory of their son, Nicholas. That year the *Times-Democrat* noted that work had begun on the "four-story fireproof brick structure with stone trimmings" in the "Collegiate Gothic" style (Marquette Hall). Mrs. Louise C. Thomas funded the building of Loyola's second new building, a residence hall (1911), also designed by the DeBuys firm.

To make room for the new college structures, "Little Jesuits," the original parish church, was moved in 1910 to a new location only sixty feet down on St. Charles Avenue. During the move, Father Biever remained in the building as it rolled down the street. As work progressed on the two new buildings, the Queen Anne style rectory, which adjoined the church, was moved to Marquette Place. From these university buildings which, with the soon-to-be built new Church of the Holy Name, form a cloister, the uptown Jesuit university grew into a recognized university, noted for its schools of music, journalism, and law, as well as for its general liberal arts curriculum. In 1912 Loyola College was chartered by the state as a university; and in the early 1920s, Loyola University launched a building campaign to raise money for new buildings. On March 21, 1922, this fund drive was the subject of Louisiana's first licensed radio broadcast. A huge clock tower, constructed on a portion of the Canal Street neutral ground, proclaimed "LOYOLA UNIVERSITY WILL BE BIG ENOUGH IF YOUR HEART IS." The campaign, however, netted only enough money to build Bobet Hall (1924), used for biology, a chemistry library, pharmacy college, and temporarily for the schools of law and dentistry.

The Church of the Holy Name of Jesus

By the early 1900s, "Little Jesuits" seemed small and perhaps not architecturally suited for its position as a church serving a growing, affluent parish and an important Jesuit university. In 1913 Kate McDermott responded to the church's needs and donated $100,000 for the building of a church in memory of her sugar broker brother, Thomas McDermott. Miss McDermott later increased her bequest by $50,000 and made the Jesuits her residual heirs. The terms of the will were contested by other heirs who charged that Hugh McCloskey and William P. Burke (who lived across the street from Holy Name Church at 6300 St. Charles Avenue), the testamentary executors, had unduly influenced Miss McDermott in changing her will in favor of the church. Although work began in 1913, the McDermott Memorial Church, also designed by Rathbone DeBuys in brick with limestone detailing to complement the Jesuit cloister, was not completed and dedicated until 1918, four

Fig. 26. Holy Name Church.

years after the death of its benefactress (Figure 26). The thirty-year-old "Little Jesuits" made its second—and last—move in 1922, when it traveled across the river to serve as the Church of Our Lady of Prompt Succor in Westwego.

Tulane University

The newly endowed, renamed, and reorganized Tulane University came uptown in the early 1890s. On April 27, 1891, almost eighteen months after the Jesuits purchased their school and church site, Tulane's Board of Administrators acquired a portion of the Foucher tract, measuring 407.8 feet on St. Charles Avenue, from the heirs of William Henry, just on the uptown side of the Holy Name property. The $37,500 purchase price, compared with the $22,500 paid by the Jesuits, reflects the increased desirability of the area. Indeed the site for the new university was reportedly decided upon after Tulane physics professor Brown Ayres plotted the city's population trends to show that Audubon Park was the neighborhood of the future. In 1893 the board added to the original purchase by paying $30,000 to the heirs of Samuel P. Blanc for an adjoining slice of the Foucher tract, fronting 175 feet on the avenue. With the rise in property values, no wonder Father O'Shanahan lamented not having bought the entire northern portion of the Foucher tract for the church! The Tulane board, however, did not exercise its option to buy another portion of the avenue-fronting Foucher tract, which shortly would become the site of Audubon Place's mansions.

Like Loyola University, Tulane's roots go back downtown: to the Medical College of Louisiana, founded in 1834 by a group of physicians in hope of combating the city's ravaging tropical diseases, and to the University of Louisiana, enabled in 1845 by the state constitution but left financially destitute after the Civil War. The true origin of the uptown university, though, lies in the generosity of Paul Tulane. A New Jersey native of French Huguenot descent, Tulane amassed a fortune in antebellum New Orleans selling hats and men's clothing and buying real estate.

Tulane eventually moved back to his native state, and in 1881 the old man summoned the patrician Louisianian Randall Lee Gibson to his home in Princeton. Tulane told Gibson, at the time a congressman from Louisiana, that he wanted to foster the education of youths in Louisiana, something he found lacking during his stay in the southern state. As a result of this tete-a-tete between Tulane and Gibson, the Board of Administrators of the Tulane Education Fund met for the first time in the spring of 1882. Money this board had, but what to do with it was another matter: establish a new institution or shore up the sinking public University of Louisiana? And what should the curriculum of the school be—liberal arts, technical, professional, or all three? The benefactor's preferences, other than that the school must be non-sectarian but not antagonistic to Christian tenets and free from political control, were yet unknown.

Although Tulane soon expressed his opposition to supporting the existing university's academic curriculum, his adamant refusal to have taxes levied on his gift resulted in a compromise arrangement whereby an 1884 legislative act (43) gave the Tulane Education Fund administrators "full direction, control and administration." In exchange, a number of tuition-free scholarships would be given to students from the state's political districts. Paul Tulane died in 1887 before a legislative act of 1890 authorized the board to sell or lease the downtown campus on Common Street. In 1891 the board of administrators of the Tulane Educational Fund acquired its uptown site across from Audubon Park and appointed a subcommittee to oversee planning for the new campus.

In November 1891, Tulane President William Preston Johnson reported to the board that he had visited various colleges in the Northeast and had been advised to consult the firm of McKim, Mead and White of New York, who are regarded "as the best architects in the United States." Although the cost of McKim, Mead and White's proposed Tulane campus, described in the July 1892 issue of *American Architect and Building News* as "a very imposing group of buildings in the Italian renaissance style," exceeded the

institution's budget, these plans rank as the firm's first experiment in collegiate work.

In early 1892, President Johnson reported that "a large number of architects from this and other states are preparing plans for our main building in the Henry tract fully twenty in number and I have named May 1 as the day for them to be handed in." Submitting architects included Lambert and Monneron, McDonald Brothers, Louis H. Lambert, William Freret and Son, James Freret, Duval and Favrot, Allison Owen, "Mr. Chanitel of New Orleans and Mr. Aiken of Cincinnati, Ohio, George T. Reed of Springfield, Missouri and Torgenson & Sutfliffe of Birmingham, Alabama." Finally, in June 1892, building committee chairman William Walmsley announced that the board had chosen the local firm of Harrod and Andry for their design, which he described as "commodious, adopted to the requirements of the situation and a very handsome structure."

Work began in early 1894 on Tulane's first structure, the arts and science building named Gibson Hall (Figure 27) after the man selected by Paul Tulane to be the chief custodian of his gift. Harrod and Andry chose Richardsonian Romanesque, the style developed by Louisiana native Henry Hobson Richardson, for the design of the monumental stone structure, thereby setting the style for the remainder of the front quadrangle located between St. Charles Avenue and Freret Street. The Physics Building

Fig. 27. Gibson Hall shortly after construction. (Courtesy TULC)

Fig. 28. Mechanical & Engineering Building (upper), Physical Laboratory, Dining Hall, Dormitories, Chemical Laboratory (lower). (Courtesy TULC)

(now F. Edward Hebert Hall), the Richardson Building, constructed for chemistry laboratories and classes, and the mechanical engineering complex, all designed by Harrod and Andry, also date from this initial spurt of construction in 1894. The siting of these buildings derived from the north-south orientation of the Physics Building for natural lighting

and for convenience in using magnetic equipment. Both the physics and chemistry buildings similarly use brown brick and ribbed limestone rather than the more expensive rock-face stone of Gibson Hall.

The early-twentieth century marked a period of continued expansion for the university and resulted in new construction in the front portion of the campus. Andry and Bendernagel designed Tilton Memorial Hall (1902) (Figure 29), a refectory (1902), the Social Work Building (1902), the Richardson Memorial Building (1908), and Stanley Thomas Hall (1911). The Romanesque Revival exterior of the Tilton library, given by Caroline Tilton in memory of her husband, Frederick, impressively displays lions, cartouches with the university's monogram, and human faces, all executed in Bedford stone. Its interior includes two Tiffany windows dominating the main staircase landing. The Dutch renaissance style of the refectory, now the Social Science Building, dramatically departs from the remainder of the campus, as does the similarly styled Social Work Building. Funds for the Richardson Memorial Building (Figure 30), built as the medical school, came from Ida Richardson, wife of Tobias Gibson Richardson, M.D., who also financed the 1908 Richardson Memorial Dormitory for medical students (now Alcée Fortier Hall). DeBuys, Churchill and Labouisse, architects for the neighboring Jesuits, designed this structure. Moise Goldstein and Associates used the Elizabethan motif for the Science Building, constructed in 1923 near Gibson Hall. The name for the latter structure was changed in 1936

Fig. 29. F.W. Tilton Library. Adolph Selige Publishing Co. (Courtesy Robert Cangelosi, Jr.)

Fig. 30. Richardson Memorial Building.

to honor Dr. Albert Bledsoe Dinwiddie, president of the university from 1918 to 1935. Also during the early 1900s, Tulane acquired the portion of the Foucher tract owned by the Jesuits, extending from Freret Street to South Claiborne Avenue, over sixty acres, which became the site of a stadium, gymnasium, and athletic field. Later in the twentieth century, construction filled in the middle portion of the campus, stretching between Freret and Willow streets, with a stylistically unrelated assortment of buildings for Tulane, as well as with a more coherent grouping of buildings for Newcomb College.

Newcomb College

Around the time that bulldozers cleared land and moved dirt to finally implement Olmsted's landscaping plan, other developments took place across the avenue, on a rear portion of the Foucher tract and neighboring property. In early 1917, piles were driven and construction begun on three buildings that would comprise the heart of Newcomb College's new campus. The Broadway Street campus was actually the third home for the women's college which, in

the words of its first president, Brandt V.B. Dixon, originated in a "bereaved mother's grief for her daughter and desire to commemorate her."

New Yorker Josephine Louise Le Monnier Newcomb lost her husband in 1866 and her daughter in 1870, and devoted the rest of her long life to making money and memorializing her daughter. The concept of endowing a coordinate college for women within the framework of a university for men came from Mrs. Tobias G. Richardson of New Orleans. In 1886 Mrs. Newcomb donated $100,000 to Tulane's Board of Administrators for the purpose of establishing the H. Sophie Newcomb Memorial College. Further contributions made before her 1901 death and through her will totaled over three million dollars.

The college first opened in 1887, the year of Paul Tulane's death, and occupied an Italianate mansion downtown at Camp and Howard streets. Between 1890 and 1918, the Newcomb campus was located in the Garden District, centered around the grand Robb (or Burnside) mansion at Washington Avenue and Sixth Street. On this campus the "old Newcomb" expanded and gained recognition, especially for its art school under the direction of New Englander brothers William and Ellsworth Woodward. The ceramics department gained international attention at the Paris Exposition of 1900 where its arts-and-crafts-inspired pottery won a bronze medal and launched the reputation of Newcomb pottery.

Newcomb's move from its Garden District campus came reluctantly and slowly. Property on Napoleon Avenue was acquired but later sold when the decision was made to find a campus nearer the Tulane campus. In 1908 the Tulane Educational Fund began financing the purchase of the final site for the new campus, consisting of the entire second block of Audubon Place and two additional squares (not part of the Foucher estate) between Zimple, Broadway, Plum, and Audubon Streets. In 1911 James Gamble Rogers, later the designer of many of Yale University's colleges, won a design competition for the new campus. Rogers associated with local architect Paul Andry, and on May 30, 1914, *Building Review* reported that "plans for the Administration, Music, Arts and Dormitories were on the market to a list of four local contractors."

Not until 1917, however, did work actually begin, with George J. Glover acting as contractor. The delay in construction came as a result of the board's rejection of bid prices and a lack of funds. Finally, in 1918, the Newcomb students moved to the new campus, made up of Newcomb Hall (administration) (Figure 31), the Arts Building (Figure 32), and the Josephine Louise House (residence). Unlike the heavy neo-Romanesque used for many of Tulane's buildings, for the women's college, Gamble employed a lighter neoclassical mode, executed in pressed red brick

Fig. 31. Newcomb Administration Building.

Fig. 32. Arts Building, just after completion. (Courtesy TULC)

with limestone trim and tiled roofs. In the next two decades, the following were added to the campus: New-comb Gymnasium (1923), architect Frank Churchill; Dixon Hall (1928) (Figure 33), architect Emile Weil; and the wrought iron Broadway Avenue gate (1934), architect Richard Koch.

Fittingly, when the Foucher estate passed from its ancestral owners into the hands of the new breed of New Orleanians who fueled the uptown expansion, the old plantation was treated holistically. Audubon Park and its educational and religious neighbors play complementary roles. In the beginning the institutions chose to move uptown, largely because of the promise of the yet unfinished park site. Then when Olmsted devised his landscaping plan, he responded to the church and school buildings that had already been constructed across the avenue. Thus, today the vista sweeps across the park to catch a glimpse of a steeple or gable, symbols of civilization. And Loyola and Tulane Universities have the prospect of an Olmstedian creation as their front yard.

Fig. 33. Dixon Hall.

RESIDENTIAL PARKS

ROBERT J. CANGELOSI, JR., A.I.A.

Before the nation's first comprehensive zoning was adopted in 1916 in New York, developers relied on residential parks as zoning tools. Nineteenth century planners created residential parks to prohibit commercialization of their developments and to control the quality of the neighborhood with restrictions covering orientation, setback, height, construction cost, and occupancy of the houses. Although New York developers created the first private residential park with St. John's Park in 1803, the concept was perfected later in St. Louis with such developments as Portland Place and Westmoreland in 1888. New Orleans was introduced to residential parks in 1891 with the announcement of Rosa Park (Figure 1).

The University Section grew rapidly after the 1884 World's Industrial and Cotton Centennial Exposition. Electrification of the streetcar and the subsequent advent of the automobile (Figure 2) helped to hasten the rapid expansion of the city. The January 25, 1891, *Times-Democrat* reported that "improvement is very marked in many of the districts, particularly in the Sixth, where the advance in the value of real estate has caused a veritable 'boom' in the price of resident [*sic*] property." Although the mixture of residential and commercial was successful in older, denser areas of the city such as the Vieux Carré and Faubourg St. Mary with the shop-residence, and in less dense neighborhoods such as Faubourg Annunciation and Tremé with the corner store, the demographics of the city were changing as its boundaries expanded. Neighborhood establishments were rapidly replaced by larger businesses serving the entire city, and as the variety of goods and services increased, commercialization and urbanization and the associated congestion, traffic, and pollution became major concerns. Consequently, there was a growing desire for detached housing in suburban areas that were free of commercial development. In New

Fig. 1. Rosa Park, Rotograph Co. post card, 1906. (Courtesy TULC)

65

Fig. 2. Rosa Park, with horse and buggy and early automobile. (Courtesy TULC)

Orleans, like the rest of the country, planners turned to private residential parks.

Three years after Rosa Park was established, Audubon Place became the city's second residential park in 1894, followed by Richmond Place in 1905, Everett Place in 1906, Audubon Boulevard in 1909, Dunleith Court in 1910, State Street Drive in 1914, Vincennes Place in 1915, Newcomb Boulevard in 1917, Wirth Place in 1919, Trianon Plaza in 1925, and Versailles Boulevard, also in 1925. Residential parks were also a real-estate concept in Jefferson Parish, with developments such as Oakridge Park, Farnham Place, and Livingston Place.

Before discussing the development of the University Section's parks, it is worthwhile to first examine the context of local governmental control. Prior to adopting comprehensive zoning in 1929, New Orleans employed the "police power" of the city to promote the public welfare, health, and safety. In the nineteenth century, the city charter gave the city the authority to regulate the conduct and location of certain businesses deemed detrimental to public health, morale, peace, and safety. In 1900 New Orleans passed various ordinances in an effort to protect many of its major streets. In the University Section, the city banned various businesses such as blacksmith shops, forges, wood and coal

AT RIGHT: Fig. 3. Richmond Place.

yards, laundries, oyster shops, and fruit shops on Nashville Avenue, State Street, and Henry Clay Avenue between Tchoupitoulas and Saratoga streets, and on St. Charles Avenue between Lee Circle and Carrollton Avenue. Five years later, the city council banned tanneries, livery stables, box factories, sash factories, "rendering establishments," and manufactory establishments from numerous streets, including St. Charles Avenue, Palmer Avenue, State Street, Henry Clay Avenue, and Webster Street.

From 1910 to 1918, New Orleans passed ninety-three laws and seven amendments regulating specific businesses in various sections of the city. Most of these regulations were to restrict these areas to residential use; other ordinances prohibited the erection of awnings, signs, sheds, and hitching posts. During this early phase, and even during the next phase, 1919 to 1923, court decisions often went against the city, and ordinances had to be redrafted, reflecting changing state enabling legislation.

A 1910 city ordinance prohibited grocery stores, barrooms, and livery stables on Broadway between St. Charles and Claiborne avenues. The following year, the same type of establishments were banned from Audubon Street between St. Charles Avenue and Magazine Street and from Calhoun Street between St. Charles and Mobile Street, now South Claiborne Avenue. Additionally, sheds over the sidewalk on Audubon Street were prohibited.

In 1912 regulations were put in place banning virtually all businesses on Palmer Avenue between St. Charles and Claiborne, on Hurst Street from Octavia Street to Exposition Boulevard, and on St. Charles from Lee Circle to Carrollton Avenue. The following year, Webster Street between Magazine and St. Charles was protected in a similar manner, and on Audubon Street, existing sheds were required to be removed from the sidewalk between Magazine and St. Charles.

In 1914 the city passed additional ordinances in an effort to establish residential zones on Audubon Street from Freret Street to Green Street, on Walnut Street from St. Charles to the river, on State Street from Magazine to Claiborne, on Perrier Street from Jefferson Avenue to Audubon Park, on Prytania Street from Jackson Avenue to Audubon Park, and on St. Charles from Lee Circle to Carrollton Avenue.

In 1915 the city council banned banners, signs, and sheds or other obstructions from St. Charles Avenue and required existing ones to be removed. The following year, businesses were banned from Broadway between St. Charles and the river and between South Claiborne Avenue and Fontainebleau Drive, except for drugstores, hotels, and boarding houses. In 1918 a new prohibition was placed on businesses on Webster Street between Magazine and St. Charles, and one was instituted for Hurst Street between Octavia Street and Exposition Boulevard.

The Louisiana state legislature passed Act 27 in 1918

Fig. 4. 642 Broadway (demolished). (Courtesy HNOC 1979.325.1279)

giving broad authority to regulate construction through building codes and zoning to cities with a population of over 50,000. The 1921 state constitution gave all municipalities the authority "to zone their territory; to create residential, commercial, and industrial districts, and to prohibit the establishment of places of businesses in residential districts." During this time, there was a growing demand for residential districts. 1923 was an important year for zoning in New Orleans, for that year the city won its first major court case, *State ex rel. Civello v. City of New*

Fig. 5. State Street, from the *Daily Picayune,* September 13, 1908. (Courtesy TULC)

Fig. 6. Palmer Avenue, 1910. (Courtesy TULC)

Orleans, upholding the city's right to establish residential districts. In 1923 the city also created its first Planning and Zoning Commission.

With the changing enabling legislation for zoning, New Orleans passed more ordinances on a piecemeal basis. In 1920 ordinances prohibited various businesses on St. Charles between Lee Circle and Carrollton, State between Magazine and Claiborne, Audubon Street between St. Charles and the Newcomb property line, Calhoun between St. Charles and Claiborne, and Magazine between Eleonore and Webster. In 1922 the city created the first University Section residential zone broader than a single street—the area was bounded by Green Street, South Claiborne Avenue, Broadway, and Audubon Boulevard. However, the majority of zoning regulations continued to focus on individual streets in the University Section, such as Prytania from Felicity Street to Audubon Park, Palmer from St. Charles to Claiborne, Audubon Street from Green to Fontainebleau, and Magazine from Henry Clay to Exposition.

By 1923 the city had begun a policy to actively enforce all zoning ordinances through the City Engineer's Department, and continued to create new zoning restrictions for Broadway from St. Charles to the river, St. Charles from Lee Circle to Carrollton, Audubon Street from St. Charles to Magazine, Broadway from General Hood (Perrier) to St. Charles, Eleonore from St. Charles to the river, State Street Drive from South Claiborne to Baldwin (Fontainebleau), and new residential districts including the areas bounded by Annunciation, St. Charles, lower Foucher line, Jefferson, and South Claiborne; South Claiborne, Jefferson, South Carrollton and the Yazoo and Mississippi Valley Railroad right-of-way.

In 1924, Audubon Place and Audubon Boulevard from St. Charles to Apricot became a residential zone. That same year, the first governmental setback requirements were established for the University Section, requiring a fifteen-foot setback on State Street between St. Charles and South Claiborne. The following year, a similar setback was established for Henry Clay Avenue from St. Charles to 120 feet north of Magazine and for Palmer Avenue between St. Charles and South Claiborne, and a height limit of three stories was imposed on apartment buildings. Also in 1925, the city created a residential district for the area bounded by Annunciation, St. Charles, lower Foucher line, and Jefferson, and banned businesses from the intersection of Joseph and Hurst streets, and revised it early the following year.

From 1918 to 1929, 164 residential protective ordinances and 112 amendments, 14 special laws and amendments, and 50 setback ordinances and amendments were passed citywide, creating a confusing mess of piecemeal zoning regulations. In 1926 the new administration of Martin Behrman greatly advanced the cause of zoning by employing Harland Bartholomew and Associates of St. Louis as technical advisors for a comprehensive zoning plan. The state legislature that year revised the enabling legislation for the Planning and Zoning Commission, and the city followed suit in revising its legislation. Also in 1926, the city banned business in two new residential zones, one for Versailles Boulevard between South Claiborne and Pritchard, and one for the area bounded by Calhoun, Palmer, St. Charles, and Claiborne.

On February 24, 1927, the city reorganized the City Planning and Zoning Commission to conform with the new state act. Two months later, the council established a moratorium on new zoning districts, pending receipt of a comprehensive zoning plan. In June that year, Bartholomew and Associates submitted the findings of its study and began the review and comment process. In July 1928, the consultants submitted a zoning plan to the city council, which began its own review process, finally adopting it on June 1, 1929. Two months later, the Board of Zoning Adjustments was created on August 26, 1929. The new plan created twelve classifications of districts—four residential, three commercial, one Vieux Carré, three industrial, and one "unresolved."

In the University Section, the Zoning Board designated the vast majority of the area as "A", single-family and duplex residential, and "B", residential for up to four-unit boarding houses and lodging houses. The board zoned St. Charles Avenue as "C", apartment district for multiple dwellings and apartment hotels. Commercial districts comprised a small percentage of the area, concentrated along Magazine, Tchoupitoulas, the river and lake ends of Broadway, and isolated pockets on Lowerline, between Cohn and Hickory, and on Calhoun, just north of Claiborne. Industrial development was limited to the riverfront.

In "A" and "B" districts, the plan limited residences to thirty-five feet or two-and-one-half stories, with a twenty-foot setback in "A" and fifteen in "B", permitting a ten-foot encroachment of steps and similar projections in "A" and five in "B". The rear yard was to have a depth not less than 20 percent of the total lot depth, but in any case not less than fifteen feet or more than twenty-five. Side yards had to have a combined width of 20 percent of the lot width, but not less than three feet each side, and the combined total did not have to exceed twelve feet.

In "C" areas, apartment districts, the plan limited buildings to three stories, not to exceed forty-five feet in height, with similar front, rear, and side yards requirements as "A", residential. For apartments exceeding thirty-five feet in height, the side yard had to be at least six feet, and increased by six inches for each additional foot of height.

Today, the zoning pattern of the University Section is basically the same. It has seven residential classifications, two business ones, a medical services district, and a light industrial zone.

Comprehensive zoning rendered obsolete the restrictions that had been imposed by residential parks, with the exception of housing discrimination, which was not outlawed until 1968 with Title 8 of the Civil Rights Act.

Rosa Park

Rosa Park is New Orleans' first residential park, created in 1891. Durant da Ponte and John M. Bonner acquired this tract with a house on it on March 30, 1887, from Minerva Flower. The two apparently subdivided Rosa Park in 1890, as a plan appears in an advertisement for the subdivision placed by real estate agents Robinson and Underwood in both the *Daily Picayune* and the *Times-Democrat* on January 25, 1891 (Figure 7). The advertisement illustrated a twenty-seven-lot subdivision in a modified cul-de-sac plan, similar to the St. Louis residential park, Benton Place, established in 1868. The advertisement read, in part:

> "Rosa Park" will be about 100 FEET WIDE, and beautified with terraced mounds, fountains, etc., the walks to be "SCHILLINGERED," thus making the lots facing the Park quite as desirable as those fronting on ST. CHARLES AVENUE and State street . . . The DRIVES and PARK will be for the exclusive use of purchasers of this land. . . . The entire tract is studded with magnificent trees, shade and ornamental, while ST. CHARLES AVENUE and State street have a row of stately shade trees. There is a comfortable two-story frame house on the grounds for sale.

The house mentioned is that which stood in the square and is shown on the Robinson *Atlas* as a masonry cross plan house owned by J.A. Peel.

An article accompanying the advertisement in the *Daily Picayune* noted that "this novel plan will surely induce purchasers to secure sites to build homes, for no such an opportunity to acquire residence lots has ever been offered." It also described a "garden spot" in the center of the subdivision, with a terraced mound and artistic fountain. Whether or not a fountain was ever constructed is unknown; there are, however, a decorative, cast iron urn and an Edison Electric Company light standard in the neutral ground today.

The article in the *Times-Democrat* stated that "although these lots have been on the market [but] a week there has been quite a demand for them and in a short time the entire tract will pass into the hands of small holders who will built residences there."

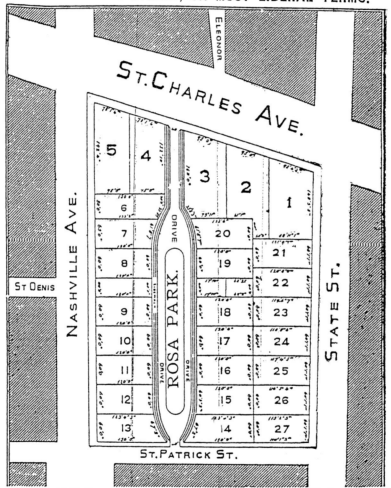

Fig. 7. "For Sale (advertisement for the sale of lots in Rosa Park), from the *Daily Picayune,* January 25, 1891. (Courtesy Microfilm Division, Howard-Tilton Memorial Library, Tulane University, hereafter TUMD)

Fig. 8. "Entrance to Rosa Park," from *Pen & Sunlight Sketches of Greater New Orleans*. (Courtesy Southeastern Architectural Archive, Howard-Tilton Memorial Library, Tulane University)

Despite the publication of this plan in 1891 and the accompanying publicity, the official plan of the subdivision by civil engineer Hunter Stewart is dated June 28, 1892, and no sales took place until 1893. That year Judge Bonner sold his interest in the property to Da Ponte, and sold five of the lots to John Dougherty on March 27, 1893. The following month, several lots were sold at auction.

In 1895 a plan was implemented to improve the St. Charles Avenue entrance to the subdivision. Property owners adjacent to the entrance donated ten feet of land, increasing the street width from forty to sixty feet. This donation was recorded on a survey by George Grandjean dated March 28, 1895. The present decorative stone and iron gates appear to date from this period. Other alterations to the subdivision were made by Municipal Ordinances 8576 CCS and 14579 CCS, in which the Danneel Street street-bed was acquired by adjacent property owners and the Saratoga Street right-of-way was purchased from Everett Place owners.

Today Rosa Park remains a private residential street with a distinctive identity due to its cul-de-sac plan, identifying gates, and consistent late-nineteenth century architecture.

Rosa Park was named in honor of Rosa Solomon Da Ponte, second wife of Durant Da Ponte. A socialite and amateur actress, Rosa was a beautiful woman whose name appeared often in local and national publications. She built a miniature theater at her residence at 3512 St. Charles Avenue, hired a director, and produced and acted in many theatrical productions. Years later her friends described to Works Progress Administration writers elaborate functions in her house, such as teas in caverns of ice and balls with Egyptian themes. After her husband's death in 1894, she went into seclusion and eventually died in New York in 1948.

Durant Da Ponte was a journalist, lawyer, soldier, and financier. Born in New York, he came to New Orleans at the age of twelve and began work as a reporter for the *Crescent.* At age sixteen, he was promoted to the editorial

Fig. 9. Rosa Park, from *Around the St. Charles Belt,* circa 1906, New Orleans and Carrollton Railroad, Light and Power Co.

Fig. 10. No. 4 Rosa Park, C.C. Swayze's residence (prior to current facade renovation). (Courtesy TULC)

department. He then moved to the *Daily Picayune,* where he became editor-in-chief, and he later established the *Delta.* During the Civil War, Durant served on the staffs of Generals Van Dorn and Magruder and was wounded at the Battle of Seven Pines. After the war, he practiced law for a brief period. One of his opinions on corporate law established the non-taxability of premium bonds. It was these bonds to which he owed his financial success. Durant then became a stock and real estate broker in New Orleans and California. He was fluent in seven languages and a charter member of the Chess, Checkers, and Whist Club and a member of the stock exchange and several Carnival organizations. Durant died at his summer home in Alameda, California.

Audubon Place

Audubon Place is the city's second residential park, and the most outstanding. Born out of controversy, Audubon Place was planned as Beauregard Place on precedents established in northern and western cities.

In 1891 Tulane University purchased a tract of land 407 feet along St. Charles Avenue by 7,000 feet in depth, adjacent to Loyola University. The University board of trustees, however, deemed the site too narrow and opened negotiations with Judge John M. Bonner for the adjacent 616 feet, securing an option for the purchase of the land at $100,000. One week prior to the expiration of the option, Tulane officials notified the judge of their intention to exercise its option.

In the meantime, however, E.E. Chase of Fort Worth, Texas, arrived in New Orleans in February 1893 bearing a letter from W.A.S. Wheeler stating that a number of St. Louis capitalists wanted to invest money in the establishment of a residential park similar to the "places" of St. Louis and other large northern and western cities. With the assistance of the real estate firm of Robinson and Underwood, Chase contacted Bonner, who for a $5,000 deposit granted them an option on the same land that Tulane wished to purchase. Soon both parties retained legal counsel and a compromise was eventually reached. Tulane decided it needed only an additional 200 feet, not the entire 616. The St. Louis syndicate offered Tulane the 200 feet for slightly less than the $100,000 it had offered for the entire 616 feet. Naturally, Tulane rejected the offer. After a series of negotiations, a compromise was reached on May 20, 1893. The *Times-Democrat* reported the following day that the St. Louis group bought the entire tract from Judge Bonner (616 feet by 7,000 feet) for the option price of $100,000 and sold to Tulane 175 feet adjacent to its property for $30,000. The syndicate also purchased from the Henry estate an adjacent, upriver tract extending to the projection of Walnut

Street and measuring 120 feet on St. Charles by 300 feet deep, paying $20,000 for it. The deal for the tract, now measuring 781 feet by 7,000 feet, was consummated in the name of Mrs. Sarah Witherspoon. She formally transferred the two lots to the Crescent Land and Improvement Company in an act dated June 3, 1893.

The Company retained surveyor George H. Grandjean to develop the plan for the subdivision of the land as far lakeward as Freret Street. His plan, dated April 10, 1894, established twenty-eight lots, each with a 100-foot front facing "Audubon Place Park," the neutral ground, with West Park Place as the road on the uptown side of the park, and East Park Place on the downtown side. Lots 1 and 2 adjacent to St. Charles Avenue had larger fronts. Lot depths varied from 189 to 210 feet, reflecting the wedge shape of the tract.

A standard printed sales form of the Crescent Land and Improvement Company listed the servitudes, reservations, restrictions, covenants, and conditions. Structures could be used only for residential purposes; they had to face Audubon Place Park, cost in excess of $7,000, and have a forty-foot setback. There could be encroachments of twelve feet for steps and porches into this setback. No fences were allowed in the setback, unless under eighteen inches in height. Rear yard fences could not exceed six feet. "Outhouses, stables or other subsidiary buildings" had to be at least one hundred feet back from the street, but not less than ten feet from the rear property line. Houses could not be built on subdivided lots less than seventy-five feet wide. Behind each lot were "East" and "West" spaces, a utility servitude of ten feet on which nothing could be built.

A board of managers or directors was established, with elections held the first Monday in January at 7:30 P.M. Each 100 feet of lot frontage or fraction thereof counted as one vote. The board managed an assessment not to exceed fifty cents per front foot per annum for maintenance of the park, roadway, sidewalks, and other improvements, and to illuminate the park. Deeds called for a meeting of property owners five years from March 1, 1895, "to decide whether the said Audubon Place Park and Places shall be dedicated to public use." Apparently, property owners voted against this, as the street remains private.

A real estate brochure prepared by Stroudback and Stern and entitled "Audubon Place: A Private Residence Park, The Most Delightful Location in New Orleans in which to Build a Home" states:

> Many residents of New Orleans have never been through this beautiful Residence park. The Magnificent Entrance Lodge and Gates on St. Charles Avenue, Opposite Audubon Park, seeming to indicate that it would require a special invitation from the owners of the Handsome Mansions already built there, to admit them.

Fig. 11. Audubon Place, "View from St. Charles Avenue," circa 1894, Seghers Survey Files. (Courtesy HNOC, 91-16-6 MSS403)

Fig. 12. Audubon Place, circa 1896. Note that only two houses are visible. (Courtesy TULC)

Fig. 13. Audubon Place. (Courtesy TULC)

This is a Mistake. They invite everybody interested in the Growth and Development of this City to make free use of its walks and parks and to show their friends through. They also invite those who wish to build a home where art and nature have been combined in beautiful harmony to come and erect a home here, and only in accordance with their means.

Under the restrictions governing this Place, this will always be the choicest spot for a home in this city.

The brochure noted that every city had a premier residential area and that New Orleans had St. Charles Avenue, but "it is being invaded by business houses and thus it loses the charm of privacy in its environments," while on Audubon Place, owners "can erect their homes without danger of having undesirable neighbors or stores to mar the beauty of their surroundings." Additional benefits cited included an elevated site, proximity to Audubon Park, and good streetcar service that put Audubon Place within twenty minutes of Canal Street.

The gates mentioned in the brochure are dated 1894 and are in the Romanesque style. They were designed by architect Thomas Sully.

Audubon Place lots sold for about $5,000, as evidenced by the sale of lot 12 in 1894. The first house was likely begun that year for Philip Rice at a cost of $12,300. The street is a parade of architectural styles, with the Colonial Revival, Romanesque Revival, Queen Anne, Mission, and Renaissance Revival being represented, and includes the works of architects Favrot and Livaudais, Toledano and Wogan, Soulé and MacDonnell, Frank P. Gravely and Company, Emile Weil, Southron Duval, Weiss and Drey-fous, Diboll, Owen and Goldstein, Andry and Bendernagle, and MacKenzie, Goldstein and Biggs.

The second phase of development was labeled Audubon Place Block No. 2 and extended from Freret Street to Willow Street (Figure 14). The plan for the extension of Audubon Place was prepared for the Crescent Land and Improvement Company by surveyor George H. Grandjean and is dated June 20, 1896. It shows 114 thirty-foot-wide lots, and two large lots at the corner of Freret. The development company experienced financial problems and was forced to sell its interest in the land to several individuals. Consequently, a new plan, dated December 28, 1899, was prepared by Grandjean for the re-subdivision of the property. Entitled "New Subdivisions of block No. 2 Audubon Place," the plan was not for subdivision of the entire block, but had only fifty lots, each only thirty feet wide, extending 750 feet lakeward of Freret. Yet another plan was developed for the subdivision of the block by Edward Pilié. Dated February 17, 1906, this survey shows ninety thirty-foot-wide lots, plus two wider corner lots.

In an undated brochure prepared by Stroudback and Stern Realtors for the sale of lots in Block 2, benefits of Block 1 were pointed out and projected onto Block 2 at a reduced cost. In Block 1, a minimum lot for building was 75 feet, and houses had to cost more than $7,000, while in Block 2, a minimum lot was 50 feet and houses were to cost more than $4,000. Lots in Block 2 ranged in cost from $1,050 to $1,500 per thirty-foot-front. The brochure stated:

Homes may be erected on these lots ranging in value from $4,000 upwards, so that at the prices placed on lots

74

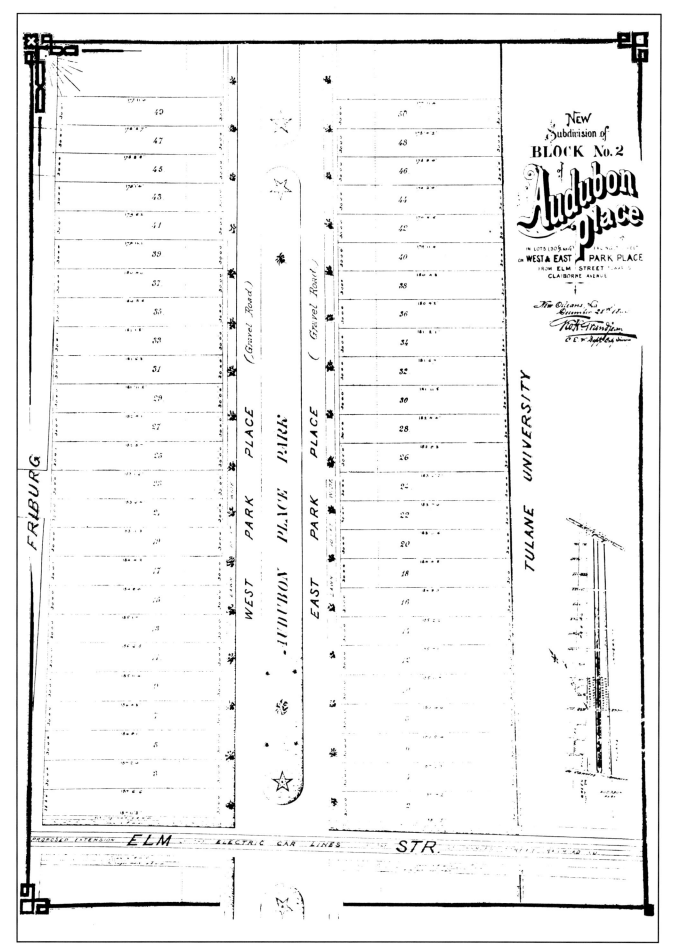

Fig. 14. New Subdivision of Block No. 2, Audubon Place. (Courtesy HNOC, 91.16.6 MSS-403)

offered by us, they will be within the reach of those who wish to secure a home in the most beautiful residence district in this city, without having to make an unusually heavy investment. It costs no more to build a home in this delightful Park than in a less desirable locality, and you are protected against all nuisances forever.

The brochure also noted that negotiations were underway to establish a branch line of the St. Charles Avenue streetcar line to service Audubon Place.

Another undated brochure, which likely postdates the one by Stroudback and Stern, was prepared by National Realty Company indicating that they were authorized to sell lots along the unimproved 750 feet lakeward of Freret and that they intended to improve the remaining 600 feet within the next ninety days. Improvements cited consisted of a "park in the centre, beautifully embellished with palms and plants, driveways, schillinger curbing and gutters, sidewalks, drainage, gas and electric lights."

Tulane University eventually acquired the whole of Audubon Place Block 2 through numerous conveyances. Commenting on the possible joining of the Tulane and Newcomb campuses, Chancellor Craighead told the *Times-*

Democrat that the two colleges would never be merged, nor would there be co-education in the undergraduate programs.

At the time Audubon Place Block 2 was absorbed by Tulane, a promotional brochure for Audubon Boulevard noted that "there are some fifteen or twenty excellent houses on the property, and these will doubtless be used for professors' residences, or perhaps temporarily, by the students of Newcomb College." Only one house survives from this development. Currently home to the dean of Newcomb College, it was built in 1908 by architect Paul Andry as his own residence (Figure 15). The Freret Street gates of Audubon Place Block 1, in the Craftsman style, likely date to the Tulane purchase of Block 2.

The area lakeward of Willow Street was lost by Crescent Land and Improvement Company as the result of a law suit filed by Eugene W. Lewis. In 1900 the civil sheriff sold the property at public auction to the Audubon Place Land Company of St. Louis. This area would eventually become Audubon Boulevard.

Audubon Place is the only residential park in New Orleans that maintains its restrictive nature, not by deeds or

Fig. 15. Paul Andry residence, 1908, now Newcomb College dean's residence.

Fig. 16. 13 Audubon Place, A.B. Wheeler residence (demolished), from *New Orleans, Louisiana: The Crescent City.* (Courtesy K&W)

Fig. 17. 8 Audubon Place (demolished). (Courtesy TULC)

BELOW: Fig. 18. "Audubon Place," by C.B. Mason, 1907. (Courtesy Robert Cangelosi, Jr.)

covenants, but by the security guards who prohibit the public from entering this private street. The neighborhood association is still active, maintaining the upscale nature of the street.

Richmond Place

The third residential park established in New Orleans was Richmond Place. Running from Loyola to Freret, Richmond Place remains a private road today but lacks the park-like setting of Rosa Park and Audubon Place. It was developed in three phases, beginning at Freret in 1905, expanding toward Loyola, and completed in 1907.

George Redersheimer sold eight lots in square No. 79, Freret Street to LaSalle Street, for $1,500 each on July 11, 1905. Purchasers included W.J. Mitchell, a banker; E. Foster, assistant U.S. attorney; Henri L. Favrot, an attorney; Frank J. Walshe, agent for Tennessee Coal, Iron and Railroad Company, Alfred F. Livaudais, a banker and broker; Charles A. Favrot, an architect; and Edward Lamberton, an agent for Southern Pacific. Henri Favrot purchased two lots, 3 and 8.

That same day, all seven owners dedicated Richmond Place as a residential park with a thirty-nine-foot right-of-way private road, according to a plan prepared by F.H. Waddill of Daney and Waddill dated July 6, 1905. Restrictions called for a fifty-foot setback from the center of the roadway. Houses could not exceed ten feet from the northern property line.

Henri Favrot acquired Square 74, Lasalle Street to Liberty Street, from Laurence Fabacher on September 8, 1905, and had it subdivided into eight lots, according to a plan by

Fig. 19. Richmond Place prior to residential construction. (Courtesy H. Richmond Favrot)

Daney and Waddill dated September 1, 1905. Favrot then sold the property to Nola Company, which, with the permission of Square 79 owners, declared Square 74 to be part of Richmond Place.

Owners of Richmond Place revised its dedication on May 4, 1906, reducing the roadway's width from twenty-five to eighteen feet and the building setback from fifty to forty feet from the center-line of the roadway.

The final expansion of Richmond Place was made on February 8, 1907, extending the street through to Loyola Avenue on the square owned by Walter Kent of Tangipahoa Parish. An undated plan by Favrot and Livaudais, architects, illustrates the full development of the street. At the intersections of Howard (now LaSalle) and Liberty streets, an eighteen-foot lawn circle was proposed. Although the two streets were shown intersecting Richmond Place, they were never cut through, and the right-of-way was eventually purchased by adjacent property owners. Two years later, lots 21 through 24 in Square 73 were re-subdivided into three one-hundred-foot lots in lieu of four seventy-five-foot lots and the setback and property line requirements removed. This established a total of twenty-three

lots on the street, with the restriction that only one house per lot was permitted.

Richmond Place was named in honor of Henri Favrot's wife, Marie Richmond (Figure 20). The Favrots lived in two houses on Richmond Place, Nos. 17 and 18, along with their two sons, Richmond and Allain. Henri Louis Favrot (Figure 21) was a state senator, prominent lawyer, father of the Boy Scouts movement in Louisiana, and veteran of the Spanish-American War. Born in West Baton Rouge Parish in 1864, he attended Louisiana State University's College of Arts and Sciences but failed to graduate due to illness. After four years as a planter and plantation store operator, he enrolled in Tulane Law School in 1888. After graduation the following year, he worked for Colonel W.L. Hughes in New Orleans and then formed a partnership with A.K. Amacker. Favrot volunteered for the Seventh Infantry Battalion of the Louisiana National Guard, where he rose to the position of adjutant. In the Spanish-American War, he became a captain and adjutant of the Second Regiment of Infantry, U.S. Volunteers. Between 1902 and 1916, he served in the Louisiana Senate, where he became an expert on road and land bonds, authored child labor

Fig. 20. Marie Richmond Favrot. (Courtesy H. Richmond Favrot)

Fig. 21. Henri Louis Favrot. (Courtesy H. Richmond Favrot)

legislation, and led the fight for the Locke law abolishing horse racing. Favrot, an anti-lottery Democrat, was also a member of the Municipal Reform Association and the Committee of Safety and worked to bring to justice those responsible for the assassination of New Orleans Police Chief Hennessey. He also served as the Commissioner of the New Orleans District of the Boy Scouts of America. The *Times-Picayune* of February 22, 1918, noted that "the growth of the Boy Scouts in Louisiana to its present large proportions began with Mr. Favrot's interest in the organization." Favrot was a member of the Chess, Checkers, and Whist Club, the Country Club, and the University Club, and was active in the alumni associations of both L.S.U. and Tulane. He died in 1918 in his home at 17 Richmond Place (Figure 22).

The entrance to Richmond Place (Figure 23) is marked by understated brick and stucco gates at Loyola Avenue, likely designed by architects Favrot and Livaudais. The street is lined with large, two-story residences, unified by a canopy of live oak trees, and terminates at Freret Street. The

Fig. 22. 17 Richmond Place. (Courtesy H. Richmond Favrot)

Fig. 23. Richmond Place.

majority of the houses on Richmond Place were built between 1906 and 1923 and represent the work of Robert S. Soulé, Sam Stone, Jr., Thomas Sully, Francis MacDonnell, and Favrot and Livaudais.

Everett Place

Edward Everett Soulé, developed the city's fourth residential park after assembling the property in three separate acts, two in 1905 and one in 1907. In his first purchase, Soulé acquired the right of joint use, enjoyment, and perpetual servitude in and to Rosa Park, its riverside neighbor. At that time, Saratoga Street was still projected through. Perhaps Soulé envisioned Everett as an extension of Rosa Park. The neutral ground is consistent with that of Rosa Park, but its architecture is of a later period.

Soulé first commissioned Daney and Waddill to subdivide the property. Their plan, dated December 1906, shows four lots on the uptown side of the street and four on the

Fig. 24. Everett Place gates, from *Pen & Sunlight Sketches of Greater New Orleans.* (Courtesy Tulane University, Southeastern Architectural Archive)

downtown side. Soulé dedicated the street to the city on January 11, 1907, making Everett Place the first residential park to do so. After he purchased an additional thirty feet along Nashville Avenue, Soulé had the site re-subdivided by Daney and Waddill in a plan entitled "New Subdivision of Everett Place," dated February 18, 1909. In the new plan, lots 2, 4, 6, and 8 on the uptown side of the street were reduced to three lots A, B, and C, and lots 1, 2, 3, and 4 were changed from 75 feet by 118 feet to varying street frontages by 118 feet.

It is safe to assume that Edward Soulé's brother, Robert Spencer Soulé, designed the Craftsman style gates and fence for the park (Figure 24). Robert, an architect, lived at 6 Everett Place.

Edward Soulé (Figure 25) was the son of Colonel George Soulé, founder of Soulé Commercial College and Literary Institute, and for many years its treasurer. Edward graduated from Soulé in 1884, from Cornell University in 1888, and from Tulane Law School in 1891. He was a member of many civic and carnival organizations, including the Boston Club, Lakeshore Club, and Rex School of Design. In 1931 Soulé was King of Carnival. Prior to his development of Everett Place, Soulé resided at 16 Rosa Park. After opening Everett Place, he purchased the 1908 Tudor Revival residence at 2 Everett Place originally built for Ernest Bornemann at a cost of $14,000, according to the design of R. Spencer Soulé (Figure 26). The remaining original houses on the street were built in 1909.

Fig. 25. Edward Everett Soulé. (Courtesy HNOC, 1979.208.226)

Fig. 26. Bornemann residence, R. Spencer Soulé, architect, from *Architectural Art and Its Allies,* July 1908. (Courtesy TULC)

Audubon Boulevard

The St. Louis firm of the Audubon Place Land Company acquired the lake end of the Foucher Estate, less lot D, on August 15, 1905, for $25,000 from Crescent Land and Improvement Company at a sheriff's sale, the result of a suit filed by Eugene W. Lewis against Crescent Land, for $50,000. Three years later, on June 30, 1908, Elias Pailet purchased the tract for $70,000, selling it, less three 90-by-170-foot lots, to Southern Land Company one month later for $109,000. According to the *Daily Picayune*, Pailet was quite active in real estate ventures at the time: "Elias Pailet, a native of Russia, was engaged in the real estate business for the majority of his adult life. He was a founder of Beth Israel Synagogue and was active in Zionist and other Jewish organizations. Pailet was noted for his charitable donations, including the gift of the site of Behrman Memorial Playground in Algiers to the city."

Fig. 27. "Audubon Boulevard: In the Residence Heart of New Orleans." Cover of Audubon Place sales brochure. (Courtesy TULC)

Southern Land Company, based in Atlanta, retained H.C. Brown to prepare the plan for the subdivision of Audubon Boulevard. The plan, dated February 9, 1909, created 307 lots in eight squares, most with a thirty-foot front, varying in depth from 55 to 168 feet. The plan, however, proved to be inaccurate, particularly with regard to lot depth. Frank H. Waddill made another survey and recalculation of the plan in November 1915.

A Southern Land brochure entitled "Audubon Boulevard In the Residential Heart of New Orleans" (Figure 28), began:

> Within the St. Charles Belt Line, flanked by the grounds of the Tulane University on the one side and by the proposed Campus and buildings of the Sophie Newcomb College on the other, and with the showy gardens and splendid mansions of the famous Audubon Place for a front yard is situated AUDUBON BOULEVARD, the highest-class residence district that has ever been laid out in the City of New Orleans, rivaled only in location and the extensiveness of its improvements by Audubon Place, of which it is a continuation.

At this time, Audubon Place Block No. 2 was still in existence, and Audubon Boulevard was in fact a continuation of Audubon Place. The brochure focused on the improvements: "For six months a force of engineers, grading men, concrete workers, paving contractors, bridge builders and landscape gardeners have been at work in the creation of Audubon Boulevard." According to the brochure, the boulevard was graded toward the Claiborne Canal, spanned by a reinforced-concrete bridge. The neutral ground was planted with grass and tropical shrubbery in order to produce the same effect as Audubon Place. Shade trees were encased in attractively designed boxes. Sidewalks and curbs were laid in "granulithic," and the street was shell-paved.

The brochure expounded on the recent and projected growth of New Orleans, the immense success of Audubon Place, to which Audubon Boulevard was connected, and the close proximity to downtown, Audubon Park, Tulane University, and Audubon Place. The brochure acclaimed the new development as a "paragon of residence districts unusual in location, neighborhood, and improvements," "the residence district par excellence of New Orleans," and "the real estate opportunity of the South." Despite the superlatives, photographs show livestock grazing in this paragon of residential districts.

Terms of sale were 10 percent cash and the balance at the rate of 2 percent per month, with interest at the rate of 6 percent per annum. With respect to restrictions, the brochure noted that "we have thrown around the sale of this property restrictions that will preserve it for all time as an incomparable section of homes and the most highly desirable residence portion of the city. These restrictions—

Fig. 28. "Audubon Boulevard: In the Residence Heart of New Orleans." Audubon Boulevard prior to residential construction. Note cattle grazing. (Courtesy TULC)

Fig. 29. Audubon Boulevard. (Courtesy TULC)

Fig. 30. Audubon Boulevard. (Courtesy TULC)

governing cost of buildings, building line, prices, etc.—will be made known upon application." Printed sales forms listed the restrictions. There was a ten-foot utility servitude at the rear of each lot known as the "East Space" and "West Space," a continuation of the Audubon Place servitude. Setbacks varied from forty feet to five feet, depending upon the square. Balconies, porches, and steps could encroach not more than twelve feet onto the setback. The minimum value of the houses ranged from $2,000 to $5,000, depending upon location. Front-yard fences could not exceed eighteen inches, and rear yard fences, six feet. Outhouses, stables, or other similar buildings could not be built within the rear servitude nor more than forty feet from the rear property line. Structures could only be used as private residences, had to face Park Place, and could not "ever be sold or leased to anyone of African descent." Houses could not be built on a parcel less than sixty feet, which meant that a minimum of two lots were required.

The *Daily Picayune* of September 1, 1909, contained an article on the development of the residential park entitled "Audubon Boulevard Success as Soon as Sale Started." Noting that Southern Land Company had "already sold over half the lots to home builders and the homes will cost from $5,000 to $40,000," the *Picayune* predicted that "What North Shore Drive is to Chicago, Commonwealth Avenue to Boston, Euclid Avenue to Cleveland, Upper Fifth Avenue and the Riverside Drive to New York, Portland Place to St. Louis, Audubon Boulevard will be to New Orleans." The article apparently relied heavily on the company brochure, using much of its verbiage. Today the article would bear the disclaimer, "Paid Advertisement."

The *Times-Democrat* reported that same year that 145 lots had been sold, bringing from $1,300 to $3,450 per pair of lots, and noted that "Restrictions under which the sites were sold make it incumbent upon the buyers to erect attractive houses. As a result, no less than twenty will in all probability be going up on the property before the end of this month. Recently, the company has succeeded in having the Clio car line extended up Claiborne street through its tract. The cars here will be operation in about six months."

Minor Leighton Realty Company placed an advertisement for Audubon Boulevard in the *Daily Picayune* in 1910 (Figure 31). It featured a perspective by architects Keenan and Weiss, captioned, "This is Audubon Boulevard as it will appear when the homes which are now under construction and those contracted for are completed." The illustration is highly conjectural, with a church and lots of Mission and California style bungalows, bearing little resemblance to how the street actually developed. This variation resulted because the majority of homes were built after World War I when the preference for bungalows waned and eclectic houses became the vogue. The advertisement predicted a

rapid increase in property value, stating, "The growth of a few years will make a lot on the Boulevard worth just as much as one on Audubon Place."

In 1916 the *Times-Picayune* reported that "Audubon Boulevard continues to build as well as a number of other of the older developments in that locality."

Aububon Boulevard maintains the feeling of a residential park without the use of entrance gates or distinctive street furniture, and despite the interruptions of Claiborne Avenue, Fontainebleau Drive, and, to a limited degree, Hickory Street. The unifying neutral ground, crowned by a canopy of oak trees, diminishes in width from 40 feet at Willow Street to 16 feet 4 inches at Walmsley and becomes more heavily landscaped. The mile-long length of Audubon Boulevard, which also narrows in width, makes it difficult to perceive its having the same intimacy as the three older residential parks, and having more than two accesses further reduces the sense of privacy and security.

Because of the sixty-foot minimum lot requirement, 72 percent of the sites developed as two-lot parcels. The first houses on the Boulevard were begun in 1910, and the majority were completed by 1930 in a variety of architectural styles common for that time frame—Colonial Revival, Mediterranean Villa, Spanish, California, Craftsman, and Tudor are all represented. The more pretentious homes with larger sites and generous setbacks are generally closest to the river, while the smaller ones are located between Fontainebleau and Walmsley, reflecting the historic diminishing size of Louisiana plantations along the river. There is no specific growth pattern on the street, with development taking place in all sections simultaneously. The work of a variety of architects is represented on Audubon Boulevard, including Jones and Roessle, Edward Sporl, Richard Koch, Favrot and Livaudais, Emile Weil, Francis MacDonnell, Moise Goldstein, Walter Cook Keenan, and Leon G. Zwikel.

Dunleith Court

Civil engineer Frank H. Waddill of Daney and Waddill prepared a survey of Dunleith Court on November 30, 1910, at the request of William S. Campbell, Jr. for Mrs. Samuel M. Wiggins. The May 25, 1911, dedication of Dunleith Court stated that Mrs. Wiggins "has caused to be made a sub-division of said [square] the building lots of these of being made to front on a private residential park, to be hereafter known as Dunleith Court. . . . That she desires to dedicate perpetually the said court or Park-way as a street and walk, for the use and benefit of the lots and property thereon."

The subdivision contains only eight lots. Among the first houses was 7 Dunleith, designed by Robert S. Soulé for insurance agent William Campbell and contracted for on July

THIS IS AUDUBON BOULEVARD

As It Will Appear When the Homes Which Are Now Under Construction and Those Contracted for Are Completed.

WOULD YOU BUY A LOT?

IF!

You were absolutely certain that your investment was safe, sound and conservative?

You were also certain that the element of chance was completely eliminated?

You knew that within the course of a few years you might realize 100% to 200% on your money?

You were open to conviction and we proved all this to your entire satisfaction and beyond all question of a doubt?

IF!

The purchase of a couple of these lots was within your means and proved an excellent saving?

We made the terms to suit you and gave you six or seven years in which to pay for it?

Among the purchasers of these lots were some of New Orleans' leading business men, well-known as shrewd real estate investors?

You knew that the most select element of this city's populace were building or were soon going to build their homes in this ideal and exclusive parkway?

OPPORTUNITY KNOCKS ONCE AT EVERY MAN'S DOOR! DON'T MISS THIS ONE!

BECAUSE

Every day in the week we hear people speak of what they could have purchased a few years back for possibly a quarter or even a tenth as much as it is worth to-day.

History Repeats Itself and, a few years hence, the prices we are asking for lots on the Boulevard will be spoken of in the same manner.

It is located in the heart of the Garden Section of New Orleans, and is a direct continuation of Audubon Place, which is the most beautiful and exclusive residential street in New Orleans.

The last lot sold on Audubon Place brought $8000.00 which establishes the value of property on this street, and shows the margin for profit.

The growth of a few years will make a lot on the Boulevard worth just as much as one on Audubon Place.

IT WILL PAY YOU TO
REMEMBER WHAT WE TELL YOU
OR YOU WILL REGRET IT.

MINOR-LEIGHTON REALTY COMPANY,

MAIN 1447.   **426 AUDUBON BUILDING.**

Minor-Leighton Realty Co.,
426 Audubon Building,
New Orleans.
Gentlemen:
    Kindly send me full page particulars regarding few remaining lots on Audubon
Boulevard ....
....

Fig. 31. Minor Leighton Realty Co. sales advertisement for Audubon Boulevard, the *Daily Picayune,* 1910. (Courtesy TUMD)

Fig. 32. Dunleith Court.

2, 1911. The house last built on the Court was 5 Dunleith, constructed for Louise Martin in 1938.

Because the small court contains a variety of architectural styles and no distinguishing street furniture, it lacks a cohesiveness that renders a definable character generally associated with a residential park.

State Street Drive

Wedged between the upper and lower lines of Bloomingdale from Claiborne Avenue back to Fontainebleau Drive, State Street Drive was created by the Interstate Land Company, according to a subdivision prepared by Daney and Waddill dated April 16, 1914. The original subdivision of Bloomingdale established State Street from the river to about South Miro Street. The new street, State Street Drive, was only forty-five feet, compared to the eighty-two-foot-width of State Street, and had 154 lots, all thirty feet wide, except lots 63 and 64. Lots A through T were shown, but dimensions were not given. In 1916 the *Times-Picayune* reported that Interstate Land Company had built many "very handsome residences and the street has shown remarkable activity in the month of August."

The purchase price of lots was reasonable. George H. Turner purchased lot 1 and half of lot 2 for $1,125 in 1917.

Interstate Land's terms were $125 down and the balance, at 7 percent interest, at $22.50 per month. Restrictions, which were to be enforced until 1975, limited construction to residences facing State Street Drive, with a fifteen-foot setback and costing at least $2,500 for singles and $3,000 for doubles. Houses had to be built on a minimum lot width of forty-five feet, meaning each house had to sit on one and one-half lots, and the developer reserved the right to place utilities in the rear ten feet of the lot. The property could not be sold or leased to anyone of African descent. The developer promised to maintain the neutral ground and roadway during the year 1915, but after January 1, 1916, would relinquish that responsibility to the property owners. Owners were to form an association wherein every thirty feet of property frontage or portion thereof would count as one vote. They then would vote for or against an assessment of thirty cents per thirty feet per month for upkeep. The major problem with this is that State Street Drive has no neutral ground.

Although developed as a residential park, State Street Drive lacks the physical attributes that impart the feeling of earlier parks. Other than its somewhat limited access, State Street Drive is like many other streets Uptown. Perhaps its late development and growing governmental control made the residential park concept obsolete.

Fig. 33. 3300 block State Street Drive.

The mile-long length of State Street Drive begins after a small jog at Claiborne Avenue and continues towards Earhart Boulevard, with partial access from Tonti Street, making another jog at Fontainebleau, which crosses State Street Drive's right-of-way (as does Walmsley and Grape), then allows partial access at Dart Street, and terminates at Earhart. The majority of houses are bungalow- and basement-types, with a few hi-los and two-story residences. It is predominantly middle-class housing, set densely together.

Southern Development Company acquired the land above Fontainebleau Drive back to Breedlove Street on December 15, 1923, with an amendment added on June 16, 1924. The tract was subdivided according to a "plan of 106 lots" dated December 13, 1923 by Frank H. Waddill.

Vincennes Place

Vincennes Place is in reality a series of subdivisions in the rear of Hurstville facing not only Vincennes but the uptown side of Nashville. This residential park is named for the Parisian forest and château. The French crown acquired the forest in the eleventh century for a royal hunting ground. Louis XV converted it into a park, and Napoleon III subsequently gave it to the city of Paris in 1860.

The narrow street that is Vincennes Place is lined with

Fig. 34. 4000 block Vincennes Place.

modest bungalows and lacks the physical attributes generally associated with a residential park. Its nine blocks extend from Miro Street to D'Artaguette (now Dart) Street, and it is in line with Rosa Park, Everett Place, Richmond Place, and Wirth Place.

Beginning at South Miro and moving away from the river was a subdivision called State Street Court, developed in 1915. Divided by Richardson Court (now Vincennes), it extended from South Miro across South Tonti Street to South Rocheblave in squares 105 and 106. Interstate Land Company acquired the property for $20,000 and had the two squares divided into thirty-foot lots facing both sides of Richardson Court and the uptown side of Nashville Avenue, according to an undated plan by S.A. Calongne's Sons, annexed to an act before C.T. Starkey dated December 1915.

The next three squares, 108, 109, and 110, extending from South Rocheblave across the closed street of York, across McKenna, to Hewes, was subdivided according to a plan by Alfred F. Théard dated November 10, 1925. In an act of exchange between the city and the three property owners, Morris Sazer, Christian D. Rodick, and Henry Uthoff, the right-of-way of York Street was exchanged for the forty-foot right-of-way of the proposed new street, Richard Court.

The single Square 111 between Hewes Street and Fontainebleau Drive was subdivided by Southern Development Company according to a plan by B.J. Oliveira dated May 5, 1923. It had three eight-foot lots facing Fontainebleau, with a narrow 28-foot-7-inch street called Baldwin Court.

The next six squares, numbers 112, 113, 114, 115, 116, and 117, of Hurstville from Fontainebleau to D'Artaguette were subdivided according to a plan dated January 7, 1926, prepared by Alfred F. Théard for the four owners, Dr. Frederick J. Wolfe, Henry Uthoff, Horace L. Montegut, and Anthony L. Montegut. They dedicated the forty-foot right-of-way for the new twenty-four-foot street, Vincennes Place, with its Schillinger walks, to the city in exchange for the closing of the rights-of-way for Walmsley Avenue, Grape Street, and D'Artaguette Street. Restrictions included a minimum construction cost of $8,500, no garages closer than fifty feet from the front property line facing Vincennes Place, and fences only of brick, concrete, trellis, or wire, no more than six feet high, and back of the fifteen-foot set-back building line. Houses were to be no closer than four feet to either side line and parallel to the side lines. The property was to be used exclusively for residential purposes and could be neither rented nor sold to persons other than of the white race.

Newcomb Boulevard

On September 1, 1916, the *Times-Picayune* reported that "An important high-class residence development of the year was the placing on the market as residence sites of the tract occupied by the Asylum for Destitute Orphan Boys and that formerly occupied by Leland University. The

Fig. 35. Newcomb Boulevard gate.

Fig. 36. Newcomb Boulevard.

buildings of Leland University are being demolished and Robert Werk, who purchased it for a consideration of $175,000, has formulated plans for converting it into a beautiful urban residential section to be known as New-comb Boulevard." Werk acquired the Leland University tract at public auction on June 22, 1916. Terms of the sale called for $87,500 down and four promissory notes due in one, two, three, and four years each for $21,875 at 6 per-cent interest, totaling $175,000 plus interest. According to the purchase agreement, Werk was to subdivide the prop-erty into thirty lots, the prices of which were to range from $6,250 to $17,000. When sales reached $40,000, he was to pay at once $20,000 to the Board of Directors of Leland, and the other $20,000 was to go toward improvements. After that, all proceeds were to go to Leland until the bal-ance was paid; however, if Werk did not sell the lots, the balance was due as per the promissory notes. Attached to the act of sale is an undated, unsigned plan for the subdi-vision of the site that includes studies of the entrance gates and "Boulevard standards." The proposed gates appear to be those actually built.

The following year, on May 2, 1917, Werk acquired por-tions of the Hampson, Maple, and Burthe streets roadbeds in exchange for the dedication of Newcomb Boulevard to the city, in accordance with a plan by Alfred F. Théard dated October 17, 1916. A plan for the subdivision of the property into thirty lots was prepared by Walter J. Seghers dated April 10, 1917. Restrictions required that houses face Newcomb Boulevard and be used only as single-family res-idences. A building line was established at 20 percent of the lot depth, and houses were to be built on lots greater than fifty-foot frontage on lots 25 to 80, and 60-foot on lots 1 to 24 and 81 to 104. Porch steps could encroach no more than twelve feet onto the setback. Fences, garages, stables, or outbuildings were not permitted in the setback, and rear fences were limited to six feet in height. On lots 1 and 104, houses were to cost in excess of $20,000; on lots 2 through 16 and 89 through 103, more than $15,000; on lots 17 through 34 and 71 through 88, more than $12,000; and on lots 36 through 70, more than $10,000. Finally, pur-chasers could not lease or sell property to "any person not of the Caucasian Race."

Newcomb Boulevard returns to the more classical con-cept of a residential park. The elaborate Renaissance Re-vival, brick and stone gates clearly identify a residential park, and limited access from St. Charles and Freret and the crape myrtles and oak trees help to define the park (Fig-ure 37). The houses comprise a variety of architectural styles, but are generally large, two-story residences of ma-sonry or stucco construction. They were built between 1920 and 1933 and reflect the design work of Francis Mac-Donnell, Weiss and Dreyfous, Morgan Hite, Edward Sporl,

Fig. 37. Newcomb Boulevard.

Nathan Kohlman, Paul Charbonnet, and Goldstein, Parham, Labouisse.

Wirth Place

Wirth Place is a subdivision of squares 81, 82, 83, and 84 in Hurstville and is in line with Arabella Street, though interrupted by Sophie Gumble, Allen, and Fortier schools. Charles Wirth acquired squares 81 and 82 between Freret and Magnolia streets on November 22, 1892. In two acts, one dated August 7, 1903, and one dated February 23, 1914, he exchanged land in order to accommodate street alignments—Freret was widened in order to connect Freret in Rickerville and Burtheville; Joseph Street was widened by twenty-five feet; and Arabella Street was closed from Freret Street to South Robertson.

On October 16, 1914, Wirth transferred this and other property to Charles Wirth Realty and Investment Company. The realty company subdivided the property according to an undated and unsigned plan attached to a June 25, 1919, act of sale.

W.E. Huger acquired the next two squares, 83 and 84, on December 8, 1921, and on June 10, 1922, transferred to the city Arabella Street between South Robertson and Mag-nolia streets in exchange for the opening of Wirth Place and the widening of Joseph Street in a manner similar to the lower two squares. There are three plans for subdivisions of the two squares, all by B.J. Oliveira and dated January 13, 1922, June 7, 1922, and July 19, 1922.

Charles Wirth, Sr. (Figure 38), was a prominent local businessman who was born in Freudenstadt, Germany, and arrived in New Orleans in 1866. He became active in the local German community, supporting the German

Fig. 38. Charles Wirth. (Courtesy TULC)

Fig. 39. 2227 Wirth Place.

Protestant Orphan Asylum, the German Protestant Home for the Aged, and the Jackson Avenue Evangelical Church, popular with German Protestants. Wirth first opened a grocery store (see Volume VII), moved on to the saloon business, and eventually became president of Standard Brewing Company. He was elected on the "Anti-Lottery" ticket to represent the 12th Ward on the New Orleans City Council from 1892 to 1896. Wirth was well-known for his real estate investments. At the time of his death in 1936, an article in the *Times-Picayune* noted:

> In the real estate business for fifty years, Mr. Wirth often said he never had lost money save once on a New Orleans investment. He followed the principal, he said, of incurring but one debt at a time and completing one project before he began another. He was interested in the development of Lakeview and was vice president of the New Orleans Land Co., he developed Wirth Place opposite the Fortier High School.

Wirth was also a developer of the Lafayette Hotel and owned a great deal of property at Canal and Marais streets. He was a charter member of Old Firemen's Homestead Association and president of Imperial Realty Company. The Charles Wirth Realty Company built many of the homes on Wirth Place as investments.

Trianon Plaza

Free-man-of-color Pierre Marly subdivided lot 1 of Macarty's plantation according to a plan prepared by Jean Communy and L.J. Pilié dated October 15, 1834, and began selling property in 1834 and 1835. Unfortunately, the original plan has been lost, but a recreation was prepared by Edgar Pilié on May 5, 1911.

Faubourg Marly was wedged between the Foucher tract and the lower line of Carrollton and ran from present-day Fontainebleau Drive to Interstate 10, just north of Friburg. However, Marly had an extra north-south street that Friburg and Greenville did not have—a problem for mapmakers. As illustrated on the 1871 "Map of the Sixth District & Carrollton," uptown-downtown streets did align, but street names were not consistent.

In 1894 George H. Grandjean and H.W. Reynolds made a new survey for subsequent owners "Jere Lyons & Moran," which indicated the property as unimproved palmetto lands, traversed only by several fences and the Yazoo and Mississippi Valley and the Illinois Central railroads. This new plan eliminated Marly Avenue and reduced the widths of the squares, probably to conform to the d'Hemecourt survey of New Orleans. F.H. Waddill testified in Louisiana Supreme Court Case No. 30260 that "Marlyville up to that time [1894] was practically a lost country and after that survey by Grandjean & Reynolds, all surveyors have followed the locations as made in that survey." The area did not develop until much later, after adequate drainage was provided.

The heirs of Jeremiah Lyons sold square 14 of Faubourg Marly to Trianon Development Corporation on September 15, 1924, for $50,000. An affidavit of Richard Lyons that accompanied the act of sale gives some insight into the rural character of the neighborhood at that time. He attested that "the late J. Lyons leased the above described

Fig. 40. Latter and Blum advertisement for Trianon Plaza, January 25, 1925. (Courtesy TUMD)

square to a Milkman for the purpose of using it as a pasture for his cattle, that the said milkman . . . was in possession of said property for more than ten years, that he surrendered possession of the property to the said J. Lyons in the spring of 1914."

Trianon Development retained surveyors S.E. Calongne and Son to subdivide the square into twelve lots, architect Morgan D.E. Hite to design the gates, street lamps, and other improvements, and real estate agents Latter and Blum to sell the lots delineated on the September 6, 1924, plan. On January 25, 1925, Latter and Blum placed an advertisement in the *Times-Picayune* for the sale of the subdivision (Figure 40); however, the only survey located for the subdivision is dated March 10, 1925, two months after the advertisement. Perhaps the advertisement was a bit premature, or perhaps an earlier survey exists. The ad read, in part:

> TRIANON Plaza is unique in the improvement offered with each site:
> Including ASPHALT PAVED STREETS, best possible sidewalks and curbing, curved roadway, underground wiring, ornamental light standards—Spanish-Moorish design, automobile circular turn in roadway, the beauty and privacy of a "court street," and all conveniences nearby.

Trianon Development began construction of the first house, 2 Trianon Plaza, in May 1925, and the last house, 12 Trianon Plaza, was built in 1928; the predominant architectural style is Spanish, with the exception of 3 Trianon Plaza, done in the Colonial Revival style. The short, three-year development time frame and the consistency of architectural styles give a cohesive appearance to the street, and the gates and light standards define the boundaries of the residential park.

The developers placed six restrictions on the property owners. First, only one single-family house, costing not less than $10,000 and occupied by "white people only," was permitted on each building site. Second, the principal facade of the house had to face Trianon Plaza. Third, a front yard of twelve and one-half feet minimum and side and rear

Fig. 41. No. 5 Trianon Plaza.

yards of fifteen feet were required. Fourth, no driveways were permitted from Trianon. Fifth, no fence was permitted on the front yard and no hedges higher than eighteen inches; rear fences had to be less than six feet, and no "featheredge" types were allowed. Sixth, an annual assessment of one dollar per foot per year was to be paid to a fund controlled by the majority of property holders.

An undated plan of the subdivision prepared by realtors Latter and Blum lists the price of lots from $5,600 to $11,600 (averaging over $6,600) and construction costs ranging from $7,500 to $15,000 (averaging approximately $8,300).

Versailles Boulevard

"Introducing-Versailles Boulevard New Orleans' Finest Residential Park Choice—Exclusive—Restricted. Versailles Boulevard, situated in the finest residential development in the entire city of New Orleans, will be an avenue of the highest type, running through the center of the area constituted by the consolidated Tulane and Morlas tracts."

So began an advertisement placed in the April 12, 1925, *Times-Picayune* by real estate agents Rhodes and Symmes.

Fig. 42. Rhodes & Symmes Real Estate advertisement for Versailles Boulevard, the *Times-Picayune,* April 12, 1925. (Courtesy TUMD)

Greater New Orleans Development Company purchased the property in 1924 from St. Vincent's Infant Asylum, which had acquired it in part from an exchange with Southern Development Company and in part by purchase from John Morlas heirs. The Morlas tract was purchased from the Société Catholic d'Education Religieuse et Litteraire (Loyola), which had acquired it from Joseph Hernandez. Hernandez had purchased it from Robert Bloomer, who, along with others, had acquired it from the Foucher estate.

Frank H. Waddill and B.J. Oliveira developed plans for the subdivision for Greater New Orleans Development Company. One plan by Waddill, dated March 19, 1925, extended from Claiborne Avenue to Fontainebleau Drive. This portion had a three-island neutral ground, flanked by 115 lots with 30-foot fronts and varying depths of 119 to 170 feet. The plan by Oliveira, dated March 18, 1925, extended from Fontainebleau Drive to Pritchard Street and had no neutral ground. Lots 1 through 8 face Fontainebleau Drive and lots 9 through 64 face Versailles. The two sections have characters of their own, lacking a unifying design. The more spacious lots between Claiborne and Fontainebleau are developed with mostly two-story or basement houses of brick, and are unified by a canopy of oak trees. The area lakeward of Fontainebleau is comprised of predominantly brick and stucco bungalows of small to medium scale.

According to an advertisement for Versailles Boulevard in the May 24, 1925, *Times-Picayune* (Figure 43), improvements included "a broad bitulithic street, paved sidewalks, water, gas, and electric connections, ten-year-old transplanted oak trees and shrubbery." Greater New Orleans Development signed a $12,600 contract to pave Versailles and provide drainage from Claiborne to Fontainebleau in compliance with "Standard Plans and Specifications of the City of New Orleans for Street Paving," adopted in 1924. On June 24, 1925, the city accepted the dedication of Versailles Boulevard.

Restrictions were noted in a 1925 advertisement: "The section has done its own zoning and business will be strictly barred. No duplex or apartment houses to be allowed. Definite building lines; minimum cost of residences; strict fence limitations and location of garages are provided for. Sites will have a frontage of sixty feet minimum." Building setbacks varied, following a line connecting a thirty-foot setback at Claiborne Avenue to a twenty-foot setback at Fontainebleau Drive; from Fontainebleau to Pritchard Street, the setback was fifteen feet, and on Fontainebleau, twenty feet. Only single-family residences were permitted, to cost at least $10,000, from Claiborne to Fontainebleau; $8,500, the first 240 feet from Fontainebleau to Pritchard; $6,500, the next 240 feet; and $5,000, for the remainder.

Fig. 43. Rhodes & Symmes Real Estate advertisement for Versailles Boulevard, the *Times-Picayune,* May 24, 1925. (Courtesy TUMD)

Fig. 44. First residence on Versailles Boulevard, the *Times-Picayune,* May 24, 1925. (Courtesy N.O.P.L.)

Building sites from Claiborne to Fontainebleau were required to have a sixty-foot frontage; those on Fontainebleau, fifty feet; and those from Fontainebleau to Pritchard, forty-five feet.

The majority of houses in the portion of Versailles Boulevard between Claiborne and Fontainebleau were built between 1925 and 1938. The first house to be constructed was described in the *Times-Picayune* of May 24, 1925, as a "mansion designed by Morgan Hite for the lovely park being developed by Rhodes & Symmes and Latter & Blum." The photograph is of a handsome Mediterranean Villa which no longer exists (Figure 44).

Versailles Boulevard is named for the palatial château of Louis XIV. Originally built from 1631 to 1634 for Louis XIII, the château was converted by his son from a hunting lodge to an enormous palace.

The extension of Versailles Boulevard from Pritchard to the Yazoo and Mississippi Valley Rail Road was College Court. It was developed by Southern Development Company according to a plan prepared by B.J. Oliveira dated February 23, 1924.

Conclusion

The developers' restrictions on these residential parks have been forgotten for the most part and are not presently enforced, or have been ruled illegal. Developers, however, continued to use restrictions as a tool for quality control. Most of the developments along Lake Pontchartrain have similar restrictions. The recent development of English Turn goes so far as to regulate design, with a design manual requiring specific architectural styles, design elements, and minimal landscaping. The developers have had limited success with their requirements, with the majority of houses meeting a minimum common design standardization, proving that no amount of regulation can produce good design.

The success of older residential neighborhoods of Uptown New Orleans lies in good designs, well-proportioned and detailed, rather than as the result of developers' restrictions. The overlying zoning, however, has been a guide for placement, usage, and height of the designs, which has proven its usefulness.

AT RIGHT: **Historic New Orleans Interiors;
color photographs by Neil Alexander**

2 Audubon Place, home of Dr. and Mrs. Eamon Kelly. Built in 1908 according to designs of Toledano and Wogan for William Jay. It was remodeled in 1917 for Samuel Zemurray, with Edward Sporl serving as architect.

ABOVE: Dining room.
AT RIGHT: Library.

10 Audubon Place, home of Mr. and Mrs. James Coleman, Sr. Built in 1899 for Hugh Vincent, this house was designed by Frank P. Gravely.

AT LEFT: Detail, entry hall millwork.
BELOW: Hallway.

22 Audubon Place, home of Dr. and Mrs. Calvin Johnson, Jr. Frank P. Gravely designed this 1904 house for Darwin Carré.

ABOVE: Dining room, looking to living-stair hall.

460 Broadway, home of Mr. Roger Ogden.
Built in 1897 for Herman Gogreve, the house was remodeled in 1931 for Dr. William Bradburn according to the designs of Goldstein, Parham and Labouisse.

AT LEFT: Library with 1897 mantel.

1711 Palmer Avenue, home of Mr. and Mrs. Andre Grikitis. John Clark had this house built in 1906 according to the designs of architect Frank Gravely.

AT RIGHT: Dining room.
BELOW: Living room, looking to living-stair hall.

15 Rosa Park, home of Dr. and Mrs. Elmo Cerise. George E. Dickey and Son designed this 1897 house for Samuel Diamond. ABOVE: Living-stair hall.

5824 St. Charles Avenue, home of Mrs. F. Evans Farwell. Antonio Palacios commissioned architect Henry Howard to design this 1867 house.

AT LEFT: Living room.

5809 St. Charles Avenue, home of Mr. and Mrs. Nicholas Chisesi.
Built in 1896 for Nicholas Burke according to the design of Toledano and Reusch. The house burned and was "re-built" in 1907 under the direction of architects Toledano and Wogan.

ABOVE: Front door.
AT RIGHT: Living-stair hall.
OPPOSITE PAGE, TOP: Dining room.

6330 St. Charles Avenue, Round Table Club.
Built in 1896 for Christopher Doyle.

AT RIGHT: Living-stair hall.

6020 St. Charles Avenue, home of Mr. and Mrs. Michael Meyer. Built in 1903 for Judah Seidenbach, this house was designed by Favrot and Livaudais. ABOVE: Dining room. BELOW: Living room, looking to living-stair hall.

BUILDING INDEX

Address	Owner	Builder	Architect	Date	Cost
ANNUNCIATION STREET (JERSEY)					
5600-02, 5604	JACKSON HOMESTEAD	EUGENE HYMEL	EUGENE HYMEL	1926	5,000
5624	EQUITABLE HOMESTEAD ASSN.	DENIS & HANDY		1925	5,600
5817 & 5821	C.A. HOLDWITH	PAUL LAGASSE		1913	
5918-20	LOUISE WARTMANN	ALEX DREYFUS	ARMSTONG & KOCH	1928	6,200
5932	F. ZEIGLER	M.E. FERRAND		1913	
5955	W.H. SMITH	W.H. SMITH		1914	
6015-17	SIXTH DISTRICT BUILDING & LOAN	HENRY HAFFNER	HANS DIETTEL	1908	2,850
6051-53	DAVE WITKOFF	DAVE WITKOFF		1913	
6052-54, 6056-58	A. WENGE			1896	3,600
6024	A. MUSTACHIA			1899	2,000
6037-39	C.N. LUKINOVICH	C.N. LUKINOVICH		1912	
6046	MRS NICHOLAS SCHWALL			1895	1,200
6060-62, 6064-66 6068, 6070 6072-74	ADA MENGE			1895	
6227-29	LOUISE LAGMANN			1895	800
ARABELLA STREET					
223	JAMES ADOLPH	EDWIN SLATE	EDWIN SLATE	1927	5,300
418	G. ROMBACH	BOBB & LIMBURG		1895	1,000
423-25	WILLIAM KILLEEN	HENRI DEFRAITES		1927	5,190
504	M. FARAN			1884	
530-32	AMERICAN HOMESTEAD CO.	WILLIAM O'BRIEN		1923	3,600
712-14	J.M. DEFRAITES	J.M. DEFRAITES		1913	
716-18	J.M. DEFRAITES	J.M. DEFRAITES		1913	
724-26	J.J. CARRON	J.J. CARRON		1912	
728-30	R.T. CLAYETT	SEYBOLD BROS.		1915	
732-34	R.T. CLAYETT	PHILIP SEYBOLD		1912	
928	C.W. STRUMBORG	PEARCE CO.		1924	6,358
936	ELLA WALKER			1890	
1002	DAVID DESEMAN			1895	750
1015-17	H. BROAD	F.T. DANNET		1914	
1027, 1031-33 1035-37	WILLIAM. P. BRADLEY	HENRY HINRICHS		1895	4,650
1030-32	MORRIS SAZER	MORRIS SAZER		1912	

Address	Owner	Builder	Architect	Date	Cost
ARABELLA STREET					
1107-09, 1111-13, 1115, 1121-23, 1125-27	MUNICIPAL IMPROVEMENT CO.			1895	6,800
1129-31	SIXTH DISTRICT BUILDING & LOAN	SEYBOLD BROS.	PHILIP SEYBOLD	1910	3,700
1205	H.E. WILMONT			1909	2,700
1211	CITY OF NEW ORLEANS	FRANK NOULLET		1906	9,987
1300	E.M. FOX				2,000
1303, 1307, 1311 1321-23	MAX SAZER			1917	7,000
1337	WILLIAM S. DIRKIN			1905	3,000
1456	LUTHER BARNES	CHARLES NEWALD		1925	10,805
1468	GEORGE SUMMEY			1906	3,500
1504, 1510	LOUIS LAMBERT	LOUIS LAMBERT	LOUIS LAMBERT	1887	12,000
1516	C.B. GRIBBLE	C.B. GRIBBLE		1913	
1619	S. CLARK			1912	
1624	WILLIAM A. WEST		GOLDSTEIN, PARHAM & LABOUISSE	1948	
1625	LEON SALMON		DIBOLL, OWEN & GOLDSTEIN	1912	
1630	HENRY JACOBS			1846	
1631	JESSIE SCHWABACHER			1912	
1639	H.L. GARLAND			1900	2,500
1700	FRANK ANDERSON		F.D. PARHAM & M.H. GOLDSTEIN	1939	
1727	WILLOUGHBY FOX		F.D. PARHAM & M.H. GOLDSTEIN	1940	
1739	ROBERT MILLING		F.D. PARHAM & M.H. GOLDSTEIN	1940	
AUDUBON BOULEVARD					
1	K.V. RICHARD			1909	3,000
3				1925	
4	HARRY L. SWIFT	NEW ORLEANS CONSTRUCTION CO.	JONES, ROESSLE & OLSCHNER	1924	
7	CHARLES A. STAIR			1911	
10	CHAUCHER FRENCH			1913	
14	LUCA VACARRO		EDWARD F. SPORL	1917	
15	WILLIAM R. GILBERT	WILLIAM R. GILBERT		1913	4,000
16	J.M. TOBIN			1909	
17	JOHN REISS			1937	
21	B.W. SEAUREE			1921	
25	JOHN F. ROTH	J.A. RODICK		1922	14,000
26	LEONARD M. WISE			1922	
27	CASSIUS V. RICHARD			1921	
30	WALTER DWYER	PAUL CHARBONNET		1926	18,500
33	W. HASPEL			1924	
34	EDWARD HASPEL	JONES & ROESSLE	JONES & ROESSLE	1922	10,500
35	CLARENCE E. FETTIS	CLARENCE E. FETTIS		1915	
39	ALFRED EVANS			1950	
40	RICHARD R. FOSTER		RICHARD KOCH	1922	

Address	Owner	Builder	Architect	Date	Cost
AUDUBON BOULEVARD					
43	DR. CARROLL W. ALLEN	M.J. WARD, JR.		1916	8,352
44	D.B. HORN			1922	
48	H. MITHOFF	H. MITHOFF		1913	
49	FRANCIS E. LEJEUNE			1923	
50	E.G. RINS			1923	
55	JAMES FLINN, SR.			1925	
56	F.M. LASSEN			1919	
60	PARKS A. PEDRICK			1948	
65	HENRY B. MATTHEWS			1924	
70	ARTHUR MCGUIRK			1912	
71	WILLIAM R. GILBERT			1915	
73	W.E. JENNEY			1919	
75	WILSON S. SHIRLEY	THOMAS BROCKMAN		1940	14,168
77	CUTHBERT S. BALDWIN		FAVROT & LIVAUDAIS	1924	
81	SPENCER TALLMADGE			1925	
84	IRWIN H. ISAACS		FAVROT & LIVAUDAIS	1928	
89	HENRY GRADY PRICE		RICHARD KOCH	1935	
100	SIDNEY J. BESTHOFF	J.A. HAASE, JR.	EMILE WEIL & ASSOC.	1928	56,430
119	DR. HERMANN GESSNER	DR. HERMANN GESSNER		1914	
124	RALPH H. FISHMAN		MOISE FISHMAN	1954	
129	R.H. HALZER			1925	
138	GEORGE E. DEMACK	GEORGE E. DEMACK	FRANCIS MACDONNELL	1912	
144	JACOB LEVY			1925	
149	JOHN GATLING		MOISE GOLDSTEIN	1920	
154	A.M. SARAGE			1910	
155	HY. LANGE			1911	
166	A. WEINFIELD			1924	16,000
170	AUGUSTUS R. VREELAND			1925	
171	WALTER MOSES		CURTIS & DAVIS	1948	
193	CARL G. MUENCH			1922	
195	MICK ANDREWS	MICK ANDREWS		1914	
196	MAURICE COURET		ARMSTRONG & KOCH	1922	
199	CARL DAHLBERG			1926	
208	H.M. VORIES			1917	
212	LEWIS G. SCHWARTZ			1923	
217	B. PALMER HARDIE		WALTER COOK KEENAN	1916	
220	PROVIDENT BUILDING & LOAN	JOSEPH L. RHODES	KEENAN & WEISS	1910	4,000
223	JOHN E. KOERNER	HORTMAN & CO.		1916	
225	A.S.A. VERLANDER			1924	
227	HERBERT BOWERS			1924	
228	ST. DENIS DEBLANC			1922	
232	A.A. HARING			1921	
236	WILLIAM R. GILBERT	WILLIAM R. GILBERT		1915	

Address	Owner	Builder	Architect	Date	Cost
AUDUBON BOULEVARD					
238	WILLIE MINTZ		LEON G. ZWIKEL	1925	
246	ARTHUR L. JUNG	LOUISIANA CONTRACTING CO..		1916	
248	JULIUS STEGER			1927	
252	J. HOHMEYER			1910	
254	EDWARD THROUNK			1927	
258	THORP, INC.			1927	
260	ARNOLD J. KOLZER			1919	
264	HUGH J. CAREY			1924	
265	D. EDMONTON			1922	
275	JOHN A. VESY			1921	
278	HUGH J. CAREY			1925	
279	FELIX E. GOLIAN			1910	
281	CLEVELAND J. STOCKTON			1923	
282	WILLIAM C. CAMPBELL	JACOB KIRN	LOUISIANA CONTRACTING CO.	1916	2,679
285	SAMPSON BUILDING & REALTY			1919	
290	WALTER C. KEENAN		WALTER C. KEENAN	1916	
293	JOHN HENRY	ALEXANDER SMITH		1916	3,040
296	WILLIAM J. TESELLE	CHARBONNET BUILDING CO.		1923	14,600
297	CHARLES CALHOUN			1915	
299	U. BRECHT			1924	
302	FLOURNOY J. JOHNSON			1926	
303	JACKSON BUILDING & LOAN	STEVEN J. HOLZENTHAL	NEWTON MORTORLY	1921	7,000
306	FARLEY PRICE			1917	
307	ADELE C. WHITE			1916	
311	JOSEPH C. RHODES			1920	
312	NELSON E. CHURCH	ALEXANDER SMITH		1915	
314	DANIEL R. MCINES			1926	
317	FREDERICK G. GASSWAY			1915	
321	J.A. WALTER			1925	5,000
325	E. HOGUE			1925	
326	ALICE BOWMAN		LOUISIANA CONTRACTING CO.	1918	5,000
330	J. NORTON JACKSON			1927	
333	ISAAC S. HELLER			1926	
334	WALTER M. GEARY			1924	
335	H. BALL BOWERS			1926	
336	LAWRENCE C. DECKBAR	ROBERT KETTERINGHAM		1925	8,600
339	SAMPSON BUILDING & REALTY			1926	
340	CHARLES A. WRIGHT			1921	
420	ROBERT L. HILL			1922	
422	CHARLES DAMERON	R. FLETCHER		1895	800
424	DAVID J. MADDOX			1926	
425	HAROLD GUTHANS			1923	

Address	Owner	Builder	Architect	Date	Cost
AUDUBON BOULEVARD					
435	E. MARTIN HART			1916	
442	ROBERT BERKELEY			1924	
445	HARRY HENBERG		BENSON & RIEHL	1962	
448	ALEXANDER SMITH			1923	
449	JAMES LEE RHONE			1920	
453	J.C. HOGAN			1922	
456	J. STASSE			1930	
457	G.E. GEPT			1930	
459	PERCY B. LUSK			1930	
470	JAMES W. WARREN			1930	
480	MALSNIA REALTY CORP.			1934	
AUDUBON PLACE					
1	WILLIAM S. PENICK		FAVROT & LIVAUDAIS	1911	
2	WILLIAM T. JAY		TOLEDANO & WOGAN	1908	15,000
3	JOHN B. HOBSON		FAVROT & LIVAUDAIS	1900	2,000
4	J.J. MANSION			1895	12,900
5	JOHN LEGENDRE		FRANK GRAVELY	1899	9,750
6	CHARLES MANSON		SOULE & MCDONNELL	1904	25,000
7	EMILE LEGENDRE		FAVROT & LIVAUDAIS	1901	15,000
8	WILLIAM F. HOWELL	W.M. BERING		1895	7,250
9	C. EDMUND KELLS, JR.			1895	9,000
10	H. DEL VINCENT			1899	10,000
11	ROBERT CRAIG		EMILE WEIL	1922	
12	AUGUSTIN B. WHEELER		SOUTHRON DUVAL	1896	15,000
15	TULLIS C. WALKER			1899	
16	J.W. HEARN		TOLEDANO & WOGAN	1903	14,000
17	FELIX J. DREYFOUS		WEISS & DREYFOUS	1921	
18	HERMAN WEIL		EMILE WEIL	1910	20,000
19	ALICE B. VAIRIN	LOUIS PRECHTER	DIBOLL, OWEN & GOLDSTEIN	1913	25,000
20	MORRIS BUILDING LAND & IMPROVEMENT	ASCHAFFENBURG CO.	DEBUYS CHURCHILL & LABOUISSE	1906	13,000
21	LEVI M. ASH			1925	
22	D.B. CARRERE		FRANK P. GRAVELY & CO.	1904	8,500
23	FERDINAND KATZ		MOISE H. GOLDSTEIN	1913	
24	WILLIAM W. WALL		C. MILO WILLIAMS	1905	7,000
25	SALLIE D. HAVARD			1912	
26	C.W. ROBINSON		SOULE & MACDONNELL	1903	15,000
27	HENRY C. FLONACHER		WEISS & DREYFOUS	1927	
28	EDGAR A. FORDTRAN			1914	
AUDUBON STREET (CHESTNUT; MARIE; MARTHA)					
204-06	GEORGE STEIN	H. HAFNER		1919	
227	KENNETH COLOMB	EMILE BREHM		1921	1,700
240	A.L. BISSO	GEIER BROS.		1913	

Address	Owner	Builder	Architect	Date	Cost
AUDUBON STREET (CHESTNUT; MARIE; MARTHA)					
307	WILLIAM MARKEL	ROBERT W. MARKEL		1914	
316, 320	N. FREED	JOHN MINOT		1912	
325	A.A. DIETTEL	HANS DIETTEL		1916	1,400
330	ISIDORE JACOBSON		WEISS, DREYFOUS, SEIFERTH	1928	
338	GEORGE W. BRYANT			1916	
346	WILLIAM MCGRAW	H. KRENTEL		1895	1,100
356	HENRY ERVIN	E.J. STEWART & CO.		1925	6,595
402	JOHN O'NEIL	HERMAN MAKOFSKY	ADLOE ORR	1903	3,195
421	L. MOORE			1914	
435	SECURITY BUILDING & LOAN	EMILE HEBERT	WILLIAM FITZNER	1900	2,835
440	PETER MONROSE			1928	
447	E.T. BARRY	J.A. RODICK	FRANCIS MACDONNELL	1911	
452	RAY VAN WART		FRANK G. CHURCHILL	1918	
456	CARRIE HOBSON		GOLDSTEIN, PARHAM & LABOUISSE	1949	
459	THOMAS HENDERSON	J. RODICK	ANDRY & BENDERNAGEL	1912	7,815
460	FELIX DREYFOUS		WEISS DREYFOUS SEIFERTH	1929	
479	EMILE DREUIL			1902	4,000
497	JOSEPH DREUIL		SOULE & MACDONNELL	1903	4,000
501	WILLIAM P. NICHOLLS			1905	3,000
520	W. SYLVESTER LABROT, JR.		ARMSTRONG & KOCH	1928	
532	FREDERICK W. SINCLAIR	JONES & ROESSLE	JOHN BAEHR	1922	19,500
533	CORINE ABNEY		WEISS & DREYFOUS	1922	
540	JOSEPH HASPEL, JR.		PAUL CHARBONNET & SON	1941	14,866
550	SAMUEL COLVIN	PAUL CHARBONNET & SON	E.L. DONALDSON	1941	12,462
555	J.A. AIREY		SOULE & MACDONNELL	1905	6,100
560	EZRA NAMAN			1923	
571	EDWARD MARTINEZ			1889	
576	M.M. AIREY		WALTER COOK KEENAN	1915	
582	HENRY SCHROEDER		EMILE WEIL	1908	
618	VIRGINIA MARION			1906	2,500
638	A.C. LAWRENCE	T.L. YOUNG		1916	4,000
916-18	ROSALIE LUCIA	HENRI DEFRAITES		1931	6,850
1036	ELIZABETH WHERRITT	WALTER GEARY	WILLIAM NOLAN	1910	5,400
1040	BETA THETA PI		MACKENZIE, EHLIS & JOHNSON	1911	8,000
1415-17	BERTHA LASER	JOHN & JAMES COLLINS	ALBERT BEAR	1922	10,950
1418	WILLIAM R. GILBERT	WILLIAM R. GILBERT		1913	
1433-35	INDUSTRIAL HOMESTEAD	CHARLES PFISTER		1922	9,253
1437	CHARLES NEWALD	GEORGE LEAHY	JOHN BAEHR	1920	18,000
1504	BIENVILLE REALTY CO.	WILLIAM R. GILBERT		1913	
1508	WILLIAM E. LACY	ALEXANDER SMITH		1914	
1512		WILLIAM R. GILBERT		1913	
1515	PROVIDENT BUILDING & LOAN	ROBERT W. MARKEL	HENRY G. MARKEL	1918	6,740
1516	WILLIAM R. GILBERT	WILLIAM R. GILBERT		1913	

Address	Owner	Builder	Architect	Date	Cost
AUDUBON STREET (CHESTNUT; MARIE; MARTHA)					
1517-19	FREIDA BEYER	LOPEZ & BREMERMANN	JOHN BAEHR	1923	11,702
1520		WILLIAM R. GILBERT		1913	
1604	WILLIAM R. GILBERT	WILLIAM R. GILBERT		1914	
1605	CARTER EARHART		DIBOLL & OWEN	1921	15,000
1610	WILLIAM R. GILBERT	WILLIAM R. GILBERT		1914	
1621	H.W. CARR	H.W. CARR		1916	2,500
1628	M. FERRAND		E.F. SHORE	1919	4,900
1631	T. SEMMES WALMSLEY	WALTER C. KEENAN	WALTER C. KEENAN	1916	5,000
1632	HENRY L. STOUTZ	WILLIAM R. GILBERT		1916	2,500
1704	ANGELINA ONORATO	A. DANNER	A. DANNER	1907	3,400
1710	VIOLA C. RARESHIDE	VIOLA C. RARESHIDE		1916	2,000
1714	J.A. CLEMENT	SEYBOLD BROS.		1916	2,250
1736	LODILLA AMBROSE	CLAY LAINE		1923	7,025
1803	AGNES LUCY	THEARD & REILLY	THEARD & REILLY	1915	3,500
1815	J. DENTON	GEIER BROS.		1913	
1819-21	A.E. LUCY	THEARD & REILLY		1916	4,000
1820	E. STANLEY			1922	6,600
1906	DESIRE CHAUVIN	A.C. BABIN & SONS	ARMSTRONG & KOCH	1922	4,500
1932-34, 1938	FLORENCE LEVY	GUND CO., INC.		1925	8,150
2019	LENA MANSON	PAUL CHARBONNET	PAUL CHARBONNET	1929	12,660
2032	MILES HUTSON	GEORGE MILEAHY	JOHN BAEHR	1922	6,500
2037	SECURITY BUILDING & LOAN	B.S. NELSON & CO.		1922	6,500
2131-33	CHARLES WHITMAN			1922	
2425	GEORGE STEIN	H. HAFNER		1919	
2727	HELEN BLOCK	JOHN CHARLTON		1926	6,300
BENJAMIN STREET (FELICIA)					
6018	CARRIE PESSOU			1889	
6033	HUGH KOHLMEYER	EDWIN MARKEL		1927	
5125-28	TUTTLE & SEEMANN			1926	12,085
7321	WILLIAM WOODWARD			1897	2,600
BIRCH STREET					
7035	RENE SALOMON			1924	7,400
7102	WILLIAM R. GILBERT	WILLIAM R. GILBERT		1914	
7329	FRANK PALMISANO	FRANK PALMISANO		1914	
BROADWAY STREET (ALMONASTER; MAGNOLIA)					
139	JAMES A. SAMPLE	JAMES A. SAMPLE		1912	
231-33	BURNETT BROWN			1885	
255-57, 259-61	W.J. SUTHON	B.W. SCHNEIDAU		1913	
265-67, 269-71	W.J. SUTHON	B.W. SCHNEIDAU		1913	
345	ALFRED H. WHITE			1896	2,800
350	WILLIAM FLETCHER			1929	
353	J. CHADWICK	H. HULSE		1895	800
359-61	E.M. HOWELL	JOHN CHARLTON		1922	9,000

Address	Owner	Builder	Architect	Date	Cost
BROADWAY STREET (ALMONASTER; MAGNOLIA)					
360	VALENTIN K. IRION		FAVROT & LIVAUDAIS	1905	4,500
359-61	E.M. HOWELL	JOHN CHARLTON		1922	9,000
371	EMMA D. MONTGOMERY			1897	2,000
388	COLLIN MCNEIL			1902	8,000
389	COLLIN MCNEIL			1905	3,000
411	J.R. BUCHANAN			1896	2,500
428	ORLEANS PARISH SCHOOL BD.	JAMES PETTY		1922	116,485
444	JOSEPH E. BLUM		FAVROT & LIVAUDAIS	1932	
460	HERMAN R. GOGREVE			1897	4,000
478	LEO WEIL		DREYFOUS & LEVY	1937	
505	FELIX KUNTZ	DENIS & HANDY	DENIS & HANDY	1924	10,000
515	CHRISTIAN ROSELIUS			1852	
579	NELSON WHITNEY	JOHN RUESCH	DEBUYS, CHURCHILL & LABOUISSE	1910	9,708
626	THOMAS WALSHE	EDWIN MARKEL		1927	18,225
700	ADOLPH KATZ			1913	
712, 716, 718	THOMAS CAPO	JOHN MINOT		1912	
726	J.H. HAMMUETT	GEIER BROS.		1913	
819-821	SARAH ROTHERY	JAMES DICKINSON	J. MCNALLY	1905	2,500
834	MRS. R.L. ROGERS			1903	2,900
900	M. CAHN	HENRY HINRICHS		1913	
912	DR. PHILIP ASHER	DR. PHILIP ASHER		1913	
918	GEORGE LAWES	EDWIN MARKEL		1926	12,500
922	ELIZABETH LAWES	THOMAS CARSON		1920	3,230
928	WILLIAM LATHROP	EDWIN MARKEL	EDWIN MARKEL	1913	6,115
936	JOHN J. THOMAS	JULES MARKEL		1909	4,050
939	SAMUEL HELLMAN	E.W. MCKEE		1922	16,200
1007-11	JOHN B. LEVERT	J.A. HAASE		1914	
1018-22	JAMES SEWELL	NAPOLEON CONSTRUCTION		1922	9,950
1029	SECURITY BUILDING & LOAN	JONES & ROESSLE	JONES & ROESSLE	1910	
1030-32	A.L. COLLINS	HANS DIETTEL		1916	7,000
1038	A. WILLOZ	JOHN CHARLTON		1913	
1134	S. ABRAMS	L.C. WEIL		1914	
1238	ADELINE GILBERT	ADELINE GILBERT		1912	
1308	MABEL & IONE SHERMAN	SAM SIMONE	LOUISIANA CONTRACTING CO.	1915	3,000
1338	DR. CHARLES C. BASS	LOUIS PRECHTER		1913	
1432	SIMON LEVY	WINTON & AVEGNO		1924	14,886
1438	WILLIAM SONNEMANN	SAM SIMONE	SAM SIMONE	1920	4,000
1439	BIENVILLE REALTY CO.	BIENVILLE REALTY CO.		1913	
1503	H.C. SMITH	JONES & ROESSLE		1913	
1514	FRED E. STERN		JONES & ROESSLE	1922	8,000
1516	F. PALMISANO	F. PALMISANO		1914	
1601	CRESCENT CITY BUILDING & HOMESTEAD	JOHN B. RILEY		1929	3,950

Address	Owner	Builder	Architect	Date	Cost
BROADWAY STREET (ALMONASTER; MAGNOLIA)					
1624	EMANUEL BODENHEIMER	EUGENE BARROUSSE	EUGENE BARROUSSE	1925	14,300
1701	HOWARD CROMWELL			1923	
1738	WILLIAM R. GILBERT	WILLIAM R. GILBERT		1914	
1840-42	VITO SANTANGELO	E.W. ULLRICH GLASS CO.	BURK & DUFRECHOU	1922	8,400
1901-03	LOUISIANA APARTMENT HOUSE CORP.	ALEXANDER SMITH	A. SMITH	1920	14,000
1907	FIDELITY HOMESTEAD ASSN.	DENIS & HANDY		1919	3,000
1911	FIDELITY HOMESTEAD ASSN.	DENIS & HANDY		1919	3,500
1915	FIDELITY HOMESTEAD ASSN.	DENIS & HANDY		1919	5,250
1918-20	J.R. KEIFFER	ALBERT PETERSON	SAM SIMONE	1923	16,000
1921	FIDELITY HOMESTEAD ASSN.	DENIS & HANDY		1919	5,000
1923	FIDELITY HOMESTEAD ASSN.	DENIS & HANDY		1919	3,000
1927-29	FIDELITY HOMESTEAD ASSN.	DENIS & HANDY		1919	4,000
1932	FRED C. SCHMITT	JOSEPH E. CHAPMAN		1921	6,700
2001-03	THOMAS WALSHE	RUDOLPH GIEFERS	CHARLES PUMILIA	1923	13,000
2008-10	M.L. BATT	HARTMAN & TOUPS		1915	
2009-11	THOMAS WALSHE	RUDOLPH GIEFERS	CHARLES PUMILIA	1923	11,574
2016	EDWIN HAGARDORN	RUDOLPH GIEFERS		1919	5,900
2047-49	R. RATHE			1925	7,200
2110-03	THOMAS WALSHE	RUDOLPH GIEFERS	CHARLES PUMILIA	1923	13,000
2102-04	N. BELLAMORE		JONES & ROESSLE	1916	6,000
2121	JANE SOMMERSON	SAM SIMONE	SAM SIMONE	1924	3,000
2138	N. BELLAMORE	JONES & ROESSLE		1916	6,000
2216-18	J. ARGOTE	SEYBOLD BROS.		1916	
2313	F. JUNKER	J. PALMISANO		1912	2,330
2318	GENEVA BILLINGSLEY	JOHN WYCOLLINS		1925	10,900
2425-27	J. PALMISANO	J. PALMISANO		1914	
2511	E.W. LECHE	E.W. LECHE		1916	
2512	J.C. O'BRIEN	WALTER C. KEENAN		1913	
2516	PHOENIX BUILDING & LOAN	LOUISIANA CONTRACTING CO.		1916	3,800
2523	MUTUAL BUILDING HOMESTEAD	J.E. SELFE		1915	
3108-10	WILLIAM BOHNSTORFF	JAMES SAMPLE		1920	8,292
BURTHE STREET					
7219	WILLIAM THOMPSON			1873	
CALHOUN STREET (EDMUND)					
416	JOHN HAMMER	PAUL SEYBOLD		1940	3,600
438	D.C. CASEY			1883	
439	ANTHONY GRAFFAGNINO		WILLIAM T. NOLAN	1927	
821-23	JULIUS MANGER	JULIUS MANGER		1896	3,000
827	HONORIA NAPP	HENRY COOIL	HENRY COOIL	1902	1,057
1208-10	EXCELSIOR HOMESTEAD	ALEXANDER SMITH	ALEXANDER SMITH	1925	20,000
1214-16	EXCELSIOR HOMESTEAD	ALEXANDER SMITH	ALEXANDER SMITH	1925	20,000
1220	ROBERT REYNOLDS, JR.	J.E. SHAW & SON		1924	5,795

Address	Owner	Builder	Architect	Date	Cost
CALHOUN STREET (EDMUND)					
1321	IDA P. BOWEN		FRANCIS J. MACDONNELL	1907	
1325	W. WINANS WALL		ANDRY & BENDERNAGEL	1900	5,227
1335	ANDERS E. UGLAND	HAY & HULSE	WILLIAM FITZNER	1896	5,200
1444, 1448, 1452, 1456	EDWARD DEMAREST			1895	10,000
1459	BLANCHE M. CARTER			1909	5,200
1510-12	CHARLES NAPP	H.F. FOSTER		1895	4,000
1527	THOMAS G. MACKIE			1895	2,450
1530	WILLIAM VON PHUL		FAVROT & LIVAUDAIS	1931	
1545-47, 1551-49, 1553	ARTHUR MCLAUGHLIN			1893	9,000
1556-66	W&C WOOD			1891	
1586	JAMES MCCONNELL		FAVROT & LIVAUDAIS	1902	
1705	BERNARD MENGE			1895	4,200
1733	MORTIMER N. WISDOM			1900	5,000
1819	FRANK E. RAINOLD			1896	3,500
1828	MRS. W. R. ROSS	M.N. ANDERSON		1895	3,310
1915-17	ANNIE FRITH	JOHN MINOT		1896	3,250
2011	L.G. LEBEUF	T.L. & J.D. YOUNG		1915	5,250
2101-03, 2107-09	FLORENCE LOEBER	DENIS & HANDY		1922	10,000
2119	JAMES GAUDET	A.C. BABIN		1914	
2126	PETER KLOPPENBURG	JOHN MEYER		1923	5,187
2133	JAMES GAUDET			1923	10,954
2204	F.W. CARNAHAN	G.L. HEATH		1914	
2213-15	B.F. GENNISON			1911	
2220-22	PEOPLES HOMESTEAD		RUFFIN WALKER	1927	9,500
2224-26	PEOPLES HOMESTEAD		RUFFIN WALKER	1927	9,500
2225	GEORGE BROWN	PAUL CHARBONNET		1921	8,900
2319	ANDREW O'DONNELL	WILLIAM O'BRIEN		1926	6,850
2401	A.N. PEIRCE	ALEXANDER SMITH		1913	
2411	J. BONNER GLADNEY	NELVIL SETTON		1922	
2432	WILLIAM R. GILBERT	WILLIAM R. GILBERT		1913	
2436-38	GREATER NEW ORLEANS HOMESTEAD	DENIS & HANDY	A.M. PUMILIA	1921	9,000
2513-15	ERNEST SCHERER	JOHN O'BRIEN		1924	7,900
2529-31	SIXTH DISTRICT BUILDING & LOAN	PAUL FORNERETTE	ADLOE ORR	1907	2,720
2530	GEORGE CAMBIAS	HENRI DEFRAITES	HENRI DEFRAITES	1929	11,642
2538	GUS BLANCAND	OTIS SHARP	D.S. BARROW	1925	16,400
2600	GEORGE J. STEVENS		T.L. YOUNG	1912	
2601	JOHANNA CURREN	A.C. WILLIAMSON	JOHN DERLIN	1922	5,990
2604	A.M. SHAW	GEIER BROS.		1912	
2734	LAWRENCE BARRETT	EDWARD BARRETT		1922	5,500
2738	VICTOR BARBIER	JOSEPH LAGARDE	JOSEPH LAGARDE	1923	6,600
2747-49	HENRY PFLUG	OCTAVE HARANG		1937	7,610

Address	Owner	Builder	Architect	Date	Cost
CALHOUN STREET (EDMUND)					
3132-34	MAURICE BOURGEOIS	WALLACE WALKER		1939	7,960
3135	R. ROBERTS	R. ROBERTS		1916	
3225-27	HENRY SALASSI	RUSSO & MENDENEZ	ARTHUR ROUX	1940	7,524
3316	J. BERTUCCI	J. BERTUCCI		1913	
3402-04	SIXTH DISTRICT BUILDING & LOAN	AUGUST FAUST	AUGUST FAUST	1911	1,100
3509	J. CASIMIA	J. CASIMIA		1915	
3537	LILLIAN HUGHES	ROBERT GUESNON		1937	28,885
CAMP STREET (GREENWICH; MARKET; MEADOW)					
6121	GEORGE C. BOLIAN			1906	3,000
6216-18	JOHN BAEHR	JOHN BAEHR		1917	1,500
6302-04, 6306-08	JOHN BAEHR	JOHN BAEHR		1917	4,000
6314	JOHN BAEHR	JOHN BAEHR		1911	
CHESTNUT STREET (CHATHAM; ELIZABETH; PLAQUEMINE)					
5923	CHARLES POST			1901	
6019-21	PETER BONURA	PETER BONURA		1916	2,700
6031	OCTAVE LAGMAN			1898	2,000
7035	AETNA HOMESTEAD ASSN.	ARTHUR SCOTT		1924	9,600
7037	EDWARD MURPHY	JAMES MURPHY	JAMES MURPHY	1927	9,800
CLAIBORNE AVENUE, SOUTH (MOBILE)					
5707	CAROLINE DEJEAN	WILLIAM DURNING		1928	22,000
5713	ORLEANS PARISH SCHOOL BD.	J.A. PETTY & SON	E.A. CHRISTY	1930-32	
5821	JULIA SIEBEN	CHETTA & DUREL		1940	7,840
6423	ROBERT EWING	PAUL CHARBONNET		1928	14,000
CLARA STREET					
5717-21	B. ROBINSON			1925	4,000
5817-19	SIXTH DISTRICT BUILDING & LOAN	JAMES HAGAN	MAURICE REILLY	1925	21,525
5828-30-32	PHOENIX BUILDING & HOMESTEAD	EDWARD F. SPORL	EDWARD F. SPORL	1923	8,300
6216	PAT BASS	MALCOLM COCO		1945	5,109
COLISEUM STREET (FERDINAND)					
5920	JOSEPH C. MAURER			1903	2,800
6021	JOHN F. TOULMIN			1906	2,000
6029-31	TEUTONIA BANK & TRUST	ROBERT MCCANTS	JAMES HUMPHREYS	1909	4,100
6038-40, 6042-44, 6046-48	A. BILLIET	A. BILLIET		1913	
7080	SIXTH DISTRICT BUILDING & LOAN	SAMUEL MCRELL	HANS DIETTEL	1898	1,620
CONSTANCE STREET (LIVE OAK; MAIN)					
5700-02, 5704-06	CHARLES WOODCOCK	CHARLES WOODCOCK		1916	1,800
5701-03,5705-07, 5709-11, 5713-15	E.J. STEWART			1925	10,000
5920, 5926	JULIUS MANGER	JULIUS MANGER		1897	5,500
5947-49	J. GONDOLF	BAEHR BROS.		1916	1,800
6036-38, 6040-42, 6044-46, 6048-50, 6052-54, 6056	JOHN BAEHR	JOHN BAEHR		1905	11,500

Address	Owner	Builder	Architect	Date	Cost
CONSTANCE STREET (LIVE OAK; MAIN)					
6301-03	CITIZENS HOMESTEAD ASSN.	T.L. & A.J. YOUNG	F.L. GOODWIN	1914	
6315	JOHN BAEHR	JOHN BAEHR		1913	
6319-21	CITIZENS HOMESTEAD ASSN.	T.L. & A.J. YOUNG	F.L. GOODWIN	1914	3,200
DELORD STREET					
6320	GUS P. BLANCHARD			1926	16,400
DUNLEITH COURT					
1	JOSIAH E. PEARCE		DEBUYS, CHURCHILL, LABOUISSE	1912	
2	LAWRENCE FABACHER		FRANCIS MACDONNELL	1912	
3	L.E. ARBICHAUX			1911	
4	EDMUND M. IVENS			1927	
5	LOUISE MARTIN			1938	
6	J.W. HOKENSTIEN			1920	
7	WILLIAM S. CAMPBELL		ROBERT S. SOULE	1911	9,000
8	ADDY LOHMAN			1913	
ELEONORE STREET					
208	STEPHEN ALLAIN	PAUL SEYBOLD		1939	4,128
401-03, 405-07	C.A. HOLDWITH	PAUL LAGASSE		1913	
500	SALVADOR TUSA	WEST & DIECK	S. TUSA	1899	
504-06	B. LICCIARDI	J.E. NELSON		1915	
518	FRANCIS THOMAS			1869	
624	MARY TALLIEU	HANS DIETTEL	HANS DIETTEL	1897	1,200
629	THEODORE POWELL	WILLIAM BENNY	W. ANDRUS	1897	1,975
635	FREDERICK BEYER	B.J. SCHINDER		1895	2,700
700-01, 704-06, 708-10, 712-14 716-18	JOHN BAEHR			1906	11,875
709-11	EDWARD BAEHR	LORENZ JENSEN	WILLIAM ROLFES	1909	3,500
717-19,21-23, 727	JULIUS MANGER			1897	5,600
720	P. LEE	P. LEE		1914	
721-23,25-27, 731	JULIUS MANGER			1897	5,600
737	JULIUS MANGER	JULIUS MANGER		1898	2,200
905	RELIANCE HOMESTEAD	JOHN DAVIDSON	A.J. NELSON	1924	4,845
925	H.C. HEITH			1914	3,400
1033-35	CECILIA NIXON	JOHN FOOLKES		1889	1,200
1037	CECILIA NIXON			1895	
1101	W.W. VAN METER			1906	3,300
1116	A.D. HENRIQUIS			1909	4,338
1122	MATHEW M. GRAY			1909	3,200
1241-43	JOHN LOWE			1895	1,100
1319	ALBERT BENDERNAGEL		ANDRY & BENDERNAGEL	1908	
1404	WILLIAM JONES		W.W. VAN METER	1914	
1435	EUREKA HOMESTEAD	POLLOCK & KILLEEN		1914	

Address	Owner	Builder	Architect	Date	Cost
ELEONORE STREET					
1443	CHARLES W. FOX, JR.			1906	3,000
1455	THOMAS R. WATT		FRANCIS MACDONNELL	1911	
1461	A.J. PUGH	A.J. PUGH		1912	
1465	MILTON S. STANDIFER	GEIER BROS.	FAVROT & LIVAUDAIS	1912	
1519	P. KANE	G.W. O'MALLEY		1913	
1535	A.T. LANAUX	FRANCIS MACDONNELL	FRANCIS MACDONNELL	1917	
EVERETT PLACE					
1	J. BAUMANN			1909	
2	ERNEST BORNEMANN		R. SPENCER SOULE	1908	14,000
3	EMILE CHRIST			1909	
4	EDWARD SOULE		R. SPENCER SOULE	1908	
5	JAMES V. DUNBAR			1909	3,000
6	R. SPENCER SOULE		R. SPENCER SOULE	1908	
EXPOSITION BOULEVARD (BOULEVARD STREET)					
405-07	M. GRILLO	O.M. BUSH		1915	
429	T.S. RAPP			1924	4,500
523-27	CITIZENS HOMESTEAD ASSN.	EDWARD MURPHY		1924	
631-33	HARRY BARKER			1906	3,500
701	MARY COCKS			1908	
725-29	R. OTIS	R. OTIS		1914	
735	JOHN J. HECKER			1905	5,000
1315	CARRIE PAYNE		H.L. BURTON	1922	
1433	GUY MENDES		R. SPENCER SOULE	1908	12,000
1451	EDWARD DEMAREST			1896	10,000
1507, 1513, 1519, 1525	EPPIE BARR			1892	
1531	EDWIN POWELL			1910	
1539	MARY ABBOTT			1894	
1543	GEORGE C. SEARS	CAREY & LECORGNE		1893	4,079
1545	GEORGE C. SEARS		CAREY & LECORGNE	1893	4,079
1565	MARY B. TUPPER		RATHBONE DEBUYS	1905	6,000
1571	WILLIAM B. REILY		CROSBY & HENKEL	1909	12,000
1591	FRED PARAMORE		MACKENZIE GOLDSTEIN & BIGGS	1907	
FONTAINEBLEAU DRIVE (BALDWIN; JAMES)					
78	HENRY FRANZ	DENIS & HANDY	DAVID BARROW	1925	10,540
81	CHARLES AYALA	EDWIN MARKEL		1931	7,500
83	OSCAR C. TURLINGTON			1922	8,500
87	PETER WILSON	EDWIN MARKEL		1927	10,500
90	STELLA DOYLE	THEARD & REILLY		1915	2,750
92	CHARLES L. PEARSON		ABRAHAM MOISE	1916	
5801	EDWARD MAHER	GEORGE LUPO		1937	10,967
5822	ARTHUR SHUBERT	W. OSBORNE	W. OSBORNE	1937	5,650
5843	FRANK MALTRY, JR.	JOSEPH E. CHAPMAN	HORTURAN & SALMEN	1927	7,800

Address	Owner	Builder	Architect	Date	Cost
FONTAINEBLEAU DRIVE (BALDWIN; JAMES)					
6216-18	LOUIS SCHWARZ	OCTAVE HARANG	THEODORE PERRIER	1936	8,500
6401	JOSEPH HURWITZ	PAUL CHARBONNET	PAUL CHARBONNET	1949	24,252
FRERET STREET (ELM; LONG; PINE)					
5624	ORLEANS PARISH SCHOOL BD.		E.A. CHRISTY	1930	
5929-31-33-35	FRANCIS ERLINGER	ADRIAN DE JONG		1922	12,000
5940	O. BRECHTEL	O. BRECHTEL		1913	
6028	JAMES A. ROSS			1906	3,345
6037	WALTER C. KEENAN			1925	15,000
6321	WILLIAM TRACY			1873	
7219-23	JOHN KING	JOHN KING	J.C. ROBERTSON	1910	4,800
GARFIELD STREET (ANN; BOUDOUSQUIE; JENNET; JENNETTE)					
5708	NELSON WOODY	ROBERT KETTERINGHAM	HENRY EHRENSING	1939	6,330
5901	PATRICK MCGRATH			1905	
5902	GEORGE BRADSHAW			1905	3,000
GREEN STREET					
7020	JOSEPH WEIS		ARMSTRONG & KOCH	1928	
HAMPSON STREET (WASHINGTON)					
7301	JAMES MCLOUGHLIN			1907	
HENRY CLAY AVENUE (CLAY)					
323	CONSERVATIVE HOMESTEAD	JOSEPH MACULUSO		1929	4,643
333	ADAM LORCH			1885	
400-02	F. BELERINO	K. HANSEN		1914	
438	LOUIS SELLER			1898	2,000
501	L.R. SHANKS	JULIUS MANGER		1895	2,000
503	MICHAEL SHELLY			1884	
514	LEWIS PREST			1885	2,000
529-31	SADIE VEZIEU	JOSEPH ULINA		1914	
535-37, 539-41	SECURITY BUILDING & LOAN	BRIEN & BAEHR		1917	4,500
720	SISTERS OF POOR CLARES	JEFFERSON CONST. CO.	WILLIAM R. BURK	1913	43,360
814-16	DIXIE HOMESTEAD	SAM SIMONE	SAM STONE	1909	2,373
911	S.D. BOLIAN	WILLIAM F. FULHAM	WILLIAM F. FULHAM	1915	
1019-21	AMELIA HELEMEN	CHARLES PFISTER		1922	8,700
1211	CHARLES SANTANA			1900	2,500
1234	SUSIE ELLERMANN		THOMAS SULLY	1895	
1235-37	ANITA STAIGG	DENIS & HANDY		1926	10,700
1303	CHARLES EPSTEIN			1897	2,500
1304	GEORGE A. RICE	BEHAN & O'MALLEY		1893	3,000
1310	JACOB BORN	F. HOFFMAN		1895	5,800
1311	GEORGE G. BRADSHAW			1898	3,047
1320	CHARLES J. BURT	OTIS SHARP	MORRIS DEPASS	1896	2,296
1325	JOHN A. WILLIAMS	J.W. LENNOX	SOULE & MACDONNELL	1904	5,200
1334	S.S. RUSHA			1895	3,000
1419	G.J. PLEASSANCE			1906	2,500

Address	Owner	Builder	Architect	Date	Cost
HENRY CLAY AVENUE (CLAY)					
1429	SOLOMON REINACH		LOUIS A. GANTER	1895	3,450
1435	L. REINACH	LOUIS GANTER		1894	3,450
1444	MORRIS MCGRAW, JR.		FAVROT & LIVAUDAIS	1901	
1461	ELIVRA E. MAXWELL	MOORE & JENKINS	D.A. DICKEY	1895	2,250
1469	LOUIS A. DAVIDSON		LOUIS A. GANTER	1895	3,500
1500	JOHN FERGUSON			1870	
1514	TIMES-PICAYUNE		MOISE GOLDSTEIN	1936	
1529	JONAS FRENCH			1877	
1537-39	JOHN B. LEVERT	J.A. HAASE, JR.		1917	8,400
1543	JOHN W. PUGH			1895	6,000
1557	MARY WREN			1897	
1570	AUGUSTUS MAY		FAVROT & LIVAUDAIS	1900	4,000
1582	SAMUEL GILMORE		THOMAS SULLY	1888	
1604	HENRY C. EUSTIS			1893	5,000
1612	HORATIO EUSTIS			1897	2,000
1622-24	E.J. DEMAREST	JOSEPH E. CHAPMAN		1916	1,850
1648	MICHAEL FRANK			1896	4,300
HICKORY STREET					
7022-24	GERRON ALETRINO	MAX SINGER		1925	12,000
HURST STREET (IRMA; LOUISA; MISSISSIPPI)					
5528	CHARLES HERO	DANNEMANN & CHARLTON		1901	3,400
5820	JAMES APARTMENTS		JULIUS DREYFOUS	1920	
5829	MUTUAL BUILDING & LOAN			1910	
5902, 5908, 5914, 5920	F.A. SCHNEIDAU	L.C. LECORGNE		1891	13,500
6056	BROWN & UNSWORTH		FAVROT & LIVAUDAIS	1893	
6104	HENRY C. EUSTIS		FAVROT & LIVAUDAIS	1893	5,000
6322-24	E.J. DEMAREST	JOSEPH E. CHAPMAN		1916	1,850
7316-18	EUGENIE CHALIN	FREDERICK JUNKER	ROBERT WARD	1905	2,625
7335	VIOLET ODENWALD	JOSEPH ODENWALD		1922	7,367
JEANETTE STREET					
7000-04	C.A. HANSON	C.A. HANSON		1914	
7003	C.A. HANSON	C.A. HANSON		1916	1,200
7011	C.A. HANSON	C.A. HANSON		1916	2,800
7333	CHARLES STAIR	HENRY HINRICHS & SON	HENRY HINRICHS	1919	1,175
7516	STEPHEN MANNING	GEORGE LEAHY		1920	12,100
JOSEPH STREET					
422	GEORGE PELTZ			1867	
814-16	DIXIE HOMESTEAD	SAM P. SIMONE	SAM P. SIMONE	1909	2,373
930-32	JAMES O'DONNELL	FREDERICK CRIMBLE		1907	2,300
1126	FRANK LECKERT			1900	2,300
1134	THOMAS POWELL			1900	2,200
1324-26	WILHELMINA PERLEE	A.J. ELLERBUSCH		1904	3,325

Address	Owner	Builder	Architect	Date	Cost
JOSEPH STREET					
1333	MAMIE HANNON	RABORN & BETHANCOURT		1926	4,494
1442-44	CARRIE HOTCHKISS			1886	1,500
1648	IRMA MOSES	OTIS SHARP	MORRIS DEPASS	1896	4,334
1919-21	STUART HANDY	DENIS & HANDY	ARMSTRONG & KOCH	1923	7,000
2115	JOSEPH PERLUFF			1948	
2219	SECURITY BUILDING & LOAN	EDWIN MARKEL	EDWIN MARKEL	1911	3,050
2419	CHARLES WEISER	C.M. TERRY		1922	4,400
2426-28	EQUITABLE HOMESTEAD	H.F. OBERLING	EDWARD DE ARMAS	1923	10,995
2811	JACOB GENSBURGER	LOUIS MIRAMON	LOUIS MIRAMON	1938	5,700
LASALLE STREET (HOWARD; ST. GEORGE)					
3	JEANNETTE BALLARD		FRANCIS MACDONNELL	1909	
8	J.C. LYONS		ARMSTRONG & KOCH	1922	
LAUREL STREET (JERSEY; MARKET; PATTON; UNION)					
5831	CHARLES WALKER			1869	
5913-15	A. SEARY	J.M. DEFRAITES		1912	
5916-18	GEORGE WENLING	HENRY HAFFNER		1906	3,100
5939-41	HENRY H. MARKEL	ROBERT W. MARKEL		1913	
6040	FRANCIS BROWN	LOUET TAYLOR		1940	3,088
6041	JOSEPH M. ARMBRUSTER			1902	2,285
6053	MUTUAL BUILDING & HOMESTEAD	HENRY ROST		1885	2,500
6068-70	L. SOKOSKY	L. SOKOSKY		1912	
6072-74, 6076-78	L. SOKOSKY	L. SOKOSKY		1912	
6108-10	SIXTH DISTRICT BUILDING & LOAN	WILLIAM O'BRIEN		1923	5,000
6114-16	CHARLES FORKERT			1895	
6118	PHILOMENE FRAZIER			1898	2,150
6218-20	EQUITABLE HOMESTEAD	PAUL SEYBOLD	WILLIAM T. NOLAN	1923	8,200
6221, 6223-25, 6227-29	AETNA HOMESTEAD	ALBERT ORDUNA	THEODORE PERRIER	1925	13,500
6301, 6305, 6309, 6313, 6315	JULIUS MANGER	JULIUS MANGER	JULIUS MANGER	1896	4,200
LOWERLINE STREET					
300-02, 304-06, 308-10, 312-14	PETER COPELAND	ARTHUR P. BOH		1912	5,460
301, 305, 309, 313, 317, 321, 325, 329	CHALINE MILLER		ABRAHAM MOISE	1906	
410	RELIANCE HOMESTEAD	J.D. COLLINS		1915	
436	HARRY L. LOOMIS			1904	2,450
439	A.G. BOWMAN			1899	2,850
443	W.H. WOODWARD			1897	
510	CHARLES BEIN		CROSBY & HENKEL	1907	
517	P.W. TRELANNY			1896	2,650
535	FREDERICK FISCHER			1867	

Address	Owner	Builder	Architect	Date	Cost
LOWERLINE STREET					
538	HENRY G. TRAPHAGEN	H. HECKER		1916	
625	HENRY TRAPHAGEN	H. HECKER		1916	
542-44	MARY SOMMERVILLE	AUGUST BECHTEL		1923	3,900
637	WILLIAM J. MORGAN	WILLIAM BIRD	I.K. LEVY	1894	3,000
700	A.M. ELLIS	A.M. ELLIS		1915	
727	MALVINA FLEETWOOD			1894	
816	A. MORRERE	GEIER BROS.		1912	
912-14	DRYADES BUILDING & LOAN	J.N. EMMONS		1909	
1010	EXCELSIOR HOMESTEAD	JOHN CHARLTON	JOHN CHARLTON	1919	7,551
1011	GEORGE DILLON	HENRI DEFRAITES		1931	2,610
1023	M. DETTON / GEORGE DILLON	F. HOFFMAN		1914	1,800
1111	GRAHAM S. BLACK			1909	3,000
1129	J.M. BRABAZON			1869	
1150	ANATOLE E. LADNER	ANATOLE E. LADNER		1913	
1200	FREDERICK C. SCHMITT	JOSEPH E. CHAPMAN		1916	3,000
1219-21	W.L. BILLET	WALTER C. KEENAN		1915	
1328-30	ISIDORE SINGER	ISIDORE SINGER		1912	
LOYOLA AVENUE (ST. DAVID; S. FRANKLIN)					
5625	ORLEANS PARISH SCHOOL BD.	R.P. FARNSWORTH & CO.	E.A. CHRISTY	1926	
5700	SOPHIE GUMBEL SCHOOL		MOISE GOLDSTEIN	1917	
MAGAZINE STREET (LIBERTY)					
5601	NEW ORLEANS TRACTION CO.			1895	28,000
5926	J.J. O'DONNELL			1909	3,000
5930	HYMAN BARKOFF	HENRI DEFRAITES		1927	3,100
5938	CHARLES F. STERKEN			1902	2,400
5941-43	HENRY BUTLER			1893	
6021-23	WILLIAM BACHER			1902	
6028	METROPOLITAN BUILDING CO.			1900	2,200
6055-57	JOHN EISWIRTH			1885	
6101	JOSEPH INSIRILLO	JOHN BAEHR	ESSE WEST	1900	2,100
6315-17	HILAIRE CHATRY	JOHN BAEHR		1902	2,618
MAGNOLIA STREET (ARCADIA; VICTOR)					
6217	E. VILLERMAN	E. VILLERMAN		1913	
MARQUETTE PLACE (ST. PATRICK; SARATOGA)					
6120	ROBERT HOLMES		FRANCIS MACDONNELL	1910	
S. MIRO STREET					
5828	WARREN DERUSSY	MIRAMON CONST. CO.		1941	4,600
NASHVILLE AVENUE (BEAUREGARD)					
215	OSCAR CURRY	PAUL SEYBOLD		1939	3,100
401	DANNEEL SCHOOL	MUIR & FROMHERTZ		1908	45,951
434-46	SECURITY BUILDING & LOAN	ARTHUR BOH		1910	3,280
510	ELIZA MEARES			1869	

Address	Owner	Builder	Architect	Date	Cost
NASHVILLE AVENUE (BEAUREGARD)					
520	ELIZA MEARES			1887	
538	JOSEPH SEILER			1895	1,750
604-06	C.W. ROSS			1885	
623	F.J. LETTEN			1899	2,000
624	JULIUS MANGER			1897	
631	M. MAURIN	J.M. DEFRAITES		1912	
636	WILLIAM ARMS	LAGMAN & SON		1895	1,700
700	M. NIESS	SEYBOLD BROS.		1916	3,000
704, 710	JULIUS MANGER			1896	
722-24	MICHAEL WILLEN	JACOB BAEHR		1902	3,312
725-29	L. BILLET	L. BILLET		1913	
728-30	JULIUS MANGER			1896	
731	ADRIAN J. MORAIS	ABRAHAM MOISE	ABRAHAM MOISE	1904	3,375
739	EDGAR GARCIA	ABRAHAM MOISE	ABRAHAM MOISE	1904	3,443
802	GEORGE W. WILSON	JOHN BAEHR		1902	3,780
911	WILLIAM GAISSER	EDWIN MARKEL		1905	2,690
915	A.O. REIBENTICH	JOHN LUGENBUHL		1912	
1004	PETER SIREN	A.A. DIETTEL		1913	4,788
1021-23	B.F. BURKE			1917	4,000
1027	JAMES RENTON	EDWARD BAEHR		1923	7,400
1036	PEOPLES HOMESTEAD	FEITEL & DEJONG		1917	2,775
1104	JAMES SIMEON	JOHN CHISOLM		1902	3,273
1130	PARKER MEMORIAL METHODIST CHURCH	DIBOLL & OWEN		1910	
1207	MRS. E.R. KENT			1895	2,263
1213	CHARLES E. WERMUTH		KEENAN & WEISS	1907	
1214	GEORGE H. WASSON			1904	3,300
1221	TOULMIN			1897	
1224	EDWARD RANQUETAT	THOMAS BROCKMAN		1921	10,969
1231	EDGAR SMITH		EDWARD F. SPORL	1906	
1239	T.C. BOND			1905	3,450
1300	ALBERT A. MARCHAL			1924	
1318	FRANK DANNEMANN			1903	3,000
1321	CRESCENT CITY BUILDING & HOMESTEAD	E.W. ULLRICH GLASS	SAM STONE	1924	11,500
1323-25	F.F. OSER	SEYBOLD BROS.	PHILIP B. SEYBOLD	1914	4,900
1415	M.E. HOLT			1903	3,295
1419	LOUIS MARQUEZ	ARTHUR BOH		1909	6,120
1436	FIRST CHURCH OF CHRIST SCIENTIST	J. KOELS	S. STONE, JR.	1913	
1445	FRANK DANNEMANN			1905	
1458	J.A. STORCK	JULIUS KOCH		1905	5,000
1721	MAY ROSENBERG		FRERET & WOLF	1939	
2212-14	H. GILMORE	J.A. HAASE		1915	

Address	Owner	Builder	Architect	Date	Cost
NASHVILLE AVENUE (BEAUREGARD)					
2226	GEORGE ST. PAUL	EDWARD BAEHR		1925	5,930
2310-12	LENA ROSATO	DENIS & HANDY	ARMSTRONG & KOCH	1922	10,500
2320, 2322-24	MARIA ROSATO	DENIS & HANDY	ARMSTRONG & KOCH	1923	12,900
2402	JANE MCNALLY	PAUL CHARBONNET		1922	7,125
2500-02	SIXTH DISTRICT BUILDING & LOAN	JAMES HAGAN	MAURICE REILLY	1925	21,525
2508-10	AETNA HOMESTEAD	FREDERICK PUTFARK	THEODORE PERRIER	1925	6,500
2514	PEOPLES HOMESTEAD	PAUL CHARBONNET	ADOLPH EHRENSING	1926	12,660
2609	PEOPLES HOMESTEAD	ERNEST IVES	ADOLPH EHRENSING	1928	11,000
2619	PEOPLES HOMESTEAD	EDWIN MARKEL	ADOLPH EHRENSING	1924	7,600
2623-25	PEOPLES HOMESTEAD	ERNEST IVES	ADOLPH EHRENSING	1928	11,000
2627-29	PEOPLES HOMESTEAD	KENNETH COLOMB	ADOLPH EHRENSING	1928	11,000
3015	EMILE JASTRAVE	CHARLES PFISTER	SAM SIMONE	1924	9,796
3035	RUFUS FISHER	W. OSBORNE		1937	8,425
3128	AUGUSTA ENGELBACH	JOHN CHETTA	JOHN CHETTA	1939	8,350
3201-03	HENRIETTA BOURY	A.M. PUMILIA	A.M. PUMILIA	1938	8,500
3220-22	LOUIS SCHWARTZ	OCTAVE HARANG		1941	9,987
3233	ROBERT MURPHY	DAVID PITTMAN		1939	3,352
3300	LEONARD CLESI	SHEPARD PERRIER		1939	5,000
3304	LEONARD CLESI	SHEPARD PERRIER		1939	5,000
3308	EDWARD SIREN	JOHN CHETTA		1939	5,465
3326	PRESTON DEBEN	JOHN CHETTA		1939	4,650
3515-17	ADAM JUNKER	EDWIN MARKEL		1941	7,300
3518	GORDON HERBERT	WILFRED BLANCQ	ROY NORVELLE	1939	6,788
3815-17	JOSEPH RYAN	CLARENCE CHARLTON		1938	11,859
NEWCOMB BOULEVARD					
1	GONZALO ABAUNZA		FRANCIS MACDONNELL	1921	
2	ANTHONY P. SAUER			1923	
3	CHARLES SUGARMAN		WEISS & DREYFOUS	1921	
4	RICHARD J. MARTINEZ	WALTER GEARY	MORGAN HITE	1920	
5	JACOB H. BODENHEIMER			1923	
6	B.S. D'ANTONI		EDWARD F. SPORL	1923	
7	OTWAY DENNY			1922	
9	NEIL HIMEL		GOLDSTEIN, PARHAM, LABOUISSE	1922	
10	HENRY C. FLONACHER		WEISS & DREYFOUS	1924	
12	H.E. GROFFMAN		MOISE GOLDSTEIN	1921	
11	ROBERT WERK			1920	
13	HARRY GOODMAN		NATHAN KOHLMAN	1921	
15	ROBERT WERK			1920	
16	JULIUS W.C. WRIGHT		MOISE GOLDSTEIN	1922	19,000
17	GEORGE W. BOHN		MORGAN HITE	1935	
18	THOMAS WRIGHT		MOISE GOLDSTEIN	1923	15,000
19	JOSEPH CHALINA			1920	
20	FRED C. TAYLOR			1933	

Address	Owner	Builder	Architect	Date	Cost
NEWCOMB BOULEVARD					
21	LOUIS A. WEIL		MOISE GOLDSTEIN	1922	17,000
22	OTTO GOTTSCHO		WEISS & DREYFOUS	1924	
25	SAMUEL OHNSTEIN		NATHAN KOHLMAN	1922	
26	RUSSELL C. WATKIN			1924	
27	TUDOR B. CARRE		NATHAN KOHLMAN	1925	
28	DELAWARE CORP.				
29	EPHRAIM ROSENBERG			1920	
30	DELAWARE CORP.				
31	BERYL HOLLIS	PAUL CHARBONNET		1936	10,250
34	FRAZIER L. RICE			1923	
38	DAVID SILVERMAN		WEISS & DREYFOUS	1923	
39	WALTER BARNETT	PAUL CHARBONNET		1936	9,000
41	PAPULINE & VIOLA SCOLLA			1923	
42	WALTER BURNETT, JR.		PAUL CHARBONNET	1936	9,000
44	MARY D'HAMEL BARKDULL		PAUL CHARBONNET	1921	
45	ABRAHAM SHUSHAN		WEISS & DREYFOUS	1922	
OAK STREET					
7329	W. MILLER		ALEXANDER HAY	1908	4,500
PALMER AVENUE (CLAY; HENRY CLAY)					
1625	ALBERT SIMON		M.H. GOLDSTEIN	1922	16,200
1630	JOSEPH LEVY		EMILE WEIL	1908	
1637	PAUL LEMANN		MONROE LABOUISSE, SR.	1935	
1640	SYLVAN NEWBERGER		EMILE WEIL	1908	
1644	LAZARE LEVY		MACKENZIE GOLDSTEIN & BIGGS	1907	14,000
1707	BERNARD LANDAU		FAVROT & LIVAUDAIS	1900	5,000
1711	JOHN F. CLARK		FRANK P. GRAVELY	1906	10,000
1718	BENJAMIN MORGAN PALMER	A. WELLMAN		1891	6,500
1730	BRANDT V.B. DIXON		TOLEDANO & REUSCH	1895	11,700
1806	ELMIRA RICHARD	JOHN RICHARD		1885	
1812	MARY FRANCES HARDIE		FAVROT & LIVAUDAIS	1897	
1904	CHARLES B. DICKS			1902	6,500
1907	A.Q. PETERSON			1931	
1912	CRAWFORD H. ELLIS		SOUTHRON DUVAL	1905	4,000
2007	JOSEPH W. BEER		EMILE WEIL	1903	5,000
2010	CHARLES SUGARMANN		MACKENZIE GOLDSTEIN & BIGGS	1905	10,000
2036	ASHTON HAYWARD			1905	3,450
2108	TOBY HART			1873	
2115	JOSEPH FORNARIS		ROBERT SHOPPELL	1897	3,500
2124	JAMES GAUDET		BURTON & BENDERNAGEL	1916	
2200	GEORGE W. RUEFF		FRANCIS MACDONNELL	1908	
2203	FRED L. SEAMAN	ALBERT G. BEAR		1912	
2235	A.J. O'REILLEY		TOLEDANO & REUSCH	1897	
2324	PEOPLES HOMESTEAD	JOHN WERLING		1925	6,657

Address	Owner	Builder	Architect	Date	Cost
PALMER AVENUE (CLAY; HENRY CLAY)					
2439	JOHN COUTUSIER	EDWIN MARKEL	EDWIN MARKEL	1921	8,635
2522	SUBURBAN BUILDING & LOAN	F. HOFFMAN	ANDRY & BENDERNAGEL	1908	2,950
2633	G.H. STOCKTON	G.H. STOCKTON		1915	
2634	JEANNE HATREL	HERMAN JOHNSON		1928	4,000
2735	WALTER HAMLIN	JACOB KIRN	WALTER HAMLIN	1923	5,800
2830-32	WALTER KINGSTON	PAUL CHARBONNET		1923	10,472
PANOLA STREET					
7119-21	JACOB SEELIG	ALBERT POSECAI		1932	
7321	SECURITY BUILDING & LOAN	THEARD & REILLY		1915	
PATTON STREET (UNION)					
5820-22, 5824-26	FREDERICK SCHOPP	MARTIN GUELDA	DAVID CASEY	1904	5,734
6049	JOHN WELKER			1905	2,545
6052-54	JOHN J. REYNOLDS	CHARLES KEHL		1902	2,300
6116 18	JOHN DONNELLY	ROBERT MARKEL	J.T. KIRN	1913	3,350
6122-24	CAROLINE MCCUBBIN	ROBERT W. MARKEL	ROBERT W. MARKEL	1913	3,335
PERRIER STREET (GEN. HOOD; HOWARD; OLIVIER)					
5827	ALFRED CLAY			1895	
5903	HILARY L. MITCHELL		SOUTHRON DUVAL	1906	4,500
5919	WILLIAM M. HARDING			1897	
5924	EUGENIE SPORL	SEYBOLD BROS.		1910	3,775
6020-22-24-26, 6028-30-32-34	JOHN WOODVILLE	OTTO WALTER	OTTO WALTER	1904	15,576
6029	E.L. CHAPPUIS			1906	2,500
6031	A. THIBODEAUX			1896	2,000
6033	E. HOWARD MCCALEB			1918	
6048	LASALLE SCHOOL		CAPDEVILLE & HARDEE	1901	33,390
PINE STREET					
312-14, 316	HENRY HINRICHS			1908	
342	BERTHA BOISSONNEAU		MACKENZIE EHLIS & JOHNSON	1911	5,000
355-57, 359-61	SERVICE BUILDING & HOMESTEAD	RUFFIN WALKER	A.M. PUMILIA	1928	7,500
366	EDWARD A. FOWLER	T.L. & J.D. YOUNG		1912	
372-74	M. SAZER			1914	
424	MARY COLE		H.L. BURTON		
439	THOMAS QUIGLEY	JOHN O'BRIEN	MARTIN SHEPARD	1941	4,000
444	MISS G.B. ENGLEET			1917	2,200
450	F.W. BREMER			1895	5,000
622	ALFRED ALLTMONT			1923	
630	W.B. GREGORY		LEON C. WEISS	1915	
635	EUGENE CHAPPUIS	JOHN CHARLTON	JOHN CHARLTON	1920	8,400
639	L.M. WILKINSON			1905	6,500
705	GEORGE LEAHY	EDWIN MARKEL	JOHN BAEHR	1914	6,200
715-17	GEORGE LEAHY	JONES & ROESSLE	JONES & ROESSLE	1913	4,984

Address	Owner	Builder	Architect	Date	Cost
PINE STREET					
719-21	A. ALLTMONT	GEIER BROS.		1911	
727		EDWIN MARKEL	H. JORDAN MACKENZIE	1910	4,350
739	GEORGE LEAHY	JONES & ROESSLE	JONES & ROESSLE	1913	3,055
803	GEORGE MCHARDY			1897	3,000
808-10	LILLY GEISSERT	PETTY & ERWIN		1910	5,100
823-25	GEO MCHARDY		ALEXANDER HAY	1912	4,000
1108	JOHN BAEHR	JOHN BAEHR		1915	
1118	JOHN BAEHR	JOHN BAEHR		1916	2,500
1120-22	A.T. DEISENBURG	GEIER BROS.		1913	
1228	CHARLES M. BUHLER	A.L. RILEY		1909	3,000
1314	CHARLES S. CLARK	GEIER BROS	FAVROT & LIVAUDAIS	1913	
1316	PROVIDENT BUILDING & LOAN	DELTA CONTRACTING CO.		1910	3,200
1321	M.S. MCENERY			1914	
1330	ERNEST W. JONES		JONES & ROESSLE	1912	6,000
1340	JACOB FABACHER		EDWARD F. SPORL	1912	
1508-10	WILLIAM R. GILBERT	WILLIAM R. GILBERT		1914	
1509	JAMES CHALARON		FAVROT & LIVAUDAIS	1914	
1522	CHARLES T. MCCORD	JONES & ROESSLE	JONES & ROESSLE	1913	3,800
1602	WILLIAM R. GILBERT	WILLIAM R. GILBERT		1913	
1603	WILLIAM R. GILBERT	WILLIAM R. GILBERT		1914	
1607	WILLIAM R. GILBERT	WILLIAM R. GILBERT		1914	
1614-16	WILLIAM R. GILBERT	WILLIAM R. GILBERT		1914	
1626	WILLIAM R. GILBERT	WILLIAM R. GILBERT		1915	3,500
1629-31	WILLIAM R. GILBERT	WILLIAM R. GILBERT		1915	
1704	WILLIAM R. GILBERT	WILLIAM R. GILBERT		1915	
1800	FRANK PALMISANO	FRANK PALMISANO		1916	2,000
1802	FRANK PALMISANO	FRANK PALMISANO		1916	
2026	BRYAN DEANE	FRANK DUFRECHOU		1933	2,100
2133	H.S. HOLDIN	ALEXANDER SMITH		1914	
2221-23	LOUISIANA APARTMENT HOUSE CORP.	ALEXANDER SMITH	L.P. SMITH	1920	8,500
2227	LYLE CARTER	THEARD & REILLY		1915	
2231	LOUISIANA APARTMENT HOUSE CORP.	ALEXANDER SMITH	L.P. SMITH	1920	8,500
2238 & 80-78 NERON	RELIANCE HOMESTEAD ASSOCIATION	LOUISIANA APARTMENT HOUSE CORP.	ALEXANDER SMITH	1920	14,000
2433	R. TRIGG	GEORGE LEAHY		1920	5,200
2502, 2508	JOHN NIX	ANTHONY BISSANT		1925	22,000
2503	GEORGE S. COLBY	ROBERT W. MARKEL		1913	
2515	REMY JENNES	EDWIN MARKEL		1926	10,300
2516	JACKSON HOMESTEAD	EDWIN MARKEL	EDWIN MARKEL	1926	11,050
PITT STREET (BOND; HESTER)					
5701	ADAM RAU	JOHN C. STAUB	JOHN STAUB	1899	1,875
6028	EDMUND J. GLENNY			1903	8,000

Address	Owner	Builder	Architect	Date	Cost
PLUM STREET					
7301	LEONARD KING	PAUL CHARBONNET		1927	15,000
7328	THOMAS C. HILLS		ALEXANDER HAY	1911	6,000
PRYTANIA STREET (COURTLAND; WALL)					
5819-21	GUSTAVE SEITEL	L. FROLICH		1898	1845
5828	M. BOUCHE		FAVROT & LIVAUDAIS	1896	3,000
5829	HARRY BARTLETT			1908	
5917	EDGAR E. SMITH			1903	2,000
5924	F.G. LUDLIN			1896	2,500
5925	ALFRED RAYMOND			1899	2,000
6023	HENRY MCCALL		R.S. SOULE	1906	9,500
6024	W.A. SCOTT		FAVROT & LIVAUDAIS	1909	3,000
6262	M.M. BOATNER			1908	
6306	MILDRED CORNWELL	EDWIN MARKEL		1924	17,000
6333	GEORGE WIFGAND	L.J. WOODWORTH	A.J. NELSON	1925	15,383
6334	CHARLES GILMER			1925	
RICHMOND PLACE					
1	RICHARD EUSTIS		ROBERT SPENCER SOULE	1911	9,000
2	WILLIAM REID			1910	
3	MARTIN H. MANION		ROBERT SPENCER SOULE	1911	10,000
4	SIDNEY J. WHITE		ROBERT SPENCER SOULE	1911	12,000
5	L. CHRISTIANSON			1915	
6	C.P. ELLIS, JR.		SAM STONE, JR.	1911	12,000
7	THOMAS SULLY	THOMAS SULLY	THOMAS SULLY	1915	
8	LOUIS MAZERES			1909	
9	R.B. SCUDDER	R.B. SCUDDER		1913	
11	OSCAR SCHNEIDAU, JR.			1909	
12	EDWARD RIGHTOR			1923	
14	JOHN R. JUDEN		FRANCIS MACDONNELL	1922	
15	T.K. JAMES			1919	
17	HENRI FAVROT		FAVROT & LIVAUDAIS	1906	7,358
18	CHARLES FAVROT		FAVROT & LIVAUDAIS	1906	
19	E.L. LANSING		FAVROT & LIVAUDAIS	1910	
21	RUFUS FOSTER		MACKENZIE GOLDSTEIN & BIGGS	1906	6,000
22	NATHAN KOHLMAN			1920	
23	CHARLES PESCAY			1909	
S. ROBERTSON STREET (BRESLIN; BREALIN)					
5821-23	STUART HANDY	DENIS & HANDY	ARMSTRONG & KOCH	1922	5,000
5837	MARIE LARROUX	CLARENCE MAITREJEAN	CLARENCE MAITREJEAN	1923	10,000
6128	GREATER NEW ORLEANS HOMESTEAD	RUCKSTUHL & FINK	RUCKSTUHL & FINK	1938	3,942
6320	E. KLOPPENBURG	ENTERPRISE CONSTRUCTION		1922	4,435
ROSA PARK					
1	SIMON STEINHARDT		FAVROT & LIVAUDAIS	1900	20,000

Address	Owner	Builder	Architect	Date	Cost
ROSA PARK					
8	JEFFERSON WENCK			1908	
10	EUGENE W. DEMING			1900	7,135
11	MINERVA SHAFFER	OTTO MANSKE		1899	6,000
14	MAE MILLARD			1905	8,000
15	SAMUEL DIAMOND		GEORGE E. DICKEY & SON	1897	5,000
16	EDWARD E. SOULE		GEORGE E. DICKEY & SON	1899	4,000
17	T.J. STANTON		SOULE & MACDONNELL	1903	3,490
18	W.H. WENCK	ALFRED A. ADAMS & CO.	HARROD-ANDRY-BENDERNAGEL	1898	3,325
19	J.J. SHAFFER			1899	6,000
ST. CHARLES AVENUE (NAYADES)					
5603	TIMOTHY H. MCCARTHY		SOULE & MACDONNELL	1903	8,000
5604	ROBERT RIVERS			1884	
5614	LOUISE W. LIBBY		SOULE & MACDONNELL	1905	10,890
5624	ROBERT RIVERS			1884	
5631	WILLIAM T. COATS	WILLIAM T. COATS	FAVROT & LIVAUDAIS	1913	
5700	CHARLES GODCHAUX		FAVROT & LIVAUDAIS	1901	20,000
5705	GEORGE PALMER			1941	
5718	WILLIAM GIRAULT	LOUIS LAMBERT	LOUIS LAMBERT	1889	5,750
5726	THOMAS UNDERWOOD	LOUIS LAMBERT	LOUIS LAMBERT	1889	9,000
5800	JOHN HILLMAN			1870	
5801	MAE MILLARD		ROBERT S. SOULE	1902	3,000
5807	SIMON STEINHARDT		FAVROT & LIVAUDAIS	1900	
5809	NICHOLAS BURKE	WILLIAM KRONE	TOLEDANO & WOGAN	1896	13,265
5824	ANTONIO PALACIOS	DANIEL FRASER	HENRY HOWARD	1867	9,250
5912	STELLA ADLER		EMILE WEIL	1905	12,500
5954	ST. CHARLES AVENUE PRESBYTERIAN CHURCH		W.W. VAN METER	1924	
6000	JOHN CASTLES		THOMAS SULLY & CO.	1895	9,000
6016	CHARLES STICH		FAVROT & LIVAUDAIS	1903	6,500
6020	JUDAH SEIDENBACH		FAVROT & LIVAUDAIS	1903	10,000
6026	WILLIAM LEBON			1873	
6038-40	HOLLY STEM			1926	
6100	COMMERCIAL HOMESTEAD			1887	
6110	MAE MILLARD		FAVROT & LIVAUDAIS	1905	
6126	LAK REALTY CO.	W.A. KEENE	MOISE GOLDSTEIN	1924	
6145	LOUISE MONLEZUN		FAVROT & LIVAUDAIS	1923	
6149	WILLIAM BENTLEY			1916	
6153	WILLIAM ADLER		EMILE WEIL	1903	20,000
6200	ST. CHARLES AVENUE CHRISTIAN CHURCH	J.A. PETTY	JONES & ROESSLE	1920	125,000
6226	MAYER ISRAEL		FAVROT & LIVAUDAIS	1902	12,000
6227	TEMPLE SINAI	CHARLES GIBERT	EMILE WEIL, MOISE GOLDSTEIN, WEISS DREYFOUS & SEIFERTH	1927	
6304	WILLIAM P. BURKE		TOLEDANO & REUSCH	1896	8,294

Address	Owner	Builder	Architect	Date	Cost
ST. CHARLES AVENUE (NAYADES)					
6330	CHRISTOPHER DOYLE			1896	10,000
7003	GONZALO ABAUANZA		FRANCIS MACDONNELL	1918	23,200
7004	EDWARD MARTINEZ	KELLY BROS.		1893	4,868
7022	EPHRAIM PHELPS, JR.	G.E. & T.E. REIFANN	EMILE WEIL	1916	4,935
7027	A.P. SAUER			1926	
7030	ROBERT G. EYRICH	HEINRICKS & DANNERMAN	WILLIAM BROS.	1899	8,787
7100	ST. CHARLES AVENUE BAPTIST CHURCH		FAVROT & LIVAUDAIS	1925	
7111	HENRY BLOCK		FAVROT & LIVAUDAIS	1906	10,000
7209-11	GABE HAUSMAN			1915	
7214	DOMINICAN CONVENT	G. MURRY	WILLIAM FITZNER	1882	25,000
7217-23	JOSEPH HASPEL	LOUISIANA CONTRACTING CO.		1914	9,000
7300	PETER FABACHER		TOLEDANO & WOGAN	1907	25,000
7320	M. LEVY, JR.	M. LEVY, JR.		1913	
SARATOGA STREET					
6110	HAMILTON P. JONES		ROBERT SOULE	1911	10,000
6131	F. MCGLOIN			1893	4,225
STATE STREET					
400	JOHN F. HILL			1896	2,416
403-05	DAVID JUNG & BAPTIST JUNG			1899	5,000
411,413-15, 417-19, 421-23, 425-27	BAPTIST JUNG			1899	5,000
422	PATRICK J. FINAN	HENRY HAFFNER	TOLEDANO & REUSCH	1897	2,000
631	R.V. MOISE			1897	3,000
636	C.H. MCKNIGHT			1886	
641	HENRY DANNEMANN			1903	30,000
600	EUGENE VAZ	EDWIN FERGUSON	JOHN BAEHR	1924	4,250
604-06	SECURITY BUILDING & LOAN	CHARLES ARNODT	JOHN BAEHR	1924	754
703	JOSEPH GONDOLF			1902	
715	ADAM KERBER	DANNER BROS.	HANS DIETTEL	1904	3,348
718-20	BENJAMIN HANEY	WILLIAM O'BRIEN		1923	6,475
728	REGINALD S. COCKS			1902	2,765
736	WILLIAM ARMSTRONG	J. BAEHR, JR.	JAMES DEGREY	1902	3,835
741	HENRY DANNEMANN			1903	3,000
821-23	AETNA HOMESTEAD	KENNETH COLOMB	THEODORE PERRIER	1925	8,000
900	SECURITY BUILDING & LOAN	JOHN BAEHR	WILLIAM MURRAY	1906	4,750
921, 929-31	ANNIE MANN	JOHN MINOT		1900	8,850
1002	WILLIAM B. THOMPSON			1895	3,000
1025-27	ANDREW HEFFNER	RICHARD MCCARTHY	RICHARD MCCARTHY	1905	4,000
1032	INDUSTRIAL HOMESTEAD	EDWIN MARKEL		1911	7,300
1121-23	MILLARD BLAND	PERRILLIAT-RICKEY	PERRILLIAT-RICKEY	1937	9,160
1200	FIREMEN'S BUILDING ASSN.	DANNEMANN & CHARLTON	DANNEMANN & CHARLTON	1902	3,850
1207	EDWARD MARX		FRANCIS MACDONNELL	1905	4,620

Address	Owner	Builder	Architect	Date	Cost
STATE STREET					
1218	THOMAS DOTY			1901	
1230	ROBERTA DOTY	DANNEMANN & CHARLTON	DANNEMANN & CHARLTON	1901	3,500
1236	LUCIUS C. SPENCER			1903	3,522
1237	ALLISON OWEN		DIBOLL & OWEN	1902	
1315	C.D. ABBOTT			1898	3,247
1322,28, 1334	LEON LAVEDAN			1902	
1407	MRS. COULON	M. FROMBERT		1895	5,000
1425	JOHN DAVIDSON	G.O. MALLEY		1894	4,290
1450	WILLIAM E. RAYMOND	CHARLES FAVROT	CHARLES FAVROT	1893	4,100
1462	F.D. MATHER	ATTAWAY & MOULLET	ATTAWAY & MOULLET	1893	4,700
1465	F.A. SCHNEIDAU	L.C. LECORGNE		1891	
1472	J.C. FEBIGER			1892	4,000
1505	ARTHUR NOLTE			1895	5,000
1515	STONEWALL JACKSON		ROBERT SOULE	1902	5,000
1525	B.F. GLOVER		ROBERT SOULE	1902	
1535	OMER VILLERE		FRANK P. GRAVELY	1897	6,500
1544	LOUIS KOHLMANN		EMILE WEIL	1907	
1614	EMILE KUNTZ	RUCKSTUHL & FICK	RENE GELPI	1940	12,500
1617	HUGH ST. PAUL	MARK SMITH, SR.	JULES DE LA VERGNE	1940	10,603
1621	JOHN GAUCHE			1896	
1627	I.K. LEVY	I.K. LEVY		1912	
1628	EMILE KUNTZ			1937	
1635	PAUL ALKER	OTIS SHARP		1896	5,937
1654	JOSEPH MORRIS			1904	
1655	ADOLPH GOLDSTEIN			1904	7,449
1669	BERNARD HESS	METROPOLITAN BUILDING CO.		1904	7,500
1680	S.W. BILLUPS		FAVROT & LIVAUDAIS	1912	10,000
1731	ALBERT WOLF	ALBERT WOLF		1912	
1755	SHELBY SEYMOUR		DIBOLL, OWEN & GOLDSTEIN	1896	3,950
1776	LAWRENCE DEBUYS		DEBUYS, CHURCHILL, LABOUISSE	1907	
1804	CITIZENS HOMESTEAD	PAUL CHARBONNET		1928	17,300
1810	FRANCIS ROSENFIELD			1909	
1837	LOUISE DENIS	A.C. BABIN & SON		1922	16,465
1838	MAURICE B. KREEGER		SOULE & MACDONNELL	1905	3,480
1844	FRANK SOULE		SOULE & MACDONNELL	1905	6,000
1912	G.H. CARNELSON	G.H. CARNELSON		1917	8,000
1930	ED CLEMENS		DOUGLAS FRERET	1937	
1938	PETER J. KELLY			1905	4,000
2021	HENRY C. PREVOST			1909	3,000
2022	CHARLES W. COHEN			1906	5,000
2027	O.E. BRECHTEL			1913	
2028	OSCAR A. SCHNEIDAU			1905	3,400
2032	SECURITY BUILDING & LOAN	DANNEMANN & CHARLTON	DANNEMANN & CHARLTON	1902	4,200

Address	Owner	Builder	Architect	Date	Cost
STATE STREET					
2112-14	L.E. DENIS		H.L. BURTON	1922	
2122	GEROGIA STEPHENSON	EDWIN MARKEL	EDWIN MARKEL	1928	18,100
2200	W.J. MITCHELL		FRANCIS W. CROSBY	1911	9,000
2218	LARZ A. JONES			1904	4,700
2223-25				1923	
2314-16	EDMOND HAASE	CHARBONNET BUILDING CO.		1923	7,400
2324-26-28	GREATER NEW ORLEANS HOMESTEAD	JOSEPH ARMON	JOSEPH ARMON	1923	12,500
2340	PAUL VALDEJO	CHARBONNET BUILDING CO.		1923	4,580
2401-03	IDEAL SAVINGS & HOMESTEAD	DENIS & HANDY	R.M. PUNIBA	1923	5,000
2620	THOMAS HATREL	WILLIAM O'BRIEN		1925	5,500
2635	URSULINE CONVENT	GEORGE GLOVER	ANDRY & BENDERNAGLE	1910-13	
2800	STEPHEN TULLY			1920	
STATE STREET DRIVE					
3127	HENRY PIER	ALEXANDER SMITH		1916	3,800
3145	SEIFERTH & NICAUD	JULIAN BARRIOS	AUGUST PEREZ	1941	8,740
3150	ALCEE FLOTTE	LINO DELAROSA		1922	8,200
3180-82	ROY BARTLETT	DENIS & HANDY		1926	12,000
3605	M.J. SMITH	ROBERT W. MARKEL		1915	
3609	FREDERICK KOENIGHER	JONES & ROESSLE	JONES & ROESSLE	1916	2,600
3617-19	WILLIAM COOK	EDWIN RHODES	EDWIN RHODES	1929	7,450
3802	HERBERT MEYER	EDWIN MARKEL		1928	7,950
3819	E.C. FROST	ROBERT W. MARKEL		1915	
3917	GEORGE LUCAS	PAUL CHARBONNET		1928	
3921	HARRY SCHMIDT	EDWIN MARKEL		1928	4,725
3935	ARMAND BLACKMAN	PAUL CHARBONNET	ADOLPH EHRENSING	1931	8,500
4150-52	MELVIN MATHES	REIMAN CONSTRUCTION	EARL MATHES	1940	8,300
4201	VERNON WATTS	JOHN JOHNSON	RALPH LALLY	1940	6,284
STORY STREET					
6120	JEANNIE HATZEL	HERMAN JOHNSON		1928	4,000
6316	JACOB ELSTRUTT	PAUL SEYBOLD	F.L. GOODWIN	1917	3,200
SYCAMORE STREET					
7100-02	FIDELITY HOMESTEAD	DENIS & HANDY	H.C. ZANDER	1922	4,300
7317-19	J. SINGERSON			1917	1,800
7329	FIDELITY HOMESTEAD ASSN.	THEARD & REILLY		1914	
TCHOUPITOULAS STREET (FRONT; LEVEE; NEW LEVEE; PUBLIC ROAD)					
5731-33	MATTHEW CONEY	MADISON BROWN		1873	775
5904-06	JOSEPH MAYER	CHARLES LAGASSE		1941	7,730
5917-19-21-23	BARBARA LARKEN			1895	
5945	SAMUEL HARRIS			1911	
5951	J.L. MEYER			1912	
TRIANON PLAZA					
1	TRIANON DEVELOPMENT CORP.		A.J. LORBER	1926	

Address	Owner	Builder	Architect	Date	Cost
TRIANON PLAZA					
2	TRIANON DEVELOPMENT CORP.			1925	
3	GEORGE B. JURGENS			1928	
5	ALBERT G. JOACHIM			1928	
6	J.A. JENNESS			1923	
7	HAROLD BLOOM			1926	
8	J.A. WALTER			1925	
VERSAILLES BOULEVARD					
1	G.J. HOUERE			1926	
2	ANEES MOGABGAB			1931	
3	MORRIS BAAR			1932	
5	DAVID VERLANDER			1927	
7	BARNARD SCHOTT			1935	
8	GEORGE DENINGER		WEISS, DREYFOUS, SEIFERTH	1928	
9	JENNY DELUCAS	PERRILLIAT RICKEY		1937	12,000
10	ROBERT H. BOH		GEORGE RIEHL & DONALD GRAVES	1963	
11	ANTHONY APRILL			1928	
12	J. LAPRYN			1926	
14	FISHER SIMMONS			1927	
15	ROY M. STRECKFUS			1935	
16	GERVAIS F. FAVROT			1927	
17	JAY WEIL, JR.	PAUL CHARBONNET	PAUL CHARBONNET	1938	25,000
19	ALBERT TUJAQUE		WEISS & DREYFOUS	1924	
20	JOHN POTTHARST			1928	
21	JULES L. VIDEAU			1934	
23	SAUL STREIFFER			1927	
24	AMEDEE GRANGER			1927	
25	ALBERT C. JACOBS, JR.			1931	
26	JAMES H. KEPPER			1929	
27	CLEO BABINGTON			1928	
28	WILLIAM GEORGE			1930	
29	RALPH C. LALLY	HERMAN MAKOFSKY	CHARLES PUMILIA	1928	4,000
32	STASSY GOLDMAN			1934	
33	JAMES WARE			1929	
34	GEORGE CLAY			1926	
35	WILLIAM A. GILLASPIE			1928	20,000
36	GEORGE DERBIGNY			1924	
37	HERBERT H. REIN			1928	
40	MOISE CAHN		WEISS, DREYFOUS, SEIFERTH	1929	
41	JOSEPH RAU			1928	
43	JAMES J. GILLY, JR.			1928	
44	EDWARD C. BAKER		HERBERT A. BENSON	1927	
46	WILLIAM W. CARTER			1928	
47	JOHN J. MCGOEY			1928	
48	R.R. ATKINSON			1928	

Address	Owner	Builder	Architect	Date	Cost
VERSAILLES BOULEVARD					
51	JERRY FITZPATRICK	NEW ORLEANS CONSTRUCTION CO.		1928	15,000
53	JEFFERSON C. WENCK	PAUL CHARBONNET		1929	11,430
55	ALBERT TUJAQUE			1928	
57	ED. L. LILLY			1926	
63	JOSEPH FABACHER		WEISS, DREYFOUS, SEIFERTH	1928	
68	BLANCHE KING			1927	
72	CECIL ROBERTS	ERNEST MONTEL		1938	6,440
77	MAUDE PIERCE	PAUL CHARBONNET	A.H. EHRENSING	1934	10,000
3325	MARY SCHMIDT	INTERSTATE LAND CO.		1918	3,000
3329	JANIE LAPEYRE	CHARLES BACKER		1918	2,100
3528	MARGARET BURKE	W. OSBORNE		1928	4,875
4020	RALPH TAYLOR	LINO DELAROSA		1929	14,500
4036	HENRY SCHAUMBURG	LOUIS HAMMER	LOCKETT & CHACHERE	1926	14,500
4123	ALLAIN ANDRY, JR.	C. EARL COLOMB, INC.		1940	7,225
4230	MARY DISCOM	WILFRED BLANCQ	A.H. EHRENSING	1930	8,500
4235	CHARLES DRAPEKIN	ROUX CONSTRUCTION CO.	JOSEPH MILLER	1946	16,361
WALNUT STREET (PARK)					
259	SIXTH DISTRICT BUILDING & LOAN	GEARY-OAKES CO.	GEARY-OAKES CO.	1924	6,900
266	A.B. BUTTERWORTH	WILLIAM WALLACE		1926	14,160
295	MARGARET PESCUD			1917	
298	R.H. WELSH			1924	12,000
299	EDWARD H. KEEP		FRANCIS MACDONNELL	1909	4,500
304-06	VERA LIENHARD	A.C. WILLIAMSON CO.		1925	10,300
325	HILLIARD MILLER		FAVROT & LIVAUDAIS	1927	
330	KATIE ALCORN	JOHN CHARLTON	JOHN CHARLTON	1920	16,164
333	BILL PENICK		PARHAM & GOLDSTEIN	1926	
342	W. SPREEN			1895	900
353	EDWARD H. KEEP		FRANCIS MACDONNELL	1911	
357	F. RALF MICHEL	RUFUS S. EWING		1916	
374	LOWELL HASPEL	MARK SMITH		1938	13,917
383	GEORGE H. DAVIS	GEORGE H. DAVIS	FRANCIS MACDONNELL	1915	
386	ALONZO M. WEST		M.H. GOLDSTEIN	1922	20,150
419	W. SCOTT BRYAN		FRANCIS MACDONNELL	1911	
429	CHARLES KELLS, JR.			1909	8,500
437	E. HOWARD MCCALEB, JR.		R.S. SOULE	1902	2,500
440	ALICE WOLCOTT			1924	
441	HENRY A. OTIS			1913	
472	ROBERT CONNER		R.S. SOULE	1912	
474-76	JACKSON & PROVOSTY	EDWIN MARKEL		1924	14,000
496	A.D. GAUDET	W.L. KEIFE		1911	
498	E. HOWARD MCCALEB, JR.		R.S. SOULE	1911	9,000
500	GEORGE W. YOUNG		GEORGE E. DICKEY & SON	1897	

Address	Owner	Builder	Architect	Date	Cost
WALNUT STREET (PARK)					
508	CLEMENT B. PENROSE			1899	3,500
512	FRANK FORD		JOHN CAMPBELL	1905	9,032
514	LEOPOLD VON TRESCKOW		R.S. SOULE	1911	8,000
518	SOL WEISS	SOL WEISS	WEISS & DREYFOUS	1921	60,000
570	GEORGE MOORE			1896	3,000
574	GERVAIS LOMBARD			1895	2,200
WEBSTER STREET					
404	JOSEPH RODRIGUEZ			1895	750
405	H.S. ROBERTS			1912	
414	MATHIAS J. ROTH			1895	2,250
417-19	D. WITKOFF			1912	
700	EXCELSIOR HOMESTEAD	EDWIN MARKEL		1911	3,500
704-06	HENRY STRECK	JACOB BAEHR	ABRAHAM MOISE	1909	3,720
722-24	GEORGE GEIER	CHARLES GEIER		1926	5,350
828-30	P. BECKER			1905	2,900
919	GERMAN PROTESTANT ORPHAN ASYLUM		CHARLES HILLGER	1869	
1009-11	LEONARD FRANS			1909	5,450
1015	M. ABBOTT			1914	
1029-31	A.M. BOENES	J.M. DEFRAITES		1917	2,500
1134	JAMES W. WARREN		WILLIAM NOLAN	1927	
1200	THOMAS MADDEN	HENRY HINRICHS	H.L. BURTON	1903	5,450
1207	CHARLES. A. ERNST			1898	3,000
1217	M.E. SCRATCHLEY			1900	2,765
1221	STANLEY D. GRAHAM			1897	2,775
1231	EUREKA HOMESTEAD			1897	
1306	SAMUEL RUSHA	CONRAD BOPP	WILLIAM FITZNER	1894	5,000
1323	EDWARD A. WHITE			1897	2,500
1333	MISS E. JOBIN			1895	6,100
1421	JAMES D. KITCHEN		FAVROT & LIVAUDAIS	1903	
1447-49	HAROLD WALKER	CLARENCE CHARLTON	CLARENCE CHARLTON	1938	9,500
1452	ALFRED M. CONWAY			1899	3,000
1535	RATHBONE E. DEBUYS		DEBUYS, CHURCHILL & LABOUISSE	1906	4,500
1536	DORA BAECKLEY			1900	2,400
1566	F.L. GUSTINE	L.C. LECORGNE		1891	5,000
WILLOW STREET (HENRY)					
5531-33, 5535-37	DAN POLESKY	SALVADORE LAROCCA	LOCKETT & CHACHERE	1926	13,300
5709-11	SIXTH DISTRICT BUILDING & LOAN	JOSEPH DUBE	JOSEPH DUBE	1924	6,300
5713-15	WESLING HILLE	DENIS & HANDY		1925	7,000
5719-21	J.O. GAITHER	A.C. WILLIAMSON CO.	F.S. WHITE	1925	10,500
7120	PROVIDENT BUILDING & LOAN	CHARLES AMMEN	WALTER C. KEENAN	1927	32,000
ZIMPLE STREET (MAGNOLIA)					
7008	SOUTHALL TATE	NEW ORLEANS CONSTRUCTION CO.	JOHN BAEHR	1923	14,200

SELECTIVE ARCHITECTURAL INVENTORY

ANNUNCIATION (Jersey)

6060-62, 6064-66, 6068-70, 6072-74 ANNUNCIATION, BURTHEVILLE

Typical of many double shotguns in the University section, these four double shotguns feature large, decorative brackets and ornate cornices. Built as rental property, they were likely constructed for Ada Menge, who purchased three lots on June 24, 1895, from Adolph Fleisch for $1,000. Tax records for 1895 indicate four new double "box houses" assessed at $350 each. The houses remained in the Menge family until 1905.

ARABELLA

936 ARABELLA, HURSTVILLE

This two-story residence dominating the neighborhood was probably built by Ella Knight Walker

in 1890. Her husband, George Walker, paymaster for the Southern Pacific Company, is listed in the 1891 city directory as residing at "Chestnut sw cor. Arabella."

Turned colonettes set on non-original bases with delicate brackets above are combined with small spindle elements. The spindle railing on the upper level appears to be original, but the lower-level railing has been removed. The iron fencing, typical of the period, is intact. There are remnants of a cistern foundation in the rear yard.

After two interim owners, Herman Stumborg bought the property in 1922, and his family retained ownership until 1980, selling to Bryce Williams Revely, the owner as of this writing.

1630 ARABELLA, HURSTVILLE

In 1846 free-man-of-color Henry Jacobs purchased this entire square No. 63 along with nine others from Josephine Olivier, widow of William Boswell. In a letter dated April 17, 1847, Jacobs described his property as "ten squares of ground purchased by me last summer per act before Barnett notary publick [sic], which is now enclosed and otherwise improved with a dwelling and other outhouses, all of which has been paid for." The house mentioned in this letter may in fact be the subject house, as the tax receipt of 1851 lists this square as having the highest valuation of the ten squares. At that time, the subject house faced St. Charles Avenue.

After two interim owners, Judah P. Benjamin and his brother Joseph purchased Squares 63 and 64 in 1853. Their sister, Mrs. Rebecca Levy, lived here and maintained the house until August 20, 1863, when federal troops seized it. Judah P. Benjamin was a prominent New Orleans attorney who served as Louisiana's United States senator, U.S. secretary of war and secretary of state, and attorney general of the Confederacy. After the Civil War, he fled to England with a bounty on his head. There he eventually became Queen's counsel and codified English laws on sales in an 1868 book entitled *Benjamin on Sales.*

In 1864 Reconstruction Lt. Gov. James Madison Wells purchased the house for delinquent state taxes. Less than a year later, he sold the house to L. Madison Day, who lost it in a sheriff's sale to James Zuntz. In 1892, after three subsequent owners, John Bonner

sold to Carrie Newsom, wife of Alphonse O. Pessou, the present lot minus five feet and "the house situated on the center of the square, together with the contents of said house and all cisterns, foundations, and appertenances [sic] connected with said house, which said building, contents and appertenances are to be removed by the purchaser at her own expense." It was at this time that Pessou moved the house to its present location.

There have been four subsequent owners, all of whom have undertaken extensive renovations to the house: Dr. Henry Octave Colomb, 1896-1919; Mrs. Carla Bornemann, 1919-1962; Mr. and Mrs. A.L. Schlesinger, 1962-1995; and Mr. and Mrs. Edwin O. Schlesinger, 1995 to present.

Among the alterations to this Greek Revival center hall cottage have been the replacement of the original gallery railing with a flower-motif cast iron railing, and the likely replacement of the porch columns with the present Corinthian columns. A recent renovation of the house has revealed that the rear portion is older than that facing Arabella. Colombage construction was discovered and there was likely brick infill, as a few bricks were found above the sill. Ceiling joists in the rear portion are beaded, and the attic floorboards were exposed from below. The front portion of the house is of a standard stud construction, with plaster ceilings. It is possible that the rear portion is the original circa 1847 house built by Jacobs and that the front was added to it.

The house is a landmark, designated by both the Orleans Parish Landmarks Commission and the New Orleans Historic District Landmarks Commission.

1631 ARABELLA, HURSTVILLE

Jessie Schwabacher, wife of William Feingold, purchased this site in two separate transactions in 1912 from Robert Guerard and built the present two-story Craftsman residence. The 1913 city directory

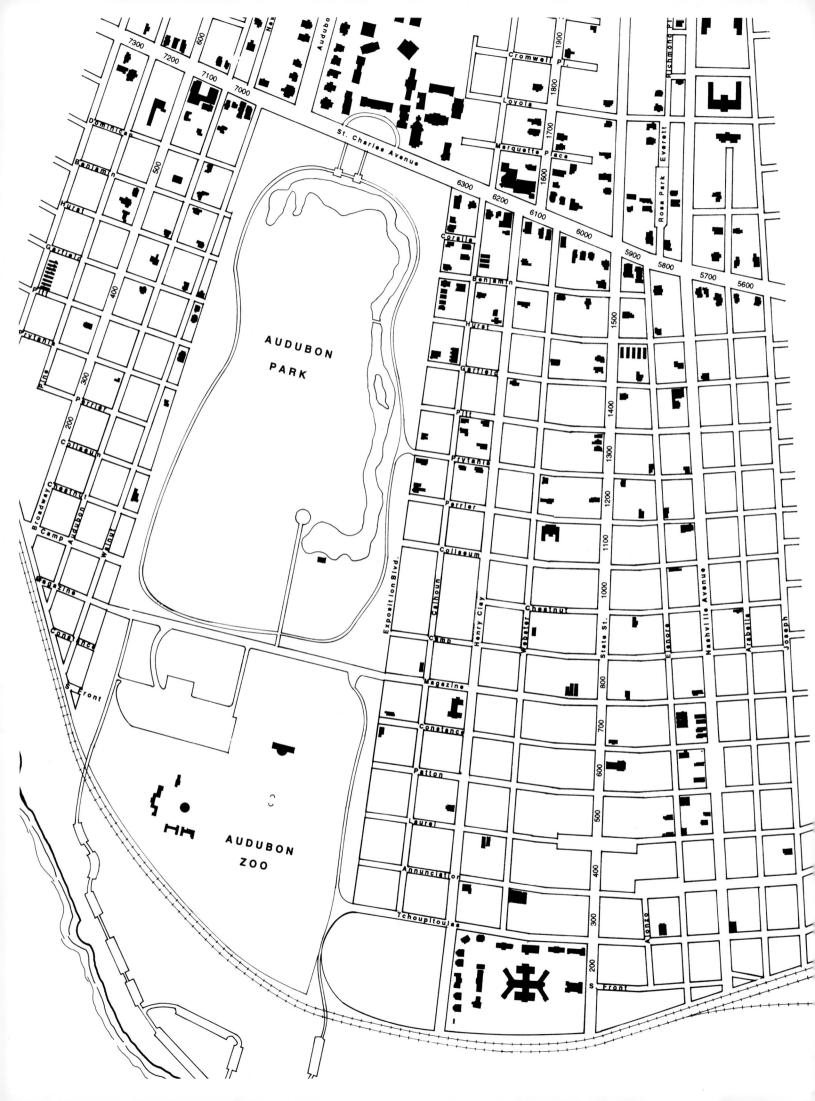

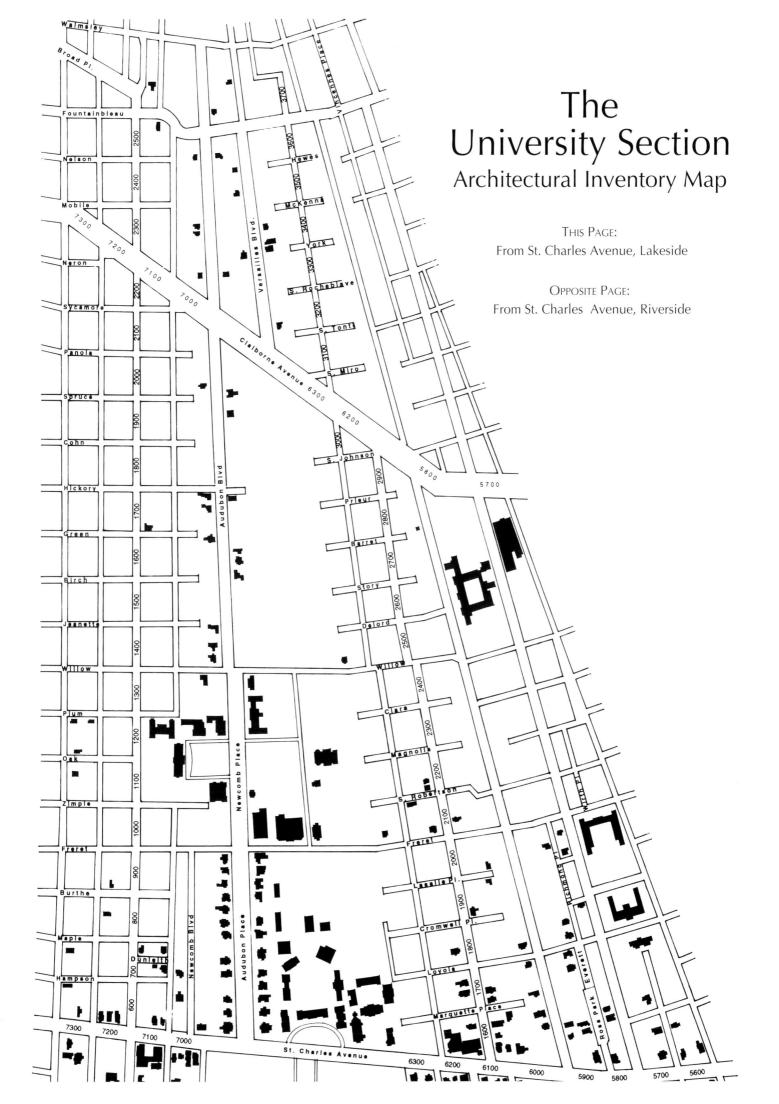

The University Section
Architectural Inventory Map

THIS PAGE:
From St. Charles Avenue, Lakeside

OPPOSITE PAGE:
From St. Charles Avenue, Riverside

lists William Feingold with Levy, Loeb and Company, dry goods, as residing here. Five years later, Clemencia Levy, wife of Isidore Marks, bought the property, and it remained in the Marks family for forty-nine years. The E. Howard Read family has owned the house since 1967.

Like many Craftsman houses, it is built of concrete block and has exposed rafter ends and a red tile roof. This style of architecture was most popular in New Orleans during the second decade of the twentieth century, but continued to be used until World War II.

1700 ARABELLA, HURSTVILLE

On July 19, 1939, cotton broker Frank Anderson purchased this site from Arabella Properties for $13,350 and commissioned F.D. Parham and M.H. Goldstein, architects, to design this French Eclectic house that same year. The French Eclectic style became popular after World War I and remained in fashion until World War II. According to the June 1918 issue of the local magazine *Building Review*, American soldiers were in "intimate contact with the real architecture of the French people" during the war and upon their return wanted French-style houses.

In 1968 Anderson sold the house to Alice Gross Newhouse, who sold it to Brenda Pumphrey in 1982. Two years later, Katherine and Richard Buckman purchased the house, selling it to Marc and Lisa Winston in 1990.

AUDUBON BOULEVARD

4 AUDUBON BOULEVARD, FOUCHER TRACT

Harry Swift, manager of L.B. Price Mercantile Company, purchased this site in 1922 and obtained a sewerage and water permit for the house in 1924. The Swifts sold the house four years later to Dalton Barranger for $53,250. After two subsequent owners, it was puchased by Her Majesty's Minister of Public Buildings and Works of the United Kingdom of Great Britain and Northern Ireland.

The house is Colonial Revival in style, with Georgian influences. The elaborate doorway with its broken pediment is typical of the Georgian style, while the two side porches, now altered, are common to the Colonial Revival.

10 AUDUBON BOULEVARD, FOUCHER TRACT

Chaucer French, first vice-president of Woodward Wight & Company, purchased this site in 1913 from Luke Boudreaux for $5,400 and, according to Sewerage and Water Board records, constructed the present house in 1913. The Frenches retained the house until 1961 when George Bohn, Jr. purchased it for $68,000. Five years later, Bohn sold the house to Fred Kahn II, who sold it in 1977 to Dr. and Mrs. Harold Fuselier, the owners as of this writing.

The house is Mediterranean in style.

14 AUDUBON BOULEVARD, FOUCHER TRACT

In 1916 Luca Vaccaro purchased Lots 22 and 24 from Louis C. Frantz for $3,500 and lots 16, 18, and 20 from Charles Duval for $5,400. Architect Edward Sporl designed a residence for this site, which tax records indicate was never built. Sporl's drawings for the house are preserved in the Southeastern Architectural Archive at Tulane University.

In 1923 investment counselor Simon J. Shwartz, Jr. purchased the site for $15,000 and commissioned Emile Weil to design the present Spanish Eclectic house. The original ornament of the house built by contractor Charles Gibert is concentrated at the main entrance.

Gov. Huey Pierce Long acquired the house from Shwartz in 1932. Upon Long's assassination, his widow sold the house to the State of Louisiana, which operated it as a museum in Long's memory and later as the home for the chancellor of Louisiana State University Medical School.

In 1979 the house returned to private ownership and was designated a landmark by the New Orleans Historic District Landmarks Commission. In 1990 the Orleans Parish Landmarks Commission marked this residence with a bronze plaque.

49 AUBUDON BOULEVARD, FOUCHER TRACT

Aline Fayers, wife of Robert Hogsett, probably built this Spanish Eclectic house in 1923 and sold it the same year to Anne Lejeune, wife of Francis Lejeune. The Lejeune family, as of this writing, still owns the property.

Solomonic columns, a popular detail of this style, articulate the entrance bay and relieve a rather austere facade. Other characteristics of the style employed in this house include a stucco facade, red tile roof, wrought iron balconies, and arch-headed

openings. Locally, the Spanish Eclectic style was most popular during the 1920s.

55 AUDUBON BOULEVARD, FOUCHER TRACT

Built in 1925 for Dr. and Mrs. James Flinn, Sr., this Mediterranean style stucco residence sports an elaborate entrance surround. Such detailing was made popular by the San Diego Exposition of 1915 and consequently is often referred to as "Exposition Style."

Mrs. Flinn retained the house until 1945 when it was sold to Theodore Dendinger for $38,000. It remained in the Dendinger family until it was bought by Norman and Maryanne Mott in 1993.

65 AUDUBON BOULEVARD, FOUCHER TRACT

This L-shaped Dutch Colonial Revival house is built on two lots. The distinctive gambrel roof and gable-end chimneys with quarter-round windows are hallmarks of this style. Henry Burke Matthews purchased these lots for $5,150 and obtained the sewerage and water hookup on September 28, 1924. That same year, a new house was assessed for $11,340. After four interim owners, Mrs. Anna Louise Cabrera inherited the house in 1960.

70 AUDUBON BOULEVARD, FOUCHER TRACT

This Mediterranean villa dates to 1912 when attorney Arthur McGuirk incorporated architectural elements from his previous house at 2438 Esplanade. When McGuirk sold his Esplanade property in 1911 for Esplanade Girls High School, now John McDonogh Senior High School, he retained the right

to either old or New England or Southern California for ideas and inspiration."

In 1927, the *Times-Picayune* interviewed several local architects about the possibility of reviving the local colonial architecture and quoted Richard Koch:

The question of the adaptability of the old French colonial plantation houses like Mrs. Schertz' [old Spanish Customhouse] on Bayou St. John is being asked of architects repeatedly, and the reason why such houses are not built is due to the high cost of construction. The average person cannot afford to build such a house, and with our present land values, with rare exceptions, it is nearly impossible.

There is no doubt that it is the ideal house to build in this climate, for the porch in our long summers breaks the heat and gives us a home that is delightful to live in. However, there has been an awakened interest in this type of house and a tendency for some people to make sacrifices so that they may live more comfortably, and I feel that the next few years will show a distinct trend toward buildings in this part of the country that are adaptable to our climate and not copies of what is being done around New York.

The Prices sold the house in 1946 to George Davidson, who sold it to Morris Burka in 1951. In 1992 Laura and Darryl Byrd purchased the house.

100 AUDUBON BOULEVARD, FOUCHER TRACT

This French Eclectic house was constructed in 1928 for Florence Stich Besthoff, widow of Sidney J. Besthoff, Sr., founder of Katz and Besthoff Drugstores. Built at a cost of $5,430.08 by J.A. Haase, Jr. Construction Company, it was designed by Herbert A. Benson of Emile Weil and Associates, a prominent, early-twentieth century firm that designed such New Orleans landmarks as the Saenger Theater, Whitney Bank, and First National Bank of Commerce.

The steep roof, smooth facade with quoins, casement windows, and basket wrought iron balconies were inspired by the chateaux of eighteenth century France. The French Eclectic style was popularized by numerous architectural books of the 1920s, such as *A History of French Architecture* (1921) and *Small Manor Houses and Farmsteads in France* (1926), and embraced by many returning World War I veterans.

The Besthoffs made alterations to the house in 1933, according to the designs of Weiss, Dreyfous, and Seiferth. In 1982 Mrs. Sidney Besthoff, Jr. sold the house to Dr. and Mrs. Noel Mills.

199 AUDUBON BOULEVARD, FOUCHER TRACT

This two-story stucco residence, with tile roof, prominent cartouche, and rusticated entry, is uncommitted as to style, although Mediterranean might be most appropriate. Large hedges obscure most of the ground-floor design.

to remove the improvements on the site within four months of the act of sale. This large brick house was originally constructed in 1858 by builders Little and Middlemiss according to the designs of Henry Howard and Albert Diettel for William Vredenberg. Floor plans of the original Esplanade Avenue and this Audubon Boulevard house are similar, and original specifications match details found in this Audubon Boulevard residence. The rough stucco exterior and red tile roof were not part of the original reconstruction on Audubon Boulevard, but were added by the Geoghagen family after they purchased the house in 1924.

A long-time resident of Audubon Boulevard told subsequent owners of the house, Mr. and Mrs. John Roy, Jr., that she remembered that the house was moved in mule-drawn wagons, piece by piece, down Claiborne from Esplanade and erected here. The Roys bought the house in 1975, selling in 1994 to Daniel O. Conwill IV, who has recently undertaken a major renovation of the house that is not complete as of this writing.

84 AUDUBON BOULEVARD, FOUCHER TRACT

In 1928 the local architectural firm of Favrot and Livaudais employed the French Eclectic style for Irwin Isaacs' new home. The architects had experimented with the style in their design of the residence at 325 Walnut the previous year, but this is a more restrained example of the style that was popularized by soldiers returning from France after World War I.

Favrot and Livaudais had an established relationship with the Isaacs family, having designed many of their houses, such as 5120 St. Charles Avenue (Volume VII) as well as their business, a Canal Street department store. Descendants of the Isaacs family sold this imposing residence in 1967 to Dr. John Ochsner, a prominent physician and 1990 King of Carnival.

89 AUDUBON BOULEVARD, FOUCHER TRACT

Dr. and Mrs. Henry Bartlett built the first house to occupy this site in 1920. According to the building contract of that year, it was a one-and-one-half-story residence costing $13,500. However, in 1934 when Henry Grady Price purchased the site for $5,610, the house no longer existed.

Richard Koch designed the present house for Price in 1935, shortly after dissolving his architectural partnership with Charles Armstrong. Koch's precedent for this French Colonial Revival residence was the so-called "Spanish Customhouse" on Bayou St. John.

Building Review, a local architectural magazine, printed a letter in 1919 from New Orleanian Nathaniel Curtis, then a University of Illinois architectural professor, who observed that the influence of New Orleans architecture was spreading nationally since the 1913 American Institute of Architects convention there. However, the French Colonial had not become a revival locally. Curtis argued that it would take only one good example before a client would not have "to send his architect in imagination

Carl Dahlberg, president of the State Agricultural Credit Corporation, built this house in 1926. As of this writing, it remains in the Dahlberg family.

217 AUDUBON BOULEVARD, FOUCHER TRACT

Architect Walter Cook Keenan designed this Craftsman house, which was featured in a local architectural magazine, *Building Review,* shortly after construction in 1919. A comparison of the present house with the photographs in that publication shows little change, other than the loss of decorative joist ends at the belt course.

B. Palmer Hardie, secretary-treasurer of Williams-Richardson Company, wholesale dry goods, was the first owner of the house. Subsequent owners were Paul Thomson (1924-34), Harris Hyman, Jr. (1935-52), Shepard Shushan (1952-79), and Ann Bremermann Holden (1979-81). Since 1981 the house has been owned by Leslie Newman, wife of Edward Kohnke IV.

220 AUDUBON BOULEVARD, FOUCHER TRACT

The original fieldstone columns supporting the wraparound porch of this California Style bungalow have been replaced by boxed wood columns. The stones were similar to those employed in the chimney.

Built in 1910 for Joseph Rhodes, the house remained in the Rhodes family until 1957 when Sina Blumenfeld, wife of Maurice Blumenfeld, purchased it for $44,500. As of this writing, there have been three subsequent owners.

This is perhaps one of the oldest California bungalows in the city. 1911 was long considered the date of the first California Style bungalow here, as cited by *Building Review,* a local architectural magazine. This example predates by one year the two cited by that publication.

258 AUDUBON BOULEVARD, FOUCHER TRACT

On June 30, 1927, Thorp purchased lots 8 and 10 from Jackson Homestead for $9,000 and later that year built the present house, according to Sewerage and Water Board records and tax rolls. In 1940 the house was transferred to James Thorp. In 1945 his succession sold it to John Whitty for $26,200. Two years later, Agnes Murphy and her children, William and Edna, purchased the house. In 1955 the Murphys sold it to Marilyn and Basil Rusovich, Jr., the owners as of this writing.

The pressed brick Mediterranean Villa was assessed at $10,000 when first built. Like most houses of this style, it employs round-headed first-floor openings and square-headed second-floor openings. Typical period ornament is seen in the transoms of the first-floor openings adjacent to the lake-end entry and beneath the central second-floor window.

265 AUDUBON BOULEVARD, FOUCHER TRACT

Here is yet another Mediterranean Villa, employing a standard design formula with slight variations. This example features a Palladian entry with a decorative central window.

On September 1, 1921, Dorothea Gillespie, wife of attorney Prentice Edrington, Jr., purchased five lots from James E. Edmonds and on January 20, 1922, entered into a $16,500 building contract with Frank Bowers for the construction of the house. Four years later, Edrington sold it to Donald Yarbrough for $33,000. A November 15, 1925, advertisement for the sale of the house described it as

> built of the finest material under supervision of a leading architect. . . . There is a tiled entry and terrace, large living hall, tiled sun room, music room, elegant dining room opening onto tiled terrace overlooking garden, butlery, kitchen, 3 bedrooms, glass enclosed sleeping porch, 2 well appointed tiled baths, automatic hot air heat, a perfect home.

In 1930 Paul Maloney purchased the residence, selling it thirteen years later to Nelson Hawkins, who sold it three years later to Richard Montgomery. As of this writing, it is still owned by the Montgomery family.

290 AUDUBON BOULEVARD, FOUCHER TRACT

Architect Walter Cook Keenan designed this Swiss style residence as his own domicile. Keenan acquired the site in 1913 from the developer of Audubon Boulevard for $2,200 and apparently built the present house three years later, according to Sewerage and Water Board records. The house remained in the Keenan family until 1937 when it was sold to Zenith Realty along with six lots in Carrollton and

stock. Zenith Realty sold the house in 1966 to Rose Bayola Geeck, and the Geecks retain ownership as of this writing.

296 AUDUBON BOULEVARD, FOUCHER TRACT

Although this house does not have a gambrel roof, it is still considered to be Dutch Colonial Revival. The use of an apron roof at the mid-point of the facade is a variant form of this style, as seen in period pattern books.

William J. Teselle purchased this site in 1910 for $2,700 and built this house in 1923, according to a building contract passed before the notary A.D. Danziger. The contract called for Charbonnet Building Company to build the house in less than ninety working days at a cost of $14,600. Original title restrictions required that buildings must cost in excess of $3,500 and have a twenty-five-foot setback and ten-foot rear yard, and allowed no businesses or Negroes. The house remained in the Teselle family until 1967 when it was sold to Charles L. Brown, Jr. Fifteen years later, Dr. and Mrs. George M. Haik, Jr. bought the residence and own it as of this writing.

333 AUDUBON BOULEVARD, FOUCHER TRACT

In 1927 attorney Isaac S. Heller purchased this site with the house on it from Clio and Rufus Perkins for $22,000, although Sewerage and Water Board records indicate Heller obtained the permit on September 6, 1926. The Heller family lived in the house

more than sixty years, selling it in 1993 to Mr. and Mrs. Herbert McCall.

This two-story stucco Mediterranean Villa is typical of many residences in the University section, following a standard design formula that includes a large tile roof, well-detailed front door, round-headed first-floor openings, and square-headed second-floor openings pushed close to the roof.

334 AUDUBON BOULEVARD, FOUCHER TRACT

This is another variant form of the Dutch Colonial Revival style, similar to 296 Audubon Boulevard. Contractor Walter M. Geary purchased the site on June 14, 1924, and obtained sewerage and water hookup two days later. The 1924-25 tax rolls cite the house as extant. Geary retained the house for only three years, selling to Arthur Rosenfeld for $22,000. A 1926 advertisement for the sale of the house placed in the *Times-Picayune* for Geary by realtor Harold Stream describes it as

artistic Two Story Home Green Tiled Roof Dutch Colonial Architecture. . . . A-1 condition, shady side of street, large lawn, garden & shade trees, terraced front tiled approach, long stylish living room with paneled walls, tiled sun parlor, dining room, breakfast room, pantry, kitchen, built in features, hood over stove, hardwood floors, American radiator, hot water heat, hot and cold water. Four well ventilated corner bedrooms, two handsome tiled baths, shown clothes closets, linen closets, birch doors, ivory woodwork, neutral tone walls. Laundry with stationary tubs, servants toilets, etc. Large double garage.

The Rosenfeld heirs sold the house in 1943 to Stanley Lemarie at a $5,000 loss. Mr. and Mrs. John Lewis purchased it in 1962, selling it in 1968 to Elise and Milton Walther, the owners as of this writing.

425 AUDUBON BOULEVARD, FOUCHER TRACT

Here is a novel variation on the Colonial Revival bungalow, popularized by *Craftsman Magazine*. The inspiration here is the modest scale of a Cape Cod cottage; however, it in no way duplicates one. Employed are a red concrete tile roof, stone and brick chimney, hooded front door, oversized columns supporting a pergola-like roofed side porch, and mitered siding at the corners.

On January 23, 1923, Harold Guthans purchased lots 9 and 11 and obtained a Sewerage and Water Board hookup on April 4, 1923. Guthans is never listed as residing here; in 1929 he recorded a twelve-month lease with J.H. O'Dowd at $100 per month.

In 1930 Guthans sold the house to Abraham Goldberg, who sold it in 1937 to Miriam Cohen. In 1942 Hilda and John Lea purchased the house for $9,500, selling it in 1951 to Leonard Moore, who sold it in 1954 to Dr. Gustave Weber, whose family retains ownership as of this writing.

AUDUBON PLACE

1 AUDUBON PLACE, FOUCHER TRACT

Favrot and Livaudais designed this imposing house for attorney William S. Penick in 1910. Penick was also the president of Penick and Ford, sugar and molasses manufacturers, and founder of H.G. Hill grocery stores, subsequently acquired by Winn-Dixie.

The architects employed a green tile roof, large brackets visually supporting a generous overhang, and brick porch columns with decorative cartouches for this Mediterranean Villa. The second-floor porch railing is not part of the original design. Tax records for 1911 list among the numerous rooms of the house a living room, dining room, side porch, sun porch, library, reception hall, kitchen, servants' dining room, back hall, four bedrooms, upper hall, and pantry. The *Daily States* of August 31, 1911, describes the recently completed house thusly:

Designed in Spanish Renaissance and is of brick and frame construction with artistic tile roof. The interior finishing with hardwood floors is in Colonial classic and French Renaissance, most artistically done. . . . It is classed as one of the handsomest as well as largest private residences in the city, and has attracted a great deal of attention, even among its many pretentious neighbors closely adjacent.

The house remained in the Penick family until 1946 when the present owners, the Lester Lautenschlaeger family, acquired it. Lester Lautenschlaeger was the recipient of the 1970 Times-Picayune Loving Cup.

2 AUDUBON PLACE, FOUCHER TRACT

William T. Jay built this impressive Southern Colonial house in 1908, according to the designs of Toledano and Wogan, at a cost of $15,000. *The Daily States* on August 31, 1908, reported on the construction:

This handsome dwelling which is in colonial style of architecture, two stories and a basement in height is now under construction. It is built of wood with pressed brick veneering and contains seven bedrooms. Besides these there are the

garage house for the automobiles and the stables for the livestock. The interior of this palatial residence will be entirely in mahogany with frescoed walls. The reception hall is to be elaborately ornamented in the most artistic plaster relief work.

In keeping with the Colonial style, the red pressed brick was unpainted, as seen in the old photographs, which also illustrates the roof railing that has since been lost. Because of developers' requirements that the house face Audubon Place and the owner's desire to face St. Charles Avenue, the house actually has two major entrances.

Jay, a cotton broker with Keplinger and Brown and vice president of Union Lumber Company of Madisonville, Louisiana, sold the house in 1917 to produce importer Samuel Zemurray for $60,000. Zemurray, the driving force of United Fruit Company and recipient of the 1938 Times-Picayune Loving Cup, remodeled the house in 1917 under the direction of architect Edward Sporl. Zemurray's widow donated the house in 1965 to Tulane University for use as the president's residence. See color interior photograph section for interior view.

3 AUDUBON PLACE, FOUCHER TRACT

This is the second house built by the Hobson family on this site. In 1894 Carrie Thorn, wife of John H. Hobson, a broker with the firm Fairchild and Hobson, purchased the vacant site for $7,500 with her separate funds. The original house, which she had constructed two years later by builder Otis W. Sharp at a cost of $13,400, was destroyed by fire. In 1900 the Hobsons built the present spacious, Queen Anne stuccoed residence, according to the designs of Favrot and Livaudais. The house remained in the Hobson family for forty-eight years until William Gordon Hayward purchased it. In 1984 Rosalyn and Charles Steiner bought the house.

4 AUDUBON PLACE, FOUCHER TRACT

James Jackson Manson of Manson Bros., a salt company, purchased this site from Crescent Land, developers of Audubon Place, in 1894 for $7,000 and built the present residence in 1895 at a cost of $12,900. An 1898 fire gutted the house, and it was rebuilt in 1899 at a cost of $11,000. It remained in

the Manson family until 1971 when Mary and Anthony Valentino acquired it.

The house is an unusual expression of the Queen Anne, with minor overtones of the Richardsonian Romanesque notable in the column capitals, the cavernous entrance, and the stone veneer.

5 AUDUBON PLACE, FOUCHER TRACT

The same 1898 fire that destroyed the original house at 3 Audubon Place also destroyed the original house on this site, which had been designed by architects Sully, Burton and Stone Company and built at a cost of $9,779 by contractors Darantel and Diaselles for James Legendre, an attorney and president of the Morris Building and Land Improvement Company.

After the fire, Legendre changed architects, commissioning Frank Gravely to design the present house, which was built in 1899. Gravely also designed 22 Audubon Place, which is more typical of his work, and 7 Audubon Place. In this Queen Anne design, Gravely employed a tower, a massive roof with gable bay window, half-timbering, and gooseneck porch railing.

The house remained in the Legendre family until 1926. After five transactions, it was purchased in 1991 by Mr. and Mrs. James Reiss, the owners as of this writing.

6 AUDUBON PLACE, FOUCHER TRACT

This is the second residence to occupy this site. The original house, designed by Suthron Duval, was built in 1894 for Lucie and Philip Rice at a cost of $12,300. Lucie Rice purchased the vacant land with her separate funds from the developers for $5,000. In 1896 Rice, manager of Rice, Born and Company, hardware dealers, sold the house and site to William F. Howell for $15,000. It was returned to Philip Rice in 1900 for back taxes. In 1902 Lucie Rice intervened, asserting that all of her husband's acts regarding 6 Audubon Place were invalid, as she was the sole owner. The same year she sold the property to sugar-broker Charles Manson for only $5,000, as an 1899 fire had destroyed the original house.

The *Daily States* in 1903 reported on Soulé and MacDonnell's design for Charles Manson's new house: "This building which is two stories and an attic in height, contains ten spacious rooms, bedrooms, parlor, dining room, library, drawing room, etc., with baths and servants quarters. The style of architecture is very graceful, the stone veneering adding to the effect. Completed it cost about $17,000."

Following its construction in 1904, the house remained in the Manson family until 1950. After an interim owner, it was purchased in 1977 by Loving Enterprises, a Coleman family company. Today it is the residence of Mr. and Mrs. James J. Coleman, Jr.

7 AUDUBON PLACE, FOUCHER TRACT

Favrot and Livaudais designed a residence for Anais Armant, widow of Emile Legendre, for this site,

as reported in the *Daily Picayune* of September 1, 1901. According to the tax records, this house burned in an 1899 fire either while under construction or shortly after it was completed.

Late in December 1908 and early 1909, Emile Legendre signed contracts for carpentry, brick, and concrete work for the present house, according to architect Frank Gravely's plans. A 1912 photograph of the house indicates that the dormers have since been altered, the original wood second-floor porch railing replaced by an iron railing, and the house enlarged toward Freret Street.

In 1915 the Legendre heirs sold the house to Paul F. Jahncke, vice-president of Jahncke Navigation Company. It remained in the Jahncke family until 1966. After two subsequent owners, ladies fashion shop owner Yvonne LeFleur and her husband, James C. Walsh, purchased the house in 1986.

9 AUDUBON PLACE, FOUCHER TRACT

Dr. C. Edmund Kells, Jr., a dentist, purchased this site in June 1894 for $5,500 from the developers of Audubon Place. The *Daily Picayune* of September 1, 1895, reported that Kells obtained a building permit during the previous twelve months for a two-story dwelling costing $9,000. This house apparently survives as the oldest residence on Audubon Place.

This highly fanciful Queen Anne residence features an unusual stone chimney balanced by a corner tower with decorative lightning rod and wrought iron porch rail with a flame motif which is repeated on the porch. True to the style, the facade is very picturesque, textural, and imaginative.

In 1908 Charles W. Ziegler purchased the home for $26,500. Fourteen years later, Cecile Ware bought the house with her own funds, independent from her husband, Walter Ware, for $28,000. The following year, in 1923, the Wares sold the house to Henry J. Porter for a substantial profit.

During the Great Depression, Porter's widow transferred the house to Frank Realty with an agreement to buy it back in 1935; however, she never regained ownership. In 1938 Fortune Jaubert, Jr. purchased it for $18,360 and retained it until Neil Johnson purchased it in 1950. In 1976 Loving Enterprise, a Coleman family company, acquired the property, and it remained in the Coleman family until Ann and James Holden bought it in 1981.

10 AUDUBON PLACE, FOUCHER TRACT

This house does not fit neatly into any stylistic category. The rough-hewn stone is reminiscent of the Richardsonian Romanesque style, and the millwork of the Colonial Revival. Frank P. Gravely and Company, which designed this house for cotton factor Hugh Delacey Vincent, employed a similar noncommittal motif for 4534 St. Charles Avenue (see Volume VII); however, there the mixture is more Romanesque and Mediterranean Villa while this example is more refined and imposing. As evidenced by old photographs, the house has lost its original widow's walk.

Tax records for 1899 indicate that Vincent was assessed for a new residence, and the *Daily Picayune* that year reported that he had obtained a permit for a two-story frame-and-stone residence on Audubon Place costing $10,000. The house remained in the Vincent family until 1964 when the Coleman family acquired it. As of this writing, it is home to Mr. and Mrs. James Coleman, Sr. James Coleman was the 1980 Times-Picayune Loving Cup recipient. See color interior photograph section for interior view.

11 AUDUBON PLACE, FOUCHER TRACT

One of the best-designed houses on Audubon Place, this monumental Renaissance Revival structure reflects the wealth of its first owner, banker Robert E. Craig. Local architect Emile Weil's 1922 design exhibits the planning and detailing of the Ecole des Beaux Arts, more typical of an earlier decade. Drawings for the house are preserved at Tulane's Southeastern Architectural Archive.

A previous house on this site documented in the *Illustrated Sunday Magazine,* was the residence of bank president Augustin Wheeler. He purchased two lots from the developers, Crescent Land, in 1895 and commissioned Suthron R. Duval to design a two-and-one-half-story stone-and-wood residence, which was built on one lot by G.W. Van Horn for $15,000. The property remained in the Wheeler family until 1911 when it was sold to banker Chapman Hyams and his wife Sarah. Apparently the house was destroyed in 1919 because the property value of the lot on which the house stood dropped radically and it is noted as a vacant lot.

Through two separate transactions, Robert E. Craig purchased the original two Wheeler lots in order to build the subject house. Tax records for 1925 indicate the house was under construction that year. The Craig family retained the house until 1944 when the Mossler family acquired it. In 1993 Elizabeth and Michael Carbine II purchased it from the succession of Evelyn Kizer Mossler.

12 AUDUBON PLACE, FOUCHER TRACT

Yet another Frank P. Gravely and Company design, this house demonstrates another early-twentieth century eclectic style—Tudor Revival. The first floor is of stone veneer while the upper portion is of half-timber design. The steep roof, a dominant design element, is a very practical solution to New Orleans' excessive annual rainfall. A fire in the house destroyed the elaborate third-floor, street-facing dormer.

Mamie Folwell Legendre, wife of Emile Legendre, purchased the vacant land in 1894 from Audubon Place developers, built the present house in 1909, and in 1926 sold the residence to Mary Louise Penick, widow of James Polk. Three years later, J. Blanc Monroe acquired the property. Upon his death in 1960, the house was donated to the Tulane Educational Fund. In 1967 shipping magnate Erik Johnsen, who reigned as Rex in 1991, bought the house and retained it until 1994 when a company owned by John Havens acquired it.

15 AUDUBON PLACE, FOUCHER TRACT

This massive stone house was likely built in 1899 for Tullis C. Walker. It is dominated by an overpowering hip roof with two large dormers facing St. Charles Avenue and an unusual wall dormer facing Audubon Place. The conical roof of the tower and an original dormer atop the wall dormer have been lost. The roof is balanced by the wraparound stone porch on the uptown-river corner of the building.

In 1903 Walker sold the house to George Dodge. His family sold it the following year to John Warfield, whose widow lost it to Charles Dennery in a suit filed by Union Title Guaranty. Dennery quickly sold the house to Albert B. Patterson, president of New Orleans Public Service, Rex in 1937, and 1944 recipient of the Times-Picayune Loving Cup. Patterson's heirs sold the property to the James Coleman family in 1975, and it is owned at this writing by the Thomas Coleman family.

16 AUDUBON PLACE, FOUCHER TRACT

The *Daily States* in 1903 boasted that this Toledano and Wogan-designed house was a model of "architectural beauty and thoroughly up-to-date in every particular." Its present facade, executed for owner Harry Spiro, lacks sympathy for the original design as seen in the old photograph. Its original Colonial Revival design was indeed a fine example of the style's transitional period from free-spirited to academically correct replication.

The house was originally designed for Angie and James W. Hearn and built in 1901 at a cost of $14,000. James Hearn was president of the New Orleans Coffee Company. Thomas J. Freeman owned the house from 1911 until 1919 when Rudolf S. Hecht, banker and civic leader, purchased it. Hecht was a founding member of the International House and was awarded the Times-Picayune Loving Cup in 1922. His heirs sold the house to Harry T. Spiro in 1960.

17 AUDUBON PLACE, FOUCHER TRACT

Attorney Felix J. Dreyfous built this Mediterranean Villa residence in 1921. Sewerage and Water Board records indicate that service was initiated on April 20, 1921, and tax records for 1922 describe the present house as a new, two-story, cement-and-stone single house with ten rooms and three baths. They also mention a two-story, tile roofed cement outbuilding with garage, two rooms, and basement.

Dreyfous's son, Julius, of Weiss and Dreyfous, architects, designed this residence with a well-articulated entry porch undercut from the main mass of the house, circular-headed ground-floor openings, red tile roof, and a glass and metal canopy on the lake side.

The house remained in the Dreyfous family until 1957 when Joyce Perez Eustis of Delcour, Louisiana, purchased it for $92,000. As of this writing, the owners are Ann and John Koerner III, who bought the house in 1986.

18 AUDUBON PLACE, FOUCHER TRACT

Herbert Camp sold this site for $12,000 in 1910 to Herman Weil, owner of Kohn Weil and Co., a Canal Street hat and trunk business. The *Times-Democrat* of September 1, 1910, reported that Emile Weil was the architect for this house and described it as "a modern residence of brick veneer, with a fine hardwood interior and all high class work throughout. The cost of the building is expected to approximate $20,000." As built, this was a two-and-one-half-story-over-basement residence with fifteen rooms, four baths, a tile roof, and a porch. The Renaissance Revival facade features a classically inspired entry porch flanked by elliptical openings with bold detailing, a well-developed roof cornice, and a green tile roof.

The house remained in the Weil family until 1971

when Thomas and Patricia Crosby purchased it. They in turn sold it to Mathilde and Prieur J. Leary, Jr. in 1981.

20 AUDUBON PLACE, FOUCHER TRACT

The Morris Building and Land Improvement Company acquired this site in 1905 and began construction of the present house the following year. The *Daily Picayune* in 1906 noted that this structure was to cost $13,000, and recorded in the Notarial Archives are the subcontracts for the plumbing and heating, carpentry, tile and plaster, and cement work totaling $8,632. The architects, DeBuys and Levy, combined a melange of architectural details, such as the Dutch Colonial gambrel roof, the Craftsman rough stucco and masonry columns, and the Beaux Arts colossal paired columns.

There have been numerous changes to the house, but the most notable is the addition to the river side, replacing a classically inspired porch.

Cora Hennen, widow of John A. Morris, resided here until 1920 when the house was acquired by Lillian Legendre, wife of Gustave Baldwin. Seven years later, Byron C. McClellan bought the property, selling to Mrs. Louis A. Meraux in 1941. Her son, Joseph Meraux, was the owner from 1944 until his death in 1992.

21 AUDUBON PLACE, FOUCHER TRACT

The architect for this California Style residence is undocumented. However, it is possibly the work of Morgan Hite, who was the most experienced architect working in this style, which is reminiscent of the work of Charles and Henry Greene, although not as sophisticated. In New Orleans the style is primarily used for bungalows and rarely for full two-story residences. An exception is 3553 Gentilly Boulevard, designed by Hite.

In 1925 Levi M. Ash purchased this site for $20,000 and late that year mortgaged the property for $30,000 to finance construction of the house. The 1926 tax assessments indicate a large, two-story frame mansion with tile roof, assessed for $31,320.

In 1930, Ash transferred the house for $10,000 to M and F, which returned it in 1932 for $5,000. From 1938 to 1943, Ash leased the house to Oliver G. Lucas for $250 per month. From 1943 to 1945, it was leased to Albert M. Stall for $255 per month, with

an option to buy within six months at $35,000. Stall exercised his option on November 18, 1943, and the house remained in his family until 1985 when Sherry and Thomas Keaty purchased it. In 1990 the Keatys sold the house to 21 Audubon Place Trust.

22 AUDUBON PLACE, FOUCHER TRACT

This Colonial Revival residence is similar to three other designs by Frank P. Gravely—one at 1524 Seventh, one at 4621 St. Charles, and one at 2006 Milan. This one was built in 1904 for lumber magnate Darwin Beach Carré, vice-president of W.W. Carré Company, one of the largest lumber suppliers in New Orleans. Many local historic houses were built with Carré lumber, as evidenced by the company's stamp found on rough framing.

Leila Carré entered into a contract with T.M. Thompson on April 29, 1904, to provide the carpentry work for this house, which was to be complete prior to October 1, 1904. In 1911 Asahal McLellan, president of Alden Mills, purchased the house for $20,000 and retained architects Favrot and Livaudais to make alterations to it. It remained in the McLellan family until 1963 when Dr. Martin O. Miller, who resided next door at 24 Audubon Place, purchased it for $87,500. In 1974 the house was sold for $228,000 to the Paul Robinsons. The owners as of this writing, Dr. and Mrs. Calvin M. Johnson, Jr., acquired the house in 1985 from the Robinson heirs. See color interior photograph section for interior view.

23 AUDUBON PLACE, FOUCHER TRACT

On June 4, 1913, notions dealer Ferdinand Katz of S. and J. Katz and Company purchased this site for $9,000 from Anna Soulé and donated it two months later to his wife. City permit records for 1913 indicate that permit #5451 was issued to Mrs. Ferd Katz for a "two story slate roof residence." Tax records for the following year show the house was assessed for $9,000.

The Renaissance Revival house is illustrated in a monograph of the works of Emile Weil from 1900 to 1928 published by his office. Weil does not distinguish between new construction and remodeling projects; however, the house is very much in keeping with his work. A comparison of the monograph with the house today indicates the loss of planters atop the well-detailed classical entry and a screened porch atop the St. Charles Avenue end wing. Also lost are the glass enclosure of this wing, originally screened, and a side entry from the driveway.

In 1917 the Katzes commissioned Moise Goldstein to make alterations to the foyer of the house in a Renaissance style. The house remained in the Katz family until 1932 when John O'Keefe purchased it for $43,750. The O'Keefe family owned it until 1949 when Frederick Vaughn purchased it for $57,500. He sold it in 1972 to Salem David, the owner as of this writing.

24 AUDUBON PLACE, FOUCHER TRACT

The Portland Cement Association of America was a great advocate of the Mission style, as its product was quite suitable for it. Architect C. Milo Williams was a great advocate of cement and employed it in this poured-in-place concrete residence for attorney W. Winans Wall. Built in an age before plywood, the house was formed up with boards, as seen in the ribbed effect of the exterior. The original design of this 1905 house has been modified by the enclosure of the one-story *porte cochere* on the St. Charles end and the addition of a second story. Behind the altered *porte cochere* a new wing has been added to the rear.

In 1940 Mrs. Wall sold the house for $22,000 to the Whitney Bank, which sold it the following year to Dr. Martin Miller for $23,500. On May 28, 1963, fire broke out in the house and did $19,471 worth of damage. As of this writing, the house remains in the Miller family.

25 AUDUBON PLACE, FOUCHER TRACT

On October 3, 1911, Sallie Littel, wife of Augustus D. Havard, exchanged three lots on Audubon Boulevard and $4,000 for this property owned by Edwin Craighead. In 1912 Havard obtained building permit #2325 for a "basement, main & semi-attic slate roof raised cottage." On October 26, 1924, the *Times-Picayune* carried an advertisement, with a photograph, for the auction of the house on November 4 that year:

This unexcelled residence is a terraced two-story, with basement, built in the English Style of Architecture (Broadmoor Type); and is erected of brick and stucco, covered with wonderful ivy. It has marble steps and approach, with front gallery,

one-half of which is screened, and side sun porch built of Spanish Tile. It contains on the first floor, large reception, living room, parlor, dining room, breakfast room, rear sun parlor, pantries, linen closet, tile and marble bathroom. All tinted and some hardwood floors. On the second floor, spacious entrance hall, four independent bedrooms, two tile and marble baths, serving room, sleeping porch and trunk room, etc. All modern conveniences such as clothes closets and chutes, intra-house telephone system, electric appliances, etc. The Basement contains three servants rooms, storage room, laundry and servants bath, triple porcelain linen laundry vessels, etc., etc.

A subsequent fire destroyed the second floor, however, and the house remained in the Havard family until 1926 when Edgar Dumont purchased it for $37,500. He sold it in 1958 to Gladys Billero, widow of Lester Alexander who reigned as Rex in 1949. The Alexander family owns the house as of this writing.

26 AUDUBON PLACE, FOUCHER TRACT

Soulé and MacDonnell were the architects for this 1903 residence. Anna Gibson Robinson, wife of Charles W. Robinson, president of C.W. Robinson Lumber Company, purchased the site that year for $3,500 with her separate funds. According to the *Daily States* of August 31, 1903:

The residence of Mrs. C.W. Robinson at 26 Audubon Place, a handsome two-story and attic frame dwelling Colonial Style, with interior finish in mahogany and oak and hardwood floors, to be lighted throughout by both gas and electricity. This thoroughly modern dwelling house cost complete $15,000.

The house was actually a rather clumsy example of the style, ill-proportioned and oddly detailed, as seen in the photograph published in the *Times-Picayune* on February 7, 1909. Tax records of 1927 indicate a fire at this site the previous year. This likely prompted the changes to the house, including the replacement of the two dormers on the Audubon Place facade with a single dormer and the loss of the large porch extending toward St. Charles Avenue.

The house remained in the Robinson family until the current owner, Harry T. Howard III, purchased it in 1988.

27 AUDUBON PLACE, FOUCHER TRACT

This Spanish Eclectic residence was built in 1927 for Henry C. Flonacher, a paper company executive. The house was designed by Weiss, Dreyfous and Seiferth and built by A.L. Fishman, being accepted on February 1, 1928. The exuberant Spanish details in the entrance bay of the front porch are noteworthy—such details were popularized by the San Diego Fair of 1915. The Flonachers in their travels would purchase components to be incorporated into the house, requiring the architects to constantly revise the plans.

Oil developer William G. Helis purchased the house from Flonacher in 1934 for $33,250, and it remains in the Helis family as of this writing.

The house has been designated a city landmark.

28 AUDUBON PLACE, FOUCHER TRACT

Anne Fordtran, wife of New Orleans Can Company vice-president Edgar Fordtran, purchased the site for $10,000 in November of 1913, and in 1914 obtained building permit #7009 for the construction of a two-story, slate roofed, veneered residence. The house was first assessed in 1915 at $10,000. In 1922 it appeared in *Building Review*, its design credited to Moise H. Goldstein. After five interim owners, Myriam Robinson purchased the house in 1990.

AUDUBON STREET (Chestnut; Marie; Martha)

356 AUDUBON STREET, GREENVILLE

This Tudor Revival, two-story residence has an animated facade, with picturesque roof line, half-timbering in the projecting gable, and a red tile roof.

This style was so popular during the 1920s, prior to the stock market crash of 1929, that it frequently was called "Stockbroker Tudor."

On July 1, 1925, Henry D. Ervin, manager of Williamson, Innon and Stribling, cotton brokers, contracted with E.J. Stewart and Company to build a one-and-a-half-story stucco house with tile roof for $6,595. Ervin accepted the house on November 7, 1925.

After five interim owners, Mr. and Mrs. Ivan Mandich bought the property in 1979 and retain ownership as of this writing.

440 AUDUBON STREET, GREENVILLE

The design precedents for this Louisiana Colonial Revival house date 100 years before its construction. Built in 1928 for Gladys and Peter Monrose, it borrows from the late 1820s and early 1830s such details as brick sawtooth cornice, decorative lintels, wrought iron railings, and arched ground-floor openings. The Monroses sold the house for $62,500 in 1950 to Charlotte Hardie, wife of Charles G. Smither.

The present house replaces an early structure built in 1893 by Frank George for W.T. Brown. Brown died during construction of the house, which his heirs could not legally claim. The court, however, ordered the homestead financing the construction to honor the contract and sell it to them at the original construction price. That house likely burned in 1900.

452 AUDUBON STREET, GREENVILLE

Building Review of the South featured this impressive Colonial Revival residence on its cover for April 20, 1918. Frank G. Churchill is identified as

the designer. Dr. and Mrs. Ray McLean Van Wart purchased this site in two transactions in 1916 and 1917 and had the present house built shortly thereafter. They are listed at this address in the 1919 city directory. In 1928 the Van Warts sold the house to L. Kemper Williams, founder and endower of the Historic New Orleans Collection. The April 8, 1928, real estate section of the *Times-Picayune* illustrated the house with the caption, "Van Wart Mansion, 450 Audubon Boulevard bought by Kemper Williams through Pipes & Johnson."

In 1942 the Williamses sold the house to Edna Stewart Farwell after moving to and restoring 718 Toulouse. Three years later, James Gibbons Burke bought the house for $40,000 and retained it until 1973 when he sold it to Travis M. Richardson for $217,000. In 1975 the house was sold to Ann and John Yarborough, Jr.

460 AUDUBON STREET, GREENVILLE

Architect F. Julius Dreyfous purchased this property in 1927 from Henry Morris for $8,500, and his firm of Weiss, Dreyfous and Seiferth designed this house as an eighteenth century château. Dreyfous, according to his partner, Solis Seiferth, had a fondness for French architecture, which their firm seldom employed since clients preferred the Mediterranean style.

The exterior of this 1928 house draws heavily from French precedents, employing casement doors and windows, bands surrounding openings, simple cornice belt course, quoins, and a mansard roof. The entrance pavilion was frequently used in French architecture to designate the center or end of a facade and replaced the tower used in Gothic designs. Ornamentation on such pavilions was commonly carved stone; however, cast stone is employed here, and is also used for the portal frame, balcony brackets, and urns. Weiss, Dreyfous and Seiferth established a reputation for employing skilled artisans to execute such well-designed details. The copper roof finials and wrought iron balcony railing are additional examples of such craftsmanship.

Dreyfous sold the house in 1945 for $35,000 to Henry Hausmann, who sold it to Roger Cavaroc in 1956. Dr. Lincoln Paine bought the house in 1969 from Cavaroc's widow.

497 AUDUBON STREET, GREENVILLE

The *Daily Picayune* of September 1, 1903, records that cotton exporter Joseph Dreuil obtained a permit for a $4,000, two-story, frame, slated residence designed by the firm of Soulé and MacDonnell. Dreuil purchased this site in 1902 from Peter Fabacher for $6,000 with the promise to maintain the buildings on the premises, indicating an existing structure. Dreuil is listed in the 1904 city directory at 499 Audubon.

In 1906 Elizabeth Kopp purchased the house for $6,000, and it remained in her family for ten years until Charles Kemper acquired it. Subsequent owners were Aline Godchaux (1920), Charles Keller, Jr. (1939), Shirley and Lee Schlesinger (1949), Leonard Nicholson (1949), Henri Favrot (1953), Gerald Pratt (1954), Ivy and John Whitty, Jr. (1962), Jeanne and Lester Edell (1965), and Duane and Harvey C. Couch (1985).

501 AUDUBON STREET, GREENVILLE

This well-proportioned house with prominent portico is partially obscured by the heavy planting of its site. Designed in the Southern Colonial style, its precedent is actually the Greek Revival architecture of the first half of the nineteenth century.

William Nicholls, secretary of the Carondelet Canal and Navigation Company, obtained a permit to build a $3,000 residence in 1905 after acquiring the site in two separate transactions. After six interim owners, William H. Henderson bought the house in 1981.

533 AUDUBON STREET, GREENVILLE

This impressive Mediterranean Villa was built for Corinne Gill Abney, widow of Francis W. Abney, after she purchased the site in 1922 for $10,500. It was designed by Weiss and Dreyfous in the style that was popular from the turn of the century to World War II. In 1948 Sadie Downman Billion purchased the house for $51,500, and it remained in her family until 1983 when the Dermot McGlinchey family purchased it.

560 AUDUBON STREET, GREENVILLE

Here is another Mediterranean Villa, built in 1923 for Ezra A. Naman, manager of Anderson Clayton and Co., cotton exporters. Tax records that year indicate construction of a single, two-story, cement house with tile roof, eight rooms, five baths, an outhouse, and a garage.

Naman had purchased the site in 1923 for $10,500. The following year he donated the lot and house, valued at $40,000, to his wife, Ann. The house sold for $25,000 in 1934 to Melanie and Jacob Goldsmith. In 1942 it was donated to their daughter, Eva Goldsmith Waldhorn. Ten years later, A.B. Freeman, Rex in 1932, purchased the property for $62,000, selling it for $72,500 in 1958 to the owners as of this writing, the William Johnston family.

571 AUDUBON STREET, GREENVILLE

This nineteenth century Southern Colonial residence is most noted for its association with Professor James Dillard, who owned it from 1906 to 1916. Dillard came to New Orleans in 1891 to join the faculty of Tulane University as a professor of Latin and eventually became dean of the College of Arts and Sciences in 1904, a position he held until 1908. He

served as president of the New Orleans Free Kindergarten Association from 1896 to 1905 and as a trustee of the city's two black universities, Straight and New Orleans. The two schools merged in 1929 to form Dillard University, named in his honor. Dillard also directed the John F. Slater Fund and the Jeanes Foundation, both of which were dedicated to the advancement of the education of African-Americans. In 1937 Dillard was awarded the Roosevelt Medal.

The house likely dates to 1889 when the entire square was subdivided by Edward Martinez, who probably built the house. The December 2, 1889, sale of the property to Robert Eyrich by Martinez cites a one-story, frame slated dwelling and one-story, frame shingled kitchen attached, valued at $2,500. This description matches the appearance of the house on the 1896 Sanborn insurance map and its present appearance. Eyrich sold the house in 1891 to Estelle Gustine Woelper, who sold it to James Dillard. Subsequent owners have been Joseph Blythe (1916), Leon Wiggins (1931), Herbert Miller (1948),

and Bemis Godfrey (1955), whose family retains the house as of this writing.

In 1974 the house was designated a National Historic Landmark.

582 AUDUBON STREET, GREENVILLE

In 1908 Henry A. Schroeder purchased lots 22 and 23 at a cost of $4,750. Tax rolls for 1909 indicate that a house valued at $5,500 was on the site. Schroeder was a well-known saloon-keeper, operating the Midway at Canal and St. Charles and another saloon at 141 Dauphine. He lived here with his wife, Millie, and five children. The Schroeders sold the house to Daniel K. Murray in 1911 for $11,000. It remained in the Murray family until 1937 when Cecile and Ladd Dinkins purchased it, selling to Mr. and Mrs. Emile Bertucci in 1965. At this writing, the owners are Dr. and Mrs. John Kenneth Saer, who bought the property in 1972.

A comparison of the house today with photos that appeared in *Illustrated Sunday Magazine* and *Architectural Arts and Its Allies* indicates the loss of a large monumental stair in front of the gallery where there is now a simpler stairway and the original concrete block fence. Emile Weil was the architect for the house.

BENJAMIN (Felicia)

6018 BENJAMIN, BLOOMINGDALE

Individually listed on the National Register of Historic Places in 1982, this raised, story-and-a-half, five-bay, center-hall cottage originally faced State Street as 1534 State, and was moved to its present location sometime prior to 1909. The move accounts for its close proximity to the sidewalk and its side entrance bay, as well as its unusual elevation above grade.

In 1889 Mrs. Carrie Pessou purchased a State Street site and built the house that same year, for the 1890 city directory lists the Pessou family at State Street, at the southwest corner of Benjamin Street. Thomas Lane Ross purchased the property in 1891 and moved the house to Benjamin, to the rear yard of the original lot, and the Ross family retained the property until 1917. After five interim owners, Mr. and Mrs. Rutledge Clement bought the property in 1980.

BROADWAY (Almonester; Magnolia)

350 BROADWAY, GREENVILLE

This brick Colonial Revival residence reflects the taste for the simplicity of the Federal style during the 1920s when it was built.

William C. Fletcher, sales manager of Consumers Biscuit Company, purchased the site in 1929 and built the present structure that year. As of this writing, the house has had only three owners and has been owned since 1956 by the Edward F. Wegmanns.

444 BROADWAY, GREENVILLE

Favrot and Livaudais designed this French Eclectic residence for Lucille and Joseph Blum in 1932 and oversaw its construction the following year when Joseph Blum, co-founder of Latter and Blum

Realty Company, purchased this site. Originally, the property extended to Pine Street. 401 and 411 Pine were created from the rear garden.

In 1972 Mrs. Blum lost the residence as the result of a lawsuit filed by Jackson Homestead Association. As of this writing, there have been three subsequent owners. In 1980 Bernard Frischertz, Jr. bought the house, and the family retains ownership as of this writing.

460 BROADWAY, GREENVILLE

This house has undergone a remarkable metamorphosis since originally constructed for German-born Herman R. Gogreve in 1897 for $4,000. As seen in the early photograph, this house reflected the late-nineteenth century taste for elaborate woodwork.

The house remained in the Gogreve family until 1931 when Dr. William Bradburn purchased it and undertook the major renovation which transformed it into the Southern Colonial style. Frederick Parham of Goldstein, Parham and Labouisse spearheaded the renovation. Bradburn sold the house in 1962 to Eugene McCarroll for $106,000. Sixteen years later, McCarroll sold it to Roger Ogden, the owner as of this writing. See color interior photograph section for interior view.

478 BROADWAY, GREENVILLE

This two-and-one-half-story stucco residence borrows many local details to invoke a regional flavor. The arch-and-ball railing pattern and the decorative transom are typical of the local parlance during the 1830s. Designed by architects Julius Dreyfous and

Emilio Levy, this residence was built in 1937, one hundred years after its inspiration, for Mr. and Mrs. Leo Weil.

515 BROADWAY, GREENVILLE

Christian Roselius, a native of Germany, purchased this entire square in 1839 and built a raised, one-story, suburban Greek Revival villa sometime thereafter. Roselius was a prominent attorney, attorney general of Louisiana, and dean of Tulane University's law school. He also had a city residence at 630 Dumaine and is not listed on Broadway in city directories until 1853. Apparently, Roselius had this house raised to a full two stories when this became his primary residence about 1852. An 1877 advertisement for the partition of his estate describes his Broadway property as a "large two-story frame house with complete dependencies, splendid garden, known as the Roselius homestead." The Robinson *Atlas* illustrates this house as the sole dwelling on the square, with both an attached and detached dependency.

In 1888 Mary Roselius Bouny's succession sold the house to Wesley E. Lawrence. The 1896 Sanborn insurance map illustrates the house as a two-story dwelling with a two-story river-end porch and a two-story Queen Anne addition on the river side where the Robinson *Atlas* indicates an attached dependency. Also illustrated is a one-story dependency with a wraparound gallery in the front yard and a one-story greenhouse, a two-story stable with an adjacent elevated tank and accompanying windmill, and a one-story octagonal gazebo.

After several interim owners, Dr. George Crozat, a prominent orthodontist and collector of Louisiana decorative arts, acquired the house in 1925 for $10,000 and undertook a major renovation. Crozat's succession sold the house to Herman Kohlmeyer, Jr. in 1967 with extensive hurricane damage. After a short, eight-month ownership, Kohlmeyer sold it to Barbara Schreier, later the wife of Dr. Clayton Edisen, who undertook a major renovation of the house. In 1989 the Edisens sold the house to J. Cornelius Rathborne.

579 BROADWAY, GREENVILLE

Reminiscent of the works of architect Charles Platt, this Mediterranean Villa imports a sense of tranquility and comfort in a subtropical setting.

A 1910 building contract in the office of the Recorder of Mortgages indicates that John Ruesch built this house in four months, according to the designs of DeBuys, Churchill and Labouisse, architects, at a cost of $9,708 for Nelson Whitney, assistant cashier at the Whitney Central National Bank. Whitney lived here only until 1918, when Buckner Chipley purchased the house. A 1928 advertisement for the sale of the house by Chipley described it:

> This is one of the finest and most attractive residences in the city. . . . Between the house wings is a pretty court paved with flagstone and surrounded by a pergola (an ideal outdoor living room). The garage accommodates two cars and has the servants quarters above. There are four bedrooms and another smaller bedroom or serving room. There is also a large living and sleeping porch upstairs opened on three sides. The reception hall, living room, library, breakfast room and dining room all open into each other by folding doors, and have attractive casement doors and windows with fanlights above.

After three interim owners, the house was bought in 1942 by the Count and Countess de Pontet-Brun, who sold it to the Herman Barnett family in 1949. Owned by William Barnett since 1976, the house was restored after a fire in 1992.

1701 BROADWAY, FRIBURG

Howard Cromwell of the Crescent Furniture and Mattress Company purchased this site in 1923 and immediately built the present Spanish Eclectic raised bungalow. The house remained in the Cromwell family until 1968.

This bungalow is one of the better ones in an area overrun with mundane bungalows. The arbor over the entrance steps and terrace adds relief to the Broadway Street facade, although it relates to the more animated Green Street facade.

BURTHE

7219 BURTHE, GREENVILLE

This circa 1873 raised cottage is very early for the area, which did not develop until the 1890s. Although a number of raised cottages were noted in the last volume of this series, this house type is rare, with only thirteen nineteenth century examples still standing in the area.

Carpenter William Thompson purchased the site in 1871 from the Fitzgerald family for $800, and the 1874 city directory lists him here, at "Burthe bet. Pine and Walk" (Broadway). The house remained in the Thompson family until 1964 when the Dieth family acquired it.

CALHOUN (Edmund)

1325 CALHOUN, BURTHEVILLE

This well-maintained, turn-of-the-century Queen Anne house reflects the growing tendency toward Colonial Revival details in the last stages of the style. Architects Andry and Bendernagel designed this house for lawyer W. Winans Wall and oversaw its construction in 1900 at a cost of $5,227. The tall, vertical massing of the house is balanced by a partial-width, one-story wraparound porch with Colonial style railing. The composition of the porch is counterbalanced by the oversized, broken-pedimented window with decorative sidelights.

After seven interim owners, Dr. and Mrs. John Ollie Edmunds, Jr. bought the property in 1978.

1335 CALHOUN, BURTHEVILLE

Here is an unusual example of architect William Fitzner's work. Fitzner, who generally designed in the Italianate style, here tried his hand at the Queen Anne. The result is a clumsy product with an awkward, three-story, truncated tower topped with a pronounced chimney. The 1909 Sanborn insurance map indicates that the present second-floor porch was originally half as wide as the lower porch, extending only to the depth of the existing overhang.

Hay and Hulse built this two-story frame dwelling for ship chandler Anders Ugland in 1896 at a cost of $5,200. The Ugland family sold the house in 1925 to attorney Meloncy C. Soniat, who wrote "The Faubourgs Forming the Upper Section of the City of New Orleans," published in the *Louisiana Historical Quarterly* in 1937, while living here. The house remained in the Soniat family until 1945. After three interim owners, Mr. and Mrs. Henry Jumonville, Jr. bought it in 1956, and the family retains ownership as of this writing.

1444, 1448, 1452, 1456 CALHOUN, BURTHEVILLE

Banker Edward Demarest, who built and resided at 1451 Exposition Boulevard, built these four two-story Queen Anne residences backing his house as rental property in 1895. 1452 Calhoun (pictured) is the most intact of the row.

1527 CALHOUN, BURTHEVILLE

Here is a comfortable Queen Anne cottage with a well-detailed projecting bay employing clipped corners, jigsaw cutout work, paneling, and a garland motif. The present porch configuration is not original, as evidenced by the 1896 Sanborn insurance map. Its detailing also suggests a later, more classical period.

According to the *Daily Picayune* of September 1, 1895, Thomas Mackie of J.C. Morris Company, a wholesale hardware company, had this house built that year at a cost of $2,450. Mackie's heirs sold the house in 1915 to Camilla Davis Parkerson, whose family owned it until 1972.

1530 CALHOUN, BURTHEVILLE

In 1931 William Von Phul replicated here his family's Port Allen, Louisiana, plantation house, "Bel Air," employing parts of the original house. Favrot and Livaudais served as architects for this Louisiana Colonial Revival, center-hall cottage. The dormers with mitered corners, the square window panes, and the front door design are subtle clues to the 1930s construction date.

The July 5, 1931, *New Orleans Item* recounts the origin of the house in an article entitled: "Replica of Famous Plantation House is erected here. William Von Phul has Charles Favrot, boyhood chum, draw plans." Von Phul, president of the New York engineering firm of Ford, Bacon and Davis and Charles Favrot, partner in the architectural firm of Favrot and Livaudais and chairman of the New Orleans Zoning and Planning Commission, grew up one-quarter of a mile apart in Port Allen, and both attended Tulane University. After graduation, Favrot would first work for James Freret, and Von Phul would go on to receive the nation's first doctorate in engineering from Tulane. According to the article in the *Item*, Von Phul's circa 1821 family home had fallen into disrepair, and he commissioned Favrot to replicate it in New Orleans. Favrot measured the house with his son, Mortimer, and produced the drawings for its replication. The "cornerstone," a brick with the dates 1821-1931, was set May 9, 1931. Apparently the front porch columns were salvaged from the Port Allen house. The roofing shingles, which appear to be wood, are actually tile.

In 1951 Elizabeth Lykes Carrere purchased the house. She sold it to Edward Haspel, and in 1993 Kathryn Bellerino Frank acquired it, selling a half interest to Robert C. Leonard that same year for an unspecified price.

Today the house serves as the prototype of many copies—even *Southern Living* features the "Bel Air" house plan.

1545-47, 1549-51, 1553 CALHOUN, BURTHEVILLE

Built for Arthur McLaughlin in 1893 for $9,000, these two double camelbacks and one single camelback have a repetitive design formula, using stock Eastlake millwork. The recurring brackets are distinguished by their placement beneath the spandrel of small spindles and the spandrel's return to the mass of the house, making these decorative brackets a less convincing structural element than on a typical shotgun.

1556, 1566 CALHOUN, BURTHEVILLE

Originally identical, these two cottages were built for brothers William and Charles Wood in 1891. 1556 Calhoun, which was home to Charles Wood, retains its original Eastlake porch detailing although much of the porch has been enclosed. 1566 Calhoun, originally the home of William Wood, has lost its original porch detailing as well as its porch dormer, projecting bay gable, and chimney caps and pots.

2133 CALHOUN, BURTHEVILLE

James Gaudet bought half this square in 1885 and initially operated a dairy here. He built this cozy Dutch Colonial house in 1923 at a cost of $10,954. The property remained in the Gaudet family until

1994 when it was sold to Suzette Sonnier and Shawn Killeen.

True to its style, the house employs a gambrel roof, a shed dormer, window boxes, mitered cornerboards, and porch benches. Aymar Embury II, the acknowledged national expert on the style, wrote in *Building the Dutch Colonial House:* "For these small houses there is probably no other style so good; it was originally devised as an architecture for small buildings. It is a fact that none of the other Colonial types was handled by the designs with anything like the freedom from traditional precedent that the Dutch work showed."

CHESTNUT (Chatham; Elizabeth; Plaquemine)

5928 CHESTNUT, BLOOMINGDALE

This three-bay, side hall cottage retains much of its authentic period detailing. The oversized dormer with jigsaw detailing and scrolls dominating the facade appears to need a heavier spandrel to counter the dormer mass. The Tuscan columns set on pedestals are a typical detail of the period.

The city directory first lists river pilot Charles Post at this address in 1902. The house remained in the Post family until 1940. After five interim owners, the Ralph M. France family has owned the house since 1965.

S. CLAIBORNE (Mobile)

5712 SOUTH CLAIBORNE AVENUE, HURSTVILLE

Eleanor McMain School is one of a few surviving Art Deco buildings in New Orleans. Other examples include the American Bank Building, General Laundry Building, Charity-Tulane-LSU medical complex, and Rabouin School.

For McMain, schoolboard architect E.A. Christy used a variety of Deco details, from zigzag patterns to stylized classic ornament to ornament inspired by Tulane University's Middle American Research Institute's Central American explorations. Contractor J.A. Petty and Sons built this reinforced concrete building between 1930 and 1932 as a school for girls.

In 1930 an article in the *Times-Picayune* described the impending project:

The new girls' high school will be built on South Claiborne avenue, between Joseph street and Nashville avenue, at a cost of about $500,000. It will accommodate 1,000 pupils. The plans call for the regular classrooms, library, study halls, four laboratories, administrative offices, cafeteria, locker rooms, an auditorium seating 1,500 persons and provisions for instruction in domestic science, serving and art. The building will be the first in the New Orleans school system to employ modernistic architecture. It will be three stories high, of reinforced concrete covered with stucco.

DUNLEITH COURT

1 DUNLEITH COURT, GREENVILLE

The *Daily States* of August 31, 1912, recorded that architects DeBuys, Churchill and Labouisse designed this "attractive residence in Colonial style" for Josiah E. Pearce. One wonders to what Colonial detailing the author was referring. Quite often Greek Revival detailing was referred to as "Southern Colonial," which seems to be the case here with respect to the front porch. Sidelights extend over the head of the three ground-floor openings in typical early-twentieth century fashion. There might have been a widow's walk atop the roof.

Pearce, owner of an "Electric Theater" on Canal Street, sold the house in 1925 to Augusta Waldhorn Dennery for $25,000. After three interim owners, Anne and Robert Walmsley, Jr. purchased the house in 1986.

2 DUNLEITH COURT, GREENVILLE

Lawrence D. Fabacher, assistant cashier at his father's business, the Jackson Brewing Company, hired architect Francis MacDonnell to design this 1912 tapestry, brick-and-patent, concrete block Craftsman house. The exposed rafter ends and purlins and the keying together of the block and brick around openings and on the porch columns are typical of the Craftsman style and of MacDonnell's work.

Fabacher sold the house in 1919 to Michael Weil, in whose family it remained until 1976. As of this writing, Joan and Gunther Michaelis own this house.

4 DUNLEITH COURT, GREENVILLE

In 1927 Edmund Ivens, a representative of Chicago Pneumatic Tool Company, purchased a vacant lot and immediately began construction of this two-story brick veneer residence. The Colonial style house reflects the appeal of the simplicity of Federal details during the 1920s and the growing prevalence of brick veneer. During this period, the side porch replaced the more fanciful and dominating front porch of the earlier phase of the style.

In 1939 Marcus Walker purchased the house and two years later sold it to J. Freyhan Odenheimer of Lane Cotton Mills, in whose family it remained until 1994 when Dr. and Mrs. Kevin McKinley acquired it.

7 DUNLEITH COURT, GREENVILLE

Robert Spencer Soulé was the architect for this Swiss Chalet residence built in 1911 for insurance agent William Campbell at a cost of $9,000. The graduated gable brackets, the second-floor jigsaw frames, and the balcony and window box details are characteristic of this rarely employed style.

Campbell financed the project through Security Building and Loan, which officially acquired the property in 1911 and sold it with the house to Campbell in 1912. Two years later, Campbell sold the house to Theophile Hirsch, in whose family it remained until 1958 when Katherine Claiborne purchased it. In 1974 Wanda and Rene Paysse bought the house. Tom Huntsinger is the owner as of this writing.

ELEONORE

518 ELEONORE, HURSTVILLE

Francis Thomas, a butcher, purchased this entire square in 1858 from Antoine Fleury and likely built the present house about 1869 when the site was part of Jefferson Parish, making this one of the earliest extant structures in the area covered in this volume.

When this house was built, Italianate was the style of choice, with its heavy detailing; in the South, however, the Greek Revival continued much longer than

in other parts of the country, as seen in the simplicity of this example.

After two interim owners, Nora O'Donnell bought the house in 1919, and it remains in the O'Donnell family as of this writing.

635 ELEONORE, HURSTVILLE

The Society of the Daughters of Charity of St. Vincent de Paul sold this site in 1895 to Frederick Beyer, a manufacturing agent, who built the present house, which appears as a double on the 1896 Sanborn insurance map.

The circa 1895 construction date is reflected in the picturesque roof line, the Eastlake porch details employing a spandrel frieze, jigsaw brackets springing from decorative columns, and the tripartite gable window.

After nine interim owners, George Guelfo, the owner as of this writing, bought the house in 1973.

717-19, 721-23, 727 ELEONORE, HURSTVILLE

As reported in the September 1, 1897 *Daily Picayune,* Julius Manger built one single and two double shotguns here for $5,600. He disposed of 717-19 and 727 that same year and 721-23 (pictured) in 1899.

The repetitive detailing of these Eastlake residences, softened by the foliage, creates a pleasant streetscape.

731 ELEONORE, HURSTVILLE

Continuing the streetscape, Julius Manger built this Eastlake side-hall cottage in 1898 for $2,200. Like its neighbors, 717-19, 721-23 and 727 Eleonore, this residence employs a great deal of stock Eastlake detailing, further complementing the street scene.

1037 ELEONORE, HURSTVILLE

Here is a typical Eastlake shotgun. Virtually all of its ornamentation is confined to the front and side porches. It was built for Cecilia Foolkes Nixon, who purchased two vacant lots in 1892. Although the house does not appear in the Sanborn insurance map of 1896, the property's tax assessment rose from $600 in 1895 to $1,800 in 1896, indicating the house was likely built in 1896.

In 1903 Nixon sold the property with the house to Walter Dupre. Nixon also built on the adjoining lot, 1033-35 Eleonore, in 1895 at a cost of $1,200. John Foolkes, likely a relative, built the double, according to an April 23, 1895, building contract. Foolkes probably was also the builder of 1037 Eleonore.

EVERETT PLACE

4 EVERETT PLACE, BLOOMINGDALE

Here is one of the many Southern Colonial residences designed by architect Robert Spencer Soulé. As seen at 5801 St. Charles Avenue and 1525 State Street, classical architecture of the Federal and Greek periods was mistakenly called Colonial during the early-twentieth century.

Soulé designed this house for his brother Edward Everett Soulé, treasurer of Soulé College, Rex in 1931, and developer of Everett Place.

The flanking one-story porches which balance the verticality of the portico are not original to the 1908 house as shown on the 1909 Sanborn insurance map, but were likely added by the Williams family, who owned the house from 1915 to 1942. After two interim owners, the Ewell Eagan, Jr. family purchased the house in 1982.

6 EVERETT PLACE, BLOOMINGDALE

Architect Robert Spencer Soulé chose to build his own house in his brother's residential park, Everett Place. He purchased the land from Edward Everett Soulé on October 24, 1907, for $3,000 and built his home in the Craftsman style. The July 1908 issue of the New Orleans-based *Architectural Arts and Its Allies* featured a photograph of the newly completed house.

R. Spencer Soulé studied architecture at Cornell University and later worked in the office of local architect Francis MacDonnell before establishing his own practice. Soulé designed numerous Uptown residences as well as some in Baton Rouge and St. Francisville and on the Mississippi Gulf Coast. During the Great Depression, he did public works projects in Audubon Park. Soulé eventually moved to Albuquerque, New Mexico, where he continued his practice until 1957 when he died at the age of eighty-three.

The Craftsman style of architecture, which Soulé selected for his own house, has its roots in the English Arts and Crafts movement, regarded as a solution to the "corrupt" values of the Victorian styles. Details which reflect the Craftsman philosophy include the lack of ornamentation, rough stucco, earth-tone bricks (now painted), red tile roof with deep overhangs, and leaded glass windows.

The Philip K. Jones family are the tenth owners of the house.

EXPOSITION BOULEVARD (Boulevard Street)

631-33 EXPOSITION BOULEVARD, BURTHEVILLE (formerly 6330 Constance)

Here is a fanciful Eastlake cottage facing Constance Street, raised on a basement and set in a lush garden. The "gingerbread" wooden ornament on this house is noteworthy.

In 1904 Harry Oswald Barker purchased this site for $500 from Mutual Building and Loan and in 1906 built the present residence with financing from Security Building and Loan. The September 1, 1906, *Daily Picayune* notes that H.O. Barker was building a $3,500 single frame cottage. The house remained in the Barker family until 1961 when Tricia and Halbert Reeves bought it. Seven years later, Charles Suhor purchased the house, selling it in 1972 to Jacqueline McPherson for $42,500.

701 EXPOSITION BOULEVARD, BURTHEVILLE

On April 11, 1908, Mrs. Mary Thompson Cocks purchased this site, and she is first listed in the 1910 city directory at this location, along with her husband, Tulane Professor Reginald Cocks.

The 1909 Sanborn insurance map indicates the house was a one-story basement residence with a two-story partial-width porch. Likely, the projecting portion of the porch had a second-floor level and partially exposed stairs coming off partially under the roof. The house is similar to one on Hillary Street designed by architect Walter Geary as his own residence, which appeared in *Architectural Art and Its Allies.*

The Exposition Boulevard residence remained in the Cocks family until 1922 when Charles Vosburgh purchased it plus additional property for $6,500. The Vosburgh family retained it until 1963 when it was sold to Charles Ward, the owner as of this writing.

1315 EXPOSITION BOULEVARD, BURTHEVILLE

This Colonial Revival residence reflects the simpler, symmetrical version of the style so popular during the 1920s. This particular example borrows from Federal precedents. It was designed by architect H.L. Burton in 1922 for Carrie Payne, widow of Julian Payne. The symmetrical facade has an emphasized entry featuring Tuscan columns and an inaccessible iron balcony. As of this writing, the house remains in the possession of Payne's descendants.

1451 EXPOSITION BOULEVARD, BURTHEVILLE

This impressive Queen Anne residence is best viewed from Exposition Boulevard. The complex facade, multitude of textures, corner tower, wraparound porch, decorative railings, oriel, clipped corners, and Queen Anne windows contribute to the picturesque effect of this late-nineteenth century home.

The wealth that made this house possible was generated from the corrupt Louisiana Lottery of the nineteenth century. Edward Demarest, who built this house in 1896, and his brother, W.J. Demarest, were the last two presidents of the lottery. In 1889, by means of two separate transactions, Edward Demarest acquired this site as well as those on Calhoun which contain 1444, 1448, 1452, and 1456. In 1895, according to the city building permits, Demarest built four "two story dwellings" for $10,000.

The following year, the *Daily Picayune* records that "E.J. Demant [*sic*] obtained a permit for a single two story dwelling, Audubon, Garfield, Calhoun and Hurst, $3,000." Corroborating this is the fact that the 1896 Sanborn insurance map notes this house as "being built."

The Exposition Boulevard house remained in the Demarest family until 1978 when Dr. John Stocks and Karen Halstead purchased it.

1507, 1513, 1519, 1525 EXPOSITION BOULEVARD, BURTHEVILLE

Here are three once-identical, and one variant, two-story Queen Anne residences. 1507 Exposition, the variant form, is the most intact, although alterations have been made to the second-floor porch.

The houses, which appear on the 1896 Sanborn insurance map, were built by Eppie Barr, who purchased the entire square in 1889. Likely, she built these four houses, along with 1503 Exposition Boulevard, over a three-year period between 1890 and 1893. In 1890 the entire square was assessed for $6,000; by 1891 the assessment had risen to $12,000, and in 1892 to $20,000, and finally in 1893 to $22,000, at which it remained for a long period of time. An 1897 photograph by John Olmstead indicates the houses were standing at that time.

Eppie Barr died in May 1903 after falling from a window of the house at 1507 Exposition Boulevard. The Barr family owned that house until 1961 when it was sold to Adele and Kenneth Salzer. The Salzers' daughter and son-in-law, Elizabeth and David Schell, Jr., retain ownership as of this writing.

1531 EXPOSITION BOULEVARD, BURTHEVILLE

Built in 1910 by clerk Edwin Powell, this Colonial Revival bungalow reflects a Southern Colonial version, although the side-projecting porch reflects the Secessionist movement, as seen in Joseph Olbrich's work and repeated locally in H. Jordan MacKenzie's work. Sleeping porches were added to the house in 1921.

The house remained in the Powell family until 1948 when Elinor Nugon purchased it for $30,000. The A.J. Nugon family retains it as of this writing.

1539 EXPOSITION BOULEVARD, BURTHEVILLE

Here is a typical Queen Anne residence of the 1890s, with fanciful massing, a variety of window types, and a complex roof line. In 1892 music teacher Mary Abbott purchased the site for $1,400 and built this house about 1894, as she is first listed at this address in the 1895 city directory. Abbott sold the house for $15,600 in 1926 to Gertrude Stiles, whose heirs sold it to Henry Williams in 1950 for $26,500. The Williams family sold it to Edna and Gilbert Grog in 1954. David Vosbein inherited the house in 1981 and sold it five years later to Catherine and Aden Burka.

1565 EXPOSITION BOULEVARD, BURTHEVILLE

Recently remodeled and enlarged to take advantage of the view of Audubon Park, this house has lost much of its original Tudor Revival-design intent. As seen in the old photograph, the front porch railing was in keeping with the original design of the structure.

Built in 1905 at a cost of $6,000, according to the designs of architect Rathbone DeBuys, this structure was originally home to Mary and Allen Tupper. Tupper, a masonry products dealer, enlarged and remodeled the house in 1928 under the direction of architect Francis J. MacDonnell, with Carl Peterson as contractor. A 1928 advertisement for the house described it as "Old English Architecture" with four bedrooms, two baths, two sleeping porches, a central hall and four clothes closets upstairs, a finished attic, and a screened porch, a large reception hall, stairway, lavatory, living room, dining room, library, buttery, storeroom, kitchen, servants room, laundry, and two coal rooms downstairs, and a double garage.

In 1930 Marie and Donald McDonald purchased the house from the Tuppers, and it remained in the family until 1947. After three interim owners, Dr. and Mrs. Joseph Sabatier, Jr. bought the property in 1967

for $85,000, and it is still in the Sabatier family as of this writing.

1571 EXPOSITION BOULEVARD, BURTHEVILLE

Crosby and Henkel were the architects for this stately Southern Colonial home built for coffee magnate William Boatner Reily in 1909 for $12,000. Copies of the original architectural drawings for this residence appeared in the May 1908 issue of *Architectural Art and Its Allies*. In 1952 the Reily heirs sold the house to Robert Beattie, who later sold it to David Oreck. In 1993 Sara and David Kelso purchased the house.

Details that place this residence in the twentieth century include windows with only the upper sash divided and the combination entrance balcony and Palladian window.

1591 EXPOSITION BOULEVARD, BURTHEVILLE

The *Daily Picayune* of August 31, 1907, described this unusual residence as "secession style."

MacKenzie, Goldstein and Biggs designed this residence for Fred Paramore in 1907. MacKenzie was an admirer of Josef Olbrich, the noted Austrian

Secessionist architect, and often patterned his designs after Olbrich's. Here he was inspired by Olbrich's Habich House of 1900. Unfortunately, the roof-top terrace and pergola, which likely leaked under New Orleans' enormous annual rainfall, have been enclosed and a gable roof added. The side porch has also been altered. The deep cove cornice and unusual door frame are typical of Olbrich's Art Nouveau architecture.

After six interim owners, Mrs. and Mrs. Richard Kartzke bought the house in 1984.

FONTAINEBLEAU DRIVE (Baldwin; James)

92 FONTAINEBLEAU DRIVE, FRIBERG

In the rear portion of the area covered by this book are a large number of bungalows, many of which are nondescript. This example, however, is particularly well detailed and is a textbook example of the California bungalow—the compact plan, the shallow roof with exposed purlins and rafters, the shingling which was originally stained rather than painted, and the "peanut brittle" stone porch columns and base are hallmarks of the style.

Architect A.H. Moise designed this 1916 bungalow for Charles Pearson, who retained it for only two years. Pearson was assistant treasurer for American Coffee Company of New Orleans.

An advertisement placed in the *Times-Picayune* on December 14, 1924, and January 4, 1925, described the bungalow as being

> between Broadway and Audubon streets, facing small proposed park. Near new car line, etc. This cozy house is without a doubt one of the prettiest and conveniently located homes on Fontainebleau Drive on the market for sale. Containing spacious front porch, large living room with stone fireplace, dining room, window seats, breakfast room, kitchen, two bedrooms with closets, pretty bathroom, hot water heater, sleeping porch, etc. Everything to make a home complete. Driveway and garage. Hardwood floors, surrounded by pretty homes and shrubbery.

Six interim owners preceded Charles C. Carlson's purchase of the house in 1938. It remains in the Carlson family as of this writing.

FRERET (Elm; Long; Pine)

5624 FRERET, HURSTVILLE

Schoolboard architect E.A. Christy designed this high school named in honor of Louisiana historian Alcée Fortier as an all-boys school. The 1930 structure employs brick and terra cotta in a handsome, yet forceful manner. Stylistically, it is a modified Renaissance design.

Fortier held a deep appreciation of Louisiana's French culture and Creole literature, folklore, history, and language. A full-time faculty member of Tulane University, he refused numerous offers to relocate although he taught in other states during the summers.

6321 FRERET, BURTHEVILLE

This Italianate center-hall cottage is unusually early for this area. William Tracy purchased seventeen lots in this square in 1870 when this was part of Jefferson Parish. The 1874 city directory lists Tracy as living on Long (Freret) near Calhoun. He sold the house and fifteen lots in 1875 to George W. Doll, who sold the property to Barbara Kuntz seven years later. After several subsequent owners, Tulane University acquired the house in 1951.

The site's lush foliage obscures this house to the casual passerby. The drop siding, sliphead windows, and cast iron railing are original to the construction while the dormer and roofline are alterations to the original design.

GARFIELD (Ann; Boudousquie; Jennet; Jennette)

5901 GARFIELD, HURSTVILLE

Built in 1905 for Patrick McGrath, a cotton weigher, this handsome house was originally two and one-half stories, as seen in the old photograph. It was lowered in 1956 by Abry Bros. for Lamartine Lamar, who wanted a one-story residence. The

Southern Colonial residence has exceptionally fine classic detailing, although the iron porch railing would be better if replaced by a wooden one as originally designed, and the portico gable would also be improved if the window were restored.

In 1910 the McGrath family sold the house to Dr. Charles Landfried for $28,000. Landfried sold the house in 1932 to Branches, which sold it to Dr. Ernest Allgeyer in 1935. Allgeyer lost the house in 1944 to the homestead, which sold it to Mrs. Dora Depass and Mrs. Mabel Depass Harris. In 1954 Dr. Abram Diaz and Dr. Edward Matthews purchased the house for $33,000. Lamartine Lamar bought it the following year and had it lowered.

GREEN

7020 GREEN, FRIBURG

Newcomb art professor William Woodward sold this property to Dr. Joseph Weis in 1927. Weis retained architects Armstrong and Koch to design the present house, with its secluded courtyard entrance. The house was completed in 1928. In 1939 architect Douglass Freret designed the garden house and fence for the residence.

In 1951 Dr. Weis' estate sold the house to Morrell Trimble, the present owner.

HAMPSON (Washington)

7301 HAMPSON, GREENVILLE

Attorney James McLoughlin purchased this site in 1904 for $4,000. At that time, he lived at 1544 State

Street in a large, two-story Queen Anne residence he had built in 1894. According to McLoughlin's diary, the family moved out of the State Street residence into a boarding house and had the Hampson Street house built with material salvaged from the State Street residence. The foundation was begun on July 9, 1907, and the family moved into the new house shortly thereafter as they are listed on Hampson Street in the 1907 city directory.

In 1922 the McLoughlins sold the house for $16,800 to Mr. and Mrs. Thomas Jefferson Feibleman who in turn sold it to Thomas Barrow in 1959. The owner as of this writing, James Noe, Jr., acquired the house in 1964.

HENRY CLAY (Clay)

333 HENRY CLAY AVENUE, BURTHEVILLE

Although the original porch deck has been eliminated, this house retains its original scale and character. The columns with their dropped capitals beneath small brackets, reflect a Mannerist detail influenced by the Neo Grec.

Adam Lorch, a clerk at Factor's Cotton Press, obtained a building permit in 1885 for this center-hall residence and retained the house until 1931. After eight subsequent owners, including Charles Feldman, Emma Feldman, First Presbyterian Church, Grace Robinson, Marion de la Houssaye, Hugh Evans, Jr., and Thomas Fiebelkorn, the Sophie L. Gumbel Guild purchased it in 1981.

514 HENRY CLAY AVENUE, BURTHEVILLE

Sugarmaker Lewis Edward Prest obtained a building permit on July 11, 1885, for the construction of this Italianate center-hall residence. The permit reported the construction cost to be $2,000. Prest, however, did not purchase the property from Catherine Prest until August 3, 1885. The act of sale stipulates that the structures being built belonged to Lewis Prest.

The house has lost a few of its original details, such as brackets above the drop-column capitals likely similar to 333 Henry Clay, or a wooden spandrel, and the porch pickets and bottom rail. The clumsy, single-dormer, segmental-window heads, window cornices, and recessed front door are typical of the 1870s and 1880s.

The house remained in the Prest family until 1932. John Paul Lozes bought the house in 1933, and his family retained ownership for fifty-five years. Since 1988 it has been the home of the Charles Sanders.

720 HENRY CLAY AVENUE, BURTHEVILLE

The Order of Franciscan Poor Clares came to New Orleans in 1885 and acquired this site two years later. The order built the present monastery between

---

1912 and 1914, replacing an earlier convent facing Magazine. Franciscan Brother Leonard Darscheid, in association with architect William Burk, designed the Romanesque Revival convent, which was designated a city landmark in 1979 by the New Orleans Historic District Landmarks Commission.

The Romanesque style in this example is characterized by the corbeled brick at the roof line, round-headed openings, rose window, and exposed brick.

1234 HENRY CLAY AVENUE, BURTHEVILLE

Thomas Sully designed this 1895 "old Colonial cottage" for Susie M.W. Ellermann. Although not a literal copy of a Colonial cottage, this early phase of the style merely hints at its precedents and is very closely allied with the Queen Anne. The house is illustrated on the 1896 Sanborn insurance map without the wraparound porch, which does appear on the 1909 map.

In 1899 Ellermann, at that time Mrs. Charles Dufour, rented her cottage to Arthur Norcross for $50 per month. A year later Norcross paid $5,500 for the property, and it remained in the Norcross family until 1912 when Helen Desmare, wife of Augustus C. Vreeland, purchased it for $10,200. The Vreeland family owned the house for fourteen years, selling to Earl S. Binnings, who in turn sold it in 1932 to Dr. Samuel Gore. Sixty-one years later, Sandra and Richard West Freeman bought the property from Dr. Samuel Gore, Jr.

1310 HENRY CLAY AVENUE, BURTHEVILLE

This well-maintained house has a decidedly vertical emphasis, with elaborate and distinctive porch detailing that is unusually flat for its construction date.

In 1895 Mrs. Wilhemina Rice Born acquired this site as a vacant lot from Angelo Burt for $2,126 and built the present house the same year at a cost of $5,800. The house remained in the family until 1922. After three interim owners, the George B. Baus family acquired it in 1961, selling it in 1993 to Kathleen and John Saer.

1334 HENRY CLAY AVENUE, BURTHEVILLE

The understated ground-floor entrance is in fact an alteration to the original design of this Queen Anne cottage, likely executed in 1925 by builder Joseph Lagarde for brothers Hermann and Eberhard Deutsch who owned it for four years. A comparison of the 1896 and 1909 Sanborn insurance maps indicates additional changes to the structure. The 1896 map notes the structure as a one-story frame residence with the same footprint as the present structure except that the front porch was only two bays wide, sans the river-side bay, and the rear wing had only a one-story porch. The 1909 map indicates a one-and-one-half-story, wood frame residence on brick basement, with the present three-bay front porch and two-story and one-story rear porches.

The complexity of this circa 1895 Queen Anne cottage is typical for its period. It has a multi-gabled roof, clipped corners on the river-side projecting bay, and brackets above dropped-column capitals.

Since 1950 this has been the residence of Dr. and Mrs. Homer Dupuy. He ruled as Rex in 1963.

1435 HENRY CLAY AVENUE, BURTHEVILLE

In 1894 Commercial Homestead purchased the corner of Henry Clay and Garfield streets for $1,000 and sold it three months later to baker Charles Oppenheimer for $4,600, an indication that the homestead built this two-story Queen Anne residence in the interim. Oppenheimer is listed in the 1895 city directory at Henry Clay, corner of Garfield.

The house is typical of the University section, with a projecting bay with clipped corners, full-width front porch with a second floor cut into a porch roof, and columns set on pedestals. *Southern Garden Magazine* for January 6, 1895, illustrated the house, stating it was erected by Louis A. Ganter, architect and builder. The article describes the exterior millwork as being of select and dry cypress, the weatherboards of dressed long leaf yellow pine; the interior millwork of selected cypress, hand oiled and rubbed down, "cut and other good quality of American glass," magnificent hardwood mantels, grates and tiles from the Sumner Building and Supply Company, an iron fence from Hinderer's, and "old Bangor slates."

The Oppenheimer family retained the house until 1919. At one time this house was owned by Alpha

Tau Omega fraternity. As of this writing, it is the home of Dr. John T. Cole and Dr. Lois Mailander.

1500 HENRY CLAY AVENUE, BURTHEVILLE

Attorney John Ferguson built this house in 1870 as the first structure on this square. Ferguson came to Louisiana from Martha's Vineyard, Massachusetts. He served in the Louisiana legislature from 1877 to 1880, at which time he became a criminal judge.

As originally built, this residence was rectangular in plan with a one-story entrance porch on the most forward portion of the house and a very elaborate verge board on a deep overhang. About 1890, as evidenced by the increase in property assessment between 1890 and 1891, the Fergusons enlarged the house with a perpendicular addition to the lake side, which appears on the 1896 Sanborn insurance map.

The house remained in the Ferguson family until 1920 when Charles Unsworth acquired it. Subsequent owners have been Hans Hellmers (1937), Wolf Hellmers (1963), Dorothea Martin (1982), and Patricia and Bret A. Clesi (1988).

In 1981 the City of New Orleans designated the house a landmark.

1514 HENRY CLAY AVENUE, BURTHEVILLE

This International style house was built in the side yard of 1500 Henry Clay in 1936 for the Times-Picayune Publishing Company to commemorate its 100th anniversary. Dubbed the "New American Home," this Moise Goldstein design featured all the modern amenities of a "dream house," such as air conditioning. Streuby Drumm, vice-president of New Orleans Public Service, convinced the publishing

company to undertake the project and then purchased the house after the promotional stint was terminated.

The International style eschewed ornament and defined space by volume rather than mass. Consequently, the exterior of the structure became the protective skin rather than a structural component, allowing window walls and windows in the corner, a key structural location. The use of brick rather than stucco, the preferred material for this style, is an unusual choice.

In 1957 Charles Kurzweg bought the house for $50,000, and his family retains ownership as of this writing.

1529 HENRY CLAY AVENUE, BURTHEVILLE

This house has been moved twice since it was originally built about 1877. Jonas H. French purchased one-half of this square in 1875. The Robinson *Atlas* indicates a house facing Benjamin Street at the corner of Henry Clay, but French is not listed in city directories.

In 1885 William Bogel purchased the site, selling it the following year to Leona Jumonville, who is listed in the 1889 directory at Benjamin, southeast corner of Henry Clay. Jumonville's 1890 succession describes a $3,000 house with parlor, front bedroom, rear bedroom, cabinet, dining room, and kitchen. Her heirs placed an advertisement in the *Daily Picayune* that described it as an elevated frame cottage, slated, with brick basement. The house was bought by Sam Henderson, an attorney, who is listed in the 1892 city directory on Henry Clay, southeast corner of Benjamin. It was likely Henderson who moved the cottage to the site at 1533 Henry Clay where the 1896 Sanborn insurance map illustrates it on six-to-seven-foot brick piers. Henderson's succession sold the house in 1916 to John B. Levert, who likely moved it a second time to its present location and lowered it, then built another house on its former site at 1533 Henry Clay.

Levert's company, J.B. Levert Land Company, sold 1529 Henry Clay to Ludo Von Meysenburg in 1926. Twelve years later, Stanley Morris purchased the house for $9,000 and owned it until 1977 when he sold it to Loretta and John D. O'Reilly for $160,000.

In 1983 Mrs. Clifford Cocram Lapeyre bought it, and in 1986 sold it to Elizabeth and James Woods.

The house has a well-detailed Greek Revival cornice, simple openings, and a porch extending down the river side with late-nineteenth century turned columns in contrast to the simpler Greek Revival boxed columns of the front gallery. The porch turnings also likely date to the late-nineteenth century.

1557 HENRY CLAY AVENUE, BURTHEVILLE

Through two separate transactions, Mary Simmons, widow of Samuel Wren, acquired this site in 1897 and built this two-story, wood frame residence that same year, as she is listed here in the 1898 city directory. The Wren family retained the house until 1912 when it was purchased by the St. Denis Villere family whose descendants are still in possession at this writing.

The comfortable house has undergone a few changes, notably the addition of an iron, second-floor porch railing and the addition and alterations to the lake side of the two-story projecting mass of the structure. Its picturesque massing is notably late-nineteenth century and typical of the Queen Anne style. The implementation of half-timbering in the Queen Anne is more closely associated with the English version than the American; half-timbering in America is more commonly associated with the Tudor Revival style.

1582 HENRY CLAY AVENUE, BURTHEVILLE

When originally built, this two-story Queen Anne residence faced the avenue as 6206 St. Charles, as seen in this old photograph. It was moved about 1912 prior to the construction of the temporary St. Charles Avenue Christian Church.

Attorney Samuel Gilmore purchased the St. Charles Avenue site in 1887 and commissioned Thomas Sully to design the subject residence. Gilmore's daughter, Martha Gilmore Robinson, who was born and lived here as a child, would later become a leader in the local preservation movement and recipient of the 1960 Times-Picayune Loving Cup. After moving the house to the Henry Clay site, the Gilmores sold it in 1919 to David Freeman, whose widow sold it to Emerson Dunbar in 1925. Two years later, Ella F. Hardie purchased it. In 1945

Hardie's succession sold it to Arthur de la Houssaye, who sold it in 1978 to the owner as of this writing, Dr. Donald Toso.

HURST (Irma; Louisa; Mississippi)

5829 HURST, HURSTVILLE

A large tile roof and "peanut brittle" front porch dominate this unusual Secessionist style residence. It is possibly the work of H. Jordan MacKenzie who was noted for his Secessionist architecture. The house is little changed since it appeared in the *Illustrated Sunday Magazine* shortly after construction.

The house was built by Mutual Building and Loan Association in 1910, as indicated by the jump in assessment in 1911, and was first the home of accountant Henry Daspit who purchased it in 1914. As of this writing, the house has had ten owners, and has been owned since 1985 by Mr. and Mrs. David Gooch.

5902, 5908, 5914, 5920, 5926 HURST, HURSTVILLE

Five originally identical Queen Anne cottages were built for a Mrs. Schneidau in 1891 by builder

L.C. LeCorgne for $18,500. Of the five, 5902 Hurst (pictured) is the most intact.

JOSEPH

422 JOSEPH, HURSTVILLE

Here is a rarity in this area of the city—a Greek Revival center-hall cottage built for butcher George Peltz in 1867 when the Greek Revival had long since given way to the Italianate and other picturesque styles. Such late examples of the Greek Revival, however, are not that uncommon in the South. The Greek-key door frame, flat-headed windows, and shiplap siding seen here are more typical of the 1840s or 1850s when this style was most popular.

This site was originally part of Jefferson Parish and bordered the service community of Jefferson City where the economy was based on butchers (see Volume VII). Gardner's directory of 1868 lists "George Beltz [sic] butcher, Joseph near Jersey" (Annunciation). The house remained in the Peltz family until 1983 when Clancy Dupepe purchased it and undertook a complete renovation. The owners as of this writing, Dr. and Mrs. Gordon McFarland, bought the house in 1988.

LASALLE (Howard; St. George)

3 LASALLE, BURTHEVILLE

Jeannette Ballard purchased this site on January 2, 1909, for $3,000 and commissioned architect Francis J. MacDonnell to design this Gothic Revival concrete residence. A photograph and first floor plan of the house appeared in the February 1910 issue of *Architectural Arts and Its Allies.* In 1919 Ballard, then married to Robert Dicks and living on Audubon Boulevard, sold the house for $8,240 to William Boatner Reily, Jr., president of Standard Coffee Company. Reily retained Armstrong and Koch, architects,

to design alterations and additions to the house which were executed in 1924 by Denegre and Woodward. In 1948 Reily's heirs sold the house to Leon Irwin, Jr. who in turn in 1965 sold to Louis Freeman.

8 LASALLE, BURTHEVILLE

This 1920 house designed by architects Armstrong and Koch garnered national attention in 1928 when G.H. Edgell featured it in his book, *The American Architect of Today.* Edgell wrote:

> No local architect, nor even client, could neglect the appropriate suggestions of the local style, and its influence appears refreshingly in many a modern building of New Orleans. As an example, we reproduce the residence of Mr. J.C. Lyons, at New Orleans . . . done by Armstrong & Koch. It would be hard to find a building that fits more perfectly into its environment. It is dignified, sheltered, yet airy. One realizes at once that it smacks of France and that it is adapted to the needs of the warm, moist climate of Louisiana.

LAUREL (Jersey; Market; Patton; Union)

5831 LAUREL, HURSTVILLE

Charles Walker, a superintendent of coal boats, likely built this cottage in 1869 after he purchased the site in 1862 for $900. It remained in the Walker family until 1973. Two years later, Chares Vick bought the house.

5940 LAUREL, BLOOMINGDALE

Mrs. Bella Reinch built this Eastlake house in 1896 as an investment, selling it upon completion to Sylvester Chuchill, who was the first occupant of the house.

6114-16, 6118 LAUREL, BURTHEVILLE

Here are a double shotgun at 6114-16 Laurel and a side-hall residence at 6118 Laurel, typical of working-class housing in the 1890s found in close proximity to the river, both uptown and downtown.

6114-16 has nice gable-end jigsaw work and 6118 has a highly decorative porch.

6114-16 appears on the 1896 Sanborn insurance map and was likely built for Charles Forkert in 1895.

6118 Laurel was built in 1898 for Philomene Frazier by the Metropolitan Construction Company, owned by J.E. Diboll and Allison Owen. After two interim owners, it was bought by Mr. and Mrs. Earl Ransano in 1965 and remains in the family as of this writing.

LOWERLINE

301, 305, 309, 313, 317, 321, 325, 329 LOWERLINE, GREENVILLE

Here are eight single box cottages built as investment properties in 1906 for Henry Chalin and John F. Miller, officers in the Henry Chalin and Company Sash, Door and Blind Factory and Planing Mill.

Architect Abraham Moise designed these simple shotguns, which demonstrate that with the advent of the twentieth century, gingerbread was used with increasing restraint and classical or colonial detailing implemented.

443 LOWERLINE, GREENVILLE

Here is an early example of a Louisiana Colonial Revival residence designed by William Woodward and built in 1897. Rather than executing a literal copy, he borrowed only certain local details from Louisiana's colonial heritage: the umbrella-like roof, cigar-shaped columns, the gallery stair, and a fanlight transom.

Originally from New England, Woodward came to New Orleans at the request of Tulane University President William Johnston in 1884 and resided there until 1912. Professor Woodward taught a night class in freehand and mechanical drawing at Turners Hall and classes at the Cotton Centennial and established an architectural engineering course at Tulane. In 1887 he moved to Newcomb College and organized the Newcomb Art School. Woodward described his residence in his memoirs as "a home near the University, among beautiful trees, planned and supervised by themselves which goes far, under modest means, towards rational improved living."

This house was designated a city landmark in 1990 by the New Orleans Historic District Landmarks Commission.

535 LOWERLINE, GREENVILLE

Here is another residence moved from its original site. This center-hall Italianate residence was built on St. Charles Avenue in 1867 for Frederick Fischer, a local sawmill owner. The Fischer family sold the property to Martha Silk Keller in 1909, at which time the house was likely moved to its present location, as is shown on the 1909 Sanborn insurance map. City directories, however, do not list Keller at this location until 1911.

True to its period, this residence has a prominent dormer, brackets and modillions in the entablature, applied column moldings, heavy window cornices, a paneled porch ceiling, beefy porch turnings, and a segmental head to the entry.

In 1913 Martha Keller bequeathed the house to her niece, Martha Beasley, who owned it until 1944.

After two subsequent owners, Mr. and Mrs. Fontaine Martin purchased it.

In 1981 the city designated the house a landmark.

637 LOWERLINE, GREENVILLE

On August 27, 1894, bookkeeper William Morgan contracted with William Bird to build this two-story Queen Anne residence designed by architect I.K. Levy. According to the contract, the $3,000 house originally had two cisterns, an outhouse, a privy, a coal house, a laundry, a "Demarest closet" in the bathroom with seat and lid, a porcelain tub, a washstand with marble top and back in the hall, a galvanized steel kitchen sink, a jib window under stairs, J. Blaffer bricks, cypress doors and windows, pine floors, and a slate roof.

Morgan sold the house to William Holden one year later for $4,000. In 1904 Mary Jane Swift Goldsmith purchased the house, and it remained in the Goldsmith family until 1920, when John Henry O'Neill acquired it for $8,250. In 1967 JoAnn and Clinton Montz purchased it and in 1974 sold it for $64,000 to Bonnie and Robert Livingston, who sold it in 1977 to Barbara and Keith Morgan.

727 LOWERLINE, GREENVILLE

Malvina Funguy, wife of John W. Fleetwood, purchased the vacant land in 1894 and built the present center-hall residence shortly thereafter, for the Fleetwoods are listed at this location in the 1895 city directory. In 1897 Malvina mortgaged the property for $4,000, stating that she owed James Fleetwood $3,800 for the purchase of the land and construction of the house. The following year she sold the house for $4,000 to James Fleetwood who in turn sold it to James Tallant in 1900. It remained in the Tallant family until 1970.

The house demonstrates the restraint of the Italianate style in comparison with the more exuberant Queen Anne and Eastlake styles popular during the 1890s.

1129 LOWERLINE, FRIBURG

The 1906 alterations by Grace McGeehan to this nineteenth century residence conceal its original appearance. McGeehan contracted with William Kiefe to make $3,350 worth of repairs and alterations to the house, including the present roof line, dormers, gable-end Palladian windows, and Tuscan columns. A 1906 survey indicates that this house had a cistern, a stable and a windmill.

The house likely dates to 1869, at which time J.M. Brabazon owned it. Directories indicate that Joseph Rau, secretary of Carrollton Insurance, resided here in 1869, although he did not purchase the site until late in 1875. Possibly, Brabazon and Rau were related, as the 1867 city directory lists them both as residing at the same St. Andrew Street residence. Rau's heirs in 1890 sold the house, along with the entire square, to James McGeehan, whose family retains ownership as of this writing.

LOYOLA (S. Franklin; St. David)

5625 LOYOLA, HURSTVILLE—Henry W. Allen School

This large, brick-and-stone Colonial Revival school replaced an earlier two-story-over-basement school fronting Nashville. According to a commemorative plaque inside, the school dates to 1926. It was designed by architect E.A. Christy, built by contractors R.P. Farnsworth and Company, and named for Civil War Governor Henry W. Allen.

This uptown educational institution was discussed in the *Times-Picayune* in 1930:

> The school board is planning another building near the present Allen School, to provide elementary work. Until this school is built, the present Allen school will give both elementary and commercial courses; the other building, to be erected on the same piece of property, probably will enable the present structure to be devoted entirely to commercial courses for high school girls.

The article notes that "the ground behind the Allen and Fortier Schools, extending for about two city blocks, will be converted principally into an athletic field." A sketch accompanying the article illustrates the H.W. Allen Elementary School on Joseph (which was never built), the H.W. Allen High School of Commerce on Loyola (the subject building), and Alcee Fortier High School on Freret, with an athletic field and stadium on Nashville.

5700 LOYOLA, HURSTVILLE

The *Times-Picayune* of February 25, 1917, reported that the Sophie L. Gumbel heirs donated $50,000 for the construction of a school to be built on the grounds of the Touro-Shakspeare Home for the Indigent. Called Sophie L. Gumbel School for the Blind and Feebleminded, it would accommodate 100 students. Its operation was funded in part by the City of New Orleans, and it drew some volunteer staff from Newman Manual Training School. According to the newspaper article:

At the commission of the Gumbels, the plan for the annex has been designed by Moise H. Goldstein, architect. It will conform in general style to the handsome Touro Shakspeare group and will be of the English collegiate type with central square tower and flanking wings. . . . The edifice will be in the rear of the existing buildings, but will front on Franklin [now Loyola] street and face the Henry W. Allen School and residence park which is to be laid out. . . . It will be more of an industrial school than an asylum, and only the indigent feeble minded and blind will be accepted. There will be no age limit, and the aim will be to help the pupils to become self supporting.

The article was accompanied by Goldstein's rendering of the building.

In 1943 the city changed the building's function to a home for neglected and abandoned children known as the Sophie L. Gumbel Home. By 1962 the population of the home was down to twenty-four children as foster-parent care replaced asylums, and the home was closed. In 1963 Retarded Children of Greater New Orleans operated here and continues as of this writing as Retarded Citizens Association of Greater New Orleans.

MAGAZINE (Liberty)
5941-43 MAGAZINE, BLOOMINGDALE

This well-preserved Eastlake residence is similar to several others in uptown New Orleans. Although converted into apartments, it retains much of its original exterior design.

The Eastlake style strived for picturesque and ornate design, as seen here in the use of boxed columns with incised ornament, dropped capitals with brackets above, a shallow balcony extending from the front porch, ornate window and door cornices, and a sunburst pattern in the roof gable.

Dairyman Henry Butker purchased eight lots in this square from Henry Lambert in 1885 and built the present residence about 1893, as 1894 is the first year the house is assessed. Butker sold the house for $1,200 to Florence Albers in 1904. Subsequent owners have been Marion Baker (1927), Marcus Korn (1928), Eureka Homestead (1930), Abe and Ida

Silverman (1943), Nicolino Alphonso (1973), and Edward William Alton Ochsner, Jr. (1974).

6021-23, 6025-27, 6029-31 MAGAZINE, BLOOMINGDALE

Here are one double shotgun and two double camelbacks typical of New Orleans housing during the late-nineteenth and early-twentieth centuries. As is the case with many of their contemporary look-alikes, most of the exterior ornament is confined to the street facade, with austere side and rear elevations.

The site for all three structures was owned at one time by the German Protestant Orphan Asylum. The site for 6021-23 was purchased from the asylum in 1902 by William Bacher who built the shotgun house that year and sold it the next year to Emelie Cuneo for $3,500. The asylum also sold the sites for the two camelbacks in 1902 to the superintendent of the asylum, Gustave Pixberg, who built one house that year and the other in 1903. A continuous cast iron fence unifies these three houses, along with others in the block, in typical New Orleans tradition.

6305 MAGAZINE, BURTHEVILLE

On August 2, 1900, Thomas O'Neil, an assistant engineer with the fire department, contracted with

John Baehr, Jr. to build this two-story, wood frame residence for $2,375. The front porch has a rock-faced, concrete block railing and columns, between which span Tudor arches. The second-floor porch deck is visually concealed from the street by an apron roof on awkward shallow brackets. The pair of stained glass windows above the front door is noteworthy.

O'Neil retained the house for only six years. After two interim owners, Dr. Darlene Bassett purchased the house in 1971 and resides here as of this writing.

MARQUETTE PLACE (St. Patrick; Saratoga)
6120 MARQUETTE PLACE, BURTHEVILLE

Francis MacDonnell designed this large, 1910 Craftsman house for cottonbroker Robert H. Holmes. Holmes purchased the site in May 1910 for $5,000 and donated it, with the house, in August 1911 to his wife, Mary Holmes. The combined value of the lot and house was $24,000. In 1919 Mary Holmes sold the house to Frederick Foxley for $19,000. It remained in the Foxley family until 1933 when the Benjamin Williams family acquired it, retaining it until 1982 when Jane and David Holtzman purchased it. The owner of the house as of this writing, Elizabeth Polchow, obtained it in 1986.

The present monotone paint scheme conceals the original design intent in which the porch columns and foundation were natural brick, the millwork painted in contrast to the stucco, and the half-timbering in the gable contrasted with the stucco. Other than the paint scheme, little has changed on the exterior.

NASHVILLE (Beauregard)
510 NASHVILLE AVENUE, HURSTVILLE

This residence was built in 1869 for Eliza Meares, wife of river pilot Hampton Meares, for they are listed in the 1870 city directory at west side Nashville, between Laurel and Jersey (Annunciation). The house appears in the 1883 Robinson *Atlas*. Meares sold it in 1902 to Morris Meares, in whose family it remained until 1941 when Mr. and Mrs.

L.C. Bisso purchased it for $4,500. The Bissos retained the house until 1965 when it was sold to Elsie and Louis F. Merz for $18,000. As of this writing, the altered house remains in the Merz family. It is a prime candidate for restoration as one of the oldest residences in the University section.

520 NASHVILLE AVENUE, HURSTVILLE

A huge magnolia provides a canopy over this quaint raised cottage. Maud Meares, wife of Thomas Elliot, acquired the property from Eliza Meares, who lived next door at 510 Nashville. The Elliots mortgaged the property to Mutual Building and Homestead Association in 1887, likely to build this house. The house remained in the hands of Meares' descendants until 1992 when Carling Dinkler III bought it.

610 NASHVILLE AVENUE, HURSTVILLE

Nashville Avenue on the river side of Magazine Street has a wonderful collection of 1890s Queen

Anne cottages. This one features a complex facade with picturesque roof line, clipped corners with decorative brackets, and a projecting entrance bay with Eastlake ornament.

Between 1896 and 1897, the property assessment increased by $600. In 1897 Julius Manger sold the site for $2,800 to William McWhirter, who two years later mortgaged the property for $1,900. The house could have been constructed by either Manger, a developer who obtained permits for three singles in this block in 1897, or McWhirter, a machinist who mortgaged the property in 1899 and is listed here in the city directory of that year. After four interim owners, Edith and Loda Crawford purchased the property for $18,000 in 1960. It is still owned by the Crawford family at this writing.

624 NASHVILLE AVENUE, HURSTVILLE

Julius Manger built this Queen Anne cottage in 1897. He purchased the site in September that year for $1,200, built the house, and sold it early in January 1898 to Ella Swain Claussen for $3,000. Although the Claussens retained the house until 1911, they never lived here, according to city directories. Philip May, the next owner, sold to Christian Fricke in 1929 and, at this writing, Fricke descendants own the cottage.

636 NASHVILLE AVENUE, HURSTVILLE

In 1895 William Arms, a reporter with the *Times-Democrat*, purchased this corner from the Daughters of Charity and built the present Queen Anne camel-

back, which appears on the 1896 Sanborn insurance map as the only house on this block. The Arms family retained the house until 1926 when Frederick Walther purchased it for $7,000. Walther lost the house in 1936 in a sheriff's sale to Home Owner's Loan Corporation, which sold it in 1939 to Clement J. Weis. The Weis family sold it in 1984 to Craig Houin and John Kain.

704, 710 NASHVILLE AVENUE, HURSTVILLE

These two identical Queen Anne cottages with Eastlake ornament complement the streetscape with their elaborate porch railings composed of spindles, diagonals, and corner blocks. The porch columns are particularly noteworthy, employing a variety of shapes.

In 1896 developer Julius Manger purchased both of these lots in separate transactions, selling 704 in 1897 to John T. Bowes and 710 (pictured) to Robert Plant, most likely after building the two cottages. The tax assessment for 704 Nashville jumps from $500 in 1897 to $2,000 the following year. The 1898 city directory lists Bowes and Plant, both river pilots, as residing at their respective addresses. The Plant family retained the house at 704 until 1987.

722-24, 728-30 NASHVILLE AVENUE, HURSTVILLE

These two Eastlake camelbacks are typical of Uptown New Orleans. Michael Willem had 722-24 Nashville (pictured) built in 1902, as evidenced by a building contract with Jacob Baehr for $3,312 and the increase in the property's tax assessment from $800 to $3,200 in 1903. In 1896, when Willem purchased the site, the entire square is shown as vacant on the Sanborn map. The 1903 city directory lists Michael Willem at 722 Nashville.

The site of 728-30 Nashville was purchased in 1896 by Julius Manger along with several other pieces of land. That same year he sold the site to Henry Cory for $3,400, likely including the present house. The house remained in the possession of Cory's heirs until 1952.

802 NASHVILLE AVENUE, HURSTVILLE
In 1899 river pilot George Wilson purchased a vacant lot on this corner and in 1902 signed a building contract with John Baehr, Jr. for a single frame cottage to cost $3,780. The 1903 city directory lists Wilson as residing here.

This Eastlake cottage has an animated Nashville Avenue facade, with a curved porch end on Magazine Street and a bay which undulates onto the porch.

1130 NASHVILLE AVENUE, HURSTVILLE
The *Daily-Picayune* of September 1, 1910, records that "although not complete as to its interior decorations and furnishings, the Parker Memorial Methodist Church in Nashville Avenue is finished to such an extent that the congregation has been worshipping in it for several months. When finally completed, it will be a very handsome church edifice."

Diboll and Owen were the architects for this modified Gothic church, which has a horizontal appearance, betraying the vertical emphasis of the Gothic style. Additionally, without employing any specific Romanesque detail, the church imparts a Romanesque massing.

1300 NASHVILLE AVENUE, HURSTVILLE
This Mediterranean Villa style residence imparts a sense of cool tranquility with its large, umbrella style red tile roof, window boxes, and casement doors and windows. Built in 1924 for Albert A. Marchal, manager of Colonial Home Furnishings, the house was designed by Weiss and Dreyfous. The house remained in the Marchal family until 1965 when Dr. Harris Hyman III purchased it.

1436 NASHVILLE AVENUE, HURSTVILLE
Samuel P. Stone, Jr. was the architect for this 1913 Renaissance Revival church built by J. Koels as the First Church of Christ Scientist. The classical detailing relates well to the many Southern Colonial residences Uptown.

1445 NASHVILLE AVENUE, HURSTVILLE
Architect Frank Dannemann built this Southern Colonial, two-story, wood frame residence in 1905 after purchasing the site for $2,600. Dannemann sold the house for $10,500 in 1909 to Mrs. Christine Hayward whose succession sold it in 1923 to Henry Bohne. The house remained in the Bohne family until 1939 when Rita Levy purchased it for $10,500. Levy sold the house in 1952 to Rowena and John Curren who the next year sold it to Adam Trowbridge. In 1967 Patricia and Frank Friedler, Jr. purchased the house from Trowbridge.

The corner pilasters, Ionic portico columns, entablature, modillions and dentils, and window

pediments are common characteristics of the Southern Colonial style.

1458 NASHVILLE AVENUE, HURSTVILLE
Dr. J. Ambrose Storck retained Julius Koch to build this 1905 Southern Colonial Revival basement residence at a cost of $5,000. The Storck family owned the house until 1977 when Bonny and Robert Maloney purchased it.

While the house incorporates a variety of stock building elements into a harmonious street facade, it imparts a feeling of being too large for the site.

NEWCOMB BOULEVARD
6 NEWCOMB BOULEVARD, GREENVILLE
This Prairie style residence is one of three designed for the D'Antoni family by architect Edward Sporl—the other houses are on Robert Street and Freret Street. The Prairie style is distinguished by horizontal emphasis and the use of Roman bricks, deep overhangs, and flat roofs. This house was completed in 1923 for Blaize S. D'Antoni who sold it for $40,000 in 1930 to Equity Security. Four years later, Morris Steinberg purchased the house for $31,200, and it remains in the Steinberg family as of this writing.

10 NEWCOMB BOULEVARD, GREENVILLE

Weiss and Dreyfous designed this house for Henry C. Flonacher, a paper company executive who had purchased the vacant lot in 1922 from Harry Latter, the 1950 Times-Picayune Loving Cup recipient. The 1922-23 tax book, under the "1924" column, notes at this address a "new single two story stucco tile roof, nine rooms, two baths, enclosed sleeping porch, $22,000." Flonacher is first listed here in 1925. The following year he sold the lot, with the house, back to Latter, who sold it in 1931 to Toga Realty, only to buy it back from Toga in 1937. In 1954 Marion and Herbert Harvey, Jr. purchased the house, and the Harvey succession sold it to Fred Larsen in 1984.

This Mediterranean Villa is topped by a large red tile roof, visually supported on shallow brackets. A loggia pierces the most forward portion of the facade, which steps back twice as it widens to the rear. A bronze sculpture adds a nice touch to the entrance porch.

OAK

7329 OAK, FRIBURG

Alexander Hay was the architect for this interesting residence on the corner of Oak and Lowerline streets. Its design follows the Arts and Crafts movement of its day, with its use of concrete block columns, exposed rafter ends, tile roof, decorative window lights, and stained woodwork, and also employs such Swiss-chalet details as decorative cantilevered bracket supports and woodwork in the stucco. Robert Gottschalk built a similar house at the corner of Freret and Burdette.

Margaret Harrison, wife of shipping merchant George Miller, obtained a permit in 1908 for this house, to be built at a cost of $4,500. The Millers sold the house to river pilot Frederick Blaslond in 1910. After two interim owners, the house was purchased by John T. Parker in 1967, and it remains in the Parker family as of this writing.

PALMER (Clay; Henry Clay)

1625 PALMER AVENUE, BURTHEVILLE

Albert Simon, a partner in Kohn, Weil and Simon, Canal Street hat and glove merchants, acquired this site in 1921 for $10,000 and engaged architect Moise Goldstein to design the subject house. A building permit that was obtained in 1922 stated the cost would be $16,200.

The house is in the Mediterranean style, which was popular at that time and also the style of Goldstein's office. The exterior of the house is typical of the style, with its large tiled roof, stuccoed walls, arched first-floor and square-headed second-floor openings, and well-articulated front door.

Simon sold the house in 1939 for $15,500 to Lois Stern Brown who sold it in 1977 to Mr. and Mrs. R. King Milling, the owners as of this writing.

1637 PALMER AVENUE, BURTHEVILLE

Here is a remodeling of an earlier, smaller residence built for Edgar Hincks, a postal cashier. After several title changes, Martha and Paul Lemann purchased the house in 1935 and engaged a young architect, F. Monroe Labouisse, Sr., to remodel and enlarge it. According to Mrs. Lemann, the precedent for the remodeling was the first floor of the "Old Spanish Custom House" on Bayou St. John. The Lemann family had a long interest in Louisiana Colonial

architecture, as did their architect. Labouisse worked for the Historic American Buildings Survey during the Great Depression, documenting such buildings as the Cabildo and Beauregard House, and his father was instrumental in creating the Vieux Carré Commission. Paul Lemann's mother donated Madame John's Legacy, a Louisiana colonial structure, to the Louisiana State Museum.

After a Lemann ownership of fifty-five years, Juliet Lemann Uhl sold the house in 1993 to Lucy and Frank Riess.

1640 PALMER AVENUE, BURTHEVILLE

Architect Emile Weil designed this house in 1908 for cottonbroker Sylvan Newburger. The eclectic design employs Tudor arches, Craftsman porch columns, and a Mediterranean Villa style roof. The Historic District Landmarks Commission designated it a city landmark in 1983.

Dr. Richard and Ann Levine sold the house in 1993 to Susan and Charles Allen.

1707 PALMER AVENUE, BURTHEVILLE

Bertha and Bernard Landau had this Colonial Revival residence built in 1900 at a cost of $5,000, according to the designs of Favrot and Livaudais, the city's leading architects at the turn of the century. Landau, a partner in the notions company of S. and

J. Katz and Company, purchased the site in 1900 for $4,125. The property remained in the Landau family until 1923 when it was sold to Robert D. Reeves for $20,500. During the Great Depression, Reeves declared bankruptcy and transferred title in 1932 to Pan American Life Insurance Company which retained the property until 1936 when Mr. and Mrs. David Dixon purchased it. In 1960 Mr. and Mrs. Roy F. Guste acquired the property, selling it in turn to Dr. and Mrs. Darrell Wolfley in 1984. The house had lost many of its original details by that time, including the front porch, and the Wolfleys undertook a major renovation, restoring many of these features under the direction of Koch and Wilson Architects. In 1992 the house was purchased by Jennifer and Paul McFadden.

1711 PALMER AVENUE, BURTHEVILLE

This residence is one of many elegant Colonial Revival designs of Frank P. Gravely that share common details, such as corner pilasters with decorative cutout designs just below the capital and third-floor wall dormers. The symmetry of this design reflects a change in taste from picturesque and asymmetrical Colonial Revival designs by Gravely as seen at 22 Audubon Place, 2006 Milan, 4631 St. Charles Avenue, and 1524 Seventh Street. The house is raised on a basement for added emphasis. The interior of the house demonstrates some of the best period detailing in the city.

Gravely was born and educated in Charleston, South Carolina, and in 1875 moved to New Orleans where he began his architectural practice.

John F. Clark, president of the New Orleans Compress and Warehouse Company, a cotton press, commissioned the construction of this house in 1906 at a cost of $10,000. The Clark family sold it in 1955 to Elizabeth Doyle for $43,000. In 1971 Mr. and Mrs. Ewell Walther purchased the house, selling it in 1994 to Elinor and Andre Grikitis. See color interior photograph section for interior view.

1718 PALMER AVENUE, BURTHEVILLE

Here is an 1891 Queen Anne residence built for Dr. Benjamin Morgan Palmer, sixth pastor of First Presbyterian Church. It has been modified into the Mediterranean style. The *Daily Picayune* of September 1, 1891, lists a "two-story frame slated dwelling for Rev. B.M. Palmer on square bounded by Henry Clay Avenue, Baronne, Carondelet and Calhoun. H. Wellman, builder, $6,500." The following year the tax assessment jumped from $2,500 to $7,500.

Although Dr. Palmer is listed at this address in the 1894 city directory and lived here until his death, he never owned the property, which was purchased in 1891 by James Caldwell. It remained in the Caldwell family until 1928 when it was sold to Charles Fenner, Rex in 1941, in whose family it remains as of this writing. An illustration of the house in a September 9, 1928, advertisement for its sale is captioned "erected by McMillan, Inc." This may refer to the conversion of the house to apartments and changes to the Mediterranean style.

The Reverend Palmer was born in Charleston to a family with a long line of ministers. After serving in Charleston, Savannah, and Columbia, Georgia, he accepted the pastorate of First Presbyterian Church in New Orleans in 1856. Known for his oratory and dynamic leadership, Dr. Palmer's sermon of November 29, 1860, in support of Southern states' rights was reprinted in the local press and often cited as swaying Louisiana to secede from the Union. In early April 1862, Dr. Palmer left New Orleans to visit the army of Gen. Albert Sidney Johnston and to attend the General Assembly in Memphis of the Presbyterian Church in the Confederate States of America. When federal forces captured New Orleans later that month and occupied the city, Dr. Palmer, looked upon as a prominent rebel, was advised by his friends not to return to the city. He did return after the war to resume his pastorate at First Presbyterian. In 1891 he succeeded in closing the Louisiana Lottery and persuading Tulane University, on whose Board of Administrators he served, to reject the Howards' offer to donate a library because of that family's involvement in the lottery.

In 1898 Henry Clay Avenue on the lake side of St. Charles Avenue was renamed Palmer Avenue in honor of the noted clergyman. Dr. Palmer died in 1902 from injuries sustained when he was struck by a streetcar at the intersection of St. Charles and Palmer Avenue.

1730 PALMER AVENUE, BURTHEVILLE

In 1892 Samuel Kreeger sold this site to Prof. Brandt V.B. Dixon for $4,000. In 1895 Dixon engaged Toledano and Reusch to design an $11,700 residence for this site. Ten years later, Dixon sold the property for $18,000 to Robbie and Benjamin Oxnard, who retained Toledano and Wogan to remodel the house. Drawings preserved in the Southeastern Architectural Archive at Tulane indicate that changes were made to the vestibule, reception hall,

dining room, and dormer and porch details. The house is somewhat unusual for Uptown New Orleans where two-story, wood frame residences proliferate. The entrance porch at the right of the brick mass is understated in comparison to the porch on the left. The roof, with its deep overhang and shallow brackets, appears to overpower the house.

In 1916 Hazel Hardin purchased the house from Oxnard for $20,000. Six years later, Hardin sold it to Eva Quin Epley who then sold it to Virginia Fenner in 1924. Dr. Howard Mahorner, Rex in 1973, purchased the house from the Fenner family in 1945 for $35,000. James Landis is the owner as of this writing.

1812 PALMER AVENUE, BURTHEVILLE

In 1896 Mary Frances Hardie purchased this lot from Hugh McCown and the following year commissioned the architectural firm of Favrot and Livaudais to design the present house. Its Colonial details are employed in a free-spirited manner, not duplicating any particular Colonial design. In an unusual approach to entry, the front door is deeply recessed on the lake side of the house. The cast iron fence is especially nice, and unusual for this area of town.

Hardie sold the house for $18,000 in 1912 to Robert Moore who two months later sold it to Augusta Solari for $22,000. In 1919 Julius Werner purchased the house, followed by Julius Mente in 1924, Dr. Albert Yenni in 1925, Louisiana Supreme Court Justice Frank W. Summers in 1961, and Stephanie and Martin Schoenberger in 1983.

The house is described in an advertisement in the *Times-Picayune* of February 1, 1925, as follows:

Across the marble porch with stately columns through massive hardwood doors, adorned with wrought iron grilles, you enter a vestibule which leads directly into the reception hall. On the left is the drawing room, paneled in dark mahogany with lovely lighting fixtures, and built-in bookcases at each end. At the end of the reception hall, and separated from it by a low iron grille is an octagonal sun parlor. This leads into the fine dining room, with oak wainscoting and tapestry above. Beyond are the spacious pantries and kitchen, all with white tiled floors, and the rear staircase. In the reception room, the drawing room and the dining room are beautiful marble mantels of rare workmanship and design.

From the hall, a fine oak staircase with a deep bay-windowed recess in the landing leads to the second floor with its five bedrooms and three baths, two of which are filled with plate glass enclosed shower and needle baths.

1907 PALMER AVENUE, BURTHEVILLE

This Beaux Arts Renaissance Revival residence is comfortably sited on a generous lot and imparts a sense of elegance without the use of a lot of details. The paired classic columns are a Mannerism detail commonly used by Beaux Arts designers. The entrance is via a Palladian arch.

A.Q. Petersen, vice-president of Southern Cotton Oil Company, Wesson Oil and Snowdrift, probably built this villa in 1931 after demolishing an earlier house that was once the residence of "Dr. Tichenor," developer of the famous "family antiseptic" made of 70 percent alcohol.

Since Petersen's death in 1979 there have been five subsequent owners, the most recent being Robert and Ruth Scott.

2108 PALMER AVENUE, BURTHEVILLE

Designated a city landmark, this whimsical Carpenter's Gothic, center-hall cottage employs relatively flat detailing in a novel manner. As seen in the old photograph, there was once a balcony adjacent to the river end of the porch.

Toby Hart, a house, sign, and ornamental painter, probably designed the house as his own residence. He is first listed here in the 1874 city directory. After more than a dozen interim owners, the house at this writing is the home of Constance and Casey Willems who bought it in 1987.

2115 PALMER AVENUE, BURTHEVILLE

Architectural pattern books were a common source of plans for nineteenth century residences, and this is an example of just that. This Queen Anne house is Residence Design No. 216 from Robert W. Shoppell's 1888 *Shoppell's Modern Houses,* except it is a mirror image of that design. Towers are commonly found on Queen Anne residences; however, they rarely comprise the entire facade.

The building contract for this house is dated June 26, 1897, in the amount of $3,673. Although the contract is between Eureka Building and Loan and A.A. Adams and Company, it was obviously for Joseph Fornaris who purchased the property from Eureka two days later. The house was completed by March 19, 1898, when Fornaris paid Eureka. Eight months later, he sold it to Augustus Chaery. In 1899 Eureka filed suit against Fornaris for defaulting on the house loan, and as a result, the house was sold at a sheriff's sale to Eureka. In 1900 Charles Weinberger purchased the house from Eureka for $4,600 and sold it eight years later to Charles Tessier for $9,500. The house remained in the Tessier family until 1924

when Hermann Mysing bought it. The Mysing heirs sold it in 1932 to Edwin Rhodes who two months later sold it to William Walton. In 1963 the Walton family sold the house to Peggy and Dr. Richard Reed. Dr. and Mrs. Andrew Rinker purchased it in 1970 and are the owners as of this writing. In 1982 the house was designated a city landmark by the Historic District Landmarks Commission.

2200 & 2212 PALMER AVENUE, BURTHEVILLE

Francis J. MacDonnell was the architect for these two Renaissance Revival "pattern stone" residences. MacDonnell became quite an aficionado of the use of concrete block, then known as pattern stone.

Both houses were built in 1908 for the Henrietta Rueff family. In 1910 a photograph of 2200 Palmer Avenue appeared in *Architectural Arts and Its Allies.* In 1952 Rueff's succession sold 2200 Palmer to Arthur Blamphin whose family retains ownership as of this writing.

The house at 2212 Palmer was purchased from the Rueff family in 1920 by George Stocker who sold it four years later to Dr. and Mrs. Paul Talbot. In 1943 the Joseph Quealy family bought it and in 1969 sold it to Elizabeth and Garland Taylor. The owners as of this writing, Catherine and Kevin McMichael, purchased the house in 1985. Unfortunately, the second-floor porch has been enclosed.

PATTON (Union)

5820-22, 5824-26 PATTON, HURSTVILLE

Frederick Adolph Schopp purchased this site for $500 on December 7, 1903, and ten days later contracted with builder Martin Guelda to construct "two double cottages" for $5,734, according to the designs of David P. Casey. Both doubles remained in the Schopp family for fifty-one years.

The two Eastlake camelbacks (5824-26 pictured) retain much of their original millwork. They are typical of many built Uptown in the late-nineteenth and early-twentieth centuries, sporting turned columns and decorative spandrels and cutout ornament on the cornices of the openings.

PERRIER (Gen. Hood; Howard; Olivier)

5827 PERRIER, HURSTVILLE

Alfred E. Clay, president of the Louisiana State Society for the Prevention of Cruelty to Children, purchased a vacant lot here in 1895 and built the present Queen Anne side-hall cottage shortly thereafter, as the 1896 city directory lists Clay at Perrier, northeast corner of Eleonore.

The house has a distinctive porch design with a Moorish arch distinguished by the entrance bay flanking a much wider side bay with an exaggerated arch. True to the picturesque nature of the Queen Anne style, the front wall of the house undulates beneath the front porch. Unfortunately, the original porch railing has been lost.

5919 PERRIER, HURSTVILLE

This 1897 Queen Anne cottage was built for William Harding, a clerk with Hoadley and Company, a wholesale fruit company. Harding purchased the site in December 1896 and had the present house completed the following year. He is first listed in the 1898 directory at this location. Harding sold the cottage in 1920 for $7,250 to Joseph Ingraham. Lester Lautenschlager, the owner at this writing, bought the property in 1984.

The asymmetrical massing, Queen Anne windows in the projecting bay and gable shingles are common traits of the Queen Anne style. The lack of "gingerbread" distinguishes it from the Eastlake style. The Gothic gable window is an unusual detail for a Queen Anne house.

6048 PERRIER, BURTHEVILLE

Now the New Orleans Center for Creative Arts,

this three-and-one-half-story brick structure was originally built in 1901 as the LaSalle School at a cost of $30,000 by W.V. Mills and Company, according to the designs of city engineers Paul Capdeville and William J. Hardee. In 1927 the school was enlarged, following school board architect E.A. Christy's plans. The present ground-floor entrance is out of character with the building's original design intent.

6333 PERRIER, BURTHEVILLE (formerly 1203 Exposition Boulevard)

This rambling Gothic residence seems out of place in Uptown New Orleans. Its tranquil setting imparts the feeling of a monastic complex, although it was never used as such.

It was built in 1918 for attorney E. Howard McCaleb as 1203 Exposition Boulevard. In 1927 a rear two-apartment addition was added. The property is still owned by the McCaleb family as of this writing.

PINE

312-14, 316 PINE, GREENVILLE

These two originally double Colonial residences present a picturesque streetscape, set in a lush, if somewhat limited, garden setting. The houses are vernacular forms of the larger Colonial Revival residences on St. Charles Avenue. Although similar, these doubles demonstrate some variant details. Both reflect the earliest mode of the style, which is picturesque and closely allied to the Queen Anne. The dentils, simple window cornices and porch railing, box and Tuscan columns, and prismatic window transoms all fall neatly into the Colonial Revival style, demonstrating a reaction to the excesses of the Queen Anne and Eastlake styles and a return to simplicity.

These houses were built in 1908 by builder Henry F. Hinrichs who purchased the sites in 1907 and sold 312-14 Pine in February 1909 to Marie Jaeger, and 316 Pine to Marie McIntyre in July 1909. The considerable increase from purchase to sale price along with tax increases indicate the houses were built at this time.

Owners of 312-14 Pine have been Mrs. Frances Hammond in 1926; John Rufin, 1946; Alfred Pittman, Jr., 1966; Clarence Gelpi, 1970; Patricia and James Watts, 1972; Elizabeth and Andrew Edwards, 1981; and Richard Dalton, Jr., 1990. Owners of 316 Pine (pictured) have been the Martin Conners family in 1925; Eleonore and George Mattix and Mimi Penn, 1964; Ralph McCullough II, 1965; JoAnn and Samuel Tournillion, Jr., 1968; Sharon and Neil Zimmerman, 1974; Jane and George Ball, 1976; Thomas S. Mahon, 1980; and John Hills, 1988.

622 PINE, GREENVILLE

This Spanish Eclectic "basement" house was built in 1923 for Alfred Alltmont, secretary-treasurer of Loeb, Lion and Felix, which assembled the site through three separate transactions totaling $5,455 between 1922 and 1923. In April 1924, Alltmont sold the property to Caroline Beer for $31,200, the price indicating that the house had been built. Also, the 1924 city directory lists Alltmont residing here, further evidence of the existence of the house.

The Spanish Eclectic style grew out of the Mission style as it exhausted the limited details of the Spanish Colonial missions of the American West. The red tile roof, wrought iron balconies, lanterns and railings, Mission gable windows, stucco walls, and well-detailed entrance are typical of the style. The river end of the house with its Palladian window was likely an open porch.

Subsequent owners of this comfortable house have been Louis Lob in 1933; Roy Schwarz, 1950; and Dr. Lawrence Arend, 1985.

823-25 PINE, GREENVILLE

This Craftsman house combines a multitude of architectural styles which the movement deems compatible with its handcrafted philosophy. Among these are Tudor, as seen in the half-timbering of the gable and the porch arch; Colonial Revival, as seen in the front door with its Adamesque garland and wreaths; and Art Nouveau, as seen in the stained glass. Typical Craftsman details include the concrete-block battered columns, porch railing and step buttresses, knee braces, exposed rafter ends, and narrow siding with mitered corners.

Insurance executive George McHardy built this house in 1912, as evidenced by tax records, after having acquired four lots in 1903 for $1,700. He sold the house in 1919 to Cora Goldsmith for $6,250. In 1924 Mrs. Albert Storm purchased it for $12,500 and in 1936 donated it to Leo DuBourg who sold it the following year to Arthur Hill for $7,000. In 1955 the Reverend Myron Madden purchased the house for $24,500, and it remains in his family as of this writing.

PLUM

7304 PLUM, FRIBURG

Tax records indicate that this house was built in 1910, as the assessment jumped from $800 that year to $3,200 in 1911. Any one of three owners could have built it—Mutual Building and Loan, builder Joseph Bichow, or architects-builders Dannemann and Charleton. Most likely, it was built by Mutual, which purchased the property for $2,000 in 1910 and sold it for $6,200 four years later to Harry Lyle,

a salesman with Eli Lilly. The transactions involving Bichow and Dannemann and Charleton include much more property and are harder to compare. Lyle is first listed as residing here in the 1914 city directory.

Two kings of Carnival have owned this house— Edgar A.G. Bright, Rex in 1956, who acquired it in 1927, and Harry B. Kelleher, Rex in 1965, who purchased it in 1941. Other owners include Amy Floweree (1920), Dr. John Dicks (1921), Alfred Alexander (1948), J. King Woolf, Jr. (1959), Henry Mason III (1964), Barbara and Hector LeBlanc III (1974), and Patricia and Richard Keyworth (1979).

The house, like its neighbor at 7328 Plum, is in the Dutch Colonial style. The gambrel roof is the most distinguishing feature of this style.

7328 PLUM, FRIBURG

This Dutch Colonial house was built in 1911 for Thomas C. Hills, according to the *Daily States*, at a cost upwards of $6,000, following the design of architect Alexander Hay. The newspaper described the house as "Dutch Colonial in design, two stories in height with a cellar, of frame construction with asbestos shingle art roof." The gambrel roof, which is often used to diminish the scale of a two-story residence, seems to overpower the first floor, especially since it extends so far beyond the footprint of the residence.

Hills, president of McDermott Surgical Instrument Supply Company, purchased the site in November 1910 for $2,000, had the house built the following year, and retained it as his domicile until 1918 when he sold it to Patrick Conway. In 1929 Rabbi Louis Binstock purchased the property for $10,000 and sold it to Simon Schwartz for $8,840 in 1941. Three years later, the Schwartzes sold the house at a substantial profit to Marie and Henry Newell for $17,500. The Newells sold the house in 1958 to Thomas McMahon who sold it to Jean and John Meade in 1979. Sandra and Laurence Crowder, owners of the house as of this writing, purchased it in 1987.

PRYTANIA (Courtland; Wall)

5829 PRYTANIA, HURSTVILLE

On December 31, 1907, dentist Harry B. Bartlett purchased two lots with improvements from Union Homestead for $3,000. The 1908 city directory lists Bartlett as residing here. The homestead built the house in 1897, as evidenced by the increase in the tax assessment from $1,000 that year to $3,500 in 1898.

Ten years later, in 1917, Bartlett sold the house to Isidore Singer who sold it the following year to Mrs. Mary Louise Hillery. In 1926 she sold it to the Charles Favrot family whose descendants retain it as of this writing. Favrot was the 1934 Times-Picayune Loving Cup recipient.

The cottage is a late example of the Queen Anne, reflecting the growing simplicity of the Colonial Revival. While maintaining a picturesque massing with a partial-width, three-bay porch abutting a projecting bay with street-facing cross gable and two pilastered dormers, Colonial detailing is reflected in the Palladian window, Ionic columns set on paneled bases, and the simple, square-banistered railing. The restrained design of this cottage is framed by lush plantings and large live oaks.

6262 PRYTANIA, BURTHEVILLE

An article in the *Daily States* of August 31, 1908, states: "The residence of M.M. Boatner, located at Calhoun and Prytania streets, is another example of highly artistic modern architecture and one of the coziest, prettiest little houses in the city. It is a frame structure two stories in height, of English style of architecture. The cost about was upwards of $9,000. A special feature of this residence is the elevated loggia on the South side."

Attorney Mark M. Boatner purchased this site in September of 1907 and had the present house built shortly thereafter. Boatner sold the house to Ernest B. Mercer in 1922 for $11,000. Mercer sold it two years later for $17,000 to Mr. and Mrs. George Matthews who sold it two years later to Mr. and Mrs. John Hobson, Jr. for $25,000. In 1950 Dr. Mercer Lynch purchased the house for $41,800, and Marsha and Henry O'Conner bought it from his widow's succession in 1979.

The picturesque, yet comfortable residence retains much of its original appearance, with its natural-brick columns and chimneys, stuccoed first floor, shingled second floor, picturesque roof line, diamond-paned upper sash, and second floor projecting over the first.

6334 PRYTANIA, BURTHEVILLE

This site was purchased on May 27, 1924, by siblings Charles Meriwether, vice-president of Marine Paint and Varnish Company, and Elizabeth Meriwether Gilmer, the *Times-Picayune* advice columnist better known by her nom de plume, Dorothy Dix. They built this house shortly thereafter, as it is first assessed in 1926 with a value of $26,120. Upon Gilmer's death, Meriwether inherited her half. In 1971 Meriwether's heirs sold the house to William Wilkins whose children own it as of this writing.

The Mediterranean Villa style house has a large tile roof, rusticated "basement" level, and entrance bay and basket balconies, all characteristics of the style. The entrance terrace has lost its original railing, which repeated details of the cast stone turning of the main living floor's basket balconies, as evidenced by a photograph preserved at Tulane University signed "Dorothy Dix sends you greetings from her new home, 6334 Prytania, New Orleans."

RICHMOND PLACE

2 RICHMOND PLACE, HURSTVILLE

This Mediterranean Villa was built in 1910 by William Washington Reid who assembled the site

through two purchases in January and March that year. On March 23, 1910, Reid obtained a water meter permit for his new house. When he sold the property to Hattie and Eugene Deming in December 1910, the act of sale specifically included the electrical, gas, and plumbing fixtures as well as appliances and window shades and screens. The house remained in the Deming family until 1920 when Leon C. Simon purchased it for $27,000. In 1935 Leland Montgomery, recipient of the Times-Picayune Loving Cup in 1913, bought the house from Simon, selling it in turn to Margaret Craig in 1944. The Craig succession sold it in 1983 to Elizabeth and John Bolles.

A comparison of the house as it appears today with a photograph from the *Illustrated Sunday Magazine* shortly after its construction shows little change, other than the fact that the uptown wing has been enclosed and glass has replaced screen in the downtown wing. The screen-enclosed division of the framing remains the same, however, and the metal trellis outlining the openings of the two wings is still intact. Although the house appears to face Loyola, its legal address is on Richmond due to deed restrictions requiring all houses to face Richmond.

4 RICHMOND PLACE, HURSTVILLE

A 1911 article in the *Times Picayune* describes this house, designed by Robert Spencer Soulé, as "of modern style of architecture done in cement construction, two stories and an attic in height, containing five large bedrooms, living room, dining room, reception hall, two servants rooms and three bathrooms. The interior finish is in mahogany and white enamel, lighted with electricity and heated with hot air." The cost was upwards of $12,000.

According to tax assessment records, the house was built in 1910 for Sidney J. White whose family retained it until 1942 when Albert Meric bought it. In 1955 state Attorney General William J. Guste purchased the house and retains ownership as of this writing.

A comparison of a photograph taken shortly after construction with the present appearance of the house shows little change. The style of the house is

best described as Craftsman, characterized by its lack of applied ornament.

7 RICHMOND PLACE, HURSTVILLE

Here is one of the many residences of architect Thomas Sully who purchased the site in 1910 from developer Walter Kent of Tangipahoa Parish. Sully obtained a building permit for this two-and-one-half-story stucco residence in 1915. This house is quite different from the more exuberant experiments in the Queen Anne and Colonial Revival styles for which Sully is more typically known, and its style could best be described as Craftsman.

In 1925 Sully sold the house to his daughter, Jeanne, and her husband, Dr. John Smyth, for $16,500. In 1967 Helen and Albert Wetzel purchased the house from Jeanne Sully West and retain ownership as of this writing.

The drawings for this house are included in the collection of Thomas Sully's architectural drawings that Jeanne Sully West donated to the Southeastern Architectural Archive at Tulane University.

14 RICHMOND PLACE, HURSTVILLE

On April 27, 1922, John R. Juden, Jr., secretary of Terry and Juden Company, purchased this site from A.Q. Pedersen for $7,750. *Building Review* of May that year noted that the plans for this house by Francis C. MacDonnell were not yet on the market. Sewerage and water connections for the new house were made in 1923.

Mrs. Juden sold the house in 1954 to her daughter, Dorothy Juden Sarpy, for $15,000. In 1976 Robert Henry Sarpy, Jr. purchased his grandfather's house.

The house is a typical example of the Mediterranean Villa style, with a generous, umbrella-like roof projecting well beyond the wall planes, simple second-story windows placed high on the wall, elliptical-headed first-floor doors, and a classically detailed entrance.

17 RICHMOND PLACE, HURSTVILLE

This is one of the first houses to be built on Richmond Place. It was designed by Favrot and Livaudais for attorney Henri Favrot, one of the original developers of Richmond Place, and his wife, Marie Louise Richmond, for whom Richmond Place was named.

This 1906 house is executed in the Southern Colonial style based on the Greek Revival architecture of Southern plantations. The *Daily Picayune* of September 1, 1906, states that H.L. Favrot obtained

a building permit for a two-story, frame, slated residence costing $7,358. On July 28, 1907, the same newspaper published interior and exterior photographs of the house, noting that "the house represents old Plantation architecture" and the "Entrance Hall is in the Colonial Style."

In 1919 Favrot's estate sold the house to James W. Smith who in turn sold it to James M. Todd in 1941 for $16,000. As of this writing, the house remains in the Todd family.

18 RICHMOND PLACE, HURSTVILLE

This Colonial Revival, two-story, wood frame residence is one of the oldest on the block. Charles A. Favrot, partner in the architectural firm of Favrot and Livaudais and one of the developers of Richmond Place, built this house in 1906. In 1931 the Favrot family transferred title to Carol Realty Corporation in exchange for 1,000 shares of stock. Carol Realty sold the house in 1948 to Raymond H. Kierr who sold it in 1974 to Dr. and Mrs. Edward Connolly.

A comparison of the house today with Sanborn insurance maps documents several changes: the present porch was added after 1933, as the porch shown on the 1909 and 1933 maps extended from the present front door all the way toward the Loyola Avenue elevation; the Loyola-end side porch was apparently added when the front porch was changed; and a two-story garage was added to the rear of the structure between 1909 and 1927.

21 RICHMOND PLACE, HURSTVILLE

Here is another house built by one of the Richmond Place developers. Rufus Foster, an attorney and U.S. district attorney, commissioned MacKenzie, Goldstein and Biggs to design this residence, which was described in the *Daily States* of August 31, 1906, as "another highly artistic and thoroughly Modern residence. . . . MacKenziesque in style of architecture, contains seven rooms with baths, is hot air heated and lighted with both electricity and gas, it cost about $6,000."

H. Jordan MacKenzie closely followed the works of Austrian Art Nouveau architect Joseph Olbrich.

Unfortunately, the house has been significantly altered, losing most of its original "MacKenziesque" detailing, including the distinctive front porch, Art Nouveau railing, and art glass above the first-floor openings.

Foster's succession sold the house in 1953 for $22,750 to Joyce and Thompson Dietz III who sold it in 1976 to Carolyn and Charles Skelton.

Demings leased the house for three years to William Jones for $90 per month, and renewed the lease in 1903 for another three years, eventually selling the house without the land to Jones whose widow purchased the land in 1925. Her descendants retain ownership as of this writing.

house into shares and, operating as Abraham Realty, sold the house in 1912 to Corinne Miltenberger for $11,000. Ernest Vincent Richards purchased the house in 1921, and transferred it in 1927 to R and L, which merged with Rochelle Investments in 1936. Rochelle Investments sold the house in 1949 to Loretto Richards whose succession sold it in 1971 to Ruth and Neal Kaye. In 1983 Charlotte and Bruce Oreck purchased the house, selling it to Diane and Lance Africk in 1992.

11 ROSA PARK, HURSTVILLE

On January 1, 1899, Minerva Shaffer entered into a building contract with builder Otto Manske to construct this stately Southern Colonial residence for $6,000. Shaffer sold the house in 1907 to Oscar Lee Putnam, in whose family it remained until 1950 when George Springer purchased it.

The so-called Southern Colonial style was based on the Greek Revival architecture of Southern plantations. It fitted into the growing reaction to the picturesque style of the late-nineteenth century by returning to classicism, symmetry, and monumental details. This house represents a very early example of this movement in New Orleans.

15 ROSA PARK, HURSTVILLE

Samuel Diamond, boss drayman for Nicholas Burke Company, built this Chateauesque residence in 1897 at a cost of $5,000. According to the *Daily Picayune* of September 1, 1897, the house was designed by George E. Dickey and Son one year after this team arrived in New Orleans from Houston.

The house is the only surviving residential example of the style in New Orleans; the only other Chateauesque building, located at 2552 N. Dorgenois, was built as a municipal structure. The term "Chateauesque" was coined by Bainbridge Bunting to describe a minor architectural movement employed in large, architect-designed residences, based on the sixteenth century chateaux of France constructed during the reign of Francois I.

The sixth owners of the house, Dr. and Mrs. Elmo Cerise, bought it in 1968. See color interior photograph section for interior view.

ROSA PARK

8 ROSA PARK, HURSTVILLE

This Swiss style house was built in 1896 for notary Jefferson Wenck who purchased the site the previous year. Its decorative "cuckoo clock" half-timbering distinguishes it from the Tudor style.

The 1897 city directory first lists Wenck at this location. The following year, he sold the house for $11,000 to Hattie Mae Deming, wife of Eugene Deming, who resided at 10 Rosa Park. In 1900 the

10 ROSA PARK, HURSTVILLE

Here is a Queen Anne house built for machinist Eugene Watson Deming in 1900 at a cost of $7,135, according to the *Daily Picayune* of September 1, 1900. The lot had been purchased in 1898 by his wife, Hattie Mae Deming. The picturesque massing, Palladian gable window, octagonal porch, oriel porch window, and projecting bay under deep-roof overhang help to define this house as Queen Anne.

In 1903 the house was sold at auction to Henry Abraham whose succession in 1907 divided the

ST. CHARLES AVENUE (Nayades)

5603 ST. CHARLES AVENUE, HURSTVILLE

Here is an excellent example of what early-twentieth century writers call Southern Colonial. The *Daily States* reported that architects Soulé and Mac-Donnell designed this 1903 house for Timothy H. McCarthy, vice-president of Ruddock Orleans Cypress Company: "This handsome residence is of frame with brick veneering and stone trimmings, in Colonial style. It cost completed $30,000." However, the surviving specifications for the house list only R.S. Soulé as the architect.

The impressive interior of this house was designed by Charles Ayars of Chicago, and reflects the influence of the then-current Art Nouveau style.

The house remained in the McCarthy family until 1940 when Dr. and Mrs. Julio Altabas acquired it, selling it six years later to Mrs. Jennie Grieshaber. The present owners, Robert and Agatha Schoen, acquired the house in 1956 from Mrs. Schoen's mother, Jennie Grieshaber.

5604, 5624 ST. CHARLES AVENUE, HURSTVILLE

Local lore maintains that these two houses were built as wedding presents for two daughters; however, like many legends, this is untrue. Col. Robert E. Rivers built these two residences as a speculative venture. Rivers, in partnership with Ed Breathitt, operated several gambling casinos, including one at the corner of St. Charles and Common. In 1870 they acquired the St. Charles Hotel and operated it until it burned in 1894. Rivers also operated the St. Louis Hotel under lease.

On May 22, 1883, Rivers' wife purchased the entire Square 59, site of the subject residences, for $5,500 and built the two Second Empire houses, as evidenced by the $6,500 increase in the tax assessment of 1884 which bears the notation: "2 two story homes $6,000" [each]. In 1886 the Riverses sold the entire square for $15,000 to James Plummer Longley who sold it back to Robert Rivers the following year.

In 1890 Rivers sold 5604 St. Charles to George Pitcher who contracted with John B. Chisolm for $3,085 in work for additions and alterations to the residence in 1897, according to the plans of W.C.

William Bros. Architects. Three years later, Pitcher sold the house to Walter Guion. It subsequently has been owned by the Allen, Burke, Trice, Stillwell, Dezendore, Haynes, and Kehoe families.

Rivers also sold 5624 St. Charles in 1890 to John Sherrouse for $5,000. Sherrouse sold the house for $13,500 in 1908 to Gabe Hausmann who sold it the same year to Samuel Diamond at a $3,500 loss. During Diamond's ownership, a photograph of the house appeared in the *Illustrated Sunday Magazine*. Since the Diamond family ownership, the Rivera, Dumont, Jaubert, and Bernanti families have owned the house.

5614 ST. CHARLES AVENUE, HURSTVILLE

Planter Joseph Libby purchased this site in 1891 from Robert Rivers who built the adjacent two houses, 5604 and 5624 St. Charles. Either Libby immediately built a house or one already existed, for he is listed here in the 1891 city directory. This earlier house is illustrated clearly on the 1896 Sanborn map.

After Libby's death, his widow, Louise Libby, built the present house in 1905 for $10,890. Soulé and MacDonnell were the architects for this Colonial Revival residence, which reflects the growing simplicity of the style during the twentieth century.

The house remained in the Libby family until 1958 when it was acquired by Albert Crutcher, Jr. who retains possession as of this writing.

5631 ST. CHARLES AVENUE, HURSTVILLE

Architects Favrot and Livaudais designed this comfortable 1913 Mediterranean Villa for William T. Coats, dealer in safes and locks. The umbrella-like green tile roof, supported on paired brackets, shades the house, providing a passive-solar design component. The entrance porch column cartouches distinguish the entry.

Two years after its construction, the house was sold by Coats' heirs to Susan Glover, wife of Randall Dugue. The *Daily Picayune* reported on September 1, 1914, that "one of the finest residences built last year was the Coates [*sic*] Place on St. Charles avenue, which has been reported sold to a California man for between $30,000 and $40,000, the death of Mr. Coates before its completion having caused the sale."

Mrs. Dugue brought back Favrot and Livaudais to make alterations to the house, which she retained until 1943 when it was sold to Jennie Grieshaber. Subsequent owners were Eugene McCarroll (1946), Robert Blum (1958), George and Marguerite Springer (1970), and Maria Springer Favor (1974).

5700 ST. CHARLES AVENUE, HURSTVILLE

The firm of Favrot and Livaudais emerged at the turn of the twentieth century as one of the city's major architectural firms. Here is another of their St. Charles Avenue designs. This design seems to share influences from both the Mediterranean Villa and Richardsonian Romanesque styles, and subsequent alterations to the porch compound the complexity of the present visual appearance.

Charles Godchaux, vice-president of the Canal Street department store of Leon Godchaux Company, in 1901 commissioned this house, which, according to the *Daily Picayune,* cost over $20,000 exclusive of plumbing and interior finishing. Godchaux retained the house until 1942 when Felix Kuntz purchased it for only $15,000. Two years later, Joseph Lucas bought the house, only to sell it the following year to Marion and Elbert Ingram. In 1949 Amelia and Marcello Monetti purchased the house for $67,700, and in 1953 sold it to Jessie Lott for $72,000. Lyonel Stone purchased it in 1976 and retains ownership as of this writing.

5705 ST. CHARLES AVENUE, HURSTVILLE

Tour buses stop here daily to see "Scarlett O'Hara's Tara." Based on the fictitious plantation home Tara in David O. Selznick's movie *Gone With the Wind,* this residence was built in 1941 for George Palmer, according to the designs of architect Andrew W. Lockett, replacing the 1894 William J. O'Donnell residence designed by Southron R. Duval.

The grounds of the 1894 house, except for three lots on Arabella Street, occupied the rest of the square.

A subsequent owner, Lawrence Fabacher, president of Jackson Brewing Company, hired architect F.N. Wilcox to add to the site a complex including a casino with swimming pool, a kitchen, a barn, a greenhouse, and a poultry shed. Architects Andry and Bendernagel were retained to revise the plans and supervise the work executed by L. Frolich. In 1911 Fabacher commissioned MacKenzie, Ehlis and Johnson to design "a monster pergola or conservatory," of which the *Daily States* wrote:

> This structure, which is to be one hundred and twenty feet high, is to be entirely enclosed with glass in the winter time and steam heated, and with wire screens in the summertime, the glass and screen sides to be portable. Even the roof is to be of glass. The floor is to be of mosaic tiles, with white marble steps, and in the center will be a large electric fountain, which also will cost a small fortune in itself. It is to be embellished with palms, potted plants and flowers.

5718 ST. CHARLES AVENUE, HURSTVILLE

Here is one of two Louis Henry Lambert designs in this block. Lambert, a native of Canada, came to New Orleans after an illustrious career in Central America. He was described in the *Times-Democrat* of September 1, 1893:

LOUIS H. LAMBERT
ARCHITECT AND BUILDER,
DECORATOR & FURNISHER

Mr. Lambert was born in Quebec where he was educated. He first studied marine architecture in the English Navy, and when he mastered that branch of the profession, he graduated in civil architecture. Casting his fortune in Central America where he knew that there was a wide field, he established himself in Honduras, and

his talents being recognized by Sato, the President of that republic, he was selected as the supervising architect, a position which he also filled successfully under Barrios in Guatemala. He also established a branch in Mexico, and still retains his interest there, visiting the City of Mexico quite frequently. In 1883 Mr. Lambert visited and finding that his style of work was appreciated here, he permanently located in this city. Among the many of Mr. Lambert's greatest achievements is the Grunewald Building owned by Mr. Louis Grunewald, of L. Grunewald Company, Limited, now in course of erection.

Mr. Lambert is not, as might be supposed, high in his charges, as a matter of fact he is most reasonable, and in addition to preparing the plans and specifications for buildings, he contracts for their erection, and is prepared to furnish a house completely, inside and out, supplying all interior decorations, bathrooms, finished in marble, walls finished with stucco, fresco or paper and put in all the plumbing and modern conveniences now so necessary in modern dwellings. As he obtains his supplies direct from first hands, he is able to give his patrons the benefits of all trade discounts and in this way is able to erect a house finished complete throughout at as reasonable a figure as was heretofore charged for an old style building. Thus it is shown that Mr. Lambert is in reality cheaper in his charges than the average.

William Girault, cashier at American National Bank, commissioned this fanciful Queen Anne residence on May 4, 1889, at a cost of $5,750. The floor plan of the house is typical for the period, featuring a living-stair hall flanked by double parlors to the uptown side and backed by a dining room. The dining room was backed by a pantry, then a kitchen. Down the rear wing was a two-story porch. Upstairs was the master bedroom with dressing room and tower niche, en suite, plus two bedrooms, one bath, one library, and one unidentified room.

In 1897 Girault sold the house to Charner Terry Scaife, superintendent of terminals for the Illinois Central Railroad who retained it until 1903 when he sold it to Philip Bodenheimer for $14,300. Bodenheimer kept the house only until 1906 when Dr. Jefferson D. Bloom purchased it for $22,000. The house remained in the Bloom family for seventy-four years. It was temporarily converted to a duplex during the Great Depression and sold by the Bloom family in 1980 to Susan and John Jones. In 1985 it was sold to Maria Carmen Palazzo.

5726 ST. CHARLES AVENUE, HURSTVILLE

The present appearance of this house denies its original whimsical design. As seen in the old photograph, the house had much more Eastlake detailing than it does now. The Nashville elevation had a wonderful porte cochere and dormer porch. The front entrance porch was a single bay wide, supported on decorative columns with a balcony above. The porch wrapped around the tower, unroofed.

The house was built in 1889 by Louis Lambert, according to his own designs, for Thomas Underwood for $9,000. The 1893 book, *New Orleans and the Industrial South,* reported:

> Mr. Lambert makes a specialty of the building of houses, for sale on time payments, and is the only person here doing this on an extensive scale. He has built 203 cottages and residences, and sold them on the installment plan, and is constructing others as fast as called for. These houses are furnished in the best style and are complete in all modern details. They are handsomely frescoed and their ornamentation includes Belgian stained glass and other extras.

Underwood, partner in Robinson and Underwood, auctioneers, and a real estate agent and president of Potthoff Paint Company, made $21,000 worth of repairs to the house in 1898. The following year, Mary Tobin acquired the house in a sheriff's sale, only to sell it two months later to Edward Godchaux of the Canal Street clothing store Leon Godchaux Company. Godchaux retained architects Favrot and Livaudais to make improvements, including exterior changes, and sold it in 1935 to Paul Kling, Jr. Five years later, Kling sold the house to Edith Haspel who sold it in 1942 to Orazio DiCristina for $12,500. The owners as of this writing, Anne and John Salvaggio, purchased the house in 1977 from the DiCristinas.

5800 ST. CHARLES AVENUE, HURSTVILLE

Set far back from the street where it can be best seen from Nashville Avenue, this handsome Italianate raised cottage suggests the suburban era of Hurstville. Its prominent, five-bay gallery has six classical Corinthian columns supporting a well-detailed entablature combining modillions and brackets, and a prominent dormer. The chief advocate of the Italianate style in America was Andrew Jackson Downing who wrote that "a villa, however small, in the Italianate style, may have an elegant and expressive

character without interfering with the convenient internal arrangement."

Cashier John Hillman built this house in 1870 when Hurstville was still part of Jefferson Parish. Hillman had lived here only five years when he sold the house to Henry Stevenson. It was sold again in 1877 and twice in 1880, the second sale that year being to music store owner Philip Werlein whose family retained the house until 1950. After two subsequent owners, Dr. and Mrs. William Rachal purchased it in 1978.

5801 ST. CHARLES AVENUE, HURSTVILLE

All major local newspapers reported on the construction of this impressive Colonial Revival house. The *Daily Picayune* wrote: "The residence of Mrs. Mae Brooks Millard, at Nashville avenue is built in old colonial style, with bright red brick and ornamental wood and stone work and is believed by many to be one of the prettiest new residences in the city. . . . Mr. [Robert Spencer] Soulé is the architect of this house." The *Daily States* reported that construction of the "only brick veneer house in the city" was begun in January 1902 and completed on July 1 that year, costing $15,000.

Mrs. Millard purchased this vacant site in 1901 and sold the property in 1904 for $27,000 to Miriam Newman Neugass after building this house. Originally, this impressive residence had a widow's walk and a roof balustrade between the dormers and corner newels.

The Neugass family lived here for twelve years, selling to Domingo Abaunza in 1916 for $25,000. Three years later, the Abaunza family sold the house to Arthur D. Parker whose family retained ownership until 1945 when Dr. and Mrs. Willoughby Kittredge bought it for $36,500. Kittredge family descendants own the property as of this writing.

5807 ST. CHARLES AVENUE, HURSTVILLE

Favrot and Livaudais designed this Colonial Revival house in 1899 for Simon Steinhardt who was with Steinhardt and Company, grain exporters and

cotton seed products and also president of Bluefields Steamship Company.

The Rosa Park elevation has an attractive side entrance with stained glass windows above. A comparison of the present house with the old photograph confirms that the St. Charles Avenue elevation has lost its original second-floor porch wood railing, a large downtown-end chimney, the extension of a pair of short windows in the bay to match the sill height of the flanking windows in the clipped corners, and the front entrance stairs. The first floor "pipe" railing, however, is original.

The Steinhardt family owned the house until 1916, selling to Joseph Rittenberg for $24,500. Twenty-one years later, John T. Holmes purchased the property for $17,500. In 1958 his widow sold the house for $47,000 to Germaine Cazenave Wells, owner of Arnaud's Restaurant and noted for her annual Easter Parade. After two interim owners, Mr. and Mrs. James Minge bought the house in 1992.

5809 ST. CHARLES AVENUE, HURSTVILLE

Unquestionably the most impressive and photographed house on the avenue, this residence is an outstanding example of the picturesque mode of the Colonial Revival style. Rather than duplicating a colonial building, this phase of the style employs colonial details such as broken pediments, palladian windows, urns, garlands, and corner pilasters in a free-spirited manner.

Wholesale grocer Nicholas Burke retained Toledano and Reusch to design this house and William F. Krone to build it in 1896 at a cost of $13,265. Shortly after construction, the house was illustrated in an advertisement for the architectural firm with a caption which read, in part:

The above residence is built according to the rich and attractive style of architecture known as "The Colonial." The finished appearance and grace of outline displayed throughout this magnificent residence denote the masterly skill and care of the architects who planned it, and under whose careful supervision it was erected.

In 1907 an electrical fire caused severe damage to the house. According to the *Daily Picayune*, Toledano and Wogan had a hand in the "rebuilding" of the Burke residence. The house remained in the Burke family and has changed little since the 1907 fire, retaining its original wall-to-wall carpeting, bathroom fixtures, security system, light fixtures, and ceiling paintings. In 1993 Rosalie and Nicholas Chisesi purchased the house and undertook a major renovation. See color interior photograph section for interior view.

5824 ST. CHARLES AVENUE, HURSTVILLE

One of the oldest structures in the University section, this Italianate center-hall cottage is well concealed behind foliage and exhibits much of the suburban character of this area when it was part of Hurstville in Jefferson Parish.

Built in 1867, according to the designs of noted architect Henry Howard, this house was described in the building contract as "a one story framed dwelling house (with unfinished garret) on a brick basement story."

Cotton factor and commission merchant Antonio Palacios paid $13,492 to builder Daniel Fraser for the construction of this elegant residence. Changes in taste from the Greek Revival to the Italianate are reflected in the segmental window heads, projecting side bays, and naturalistic cast iron porch railings.

Palacio sold the house in 1879 to Lambert Cain who sold it to Henry Roos nine days later. The Roos family retained the property until 1917 when John Lewis Phillips bought it. Phillips sold it three years later to Charles Claiborne. H. Mortimer Favrot was the next owner in 1941, and in 1953 sold to Mrs. and Mrs. Frank Evans Farwell, the owners as of this writing. See color interior photograph section for interior view.

5914 ST. CHARLES AVENUE, BLOOMINGDALE

W.W. Van Meter designed this $170,000 Gothic church, built between 1928 and 1930 as a gift to the congregation from Alice Affleck Bloomfield as a memorial to the Affleck and Bloomfield families. The rather simple facade is complemented by the more ornate tower placed away from St. Charles Avenue. According to an article in the July 29, 1928, *Times-Picayune*, the St. Charles Avenue Presbyterian Church planned this to be the first phase of a three-unit complex extending back to Benjamin Street. (Refer also to "Bloomingdale" in "The Uptown Faubourgs.")

5912 ST. CHARLES AVENUE, BLOOMINGDALE

Stella Adler acquired this site on May 18, 1905, and retained Emile Weil to design a two-story Mediterranean Villa. That 1905 house, costing $12,500, appeared in the October 1906 issue of *Architectural Art and Its Allies*. In 1907 Stella Adler sold the house to Julius Adler, but a 1921 lawsuit, *Stella Adler v. Julius Adler,* cancelled the sale and returned title to Stella Adler. She sold the house on September 15, 1921, to Lazarus Fass for $33,000, retaining the right to occupy the house rent-free except for one front room downstairs, until September 30, 1921. The sale included the window shades, curtain rods, gas logs, ceiling fans, gas heater, water heater, coal heater, and all plumbing and electrical fixtures.

In 1927 Fass sold the house for $60,000 to Electra Van Ostern, widow of Leon Soards. She sold it to Edwin Russell the following year, including in the sale "all furniture, bric-a-brac, and carpets except for the furniture in apartments B and C, the furniture in the reception hall and wall mirror in the lower hall together with a wicker set in apartment E and two chest of drawers in Apartment E," an indication that the house had been converted, altered, and enlarged into an apartment building.

Russell sold the property the next year, 1929, to Beulah and John Wallace, including furniture, bric-a-brac, and carpets, but not musical instruments and sewing machines that were the property of the tenants. In 1937 the Wallace family sold the building for $24,000 to Thelma Fabacher, wife of Robert Coffin. Harry Rosenburg purchased the building in 1944 for $130,000, and it remained in his family until 1986 when it was bought by Evangeline Associates.

6000 ST. CHARLES AVENUE, BLOOMINGDALE

The *Daily Picayune* on September 1, 1895, reported on the construction of this stately house: "We [Thomas Sully and Company] have in course of construction and nearly completed on St. Charles avenue, and State street, a two-story residence in the old colonial style for Mr. J.W. Castles."

John Castles, president of Hibernia National Bank, purchased the site in 1894 for $9,500 and had the

present house built for $9,000. The house originally had a widow's walk, a full-width terrace with wood railing and semicircular steps to the entrance porch, and a one-story uptown porch with Ionic columns, as seen in the old photograph. Its design was apparently inspired by the 1759 Longfellow residence in Cambridge, Massachusetts.

Castles' widow lost the house to John Gannon in 1910 as the result of a lawsuit. Gannon sold the house in 1920 to Victor Elsas for $45,000. After four interim owners, it was purchased by Darryl and Louellen Berger in 1978.

6016 ST. CHARLES AVENUE, BURTHEVILLE

Architects Favrot and Livaudais designed this 1903 Queen Anne house for Charles Stich, a fruit merchant who acquired the site in 1901 for $5,000. The Stich family retained the house until 1927 when Lucille White, wife of Douglas Holmes, puchased it. It was subsequently acquired by Mae and James O'Neil, Jr. who sold it in 1971 to Dr. and Mrs. Oliver Dabezies, the owners as of this writing.

Unfortunately, the original appearance of the house has been marred by the addition of a second-floor porch and replacement window sash. The half-circle, gable-end window is a surviving detail of the original design, which can be seen on original architectural drawings of the house.

6020 ST. CHARLES AVENUE, BURTHEVILLE

Judah Seidenbach, a cashier of A. Lehmann and Company, purchased the side yard of 6018 St.

Charles from the estate of Joseph H. Duggan in 1901 and built 6020 St. Charles in 1903 for $10,000. This picturesque residence, designed by architects Favrot and Livaudais, is an example of the Queen Anne style, with strong Tudor Revival influences. The rather simple exterior conceals a lavish interior that is one of the best preserved period interiors in New Orleans. The ornament of the living-stair hall is particularly fine, with griffins and grotesques peering down from the coved ceiling, a Jacobean carved oak mantel set in a Moorish arch, and stained glass windows. The living room has a fine coved ceiling with eagles incorporated into its low profile pattern, which is contrasted by the deep profiles of the wood elements. The dining room resembles an English medieval dining hall, with a wainscot, a beamed ceiling, and an ornate, carved Jacobean mantel.

In 1920 Peter Fabacher, proprietor of Fabacher's Restaurant and Hotel, purchased the property from the Seidenbach family and owned it until 1922. Between 1922 and 1953 a succession of five families owned this house: Ewing, Jordan, Mysing, Pincus, and Gray. In 1953, Mother Isabel Tejero bought the house, and it was used as a convent and boarding school for the Religious Congregation of the Daughters of Jesus until 1973 when it was returned to use as a private residence. After three interim owners, Mr. and Mrs. Michael Meyer bought the property and retain it as of this writing. See color interior photograph section for interior view.

6026 ST. CHARLES AVENUE, BURTHEVILLE

Tax records and city directories indicate that William LeBon built this two-story Queen Anne residence in 1873. LeBon purchased the site in 1871 for $1,363 from cotton weigher Aimé Gautier who lived next door at 6000 St. Charles Avenue (not the present residence). LeBon sold the house in 1880 to Carl Blankensteiner for $3,000, only to repossess it the following year and sell it to George W. Boutcher, a salesman with Delgado and Company and later its president. The house remained in the Boutcher family until 1981 when it was bought by Dr. and Mrs. Frederick Kushner.

In 1903 improvements costing $3,400 were made to the house, as indicated in the *Daily Picayune* and by a $3,500 increase in property assessment. An article in the *New Orleans Item* in 1941 about a pending family wedding discusses the house, noting that at the time of its purchase by George Boutcher, grandfather of the bride:

It was a mature house then, a raised cottage standing in the middle of the swamp. There were only two or three other residences for miles. . . . George Bouthe [Boutcher] set his mind to improving his house. It was transformed from a raised cottage into a two story residence building from below. In no time at all it looked as it does today, a dignified, graceful home complete with double parlors, dining-room, music room and reception hall downstairs and six bedrooms and a sitting room upstairs.

Whether the house was actually modified as the article indicates cannot be documented. The 1896 Sanborn map clearly indicates a two-and-one-half-story residence, and the Robinson *Atlas* that illustrates the house does not indicate the number of stories.

6038-40 ST. CHARLES AVENUE, BURTHEVILLE

An advertisement in the August 28, 1927, *Times-Picayune* states:

The splendid new duplex shown above has just been completed and in its construction Everstone brick from the American Brick Co., a New Orleans concern, were used. This duplex is at St. Charles and Webster and is one of the finest examples of this type of construction in New Orleans.

The house combines a variety of different stylistic details into an awkward, though typical design of this period.

Mrs. Holly Stem built the duplex after acquiring the site for $13,900. The 1926 tax records note, "Take old house off rolls," and the following year a large, stucco, tile-roofed duplex at this address is assessed for $5,800. Stem retained the property until 1951 when she sold it to Samuel Zemurray who sold it only three months later to Shepard Latter and Shirley Latter Schlesinger. They retained it just nine months before selling at an $8,000 profit to Chester Owens who in turn sold the house two months later at a profit of $2,000 to Gertrude and Robert Jeffers. However, in 1961, Chester Owens was declared the lawful owner, and his widow, along with Gertrude Jeffers, sold the duplex in 1963 to Helen Westerhoff. In 1972 Milton Brenner purchased it.

6100 ST. CHARLES AVENUE, BURTHEVILLE

Although altered, this two-story Queen Anne residence maintains much of its 1890s appearance. The downtown second-story addition masks the original three-dimensional quality of the St. Charles Avenue facade.

On October 11, 1886, Commercial Homestead acquired a building permit for a structure on the river side of the 6100 block of St. Charles Avenue, possibly for this residence. The tax assessment increased substantially between 1887 and 1888, indicating the house was completed in 1887. On February 29, 1888, Edward T. Merrick purchased the house from Commercial Homestead and in 1895 obtained a permit for the addition of a front gallery costing $175. Merrick retained the house until 1926 when he sold it to Dr. O.C. Cassegrain for $15,000. As of this writing, there have been four subsequent owners: John T. Sanders (1936), Charles Mackie III (1955), Marian and James Brooks (1973), and John Gottshall (1985).

6110 ST. CHARLES AVENUE, BURTHEVILLE

After building 5801 St. Charles Avenue in 1902, Mrs. Mae Millard, with "her own separate and paraphernal funds, which have at all times been separately administered by her and under her separate control," purchased this site in 1904 for $8,500 and commissioned architects Favrot and Livaudais to design this Swiss Chalet residence. The house is unique on the avenue, with fanciful woodwork reminiscent

of the Alps in the gables of the main house and entrance porch.

In 1906 the Millards sold the property, including "the gas and electric fixtures, bathtubs, etc.," to Stella Hirsch, wife of Dr. Isaac Lemann. Mrs. Lemann is noted for her donation of Madame John's Legacy, 632 Dumaine Street, to the Louisiana State Museum. She worked for many years for the preservation of the Vieux Carré as well as for many other civic causes. The Lemann family sold the house in 1974 to the John Kourians, who retain ownership as of this writing.

6126 ST. CHARLES AVENUE, BURTHEVILLE
Architect Moise H. Goldstein designed the Lake Apartments in a Spanish Eclectic style. Although the

building is four stories in height, its scale is minimized by its rusticated base and humanistic details so that it does not overpower the avenue. It was built by W.A. Keen in 1924 for Lak Realty Company, which purchased this site and demolished an existing two-story, wood frame residence built for Edward Hunt in 1899. Lak was an acronym for the company's owners, Charles Levy, Charles Alltmont, and Sol Kahn.

After three interim owners, Dorothy and Shepard Shushan acquired the property in 1978 in an unusual real estate transaction by trading property in Palm Springs, California, for this triplex, which has since been converted into three luxury condominiums.

6145 ST. CHARLES AVENUE, BURTHEVILLE
According to the local architectural magazine *Building Review* of April 20, 1918:

Miss Louise Monlezun of 4437 St. Charles avenue has purchased from Mrs. William H. Renaud the Renaud residence at 6145 St. Charles avenue. The property had been in Mrs. Renaud's family for about 35 years. Miss Monlezun paid $35,000 or upwards of $200 per front foot. It is reported she will demolish the house and erect a modern and handsome home costing a considerable sum. The deal was effected through the Bank of Orleans. The property fronts 196 feet front on the avenue and is more than 200 feet deep.

This transaction occurred on April 8, 1918. Monlezun then married Edward Schleider, president of

American Brewing Company, and commissioned architects Favrot and Livaudais to design the present Mediterranean Villa style residence. The house was built between 1923 and 1924. Tax records indicate a partial assessment in 1923 for "granite block 16 room house, $60,000 permit." Monluzen and Schleider divorced in 1924, the first year Schleider is listed at this address.

Eventually, the Dutton family acquired the house, selling it in 1972 to Dr. Charles Pearce. In 1979 Norman Johnson purchased the house and undertook a major renovation under the direction of architects Lyons and Hudson. In 1984 James and Louise Moffett acquired the house. "Jim Bob" Moffett is chairman of the board of Freeport McMoRan, an oil-minerals-chemicals-metals conglomerate.

6149 ST. CHARLES AVENUE, BURTHEVILLE

Cotton buyer William Bentley of Bentley, Joynson and Company purchased this site in September 1915 and built the present house shortly thereafter, as he is listed here in the 1917 city directory. He sold the two-story stucco residence in 1927 to Mrs. Cecil Robinson for $35,000. In 1955 Bouwe Dykstra bought the house and it remained in that family until 1994 when Mary Johnson and William L. Marks purchased it.

This residence is a good example of the Mediterranean Villa style popular during the second and third decade of the twentieth century. The green tile umbrella roof, shallow roof brackets, semicircular first-floor openings, and emphasized entrance bay are typical of the style.

6153 ST. CHARLES AVENUE, BURTHEVILLE

Emile Weil was the architect for this Renaissance Revival, two-and-one-half-story residence. The raising of the house on a pedestal, the classical front porch and terrace, and the classic dormers and cornice add an air of formality to this simple, box massing. The Palmer Street side has an interesting canopy, and the State Street side has a small projecting bay and conservatory.

William Adler, president of State National Bank and vice-president of Schwartz Foundry Company, had the house built in 1903 at a cost of $20,000 in the then-current style for a wealthy capitalist. The *Daily Picayune* of September 1, 1903, recorded its construction:

Emile Weil is in charge of the plans of the new two-story stone residence of William Adler at Palmer Avenue and St. Charles which will have fifteen rooms and a basement, perhaps the first basement in a residence in the city. The basement is constructed with concrete and will be perfectly dry. The interior finish of the house is hardwood and marble.

The house was sold in 1910 to Jacob Wilzin for $39,000. Mario Bermudez bought it in 1954 and sold it in 1973 to Geraldine and Jay Seastrunk II for $170,000. Eleven years later, Seastrunk sold the house to Beverly and Roland Von Kurnatowski. In 1988 John Bookout acquired the house, selling it in 1992 to Marcia and Gothard Reck.

6200 ST. CHARLES AVENUE, BURTHEVILLE

James A. Petty built this Renaissance Revival church for the St. Charles Avenue Christian Church in 1922 at a cost of $39,765.65. The design by architects Jones and Roessle employs tapestry brick laid in patterns creating architectural details, a characteristic of the Decorative Brick style. It was dedicated on March 4, 1923. An electrical fire that captured local newspaper headlines on January 20, 1958, caused $50,000 in damage and resulted in extensive interior renovations.

Established in 1904 as an uptown outgrowth of the First Christian Church and temporarily housed at Coliseum and Jefferson, the church moved to Soniat and Camp streets in 1905 and was known as the Soniat Avenue Christian Church. In 1914 the subject site was purchased, and a "one story frame composite roof temporary rough board tabernacle church" was constructed. The following year, through a charter change, it became the St. Charles Avenue Christian Church, and a more substantial church was built on the rear portion of the lot. This building, which serves today as the fellowship hall, became known as the "Bungalow Church." Its St. Charles Avenue facade, now obscured, combined Mission and California Style detailing. It was designed by Rudolph Roessle, a church member, while in the employ of architect Charles Charlton. It was always the intention of the

congregation to build a more elaborate church on the avenue, which was finally done in 1922.

Originally, this was the site of the Samuel Gilmore residence. (See 1582 Henry Clay Avenue.)

6214 ST. CHARLES AVENUE, BURTHEVILLE

By means of two separate transactions, Annie Aiken, wife of William Pollock Curtis, a tobacco-man-turned-real-estate-broker, acquired this site in 1887 and built the house before 1890, when the couple are first listed as residing at this location. Tax assessments rose steadily, from $4,000 in 1888 to $6,000 in 1889 to $9,000 in 1890, indicating a construction timetable spanning more than one year. Most likely, the majority of construction took place in 1889.

In 1893 Assistant U.S. District Attorney Delos C. Mellen purchased the house for $10,850. Eight years later, Augusta Baldwin bought it at public auction for $8,200 and sold it four years later to Earle Knobloch, a sugar and molasses broker, for $12,000. In 1912 George Allain purchased the house, and his heirs sold it in 1925 to the St. Charles Avenue Christian Church for $25,000 for use as a parsonage. Eric Smith, the owner as of this writing, purchased the house in 1991.

The Queen Anne residence has lost its original wraparound porch seen in the old photograph. This feature could easily be replaced to restore the architectural integrity and three-dimensional quality of the house. The house does, however, retain its original leaded glass front door, oval stained glass window, and decorative cornice block motif.

Volume I), according to the designs of Charles Hillger. On November 13, 1927, the Grand Lodge of Louisiana F&AM laid the cornerstone of the present St. Charles Avenue temple designed by Emile Weil, Moise H. Goldstein, and Weiss Dreyfous and Seiferth, associated architects. Charles Gibert was the general contractor.

The temple's exterior is best described as Stripped Classical, an abstraction of a traditional design that would become popular during the Great Depression. Over the bronze entrance doors with Biblical scenes is ornament with corn, wheat, and grapes, above which are two tablets with the Ten Commandments. The sanctuary features a marble ark, a coffered ceiling with a Moorish pattern, trompe l'oeil painted wood, Art Deco pilasters, cornices, screens, and chandeliers, a parquet floor, and stained glass windows. Original hat racks survive under the cushioned seats.

natural causes, such as storms, or through intentional redesign to simplify its appearance. Lost elements include the applied garlands of the porch entablature, the second-floor porch railing with urns and gooseneck railings, and the railing for the gable balcony of the projecting bay and the roof line, as well as the widow's walk.

On February 16, 1896, grocer Christopher Doyle purchased the site for $12,520 and built the present house the same year at a cost of $10,000, according to the *Daily Picayune*. In 1904 the Doyle family sold the house to George Keller of Pointe Coupee. It remained in the Keller family until it was sold in 1919 to the Round Table Club for $24,000.

6226 ST. CHARLES AVENUE, BURTHEVILLE

Canal Street clothing merchant Mayer Israel commissioned architects Favrot and Livaudais to design this 1902 Colonial Revival residence, which reportedly cost $15,000. The picturesque massing of the facade is more in keeping with the nineteenth century phase of the style than other homes of its period which began to reflect true replication of colonial residences.

In 1922 Israel sold the house to Eugene Atkinson for $25,000. The house remained in the Atkinson family until 1944 when Alexander Carmel purchased it. In 1964 the Marquette Association for Higher Education (Loyola) bought the house.

6227 ST. CHARLES AVENUE, BURTHEVILLE

Organized in 1870 as a reform Jewish congregation, Congregation Temple Sinai built its first synagogue in 1871 at 1832 Carondelet Street (see

6300 ST. CHARLES AVENUE, BURTHEVILLE

This Colonial Revival residence, designed by Toledano and Reusch, with a large, square tower, broken-pedimented dormers, and first-floor windows and garlanded front porch, has unfortunately lost its tower cresting railing. William P. Burke, vice-president of Nicholas Burke Company, wholesale grocers, purchased this property in 1896 and obtained a permit that year for a $8,294 residence. The house remained in the Burke family until 1991 when Colleen and John Knotts purchased it.

6330 ST. CHARLES AVENUE, BURTHEVILLE

Unfortunately, this house has lost much of its original detail seen in the old photograph, either through

The club, originally known as the Followcraft Club, was conceived by Dr. Beverly Warner in 1897 as a men's club dedicated to the discussion of literary, artistic, and scientific topics. The seven charter members were Dr. Warner, rector of Trinity Church; Professors James Dillard, John Ficklen, and Henry Orr of Tulane University; Professor Ellsworth Woodward of Newcomb College; and businessmen Henry Sloan and R.M. Westfeldt. The club first met on January 3, 1898, at 1435 Jackson Avenue in rented space that had fallen out of public favor because it had sheltered several cases of yellow fever in the epidemic of 1897. The new clubhouse on St. Charles Avenue was formally opened on April 23, 1919, with an evening reception for members and ladies following a symposium on Shakespeare. The Round Table Club continues to hold lectures here as of this writing. See color interior photograph section for interior view.

7003 ST. CHARLES AVENUE, GREENVILLE

Gonzalo Abaunza built this comfortable, two-story, stone veneer residence in 1917 at a cost of $23,200, according to building permit No. 10398, taken out on May 14, 1917. Designed by architect Francis J. MacDonnell, the house has entrances on both St. Charles Avenue and Newcomb Boulevard.

Abaunza, general manager of Mexican Navigation Company, purchased the site on April 2, 1917, and built the house that year. In 1923 he sold the house for $55,000 to Roland Thomas who sold it three months later to Williams Investments. In 1937 Horace Williams purchased the property and retained it for five years. Sybil Stevens acquired the house in 1942 for $45,000, and in 1950 sold it to her daughter, Sybil Calhoun, whose family retains ownership as of this writing.

7004 ST. CHARLES AVENUE, GREENVILLE

The dominant front porch with its decorative railing adds a three-dimensional quality to this Queen Anne house. Kelly Bros. built this two-story residence in 1896 for Carrie Taylor at a cost of $8,000. Tax

records verify this with an increase in assessment from $4,500 in 1896 to $15,000 in 1897.

Edward Martinez acquired the entire square for $10,000 in 1888, at which time an earlier house stood in the center of the square. Martinez apparently built a house here in 1893 for a permit exists for a $4,868 residence.

Known for many years as the Parkview Guest House, the structure had ten owners up to 1990 when it was sold to 7004 St. Charles Avenue Corporation, Nicholas Alan Ransom, president.

7014 ST. CHARLES AVENUE, GREENVILLE

The Alameda Apartments replaced an earlier two-story, wood frame Queen Anne residence. Most likely, the twelve-unit Spanish Eclectic building was erected in 1918 for Olive Pollock, as evidenced by the rise in property assessment from $7,750 in 1918 to $15,500 in 1919.

Pollock sold the apartment building in 1919 to Dr. John A. Majors who sold it for $16,160 in 1924 to Norman Shubert, vice president of J.A. Majors Company, medical book suppliers. The following year, Jefferson Burnett, who was involved in real estate, acquired the property and transferred it to Orleans Realty and Investment Company. In 1930 Dr. John Capo purchased the property as the result of a lawsuit. The building remained in the Capo family until 1985 when it was transferred to Alameda Associates for $600,000.

7022 ST. CHARLES AVENUE, GREENVILLE

Ephraim Phelps, Jr., a shoe store owner, purchased this site in September 1915 for $5,000 and sold it with the present structure the following September to Charles Weinberger for $17,000. Phelps obtained a permit for the house in 1916 in the amount of $4,935 in the name of St. Charles Avenue Company. G.E. and T.E. Relfann are listed as the builders of this Mediterranean residence.

During the Great Depression, Weinberger lost the house to the homestead, which sold it to Coryell McKinney for $25,000. Two months later, McKinney sold the building to Weinberger's wife for $25,000. The building remained in the Weinberger family until 1958 when it was sold to Frank Van Kirk. Two years later, the property was purchased by Dr. and Mrs. Royce Henry, the owners as of this writing.

7027 ST. CHARLES AVENUE, GREENVILLE

Built in 1926 for Anthony Sauer, president of Seaboard Refining Company (cottonseed products), this two-story brick residence has two major entrances. The Newcomb Boulevard entrance was to comply with the Newcomb Boulevard developer's restrictions while the St. Charles entrance apparently accommodated the owner's desire for a St. Charles Avenue address.

The house as it faces St. Charles is best described as in the "Southern Colonial" style, and Norman as it faces Newcomb Boulevard, though that facade is somewhat harder to categorize. This eclectic approach to design is not uncommon with homes of this period.

The Sauer heirs sold the house for $27,000 in 1937 to William DePass, president of Standard Supply and Hardware Company, whose heirs sold it in 1941 to Eugene Atkinson, Jr. for $25,000. Patton Marion acquired it from the succession of Atkinson, and Keith Capone, the owner as of this writing, bought the house in 1992.

7030 ST. CHARLES AVENUE, GREENVILLE

Joanna Eyrich purchased this site in 1889 and contracted with Heinrich and Dannemann to build this Queen Anne house with corner tower, wraparound porch, and whimsical porte cochere, according to the designs of Williams Bros. The *Daily Picayune* had reported the previous year that "in dwelling houses the Queen Anne style of architecture appears to have become quite the rage and a large number of these ornamental and comfortable yet comparatively inexpensive buildings have been added to the dwellings in this city."

City directories first list Joanna Eyrich here in 1890 with her husband, Robert, a travel agent. The house remained in the Eyrich family until December 21, 1908, when it was sold to Benton Foret for $10,000. Subsequent owners have been George Stahler (1914), Ralph Katz (1943), Ruby Pick (1944), and Toby Pick Feibelman and Julian Feibelman, Jr. (1970).

7100 ST. CHARLES AVENUE, GREENVILLE

The 1915 Panama-California Exposition in San Diego made the "Exposition Mode" of the Spanish Eclectic style popular during the subsequent years. Architects Favrot and Livaudais chose that style for the St. Charles Avenue Baptist Church, built in 1925. The ornate, terra cotta central design, flanked by similarly ornamented side entries as well as the bell tower, are common to this style. The portion of the complex along Broadway was added to the original church in 1963.

7107 ST. CHARLES AVENUE, GREENVILLE

Here is an early-twentieth century, two-story residence that combines influences of both the Queen

Anne and Craftsman styles. The roof and gable ends, with their half-timbering, knee braces, and exposed rafter ends, are clearly in the Craftsman taste while the remainder of the house is in the Queen Anne style, with such details as seen in the porch and bay window under the projecting upper floor.

Emma and Anna Lurges had this house built in 1908 after purchasing the site at auction for $3,750 in 1905. The year of construction is indicated by the increase in property assessment of $4,000 in 1908 to $7,000 in 1909. The house is illustrated on the 1909 Sanborn insurance map. M. Truman Woodward, Jr. inherited the house in 1945 and sold it for $32,000 in 1956 to Ford Thomas Hardy, in whose family it remains as of this writing

7111 ST. CHARLES AVENUE, GREENVILLE

Florence Lazard, wife of liquor dealer Henry Block, purchased this site for $1,920 in 1907 after retaining architects Favrot and Livaudais to design this Craftsman residence featuring a red tile roof, gable-end half-timbering, diamond-paned gable windows, and Doric porch columns. Unfortunately, one-third of the partial-width wraparound porch has been enclosed.

Block sold the house for $15,000 in 1918 to merchant Emanuel Wolf of St. Francisville, Louisiana, whose family owned it until 1927 when general contractor Harold Pratt Farnsworth acquired it for $31,000. He sold it twelve years later to Vincenzina Attabas for only $12,000. In 1943 Edward Falkenstein purchased the house, and in 1964 his heirs sold it to Maria and William Daly, the owners as of this writing.

7209-7211 ST. CHARLES AVENUE, GREENVILLE

In two separate transactions, one in 1911 and one in 1913, Gabriel Hausmann assembled the parcel of land for the construction of this Tudor Revival duplex, obtaining permit #8206 on May 24, 1915. The *Daily States* reported in 1908 that "a style of architecture known as English half-timbering has become very popular in New Orleans of late." A small dollhouse in the side yard mimics the style of the main house.

Hausmann, a jeweler with T. Hausmann and Sons, lived here until his death. As of this writing, the house is owned by Gail Hausmann Victor.

7214 ST. CHARLES AVENUE, GREENVILLE

William Fitzner designed this impressive structure built by G. Murry in 1882 for the Dominican nuns as Greenville Hall of St. Mary's Academy. Its original impact on the Avenue is diminished, however, by the dormitory along Broadway. The now very familiar Byzantine dormers are not original to Fitzner's Italianate design featuring a double gallery with segmental arches between boxed columns and a cupola. The *Times-Democrat* reported on September 1, 1883, that "the Dominican Convent has built a handsome front to their establishment on St. Charles avenue costing over $25,000." In 1898 Toledano and Reusch designed an addition of a chapel and wing, which no longer exist, at a cost $12,456. In 1906 another two-story addition costing $12,000 was added by B.J. Schneider. St. Mary's Academy became St. Mary's Dominican College in 1910. After the closure of Dominican College, the property was acquired by Loyola University.

A Craftsman style arbor with shrines adds a feeling of tranquility to busy St. Charles Avenue.

7217-23 ST. CHARLES AVENUE, GREENVILLE

Sisters Edith and Marion Leopold, who were married to brothers Joseph and Edward Haspel, had Louisiana Contracting Company build this Craftsman style house in 1914 for $9,000. The asymmetrical stucco duplex has window boxes and casement windows with a Union Jack light pattern. Unfortunately, the uptown-side porch has been enclosed on the second floor.

The duplex remained in the Haspel family until 1923 when the Kessler family purchased it for $20,000. In 1950 Albert Boisfontaine bought the house, and ten years later sold it to Gaston Gaudet, the owner as of this writing.

7225 ST. CHARLES AVENUE, GREENVILLE

This Craftsman style raised bungalow, designed by architect Emile Weil, dates to 1917 when clothier Jacob Levy purchased the site for $6,250. Levy is first listed at this location in the 1918 city directory.

The bungalow, illustrated in a monograph of Weil's work entitled "Illustrations of Selected Work of Emile Weil, Architect, New Orleans, La., 1900-1928," gives the appearance of being on a hill, with a terrace halfway up the St. Charles elevation. However, from Pine Street, it is clear that is merely a berm, and the bungalow is raised over a basement with a decorative street-grade side entrance. A variety of design influences are united in this bungalow by the common thread of Craftsmanship—the half-timbering in the gable ends, borrowed from the Tudor Revival style; the decorative use of tapestry brick, from the Decorative Brick style; classic, cast stone railings from the Renaissance Revival; and snakemouth ends of exposed rafters and casement windows from the California Style.

The house remained in the Levy family until 1959 when it was sold for $50,000 to Geralyn and Bertney Frick, Jr., who still own it as of this writing,

7300 ST. CHARLES AVENUE, GREENVILLE

Originally built as the home of Peter Fabacher, president and general manager of Peter Fabacher and Bros. Catering Company, this stone house is difficult to define stylistically. Architects Toledano and Wogan employed a large, umbrella-like roof cantilevering out on shallow brackets and modillions, a stone wall dormer, a wraparound porch with decorative cartouches on the columns, and a side porte cochere. When built in 1907 this house reportedly cost $25,000.

In 1917 Fabacher sold the house for $35,000 to James Wright who sold it in 1919 to John Bouden, Jr. Bouden's heirs sold it in 1943 for $45,000 to the New Orleans Dominican Female Academy. St. Mary's Dominican College bought the house in 1964 and sold it to New Orleans Dominican Female Academy in 1990.

The addition over the porte cochere mars the original design intent.

7319 ST. CHARLES AVENUE, GREENVILLE

The present appearance of this house belies its original construction date, but a discerning eye will observe that exposed rafter ends are found only on the front and on a portion of the downtown side of the house. The original configuration of the house can be seen on the 1896 Sanborn insurance map which indicates it as a one-story house with full-width front porch and a projection on the downtown side with a street-facing porch. The house likely dates to 1890, as indicated by a jump in tax assessment from $1,500 in 1890 to $6,200 in 1891.

Tulane Professor Robert Sharp, who resided next door at 7326 St. Charles in a now demolished 1886 house, purchased this site in 1890 from manufacturing agent William S. Devan and built this house. In 1914 permit No. 6866 was taken out by V.H. Elsas

for alterations to the house, transforming it to its present appearance. City directories list Elsas, assistant manager of the Fulton Bag and Cotton Mills, as residing here, but he did not own the house. In 1920 Sharp sold the remodeled house to John Bedger whose family retains it as of this date.

7320 ST. CHARLES AVENUE, GREENVILLE

Building permit No. 4838, issued in 1913, documents that "M. Levy, Jr." built a two-story, slate roofed residence here. Tax assessment records also indicate a $13,500 increase in value between 1913 and 1914.

Moise Levy, a travel agent, purchased the property on February 10, 1913, for $7,500 and built the present Gothic house. His widow sold the house to the New Orleans Female Dominican Academy in 1953 for $58,950.

STATE

210 STATE STREET, BURTHEVILLE

Opened in New Orleans in 1803 as the U.S. Marine Hospital for the Merchant Marine, this institution is the second-oldest hospital in the city. At first the hospital operated out of Charity Hospital. In 1847 Congress appropriated funds to build a Gothic style hospital in Algiers that initially was taken over by the army until 1848, and then served as the Marine Hospital until 1858. In 1855, Marine Hospital Services acquired a new site on Broad and Tulane and

built a large, cast iron building, but like its predecessor in Algiers, it was immediately occupied by the military. After a crevasse forced closure of the Algiers Hospital, Marine Services moved to Jackson Barracks where it operated between 1858 and 1861. In 1862 Marine Services returned to Charity Hospital and then moved to Hotel Dieu in 1870 and to Touro Infirmary in 1882.

In 1885 the Marine Hospital purchased the subject site, on which there existed a cottage, facing Tchoupitoulas, which likely dated to the early 1830s. Wings and a gallery were added in the late 1850s or early 1860s, as shown on the Robinson *Atlas*. The house was moved in 1930, along with several slave cabins, to its present location, on angle to the new hospital complex, where it still exists.

After purchasing this site, the government began construction of a hospital complex of seven principal frame buildings, one of which still exists, plus a stable, a laundry, and a service center, as illustrated on the 1909 Sanborn map. Known officially as Quarters No. 3, it is a six-bay, center hall, two-story, galleried, frame, Italianate residence designed by a Mr. Still, supervising architect of the U.S. Treasury. This building possibly includes a circa 1850 rear wing. The present upper gallery was added in 1903.

The present complex was built between 1931 and 1933 in the Renaissance Revival style. The main hospital is a five-story, irregularly planned, red brick building surmounted by an octagonal cupola. The Administrative Building is a three-story, sixteen-bay structure. The five Quarters Buildings are two-story, gable-ended, four-bay dwellings. There are numerous other buildings on the site, including the Gate House, Engineering and Maintenance Building, Power House, Transformer Room, Research Building, Warehouse, Smokestack, and Building No. 14.

631 STATE STREET, BLOOMINGDALE

This fanciful Eastlake camelback was built in 1897 as the rectory for St. Francis of Assisi Roman Catholic Church for its pastor, the Reverend Moise, at a reported cost of $3,000. Like many University section camelbacks, this one confines its ornament to the front of the house, even though it is not on a narrow lot. The central porch bay spandrel, with its curved cutout and gooseneck railing, is unusual.

703 STATE STREET, BLOOMINGDALE

Here is a double-galleried Eastlake residence, typical of the late-nineteenth and early-twentieth centuries. The details of the three-bay porch—boxed columns, dropped capitals, and decorative spandrels—are common to the style. The decorative iron porch railing, which may not be original, is atypical for this wooden style of architecture.

In 1901 grocer Joseph Gondolf purchased two lots here from Charles Mendelsohn and built the present house shortly thereafter, for he is listed here in the 1903 city directory. The house remained in the Gondolf family until 1946 when Mary Elizabeth Gillen

acquired it. She willed the house to the Franciscan Missionaries of Our Lady which sold it to Marcelle Bordenave and John Coogan in 1988.

1218 STATE STREET, BLOOMINGDALE

Here is another Southern Colonial residence with full, two-story Ionic columns, stately proportions, and symmetrical facade.

Roberta Weigel, wife of Thomas Doty, secretary of Stuyvesant Docks, purchased this site in 1901 from Eugene Dupre, et al., and is listed as residing here in 1902. In 1905 Dr. Stephen W. Stafford purchased the house, only to sell it that same year to Charles Dunbar. The Dunbar family sold the house to Elizabeth and George Haik in 1941. In 1948 Elizabeth Haik sold it to Mary and William McCardill. Ten years later, the house was bought by William Lewis who in 1971 sold it to Lucinda and Lester Lautenschlaeger, Jr. In 1976 Burt and Melanie Strug purchased the house, only to sell it the following year to Sandra and Marshall Oreck. Sandra Oreck sold the house in 1986 to Kristin and Benjamin Capshaw III.

1237 STATE STREET, BLOOMINGDALE

This stately Southern Colonial residence is the work of architects Diboll and Owen. It was built in 1902 as the home of architect Allison Owen who served in the U.S. Army in World War I and in the National Guard where he held the rank of major general. Owen also helped organize the New Orleans Parkway Commission, and in 1929 he received the Times-Picayune Loving Cup in recognition of his civic endeavors.

The house remained in the Owen family until 1976 when Billye Sue and Oran Carter purchased it. In 1983 the house sold to Carla and Daniel Proffitt who sold it the following year to Roy Lassus, Jr., the owner at this writing.

This Colonial house, designated a city landmark in 1988, employs a partial-width portico with four Ionic columns and decorative oval gable window. The elaborate front door has a broken pediment and unusual sidelights.

1322, 1328, 1334 STATE STREET, BLOOMINGDALE

These three, once identical, two-story Queen Anne residences date to 1902, as indicated by tax records. They were built for butcher Leon Lavedan and remained in the family until 1920.

All three houses have been altered to some degree, with 1334 State (pictured) being the most intact, having only a replacement second-floor porch. The prismatic lights of the upper window sash clearly place the house's construction date in the early-twentieth century. The attic gable vent is noteworthy.

1425 STATE STREET, BLOOMINGDALE

Here is a large, two-story Queen Anne residence with decorative, paired columns set on bases, creating a picturesque facade. The windows employ large panels of glass, which technology made possible and affordable during this period. The second-floor projecting bay has clipped corners with decorative brackets.

John Davidson, secretary-treasurer of the Board of Harbor Masters, purchased this site in 1893 and hired G. O'Malley to build the house in 1894 for $4,290. Davidson is listed at this address in the 1895 city directory. The house remained in the Davidson family until 1943. In 1945 Helen Generes purchased the property and retained it for forty years. After one interim owner, Mr. and Mrs. William Metcalf, Jr. bought the house in 1989 and are the owners as of this writing.

1450 STATE STREET, BLOOMINGDALE

Charles Favrot was the architect-builder of this large Queen Anne residence which cost $4,100 to construct in 1893, according to the *Daily Picayune*. It was first home to William Raymond, a cashier with Lucas E. Moore and Company, steamship agents. Raymond purchased four lots on this block in 1892 for $3,800, and in 1898 sold two lots, along

with the present house, to John Ferguson, a brother-in-law. The house remained in the Ferguson family until 1946 when Warren Goodspeed purchased it for $22,000. The following year, the Goodspeeds sold it to Barbara and Robert Schupp. In 1978 the Schupp family sold the house to Louellen and Darryl Berger who sold it the following year to Leslie and Harold Stokes.

The house employs a fairly standard design formula for the Queen Anne style, with a one-story, full-width porch with one end terminating in an octagonal pavilion and a projecting bay with street-facing cross gable abutting a second-story porch.

1462 STATE STREET, BLOOMINGDALE

Attaway and Moullet, builders and architects, built this house in 1893 for Thomas Mather at a cost of $4,700, according to *Daily Picayune*. Its massing is typical of the Queen Anne style, except for the shallow porch gable.

Thomas Mather purchased this site in May 1893 and immediately began construction of the house. The house remained with the Mather heirs until 1974 when Colleen and Roy Ingraffia purchased it. Ten years later it was sold to Sofia and Alfredo Botero.

1525 STATE STREET, BLOOMINGDALE

Based on Thomas Jefferson's University of Virginia, this Southern Colonial residence was designed by architect Robert Spenser Soulé for Mary and Josephine Glover in 1902. The following year the Glovers sold the house for $9,500 to Henry Toutant Beauregard who sold it seven years later for the same amount to Joseph LeBourgeois. LeBourgeois lost the house to Mollie McQuoid in 1930 as the result of a

lawsuit filed by Archibald Suthon. The house remained in the McQuoid family until 1939. After two interim owners, it was acquired in 1961 by Dr. William Beatrous. Gayle and Leonard Glorioso, the owners as of this writing, bought the house in 1993.

As originally built, this residence was symmetrical, with two flights of stairs approaching a small entrance stoop independent of the Doric columns. The river-end porch is not original.

1544 STATE STREET, BLOOMINGDALE

This large Beaux Arts/Renaissance Revival residence appears to have been transported from St. Charles Avenue to this ample site. The massive size of the house is diminished by the partial-width front porch with its paired Ionic columns and segmental spandrels. An examination of old photographs indicates that the two river-end, second-floor openings have been changed from windows similar to those on the lake end to French doors with transoms, as has the single, river-end, first-floor opening. The three first-floor openings on the lake end have a Queen Anne-like pane configuration. An illustration in the May 1907 issue of *Architectural Art and Its Allies* testifies to the lavish interior of this house, done in an Empire style.

Designed by noted local architect Emile Weil in 1907, this house was first home to William H. Kohlmann, a physician, and Louis Kohlmann, president of Kohlmann Cotton Mill and Manufacturing Company. In 1922 Miss Clemence Kohlmann sold the house to Leon Heymann who retained it until 1955, selling it to Fisher Simmons for $65,000. Simmons sold the house in March of 1984 to Louellen and Darryl Berger who lived in the adjacent house at 6000 St. Charles. The Bergers sold it nine months later, minus a portion of land they annexed to their property, to Shirley and Christian Voelkel. In 1987 Shirley Voelkel sold the house to Theresa and Kenneth Williams.

1621 STATE STREET, BLOOMINGDALE

This house is a typical example of a metamorphosis from a picturesque style of the late-nineteenth/early-twentieth century—either Queen Anne,

Eastlake, or early Colonial Revival—to a restrained Federal or Colonial Williamsburg version of the style in the 1920s.

The old photograph shows this house as a picturesque Queen Anne residence with gable balcony, second-story, partial-width porch cut into the roof of the wraparound first-story porch, which is supported on a pair of Tuscan columns set on pedestals, between which spans a wood railing. Today, the house has been simplified to a Federal style home, with the loss of gable porch and wraparound front porch and a change of windows to six-over-six double hung. The small entrance porch is typical of the Federal style.

The house dates to 1896 and was first home to Mrs. John Gauche who acquired the lot the previous year. The 1896 Sanborn map illustrates a two-story house with a porch only across the front, but the 1909 map illustrates a configuration like the old photograph. In 1906 Gauche transferred the house to the Gauche Realty Company, which sold it in 1916 to Julia Sliger. She sold the house in 1920 to Charlotte Mehnert who sold it the following year to her daughter, Charlotte Dietze. It was likely the Dietzes who made the changes to the house.

In 1935 Charles Nehlig acquired the house, selling it in 1943 to Jess A. McMurry for $19,000. Four years later, William Johnston purchased the house. In 1965 William Ellis bought it for $55,000. In 1976 Susan and Earl Silvers purchased the house, selling it in 1979 to Susan and Alan Horwitz. Claire and Robert Webb, Jr., the owners as of this writing, bought it in 1991.

1628 STATE STREET, BLOOMINDALE

Here is an elegant Colonial Revival residence with a well-detailed front door featuring lions resting on the transom and a beautiful wrought iron gate. The house reflects the change in style from the picturesque version of the nineteenth century to the simplicity and symmetry of the twentieth century. This particular example borrows from the Georgian style.

The house was built for Mrs. Emile Kuntz after she purchased the property in 1937 for $22,000 and has remained in the Kuntz family as of this writing.

1631 STATE STREET, BLOOMINGDALE

This Craftsman style bungalow retains its original design integrity—an attempt to be in harmony with nature and reflect handcrafted architecture—as exhibited by the berming of the site, the natural fieldstone columns and porch railing, the exposed rafter ends and purlins, and the stucco walls and tile roof.

In 1912 Ida Kaufman, wife of stationer Joseph Levy, purchased this site for $5,250 and had the present house built that year, for the family is listed as living here in the 1913 city directory.

Mrs. Levy sold the house in 1936 to Dr. Octave Cassegrain for $13,250. The house remained with Cassegrain until 1961 when he sold it to daughter Aileen and her husband, Herbert Livaudais, the owners as of this writing.

1640 STATE STREET, BLOOMINGDALE

This Italianate, center-hall residence appears out of place in this part of the neighborhood, as if it had been moved from St. Charles Avenue or somewhere closer to the river. It may in fact have been the house that appears in the Robinson *Atlas* marked "Alfred Keen" on the corner of St. Charles and State. Tax records indicate that the house possibly was moved

On July 8, 1904, Frances Forcheimer, widow of Abraham Rosenfield, purchased this site and likely built the house in 1909, as she is listed in the 1910 city directory at this location. Rosenfield's heirs sold the house in 1925 to Rosie Gerber, in whose family it remained until 1964 when Coleman Kuhn purchased it for $56,500. The Kuhn family still owns the house as of this writing.

in 1890, for the following year Mary Abbott, who had purchased it from Alfred Keen in 1883, is listed on State Street. It remained in the Abbott family for twenty years. After five interim owners, Andrew Stewart bought the house in 1909 and retained it for twenty-eight years, selling in 1937 to Rosemond Herwig, widow of Emile Kuntz, who sold it the following year to Dr. and Mrs. Guy Caldwell. The Caldwell's twelve-year occupancy ended in 1950 when Robert M. Parker bought the house. Upon Parker's death in 1966, Lawrence Deckbar purchased it for $160,000, selling two years later to Richard Freeman, Jr. In 1990 Freeman sold the house to his sister, Tina Freeman Woollam, wife of Philip Woollam. The Woollams are the owners as of this writing.

Stylistically, the house appears to date from the 1870s, as indicated by the prominent dormer and paired brackets over the Corinthian columns. This would imply that Alfred Keen was the likely builder. The 1896 Sanborn insurance map does not show the St. Charles Avenue side gallery, an indication that this is a later addition.

residence, this house was not built until 1904. That year Joseph C. Morris purchased this site for $3,000 and undertook the construction of the present house. Interior details such as a beamed dining room ceiling, horizontal-paneled doors, leaded glass front door, and coved ceilings clearly place the house within the early-twentieth century vocabulary of architectural details.

The house remains in the Morris family as of this writing.

1776 STATE STREET, BLOOMINGDALE

The Mediterranean Villa at this corner has changed little since designed by architects DeBuys, Churchill and Labouisse in 1907. A study of the photograph which appeared in the *Illustrated Sunday Magazine* shortly after its construction indicates only that the present second-floor French door onto the porch was originally a window and the first-floor porch had no railing.

Dr. Lawrence DeBuys commissioned the house after purchasing the site in March 1907 for $7,200. In 1937 the administrators of the Tulane Education Fund bought the property, selling it in 1960 to Robert Nieset. Nine years later, Nieset sold it to Irma and John Overby for $96,000. In 1988 Donna and John Rotonti, the owners as of this writing, purchased the house.

1810 STATE STREET, BLOOMINGDALE

The charming basement residence at 1810 State Street is based on Gothic architecture, as evidenced by the half-timbering, Gothic front door and porch railing and steep, pitched roof.

2635 STATE STREET, FOUCHER TRACT

The Ursuline Nuns have been in New Orleans since 1727, providing educational, social, medical, and religious services for the citizens of the city. This is the fifth home of the Ursulines, following three in the Vieux Carré and one on the river near the present-day Industrial Canal.

The *Daily Picayune* of September 1, 1909, reported that "the Ursuline Sisters also have plans

1654 STATE STREET, BLOOMINGDALE

Here is a convincing architectural imposter. Often thought to be a nineteenth century Italianate

sold it fifteen years later to Mrs. Catherine Dodd. It remained in the Dodd family until 1963 when Philip Begue purchased it for $22,500. As of this writing, the house remains in the Begue family.

drawn for the erection of their new convent and school on Napoleon Avenue, near Claiborne Street. Just when this work will begin is not known, but the architects have been preparing the plans ready for work to begin as soon as the Orleans Board shall have acquired and paid for the present site." The following year, an article in the same paper said:

Work preparatory to the erection of the new Ursuline Convent on State Street has been done under the plans drawn by Andry & Bendernagel, the contractor being in the hands of George Glover. The cost of this great undertaking has never been given out, but it will represent the outlay of a considerable fortune of money.

The convent proper will be a group of buildings attached to form a triangle with a large courtyard inside. The outside dimensions of the building will be 450 in length by 300 feet in depth.

The architecture will be of the old English Gothic. All buildings are to be of gray pressed brick, with stone and terra cotta trimmings. The main building will comprise three stories and be entirely fireproof. All of the buildings will be provided with every modern appliance and not the smallest detail will be overlooked to make the buildings the finest of the kind in the country.

In 1922 the cornerstone was laid for the Chapel of Our Lady of Prompt Succor. George Glover was the builder of this Gothic style chapel, designed by H.L. Burton and A. Bendernagel, architects.

2800 STATE STREET, BLOOMINGDALE

The facade of this unusual bungalow diminishes its true scale by the presence of a strong and picturesque gable on the two-story mass. The decorative half-timbering adds not only charm but scale to the facade.

Built in 1920, this bungalow was first home to Stephen Tully, a clerk at the cotton brokerage firm of C.P. Ellis and Company. In 1922 Thomas McDonnell purchased the house from Tully. In 1930 McDonnell's widow sold the house to Adele Seyle who

TCHOUPITOULAS (Front; Levee; New Levee; Public Road)

5731-33 TCHOUPITOULAS, HURSTVILLE

One of the older residences in the neighborhood, this four-bay, originally double cottage dates to 1879, although its classic style suggests an earlier era. Adelaide Rippo, a produce vendor at the Magazine Street Market, purchased this property in 1868 for $800. She is first listed at this location in the city directory of 1880, the same year tax records indicate that the house was first assessed. Rippo lived here until her death. Her will mentions two bedrooms and a parlor in the house.

The house remained in the Rippo family until 1887 when James Drury purchased it for $1,500. The Drury family lost the house in 1921 when it was acquired by Charles H. Vogt from Columbia Building and Loan. In 1928 Mary Habisreitinger purchased the property, along with two lots in Jefferson Parish. Three years later, Henry W. White bought the house, and in 1945 his heirs sold it to Olga and Frank Chevally. The house was purchased in 1988 by Elizabeth Burgess, the owner as of this writing.

5917-19-21-23 TCHOUPITOULAS, HURSTVILLE

In 1877 Barbara Wolf Larken purchased lots 1 through 5 in the square for $1,700. Larken is first listed in the 1880 city directory at "Tchoupitoulas N.E. cor. Alonzo." However, this was not the subject house, as it is illustrated in the Robinson Atlas on lot 1, the present-day 5933 Tchoupitoulas, while the subject house is on lots 3 and 4. The Atlas also illustrates a house on lot 5, the present-day site of 315 Alonzo.

Construction of the subject residence was begun in 1895, as evidenced by the partial assessment in the tax records of that year; 1896 tax records indicate the completion of the house. Larken retained the house until 1921.

Originally a duplex, this two-and-one-half-story, wood frame structure has an animated facade featuring an undercut gable porch with Eastlake detailing.

TRIANON PLAZA

1 TRIANON PLAZA, MARLYVILLE

Designated as a city landmark, this Spanish Eclectic house has a rambling plan, tile roof, and circular tower with wrought iron finial in imitation of a flag. A.J.F. Lorber was the architect for this house, originally built for Trianon Development Corporation. A 1926 Latter and Blum real estate advertisement in the Times-Picayune described the house as

A PICTURESQUE SPANISH HACIENDA
IN NEW ORLEANS

This unique home is an exact reproduction of the haciendas of Southern Spain, complete in every detail. To see it is like making a trip to old

California or Spain itself. The work of A.J. F. Lorber, an architect of national fame, with a record of successes in Florida and New York.

Contains a large living room with open fireplace, Spanish built-in book shelves, artistic tiled tapestry over the fireplace and rustic rough-hewn beam ceiling with polychromed iron work. Reception hall with stairing, dining room, and master's suite of large bedroom, bath and bedroom. This bath is extra large with tile and marble fittings.

Guest's suite of bedroom, bath and bedroom.

Samuel Rosman, president-manager of Security Loan Office, purchased this house in 1932, becoming its first occupant. He sold it to Jeff Rebstock in 1950 for $65,000. Twenty years later, Claude Kelly, Jr., the owner as of this writing, purchased the house from Rebstock's succession.

VERSAILLES BOULEVARD

5 VERSAILLES BOULEVARD, FOUCHER TRACT

By means of two separate transactions, one in October 1926 and the other in January 1927, David Verlander, superintendent of American Crescent Laundry, purchased this site and was assessed in 1927 for a two-story, pressed brick residence with tile roof. He sold the house in 1933 to Dr. and Mrs. Edmond Faust for $18,000. In 1944 Harold Sporl purchased the house and engaged architect Edward F. Sporl to design alterations to it. The house remained in the Sporl family until 1976 when Jennifer and Anthony Palermo, Jr., the owners as of this writing, acquired it.

The residence is in the Mediterranean Villa style so commonly employed during the early twentieth century.

20 VERSAILLES BOULEVARD, FOUCHER TRACT

This Mediterranean Villa fits neatly into the standard design formula for the style, exhibiting a big, umbrella-like roof, arched opening on the ground floor, flat-head openings close to the eave on the second, and a well-detailed front door.

On October 27, 1927, John Pottharst purchased the property for $18,000, and the present house was completed in 1928, as indicated by tax records and the city directory. The house remained in the Pottharst family until 1971 when it was purchased by the owners as of this writing, Claire and John Brennan.

27 VERSAILLES BOULEVARD, FOUCHER TRACT

Cleo Babington, wife of James Babington, assistant purser for United Fruit Lines, acquired this property in 1928 and built the present house that year, according to tax records. However, according to city directories, the Babingtons did not live here at first, but at 1234 Audubon. It is not until 1938 that they appear in the city directory at their Versailles Boulevard residence.

Howard Sporl bought the house for $16,000 in 1941 and sold it to Jesse Lott in 1945. Lott sold it the next year to Dr. Leo Schoeny. Twenty years later, Aaron Mintz purchased the house and in 1987 sold it to Cynthia and Dr. Michael Haydel.

This picturesque house has no detailing to help classify it as one style or another. It is, however, typical of many houses built during the 1920s, with an eclectic look.

29 VERSAILLES BOULEVARD, FOUCHER TRACT

This Spanish Eclectic house combines a variety of details, such as the red tile roof, solomonic columns, bas-relief details, stucco walls, and carved-like front door into a Spanish ambiance.

Produce broker Ralph Lally purchased the property in 1928 for $8,500 and built the present house that year. The 1929 city directory lists Lally as residing here, and tax records that year cite a new, two-story, raised stucco residence valued at $14,700. In 1980 Lally's heirs sold the house to Saramae and William Dalferes, Jr., the owners as of this writing.

33 VERSAILLES BOULEVARD, FOUCHER TRACT

As the Colonial Revival style evolved, the picturesqueness of the nineteenth century was abandoned for the simplicity and symmetry of Federal precedents. Like other homes of its period, this 1929 residence has a symmetrical facade dominated by a well-detailed front door, in this particular case, employing Ionic columns.

In February 1929, cottonbroker James Ware purchased this site from Daniel Williams for $9,360 and built this brick residence valued at $16,400 that year, according to tax assessment records. In 1952 Bernard Woolner purchased the house, selling it in 1959 to Dr. Simon Ward who sold it in 1982 to N'Ann and Jan Glade, the owners as of this writing.

34 VERSAILLES BOULEVARD, FOUCHER TRACT

Here is another Colonial Revival residence from the late 1920s reflecting the simplicity of the period. When cottonbroker George Clay purchased the property in 1926, there was a garage and shed on the site, as well as a restriction calling for a thirty-foot setback and a requirement that the new house have a base value of at least $10,000. The 1927 tax records indicate a new, two-story, pressed brick residence, assessed at $19,000, at this location. In 1934 Clay rented the house for one year to John McKay for $125 per month. McKay, general manager of the Board of Commissioners for the Port of New Orleans, purchased the house for $16,000 the following year. As of this writing, the house remains with the McKay heirs.

40 VERSAILLES BOULEVARD, FOUCHER TRACT

This is one of four French Eclectic houses featured in this book. The style became popular during the 1920s after soldiers returned from France following World War I.

Moise Cahn purchased this site in January 1929 and began construction shortly thereafter, as a new, single, stucco residence is assessed at $13,800 that same year. Cahn is listed in the 1930 city directory as living at 3500 Versailles, corresponding to 40 Versailles Boulevard in the present numbering system. Dr. William A. Martin purchased the house from the Cahn heirs in 1991 and retains ownership as of this writing.

68 VERSAILLES BOULEVARD, FOUCHER TRACT

The Dutch Colonial Revival was one of many eclectic styles popularly employed for small residences during the 1920s. Here, a nearly full-width

shed dormer dominates the gambrel roof, and the only decorative ornament is the broken pedimented entrance with pilasters. The entrance is flanked on the river side by six-over-six, double-hung windows, and on the lake side by French doors opening onto the small terrace.

In 1925 Blanche King purchased the site with her separate funds. At that time, the property had a fifteen-foot setback, a forty-five-foot frontage, and a $6,500 minimum cost restriction. The Kings built the house in 1927 of brick, likely because Clifford King, Blanche's spouse, was manager of Acme Brick Company. The 1927 tax assessment valued the house at $8,500. In 1934 the Kings leased the house to Philip Rittenberg who eventually purchased it in 1945 for $15,000. His heirs sold the house in 1961 for $37,000 to Helen and Paul Gillaspy who in 1985 sold it to Susan and Keith Capone. In 1988 Patricia Elise Weeks purchased the house and retains ownership as of this writing.

WALNUT (Park)

295 WALNUT, GREENVILLE

In 1903 Margaret Maginnis, wife of bank president Peter Pescud, assembled the site by means of two separate transactions and built this large, two-story, Norman-styled stucco residence in 1917.

In 1920 Margaret Pescud's succession sold the house to Mrs. Laura Penrose for $4,700. In 1924 the property was increased in size. Penrose heirs sold the house in 1944 to Richard Freeman, 1977 Times-Picayune Loving Cup Recipient and 1959 Rex, whose family retains possession as of this writing.

325 WALNUT, GREENVILLE

Architects Favrot and Livaudais designed this 1927 house for Dr. and Mrs. Hilliard Miller. It is one of the better-designed French Eclectic houses in the city from this period. Typical French detailing includes the stucco bands around the windows, quoins, and mansard roof. The double-hung windows, however, are not typical of the style. The glass canopy over the door is particularly nice.

Isabel Kohlmeyer purchased the house in 1946 and sold it to Clifford and Delphine Atkinson in

1965. In 1978 Lesa and John Oudt purchased the house. William and Elizabeth More acquired the property in 1985 and retain ownership as of this writing.

353 WALNUT, GREENVILLE

On May 22, 1897, Lewis Strong Clarke purchased this site and apparently his succession allowed Edward Keep, assistant cashier of Whitney Central National Bank, to build a house here. The September 1911 edition of *Architectural Art and Its Allies* published a photograph of the newly completed house, shown here, with the caption, "Residence of E.H. Keep, New Orleans, Francis J. MacDonnell, Architect." Keep is listed here only in the 1911 city directory as he moved virtually every year.

In 1920 the Clarke estate sold the property for $1,966 to Janet Thorn, wife of Charles Thorn, vice-president of Interstate Trust and Banking Company. The Thorn family owned the house until 1963 when Dr. and Mrs. Arthur Samuels purchased it. In 1977 Kathy and James Baskin bought the house, selling it two years later to Richard Brunswick, the owner as of this writing.

The house is an example of the Craftsman style, employing tapestry brick, concrete block, concrete roof tiles, and an Art Nouveau leaded glass door.

383 WALNUT, GREENVILLE

Francis MacDonnell was the architect for this picturesque 1915 Tudor Revival house originally built for George H. Davis. True to the style, its massing is complex, with a complicated roof and an undulating facade with a projecting upper floor and Tudor arches. What is unusual is that half-timbering is not employed.

George Davis, of the civil engineering firm of Ford, Bacon and Davis, purchased the site in 1913 for $20,000 and sold it in 1922 with the house he built to Edward Benjamin who retained architect Moise Goldstein to oversee improvements to the house. It remains in the Benjamin family as of this writing.

429 WALNUT, GREENVILLE

Here is another Southern Colonial house, featuring colossal, two-story Ionic columns. Unfortunately, the facade seen in the photograph can only be viewed from Audubon Park; the Walnut Street elevation is the rear.

Dr. Charles Kells, Jr. purchased the lot in 1906 and obtained a permit in 1909 for an $8,500 house. The house remained in the Kells family until 1952 when James Lake purchased it for $32,000. Subsequent owners have been Dr. Oscar Bienvenu, Jr. (1966), Roberta and Richard Brunstetter (1972), and Margaret and Cliffe Laborde (1984), the owners as of this writing.

437 WALNUT, GREENVILLE

The *Daily Picayune* of September 1, 1902, records that "E. Howard McCaleb, Jr. has completed a very unique house at Audubon Park and Walnut Street, which stands out by itself and on account of its quaint construction attracts great attention. Mr. [Robert Spencer] Soulé is the architect of his house." The cost of the house was reported to be $2,000. Although McCaleb, an attorney, is listed at 437 Walnut in the 1903 city directory, he never owned the property. Title research reveals that Frank Clark of Illinois purchased the site in 1902 for $2,400 and sold it to Christian Wiehe in 1905 for $5,000, indicating that the house had been built. Wiehe sold the property the same year to Harry O. Penick who six months later sold to Dr. Charles Kells, Jr. Kells, who

Robert Spencer Soulé employed the style for the exterior of this house, built in 1912 for osteopath Robert Conner and his wife, Carrie. The interior, however, is executed in a more traditional manner.

The Conners purchased the site in 1911 and entered into a contract for construction of the house on January 25, 1912. Margarita Waguespack bought the house in 1919 for $24,250 and sold it in 1945 for $17,000 to Marcelle and Charles de la Vergne. The owner as of this writing is John Haynes, who bought the house in 1991.

built 429 Walnut in 1909, sold 437 Walnut to his daughter, Florence Kells, who married J.O. Pierson, vice-president of Dameron-Pierson Company. The Pierson family retained ownership until 1966. From 1966 to 1978, the Edgar Allen Thorpes resided here, selling in 1978 to J. Byron Gathright, Jr., the owner as of this writing.

The house, which should be viewed from Audubon Park, is executed in the Southern Colonial, a style about which local architectural magazine *Building Review* wrote: "Many have appreciated the obvious dignity of the type we call Southern Colonial, the tall colonnaded portico and the severe classicism."

440 WALNUT, GREENVILLE

In April 1924 Alice Houston, wife of Robert Wolcott, manager of Lukens Steel Company, purchased this site for $15,000. The house was likely built shortly thereafter, as the Wolcotts are listed at this location in the 1925 city directory; however, Alice Houston sold the property to Abram Houston in August 1924 for the same amount she paid for the site. In 1926 Irving R. Saal purchased the property for $55,000, indicating a house definitely existed. The house remained in the Saal family until 1957 when Moise Dennery bought it. Subsequent owners have been Louise Levy (1960), George Stoner (1962), Charles Stilwell (1964), James Jones (1969), and A.T. Green, Jr. (1977), the owner as of this writing.

This large, circa 1925, French Eclectic residence, sited in a lush yard, features a steep roof, clipped eaves, quoins, a variety of window types, and a recessed entry.

441 WALNUT, GREENVILLE

Edward Keep sold this site for $8,500 in 1913 to Henry Otis who obtained a permit to build this "patent stone" house in 1913. Patent stone, or concrete block, residences are most common in New Orleans during the second decade of the twentieth century and were a favorite of architect Francis MacDonnell. In 1914 Gonzalo Abaunza purchased the house for $21,000, and three years later it was sold to Walter Gilligan for $25,500. After three subsequent owners, Benjamin R. Slater bought the house in 1972.

472 WALNUT, GREENVILLE

Here is a rare example of the Prairie style in New Orleans. It is not as sophisticated as the D'Antoni residence at 7929 Freret, or the Maunsell residence formerly at 1707 Jefferson Avenue, but it is one of a few Prairie style houses in the city which retains its original design intent. The horizontal line is the distinguishing feature of this style, as seen in the silhouette of this house against the sky, the deep overhang, and the lines of the front porch and terrace. The rough stucco, however, is not typical; a smooth sand finish would be more common. Also, heads and sills of openings are commonly unified by means of horizontal banding in the Prairie style.

512 WALNUT, GREENVILLE

On July 24, 1905, Dr. Frank B. Ford contracted with Robert B. Ward to build this two-story Queen Anne residence, according to the designs of John Campbell, for $9,032. Complete plans of the house are preserved in the office of the Recorder of Mortgages.

The house remained in the Ford family until 1923 when Lois and Leonard Nicholson purchased it for $19,000 and commissioned architect Robert Spencer Soulé to make alterations to it. Subsequent owners were Clarris Company (1935), David White (1935), Marsha and Thomas Lowrey (1982), Dr. Enrique Carvajal (1983), and Susan and Dr. Judd Shellito (1989).

Two bays of the front porch have been enclosed, diminishing the picturesque effect of the house.

514 WALNUT, GREENVILLE

Designated a city landmark by the New Orleans Historic District Landmarks Commission in 1989, this Mission style residence was designed by Robert

189

Spencer Soulé for the Leopold H. Von Tresckow family. The house is little changed since it was built in 1911 at a cost of $8,000 and was featured in *Architectural Art and Its Allies*. The tile roof, stucco walls, Mission parapet, and cloister-like entry porch are typical of the style.

In 1916 Von Tresckow donated the house to his sister-in-law, Julie Falwell, but in 1933 it was returned to the Von Tresckows. Samuel Antin, Jr. purchased the house in 1951 for $27,500 and sold it four years later to Alfonso Godoy, in whose family it remains as of this writing.

WEBSTER

919 WEBSTER, BURTHEVILLE

On June 15, 1869, the German Protestant Orphan Asylum contracted with Henry Friedrich to build an asylum in the square bounded by State, Camp, Webster, and Chestnut for $11,650. Charles Hillger was the architect. This is the sole surviving component of the complex. The 1896 Sanborn map indicates this as the laundry and stable, with the chicken house adjacent. It was designated a landmark in 1978 by the New Orleans Historic District Landmarks Commission, preventing its demolition. Two years later, Dee and Stephen Moses, the owners as of this writing, purchased the building from the asylum and retained architects Lyons and Hudson to adapt it as a residence.

1217 WEBSTER, BURTHEVILLE

This three-bay, side-hall cottage features boxed columns set on pedestals, between which spans a wood railing, a denticulated entablature, and 2/2 double-hung, slip-head windows.

1231 WEBSTER, BURTHEVILLE

Here is a whimsical version of the Queen Anne style, with two variant towers flanking an unusual central entry porch topped by a large dormer.

It was likely built in 1897 by Eureka Homestead which purchased the property that year for $1,454 and sold it the following year to William P. Johnston for $5,000. His succession sold the house in 1915 for

$8,400 to C. Lee McMillan who sold it the following year to Louis Price. As of this writing, there have been seven subsequent owners: Nellie Price Graham (1921), Allen Johness (1922), Peoples Homestead (1928), Ragnhild Brodie (1928), Olive and Royal Donavan (1944), Dr. John A. Stocks (1955), and Caroline C. Stewart (1979).

1447-49 WEBSTER, BURTHEVILLE

This "FHA Colonial Revival" duplex is typical of many built Uptown during the 1930s. A Federal doorway, simple boxed columns, and mitered corners are characteristic of this style. Builder Clarence Charlton is credited with the construction of this duplex, which demonstrates the simplicity of the Colonial Revival movement in pre-World War II housing financed by the Federal Housing Authority.

Harold B. Walker purchased this site for $3,250 in 1937 and mortgaged the property for $9,500 the following year, likely to finance construction of this duplex, which is first cited in the 1938 tax rolls. Walker sold the property for $25,000 in 1947 to Eugene Aschaffenburg who sold it the same day to Lawrence Howard for $27,000. In 1966 Zema and George Rapier purchased this duplex, and it remains in the Rapier family as of this writing.

Many duplicates of this two-family dwelling are located throughout Uptown New Orleans.

1535 WEBSTER, BURTHEVILLE

Architect Rathbone DeBuys of DeBuys, Churchill and Labouisse built this as his private residence in 1906 at a cost of $4,500. Its style is typical of De-Buys' work—hard to categorize, with both Colonial Revival and Mediterranean Villa traits. The house has a rough stucco finish, deep overhangs, and Doric columns set on stucco bases, between which spans a rose-patterned, cast iron railing. It presently is sited in a heavily planted lot.

DeBuys sold the house in 1925 to Herman Barnett who sold it in 1949 to Jack Kessels a year after making improvements under the direction of architect Richard Koch. In 1982 Darlene and Robert Fabacher purchased the house and retain ownership as of this writing.

BIBLIOGRAPHY

BOOKS

American Institute of Architects, New Orleans Chapter. *A Guide to New Orleans Architecture.* 1974. Reprint. New Orleans, 1981.

Audubon Park Commission. *Annual Reports.* New Orleans, 1894-95.

Audubon Park Commission. *History of Audubon Park.* New Orleans, n.d.

Baudier, Roger. *The Southern Plumber.* November 1930-April 1932.

Cangelosi, Robert J. Jr.; Reeves, Sally Kittredge; and Schlesinger, Dorothy 333G. *New Orleans Architecture, Vol. VII: Jefferson City.* Gretna, La.: Pelican Publishing, 1989.

City of New Orleans. *The Book of the Chamber of Commerce and Industry.* New Orleans, 1894.

Craig, James P. *New Orleans: Illustrated in Photo Etching.* 1890.

Doussan, Albert J. "History of Loyola." Unpublished manuscript. New Orleans, 1939.

Dyer, John P. *Tulane: The Biography of a University, 1834-1965.* New York and London, Harper and Row, 1966.

Edgell, G.H. *The American Architect of Today.* New York: Charles Scribner's Sons, 1928.

Embury, Aymer II. *Building the Dutch Colonial House.* New York: R.M. McBride & Co., 1929.

Engelhardt, George W. *The City of New Orleans: The Book of the Chamber of Commerce and Industry of Louisiana.* New Orleans, 1894.

————. *New Orleans, Louisiana, The Crescent City: The Book of the Picayune, also of the Public Bodies and Business Interests of the Place.* New Orleans, 1903-4.

Forman, L. Ronald, and Logsdon, Joseph. *Audubon Park: An Urban Eden.* New Orleans: Friends of the Zoo, 1985.

Goodnow, Ruby Ross, and Adams, Rayne. *The Honest House.* 1914.

Guilbeau, L.L. *The St. Charles Street Car or the New Orleans & Carrollton Rail Road.* Guilbeau, 1975.

Hardy, Donald Clive. *The World's Industrial and Cotton Centennial Exposition.* New Orleans: The Historic New Orleans Collection, 1978.

Hawkins, Donald A. *Church on the Park: Holy Name.* New Orleans, 1987.

Heard, Malcolm. *Tulane Places.* New Orleans: Tulane University, 1984.

Hennick, Louis C., and Charlton, E. Harper. *The Streetcars of New Orleans.* Gretna, La.: Pelican Publishing, 1975.

Hunter, Julius. *Westmoreland and Portland Places.* Columbia, Mo., 1988.

Irvin, Hilary, and Cangelosi, Robert. "Uptown New Orleans." Report for the Uptown National Register District for the Preservation Resource Center, n.d.

Keenan and Weiss, Architects. Brochure, ca. 1910.

Kendall, John Smith. *History of New Orleans.* 3 vols. Chicago: Lewis Publishing, 1922.

Lee, Lionel. *Architecture and People of Leland University and Leland College.* 1980.

Lemann, Bernard. *Historic Sites Inventory, New Orleans.* Rader and Associates for the Regional Planning Commission, 1969.

Lemmon, Alfred. "New Orleans Popular Sheet Music Imprints: The Latin Tinge Prior to 1900." *Southern Quarterly* XXVII (Winter) 1989.

Longnecker, Herbert E. *Great Vision Amply Justified: The Story of Tulane University.* Princeton: Newcomen Society in North America, 1968.

Men and Matters. ("A Magazine of Fact, Fancy, and Fiction. Miss Marie Evans, Proprietor and Editor"), 1894-96.

New Orleans & Carrollton Railroad, Light and Power Co. *Around the St. Charles Belt.* New Orleans, ca. 1906.

New Orleans City Guide. American Guide Series. Boston: Houghton Mifflin, 1938.

O'Conner, Thomas, ed. *History of the Fire Department of New Orleans.* New Orleans, 1895.

Reeves, William D. and Sally K. "Management Summary: Cultural Resources Survey, United States Public Health Service Hospital," prepared for U.S. Department of Health & Human Services, October 1981.

Rightor, Henry. *Standard History of New Orleans.* Chicago: Lewis Publishing Co., 1900.

Savage, Charles. *Architecture of the Private Streets of St. Louis.* Columbia, Mo., 1987.

Schuyler, David. *The New Urban Landscape: The Redefinition of City Form in Nineteenth Century America.* Baltimore and London: Johns Hopkins University Press.

Seebold, Herman. *Old Louisiana Plantation Homes and Family Trees.* New Orleans: Pelican Press, 1941.

Simms, George A., ed. *Notable Men of New Orleans.* New Orleans: George Simms Advertising Co., 1905.

Soniat, Meloncy C. "The Faubourgs Forming the Upper Section of the City of New Orleans." *Louisiana Historical Quarterly* 20 (January 1937).

Spratling, William, and Scott, Natalie. *Old Plantation Houses in Louisiana.* New Orleans: Pelican Book Shop, 1927.

Stewart, Jack. "The Mexican Band Legend: Myth, Reality and Musical Impact, A Preliminary Investigation." *The Jazz Archivist* VI (December 1991).

Swanson, Betsy. *Historic Jefferson Parish: From Shore to Shore.* Gretna, La.: Pelican Publishing, 1975.

The Story of Louisiana. New Orleans: J.F. Hyer Pub. Co., 1960.

Visitor's Guide to the World's Industrial and Cotton Centennial Exposition and New Orleans, Commencing December 16, 1884 and Ending May 31, 1885. Louisville, Ky.: Courier Journal Printing Co., 1884.

Waldo, Rudolph H. *Notarial Archives of Orleans Parish.* New Orleans, 1946.

———. *Notarial Archives of Orleans Parish: Plan Books.* New Orleans, 1946.

Weil, Emile; Benson, H.A., and Bendernagel, Albert. *Illustrations of Selected Work of Emile Weil, Architect, New Orleans, La., 1900-1928.* New Orleans, n.d.

Widmer, Mary Lou. *New Orleans in the Forties.* Gretna, La.: Pelican Publishing, 1990.

———. *New Orleans in the Thirties.* Gretna, La.: Pelican Publishing, 1989.

Wilson, Edward L. *View Album, World Exposition and Cotton Centennial Exposition.* n.d.

"World's Industrial and Cotton Centennial Exposition at New Orleans, La." May 1, 1885.

PERIODICALS

Architectural Art and Its Allies, July 1905-June 1912.

Building Review, 1913-23.

House Beautiful.

NEWSPAPERS

Louisiana Courier.

New Orleans Crescent.

New Orleans Daily Picayune and Illustrated Sunday Magazine.

New Orleans Daily Times Delta.

New Orleans Daily States.

New Orleans Item.

New Orleans States.

New Orleans States Item.

New Orleans Times Democrat.

New Orleans Times-Picayune.

Preservation in Print.

NEW ORLEANS CITY DIRECTORIES

Cohen Company. *New Orleans and Lafayette Directory.* New Orleans, 1849-52.

———. *New Orleans and Southern Directory.* New Orleans, 1856.

———. *New Orleans Directory.* New Orleans, 1853-55.

Edwards Company. *Annual Director.* New Orleans, 1870, 1871, 1873.

———. *Annual Directory.* New Orleans, 1872.

Gardner Company. *New Orleans Directory.* New Orleans, 1859-61, 1866-69, 1873.

Gardner and Wharton. *New Orleans Directory.* New Orleans, 1858.

Graham and Madden. *Crescent City Directory.* New Orleans, 1867, 1869, 1870.

Kerr. *General Advertiser and Crescent City Directory.* New Orleans, 1856.

Mygatt & Company. *New Orleans Directory.* New Orleans, 1857-58.

Polk's City Directory of New Orleans. New Orleans, 1935-94.

Soards' Directory Company. *City Directory of New Orleans.* New Orleans, 1874-1935.

———. *Soards' Elite Book of New Orleans.* New Orleans, n.d. [ca. 1907].

MAPS AND SURVEYS

"Bienville's Land Grants from King Louis XV." ca. 1725.

Casey, Edgar. "Plan of Choice Property, Sixth District." Danziger & Tessier, n.d.

"City of New Orleans and Suburbs." Theo Pohlmann, 1883.

"Gray's Map of Louisiana." 1878.

Insurance Maps of New Orleans, Louisiana. New York: Sanborn-Perris Map Co., 1896, 1909.

"Map of the Sixth District and Carrollton." William H. Williams, 1871.

"New Orleans and Its Environs." F.B. Ogden, 1829.

"Norman's Chart of Lower Mississippi River." A. Persac, 1858.

"Perspective View of New Orleans and Environs Looking from the South." H.W.W. Reynolds, 1884-85.

"Plan of the City of New Orleans." L. Pessou and B. Simon, 1855.

"Plan of Division of Part of Property of Boré." October 1832, S.[?] Bringier.

"Plan of 32 Lots of Ground Situated in Greenville." C.A. Hedin, 1847.

"Plan of Valuable Property in Greenville." C.A. Hedin and L. Reizenstein, 1857.

Robinson, Elisha. *Atlas of the City of New Orleans, Louisiana.* New York, 1883.

"Six Squares on Burtheville to be Sold at Public Auction May 20, 1867."

"Succession of D.F. Burthe, 30 Squares to be Sold at Auction May 13, 1854."

"Topographical and Drainage Map of New Orleans prepared for Joseph Jones by T.S. Hardee, Civil Engineer." 1880.

"Topographical Map of New Orleans and Its Vicinity, 1834." Charles F. Zimpel.

"T.13 S.R.11E. South Eastern District, Louisiana." Map approved by E.W. Foster, Surveyor General, La., January 26, 1872. Based on survey of 1836.

MANUSCRIPTS AND RECORDS

Civil District Court Building:
    Jefferson Parish Conveyance Office Books.
    Orleans Parish Mortgage Office Records.
    New Orleans Conveyance Office Records.
    Notarial Archives: Orleans Parish Notarial Acts.
Friends of the Cabildo:

Building Contract File.
Building File.
Building Permit File.

Historic New Orleans Collection, Museum/Research Center:
Lawyers Title Insurance Co. Records.
Photograph Files.

Lawyers Title (insurance records, prior to donation to Historic New Orleans Collection).

Loyola University Library, Special Collections & Archives.

National Archives, Washington, D.C. Records of Civil War Special Agencies: Index to Ledger of Property Seized in New Orleans and Ledger of Property Seized in New Orleans. Third Agency, Book 44: Record of Property (Real Estate and Personal) in New Orleans with Index.

New Orleans City Hall, Real Estate Office Records.

New Orleans Public Library
Louisiana Division:
Blueprint Index.
Civil District Court Records

New Orleans City Planning Commission Records.
Newspaper Index.
Obituary Files.
Photograph Files.

St. Mary's Dominican Archives.

Tulane University, Howard-Tilton Memorial Library:
Louisiana Collection:
Board of Directors Minutes.
Picture File.
Scrapbooks (newspaper clippings).
Vertical File.

Rare Books and Manuscripts Section:
Tulane Board of Directors minutes.

Southeastern Architectural Archive:
Frank H. Boatner Photograph Collection.
Louisiana Landmarks Society Photograph Collection.
Collection of Building Contracts and Excerpts, 1800-1900. Compiled by Samuel Wilson, Jr.

Fig. 1A, 1B. Interior views of 5931 St. Charles Avenue, built in 1897 for Henry Dart according to the designs of architects Toledano and Reusch. These 1910 Teumisson photographs capture the interior when this was the home of Marie Louise Schmidt, known as "Tante Mimi," widow by first marriage of Hughes Jules de la Vergne, and by second marriage of Henri Landry de Frémeuse. (Photo courtesy Louis V. de la Vergne)

Fig. 2. Tante Mimi (standing, center) with her daughter (seated to the right), Léda de la Vergne, wife of Hugh C. St. Paul, and granddaughter (seated to the left), Diane St. Paul Fricke Olivier. This photograph was taken in 1938 during one of the early Spring Fiesta celebrations. Tante Mimi, founder of Spring Fiesta in New Orleans, is wearing a nineteenth-century gown which belonged to her mother, Léda Hincks of Mobile. Mrs. St. Paul is wearing a gown which belonged to Tante Mimi. (Photo courtesy Louis V. de la Vergne)

INVENTORY
PHOTOGRAPH
CREDITS

Neil Alexander
22 Audubon Place.

Abry Brothers Inc.
5901 Garfield Street (historic photographs).

Avery McLoughlin Bassich
7301 Hampson Street.

Robert J. Cangelosi, Jr.
All contemporary photographs.

The Historic New Orleans Collection, Musesum/Research Center
6000 St. Charles Avenue. Acc. No. 1974.25.3.626ii.

Koch and Wilson Architects
Historic photographs
460 Broadway Street, from *The City of New Orleans*, by George Engelhardt, 1894.
1582 Henry Clay Avenue, from *New Orleans, Louisiana: The Crescent City*, by George Engelhardt, 1903-4.
6206 St. Charles Avenue, *Ibid.*
5726 St. Charles Avenue, from *New Orleans Illustrated in Photo Etchings*, by James P. Craig, 1892.
2108 Palmer Avenue. Office Records.

New Orleans Public Library, Louisiana Division
25 Audubon Place, from *Times-Picayune*, October 26, 1924.
210 State Street.

St. Mary's Dominican Archives
7214 St. Charles Avenue.

A.L. Schlesinger, Jr.
936 Arabella Street.

Eric Smith
6226 St. Charles Avenue.

Caroline Steinhart
5807 St. Charles Avenue (historic photograph).

Tulane University, Louisiana Collection, Howard-Tilton Memorial Library
Historic photographs
2 Audubon Place, from *Architectural Art and Its Allies*, April 1910.
5 Audubon Place, from "Beautiful New Orleans Homes," *Daily Picayune Illustrated Sunday Magazine*, December 19, 1909.

12 Audubon Place, from *Architectural Art and Its Allies*, December 1910.
15 Audubon Place, from "Beautiful New Orleans Homes," *Daily Picayune Illustrated Sunday Magazine*, no date. Photographic File.
16 Audubon Place. Photo by Seguin & Harvey. Photographic File.
20 Audubon Place, from *Architectural Art and Its Allies*, December 1907.
24 Audubon Place, from *Architectural Art and Its Allies*, June 1909.
582 Audubon Street, from *Architectural Art and Its Allies*, October 1909.
6 Everett Place, from *Architectural Art and Its Allies*, July 1908.
1565 Exposition Boulevard, from *Architectural Art and Its Allies*, December 1907.
1591 Exposition Boulevard, from *Architectural Art and Its Allies*, June 1908.
3 LaSalle Street, from *Architectural Art and Its Allies*, February 1910.
1640 Palmer Avenue, from *Architectural Art and Its Allies*, October 1909.
2115 Palmer Avenue, from *Daily Picayune Illustrated Sunday Magazine*, December 5, 1909.
2212 Palmer Avenue, from *Architectural Art and Its Allies*, February 1910.
6040 Palmer Avenue, from *Daily Picayune Illustrated Sunday Magazine*, no date. Photographic File.
6048 Perrier, from *Daily Picayune Illustrated Sunday Magazine*, January 17, 1909.
2 Richmond Place, from "Beautiful New Orleans Homes," *Daily Picayune Illustrated Sunday Magazine*, no date. Photographic File.
21 Richmond Place, from *Daily Picayune Illustrated Sunday Magazine*, March 7, 1909.
5705 St. Charles Avenue, from "Beautiful New Orleans Homes," *Daily Picayune Illustrated Sunday Magazine*, January 24, 1909.
5912 St. Charles Avenue, from *Architectural Art and Its Allies*, October 1906.
6153 St. Charles Avenue. Photographic File.
6300 St. Charles Avenue. Photographic File.

6330 St. Charles Avenue, from "Beautiful New Orleans Homes," *Daily Picayune Illustrated Sunday Magazine,* October 25, 1908.

1525 State Street, from *Architectural Art and Its Allies,* January 1906.

1621 State Street, from "Beautiful New Orleans Homes," *Daily Picayune Illustrated Sunday Magazine,* no date. Photographic File.

2635 State Street, from *Architectural Art and Its Allies,* June 1912.

353 Walnut Street, from *Architectural Art and Its Allies,* September 1911.

Tulane University, Southeastern Architectural Archive, Howard-Tilton Memorial Library

18 Audubon Place. Drawing by Emile Weil, architect.

University of New Orleans, Archives and Manuscripts/ Special Collections, Earl K. Long Library

5625 Loyola Avenue. Photo by Charles Franck.

INDEX

DePass, William, 179
DePaul Hospital, xv, 28
de Pontet-Brun, Count, 147
Derbigny, Charles, xiii
Derbigny, George, 130
Derlin, John, 112
Derussy, Warren, 119
Deseman, David, 103
Desmare, Helen, 154
Destrehan, Jeanne, 26
Detton, M., 119
Deutsch, Eberhard, 155
Deutsch, Herman, 155
Devan, William, 181
Dezendore family, 171
d'Hemecourt survey, 90
Diamond, Samuel, 99, 126, 170, 171
Diaz, Abram, 153
Diboll & Owen, 58, 109, 120, 128, 158, 162, 183
Diboll, J.E., 158
Diboll, Owen & Goldstein, 57, 74, 104, 107, 128
Dickey, D.A., 117
Dickey, George E. & Son, 99, 126, 131, 170
Dickinson, James, 110
Dicks, Charles, 122
Dicks, John, 167
Dicks, Robert, 157
DiCristina, Orazio, 173
Dieth family, 147
Diettel, A.A., 108, 120, 137
Diettel, Albert, 137
Diettel, Albert & Son, 28
Diettel, Hans, 103, 108, 110, 113, 114, 127
Dietz, Joyce, 170
Dietz, Thompson, 170
Dietze, Charlotte, 184
Dillard, James, 145, 178
Dillard University, 145
Dillon, George, 119
Dingirart, Bertrand, 25
Dinkins, Cecile, 145
Dinkins, Ladd, 145
Dinkler, Carling III, 161
Dinwiddie, Albert, 63
Dirkin, William, 104
Discom, Mary, 131
Dix, Dorothy, 168
Dixie Homestead, 116, 117
Dixon, Brandt, 63, 122, 164
Dixon, David, 164
Dixon Hall (Newcomb College), 64
Dodd, Catherine, 186
Dodge, George, 141
Doll, George, 153
Dominican Convent, 34, 127
Dominican Street, 33, 34, 35
Donaldson, E.L., 108
Donavan, Olive, 190
Donavan, Royal, 190
Donnelly, John, 123
Dorian, Josette, 33
Doty, Roberta, 128, 182
Doty, Thomas, 128, 182
Dougherty, John, 71
Downing, Andrew, 173

Doyle, Christopher, 101, 127, 178
Doyle, Elizabeth, 164
Doyle, Stella, 115
Drapekin, Charles, 131
Dreuil, Emile, 108
Dreuil, Joseph, 108, 144
Dreyfous & Levy, 110
Dreyfous, F. Julius, 117, 142, 144, 146
Dreyfous, Felix, 107, 108, 142
Dreyfus, Alex, 103
Drumm, Streuby, 155
Drury, James, 186
Dryades Building & Loan, 119
Dube, Joseph, 132
DuBourg, Leo, 167
Dufour, Mrs. Charles, 154
Dufrechou, Frank, 124
Duggan, Joseph, 175
Dugué, Aline Delachaise, 31
Dugue, Randall, 171, 172
Dumont, Edgar, 143
Dumont family, 171
Dunbar, Charles, 182
Dunbar, Emerson, 156
Dunbar, James, 115
Dunleith Court, 66, 84, 86, 114, 149
Dupepe, Clancy, 156
Dupre, Walter, 150
Dupre, Eugene, 182
Dupuy, Homer, 155
Durning, William, 113
Dutch Colonial Revival, 136, 138, 139, 142, 148, 167, 187
Dutch Renaissance Revival style, 62
Dutton family, 177
Duval & Favrot, 61
Duval, Charles, 136
Duval, R. Suthron, 74, 107, 122, 123, 140, 141, 172
Dwyer, Walter, 104
Dykstra, Bouwe, 177

Eagan, Ewell, Jr., 150
Earhart, Carter, 109
Eastlake style, 7, 148, 150, 151, 159, 160, 161, 162, 166, 167, 172, 182, 184, 186
Edell, Jeanne, 144
Edell, Lester, 144
Edgell, G.H., 157
Edisen, Barbara, 34, 146
Edisen, Clayton, 146
Edison Electric Co., 69
Edmonds, James, 138
Edmonton, D., 106
Edmunds, John, Jr., 147
Edrington, Prentice, Jr., 138
Edwards, Andrew, 167
Edwards, Elizabeth, 167
Ehrensing, Adolph, 121, 129, 131
Ehrensing, Henry, 116
Eiswirth, John, 119
Eleonore Playground, 9
Eleonore Street, xiii, xv, xvii, 9, 11, 18, 24, 68, 114, 115, 149-150, 166
Eliot, Charles, 47
Elizabethan motife (architecture), 62
Ellerbusch, A.J., 117

Ellermann, Susie, 116, 154
Elliot, Thomas, 161
Ellis, A.M., 119
Ellis, C.P., Jr., 125
Ellis, C.P. & Co., 186
Ellis, Crawford, 122
Ellis, William, 184
Elsas, Victor, 175, 181
Elstrutt, Jacob, 129
Embury, Aymar II, 148
Emmons, J.N., 119
Engelbach, Augusta, 121
Engleet, G.B., 123
English collegiate style, 160
English half-timber, 180, 181
English style, 143, 168
Enterprise Construction, 125
Epley, Eva, 164
Epstein, Charles, 116
Equitable Homestead, 103, 118
Equity Security, 162
Erlinger, Francis, 116
Ernst, Charles, 132
Ervin, Henry, 108, 144
Eureka Building & Loan, 165
Eureka Homestead, 114, 132, 160, 190
Eustis, Henry, 117
Eustis, Horatio, 117
Eustis, Joyce, 142
Eustis, Richard, 125
Evangeline Associates, 174
Evans, Alfred, 104
Evans, Hugh, Jr., 154
Everett Place, 66, 71, 80-81, 87, 115, 150-151
Everstone Brick, 176
Ewing family, 175
Ewing, Robert, 175
Ewing, Rufus, 113
Excelsior Homestead, 111, 119, 132
Exposition Boulevard, 8, 9, 43, 67, 68, 115, 147, 151-153, 166
Exposition style, 136, 180
Eyrich, Joanna, 179, 180
Eyrich, Robert, 127, 145, 180

F.H.A. Colonial Revival, 190
Fabacher, Darlene, 190
Fabacher, Jacob, 124
Fabacher, Joseph, 131
Fabacher, Lawrence, 18, 19, 77, 114, 149, 172
Fabacher, Peter, 127, 144, 175, 181
Fabacher, Peter & Bros., 181
Fabacher, Robert, 190
Fabacher, Thelma, 174
Fabacher's Restaurant & Hotel, 175
Factor's Cotton Press, 154
Fahey, James, 56
Fairchild & Hobson, 139
Falkenstein, Edward, 180
Falwell, Julie, 190
Faran, M., 103
Farnsworth, Harold, 180
Farnsworth, R.P. & Co., 119, 159
Farwell, Edna, 144
Farwell, F(rank). Evans, 18, 99, 174